Laughing matters

Manchester University Press

LAUGHING MATTERS

Understanding film, television and radio comedy

John Mundy and Glyn White

MANCHESTER UNIVERSITY PRESS
Manchester and New York
distributed in the United States exclusively by
Palgrave Macmillan

Published by Manchester University Press
Oxford Road, Manchester M13 9NR, UK
and Room 400, 175 Fifth Avenue, New York, NY 10010, USA
www.manchesteruniversitypress.co.uk

Distributed in the United States exclusively by
Palgrave Macmillan, 175 Fifth Avenue, New York,
NY 10010, USA

Distributed in Canada exclusively by
UBC Press, University of British Columbia, 2029 West Mall,
Vancouver, BC, Canada V6T 1Z2

British Library Cataloguing-in-Publication Data
A catalogue record for this book is available from the British Library

Library of Congress Cataloging-in-Publication Data applied for

ISBN 978 0 7190 8314 3 *hardback*
ISBN 978 0 7190 8315 0 *paperback*

First published 2012

Typeset in Calluna with Candara display by
Koinonia, Manchester
Printed in Great Britain
by Bell & Bain Ltd, Glasgow

Contents

List of illustrations

Acknowledgements

Over the several years that this project has been in the works we have accrued debts of gratitude to many more people than can be individually named and thanked among our colleagues, students we have taught, friends and family. We have also gained a lot from attenders and speakers of the annual Comedy conferences at the University of Salford in 2007–11. We would like to thank Matthew Frost, the readers of our proposal and all at Manchester University Press who have had a hand in shaping this book.

John would like to thank colleagues and students at the University of Central Lancashire and the University of Salford for sharing an enthusiasm for comedy and particularly to thank the School of Media Music and Performance at Salford for a period of sabbatical leave. As always, thanks to Karen, Ellyn and Alice.

Glyn would like to thank colleagues past and present for help with this project, and the following individuals, without attempting to shift any blame to them: Douglas Field, for timely reassurance; Peter Krämer, for advice on teaching comedy film; Alan Peterson, for detailed feedback; Ian W. White, for as far back as I can remember; Michaela Schoop, for retaining a sense of humour and creating the cover illustrations; and Edmund, William and Greta for learning jokes along the way.

To students of comedy

Introduction

Our aims in writing this book have been fourfold. Firstly, we want to produce a wide-ranging introductory academic book for students and teachers interested in studying comedy on film, television and radio (and for anyone else with an analytic interest in these media). Secondly, we want to discuss key issues around comedy through analysis of significant and revealing comedy texts from these media. Thirdly, on the basis of our teaching experiences, we want to show students how to respond to comedy analytically; that is, to write about it interestingly and originally, referring to – but differing from – other writers on the same or similar comedic texts. Finally, we hope to point the way for new research in the area, knowing that we couldn't possibly cover all aspects of this vast field alone.

Our focus and the choices we have made

The title of this book, *Laughing Matters*, signals both our focus on comedy and our belief in its social, psychological and cultural importance. Still a relatively mysterious form of human behaviour, laughter appears to be a universal human experience. One research study suggests that we laugh, on average, eighteen times a day, mostly in the evening, and mostly owing to common social incidents rather than formal jokes (Rappoport 2005: 25). In this book our focus is on professional comedy, and particularly the films, programmes, jokes, gags, slapstick and narrative situations that are produced by people whose job it is to make us laugh. This is not to deny the importance of what we might call everyday laughter that runs throughout all our lives, as when we share a joke with a work colleague, or laugh at some incident on the street. Such 'amateur' moments of laughable incongruity are important, but they are not something that can – or indeed should – be recreated for a wider audience since, as we often say when we attempt unsuccessfully to recount the joke, 'you had to be there'. Instead we highlight film, television and radio as the key media in delivering comedy for mass consumption. Of course 'comedy' is not just a genre but a meta-genre far beyond the scope of a project of this size to encompass entirely. Among the media and performance modes that we largely or wholly neglect are stand-up comedy, cabaret, stage comedy from revue to farce, comic novels and poems, satirical literature, blogs, periodicals (including 'comics'), cartoons, everyday face-to-face amateur joke-telling and the circulation of jokes on mobile phones and comedy clips via the internet. Even where there are strong links to the three media we have chosen to highlight, we make no apology for leaving these others out because the project is sufficiently (if not over-) ambitious anyway. We hope that what we have chosen to exclude will point others towards further research in those areas.

There are other exclusions. We have focused on British and American comedy across the media we cover. These two nations may be 'divided by a common language' but are consistent reference points for one another, more or less visible, across the Atlantic. In cinema, the relationship is usually very one-sided with Hollywood dominating, though British film productions occasionally make a splash (*Four Weddings and a Funeral*, *The Full Monty*). Contributions to Hollywood cinema by performers who began in Britain have certainly been significant (consider, for example, the careers of Charlie Chaplin, Stan Laurel, Cary Grant and Bob Hope). The few American sitcoms that establish themselves on British television have been, and are, hugely influential in the UK (from the evergreen *The Phil Silvers Show* aka *Sergeant Bilko*, to *Cheers*, *Friends* and *Curb Your Enthusiasm*), yet there are several examples of British television products making an impact in America, too (some examples might be *Monty Python's Flying Circus*, *Till Death Us Do Part* via *All in the Family* and *The Office*). While we recognise debates that argue for distinctive comic sensibilities across cultures and even within sub-cultures, and which discuss important determinants such as ethnicity, national identity and regionalism, we believe that there is sufficient Anglo-American interaction in our chosen media, whether it is direct or through translation and/or influence, for us to discuss British and American material together, noting the significant differences in production contexts where relevant. We leave it to other, more specialised, studies to excavate in depth what is distinctive about comedy in relation to particular nations (see Medhurst 2007) and regions (see Russell 2004).

It is worth noting at this point that though Anglo-American comedy is substantial and vast, it is a smaller field than English-language comedy. But to even begin to include comedies produced in Australia, Canada, New Zealand and elsewhere, most of which have not reached British or American screens, would consume too much precious word-count. Sorry *Kath and Kim* (2002–7). Once again, we hope that what we have chosen to exclude will point others towards further research in those areas.

Within the boundaries we have set ourselves, what do we actually mean by comedy? Laughing certainly matters, but comedy and laughter are not synonymous and, as we suggested above, much of our laughter is provoked by everyday social interaction, not what we might call 'professional comedy'. The link between laughter and comedy is one of both expectation and anticipation. If a film, radio or television comedy text possesses any level of ambition, it should intend to produce laughter and is usually explicit about this intent. Comedic texts are, in fact, often prepared to use any means necessary in order to achieve that goal whether it is by innovation, by boundary-challenging or by repetition, recycling and rewriting. Importantly, these mediated, performative texts provide a context for laughter, generic 'cues' that encourage laughter as a 'natural' and legitimate response.

Comedy is a commodity that develops and builds upon what has gone before in a number of generic forms within the media we cover. Film, radio and television have been recorded or are recordable in analogue and now digital forms, in ways that allow us to see both their links and lineages. This is not true of their entire histories, and absences in the history of all three media are to be lamented. However, even before reproduction was technologically possible, comedy appeared in forms that were reproducible such as sketches and routines. Gags erase their history pretty quickly with a change of performer, or of narrative context. Comedy has always recycled itself, building originality out of an intertextual combination of what has gone before (and what hasn't). This shows comedy texts having some of the characteristics of postmodernity before theoretical access to 'postmodernism' in any medium. It is certainly a uniquely complex meta-genre, as we shall see when we discuss theories of comedy below.

Creating successful comedy in our selected media requires such heterogeneous strategies and approaches because audiences, taste and times change. As William Goldman (1996: 39) has said of the film industry's ability to predict success, 'nobody knows anything', and this applies almost across the board to comedy in film, television and radio when it comes to judging what will and what won't succeed. It is also difficult to predict what will endure in audience affections and become canonised as a 'classic'. This is a way of saying that not all our choices will be well known or entirely representative and that in the future their selection may look distinctly odd (or indeed very perceptive).

Have we got room to be genuinely comprehensive within the media we aim to cover? No. We certainly can't examine everything. Comedy's essential heterogeneity would make it difficult to cover the entire topic coherently even if it were not so vast. There are exhaustive efforts to do so elsewhere for single media such as Lewisohn (1998, 2003b) on British television, Siegel and Siegel (1994) and Austerlitz (2010) on American cinema and Wertheim (1979) on radio. One of the dangers of covering comedy across three media is that of merely producing a set of shallow historical surveys ('and then … and then …') that reiterate an existing canon of material. We won't be wholly able to escape this danger since we must take our aim to be a teaching textbook seriously and deal primarily with material that is readily available, but we will select comedy texts that are illuminating in their own right and/or revealing in the way they have previously been interpreted by other commentators. Our concentration on specific texts alongside the need to survey the field is necessary, because, without attentive examination through close reading, little can be added to our knowledge of comedy material. It is the uniqueness *and* the specificity of comedy in recordable media we focus on, presenting us with one-off moments that can be enjoyed again and again and analysed.

Analysing comedy

Despite André Bazin's view that comedy is the most serious genre in Hollywood, since it reflected 'the deepest moral and social beliefs in American life' (Bazin 1982), there has been resistance to analysing comedy in all of the media we are concerned with. It is perhaps most clearly seen in relation to film, as Andrew Horton notes: 'there is a historical bias against a close and serious consideration of comedy. That comic films seldom win Academy Awards even though comedy reigns at the box office (six out of the top ten selling films in 1988) is only the latest example in a long history of criticism that has viewed comedy as inferior to other genres in Western culture' (1991: 2). If Horton's evidence seems a little outdated, then the box office top tens for both 1998 and 2008 can also be invoked and both also show five comedies earning more than $100 million in America alone. If we include Computer Generated Image (CGI) animations predicated on comedy, such as *A Bug's Life* (1998) and *Kung Fu Panda* (2008), the significance of comedy to cinema only becomes clearer.

Comedy's commercial viability and lack of critical attention seem to be related. Comedy films are seldom culturally prestigious and are usually ignored by polls of 'the best' films, but they are reliable money earners, the bread and butter of the industry, capable of spectacular success. The same appeal to audiences and relative lack of attention paid by critics is apparent in critical response to television and radio comedy, too. Stott summarises the situation in the following way: 'Comedy's denigration in academic study is a product of its populism' (2005: 148).

An academic book (to our way of thinking at least) on the 'lowbrow' subject of comedy in popular media is necessary today, but outside of the academy any publication which aims to analyse comedy and humour seems anathema to many practitioners, anti-intellectuals and cultural snobs (among others). It has its echoes in the commonly expressed fear on the part of students that if we analyse comedy it will cease to be funny for us. There are a number of ripostes to this. Firstly, the implication is comparable to saying that being able to read music inhibits one's ability to appreciate it. Secondly, the field of comedy is far broader than just the things that make us laugh personally and anyone studying it may choose to target those pieces they don't find funny in the first place. Rightly, Andy Medhurst rebels against doing this, foregrounds his subjectivity and explores what makes him laugh, confident that 'knowing how comedy works, understanding its internal conventions, its performative dimensions and its ideological implications, causes no harm to its pleasurability unless the comedy under scrutiny was flawed from the outset' (2007: 6). The fear of finding that we shouldn't be laughing at what makes us laugh, coupled with the generally low academic status of humour (not to mention the constant attacks on media as a subject worthy of serious academic study) conspires to counsel caution in analysing comedy. Who knows what we might uncover? These fears may also determine why more usual ways of writing about comedy deflect interest away from how the comedy works.

Recent writers on the subject, such as Mills (2005), Medhurst (2007) and Deleyto (2009), argue strongly that far too little criticism of comedy focuses on the actual performance, delivery and sources of the humour. The interest in and affection for comedic performers and certain comedic texts has generated a lot of writing which instead assumes biographical and anecdotal form. Nostalgia and reminiscence are clearly acceptable frames through which to view comedy, but too often this material falls prey to the tendency to make comedic performers their own auteurs, responsible for all aspects of writing, production and performance of those media they appear in. While the history of comedy certainly features several true renaissance men and women, such approaches neglect the other aspects of the production context and the performers they work with. Auteurism, star studies and the industrial reliability of comedian-led comedy also provide tracks for academic criticism to follow but these are ultimately constraining if rigidly adhered to, at least in terms of what we hope to achieve here. Certainly material must be delivered by the appropriate performer(s) and in the right medium for that humour. Thus Buster Keaton's screen persona in his silent films is a key to their success, as is the rapport and particular range of silly voices that gave British radio's *The Goon Show* (1951–60) its unique character. Performers are interesting subjects, but the period in which they are at the cutting edge of comedy, or are otherwise vitally in tune with their time, may be brief. The nexus of things that makes comedy work ought not to be reduced to individuals, even where they are a driving force. Therefore we will not proceed entirely through personalities (performers, writers, directors) but will also highlight individual texts with little regard for their authorship.

Though claims that laughter is somehow 'universal' have some validity, the historical specificity of comedy must also be acknowledged as significant. In-depth archival work on a huge scale would be required to place our selected comedic texts in full historical context for a project of this scope, but an awareness of these media products as historical artefacts is something we encourage. There is clear evidence, just from the century our chosen media have been operational, that comedy tastes change over time. Did everyone find Laurel and Hardy funny when the films were originally screened, and does everyone today still find them funny? The sustained appeal of certain performers and texts to minority audiences can certainly be instructive, but supposedly 'timeless' comedy is actually just material from the past that has an appeal to the present. Identifying what an audience will find funny today is difficult enough for contemporary comedy producers but guessing exactly what they found funny in the past is perhaps even more so. It is one reason that discussion of comedy often comes down to personalities. Box-office returns, together with listener and viewer ratings, seem to suggest that audiences have found this or that performer funny at that particular time. We may also find them more or less amusing, to a degree, but can we be sure that we are laughing at the same things that appealed to contemporary audiences? Such assumptions are sometimes quickly elided, but we need to remember they are there. In our work we have to be aware of our early twenty-first century context and the influence it has on our understanding (and lack of understanding) of historical texts.

Writing about comedy is a lesson in subjectivity. One person's sense of humour is different from the next, but even if we laugh at the same time it is not clear whether we are laughing at exactly the same thing or exactly what aspect of the thing (line, event, image) sparks our laughter. What seems certain is that being surrounded by other people laughing at comedic material (except when we are the object of their laughter) makes it easier for us to laugh. Another key factor is our awareness of genre and the way in which comedic texts establish a '"conspiratorial" relationship with the viewer (reader)' (Horton 1991: 9) or gather what Brett Mills calls 'comic impetus' (2009: 5–6). When we turn on our televisions to watch a programme called *Michael McIntyre's Comedy Roadshow*, we have a good idea of what to expect. Thus primed, we are ready for the comedy text to deliver, but our experiences of rolling in the aisles are likely to be far fewer than we might have hoped for. What are we looking for as the primary comedy experience? Whether it is the silent comedians' hierarchical categories of 'the titter, the yowl, the belly laugh and the boffo' (Palmer 1987: 101), or Ken Dodd's more concise scheme of 'titters, woofers and belters', that primary experience is laughter. Comedy's aim of producing a physical reaction from its audiences puts it in the disreputable company of other genres aiming for a physical response, such as horror (see Paul (1994) on links between horror and comedy) and pornography.

Initial critical analyses of media texts preferred to look to respectable literary models instead, and as a result, as Stott suggests: 'a recurrent problem of comedy criticism is its focus on structure and plot' (2005: 31). Narrative coherence is by no means the key to comedy. Henry Jenkins, responding to early sound film in *What Made Pistachio Nuts?: Early Sound Comedy and the Vaudeville Aesthetic* (1992), explores the differing emphases of different comedy texts in relation to gags, lead performers, performance styles and self-reflexivity. Jenkins's (1992: 129–32) criteria for analysing coherence in narrative comedy are summarised below:

1 Narrative Integration: Is the emphasis on narrative or gags?
2 Character Integration: How well do character roles fit the star personae?
3 Expressive Coherence: How coherent are the actors' individual performances?
4 Ensemble Consistency: Is there a 'homogeneity of performance style' among the performers or not?
5 Consciousness of Audience: Do the performers work as though there was a fourth wall between them and the camera or do they play to the audience?

Using these criteria, Jenkins establishes an opposition between what he calls anarchistic comedy and affirmative comedy. In an anarchistic comedy the emphasis would be on gags over narrative, star persona over character, with less than coherent performances and no homogeneity of style across the cast, who may possibly show some awareness of the audience. The opposite emphasis, on narrative, character, homogeneity and maintaining the fourth wall, is typical of the romantic comedy or what Jenkins calls 'the affirmative comedy'. The two types are never, however, mutually exclusive: 'The disintegrative aspect of anarchistic comedy – the comedy of disorder – almost always coexists with the integrative aspect of romantic comedy – a comedy of reordering – though the emphasis given the two plots shifts from film to film across historical periods' (1992: 236).

A strong, involving and affecting narrative can increase comic dividends, but as Horton points out, 'No plot is inherently funny' (1991: 1). A genuinely funny sequence, something that goes beyond a 'bit' and reaches what Palmer calls 'comic articulation' (1987: 98–113), is gold. A few genuinely effective – because they raise laughs – scenes, sequences, catchphrases or characters will sell a comedy text to audiences much more successfully than the consistent level of achievement in the film, sitcom or sketch show they appear in. The basics, beyond reception context, are then relatively simple according to Palmer: 'any event – in order to be funny – should simultaneously be surprising, implausible and plausible' (1987: 136).

Let us suggest some famous comedy sequences that illustrate this:

- a starving Charlie Chaplin eating his boots in *The Gold Rush* (1925)
- Jack Benny pausing to consider his response to a mugger's demand for 'Your money or your life' in his radio vehicle, *The Jack Benny Show* (1948)
- Del-Boy (David Jason) falling through a bar counter while attempting to 'play it cool' in the situation comedy *Only Fools and Horses* (1989)
- the exchange 'Well you started it!' 'No, you started it; you invaded Poland' in the *Fawlty Towers* episode 'The Germans' (1975)
- Cameron Diaz gelling her hair with Ben Stiller's semen in *There's Something About Mary* (1998).

Such comedy is memorable, recountable, repeatable; but why? What exactly is it that is funny about these images or scenes? There will be important details for you that we've missed out, especially for any of them that are unfamiliar. This brings the additional question about how much context do we need to know to understand the gag? Anyone attempting to recount a humorous incident from their own life which they found far funnier than any of the examples cited above may find it impossible to convey the humour to others, leaving them with the wry conclusion along the lines of 'I guess you had to be there at the time'. Content is important, but establishing the comic context is key.

As anyone who has tried to tell a joke knows, it isn't simply dependent on the narrative or the cleverness of the words; a joke has to be performed or, as it is customarily put, 'delivered'. To do this well requires a combination of distinct attitude, build-up, facial expression, body language and timing. If some of these are good enough, and if the audience is sufficiently warmed up, the quality of the joke becomes less and less important. This is why some 'much-loved' sitcoms bear repetition so well.

To focus in particular on just one of the sequences recalled above; Del-Boy's brother, Rodney (Nicholas Lyndhurst), is distinctly taller than him and may, perhaps, have been even more spectacular when toppling rigidly through the unexpectedly open counter, since he has further to fall, but the laughs (coming partly because of surprise at this particular piece of slapstick intruding into a largely verbal sitcom) are heavily dependent on Del-Boy's misplaced confidence in his being master of any situation. Punctured pomposity is funnier than sheer haplessness.

In fact in each of our examples there is a level of delusion or a refusal of reality: a way for the audience to understand some aspect of the context

1 Buster Keaton with the two loves in his life, the train and the girl (Marion Mack), in *The General* (1926). See pages 41–2.

better than the characters in each case: You can't eat boots; life *is* better than money; Del-Boy is not, as he imagines, cool; Basil Fawlty is not, as he imagines, (currently) sane; semen isn't hair gel. Does this understanding lead to feelings of superiority or of sympathy? Do we take pleasure in knowing (or imagining) we are not that hungry, that stingy, that embarrassed, that tactless or that innocent? Or do we feel relief because we recognise that while we, too, are potentially prey to hunger, robbery, accidents and misunderstandings these particular mishaps have not happened to us?

Answers to these questions would not exhaust all that might be said about any of these sequences. Comedies (and jokes) are particularly resistant to being reduced to one meaning, seemingly preferring a range of possibilities which they (and we) arbitrarily close off with an 'ending' or by wilfully imposing a single 'meaning'. Critical and cultural neglect of comedy ('It's *only* a joke/ comedy') stems from allowing the often quite arbitrary endings of comedy narratives to stand for resolution of the issues raised (see Stott 2005: 148). The more familiar we are with the ways in which comedy works, the more easily we can identify the relevant issues in the texts.

To introduce what these issues might be we need to survey the academic field of comedic study and address the critical work that has preceded ours.

The field

It has been a commonplace complaint in earlier books on comedy that the subject has suffered from analytical neglect, but this is increasingly a relative statement. In the past it has been true, partly because of belated academic recognition of the media themselves, partly because the task of attaining academic credibility ordained that areas such as comedy, perceived as frivolous in a field sometimes accused of being itself entirely frivolous, were not the first to be focused upon. Over the extended development of this project, even when chapters have been written, in addition to new groundbreaking comedies appearing and 'classic' comedies becoming hard to get hold of, despite the wonder of YouTube, new academic material has regularly been published making this a sometimes Sisyphean struggle. This problem is exacerbated because we are attempting to cover a broad area. Our approach is part film studies, part media studies and part cultural studies within a socio-historical contextualisation. Our positions within each of these academic areas could be further exhaustively broken down, but we leave those who might be interested in the results to do so. The point is that comedy is of interest to a number of disciplines.

The first critics studying comedy in twentieth-century media, finding themselves in a new field, tended to want to map the whole thing comprehensively, only to find their maps did not suit those coming after them. Gerald Mast (1979; first published 1973) begins with definitions of comedy that he knows other will protest against. He himself vehemently argues against the more metaphorical approach of Raymond Durgnat in *The Crazy Mirror* (1969), while Jerry Palmer (1987) finds Mast irritatingly eclectic and hampered by his literary obsession with plot. Steve Seidman (1979, 1981) finds early writers too unfocused, and praises Stuart Kaminsky's systematisation (2nd ed. 1985), while introducing his own concept of 'comedian comedy'. Comedian comedy, now a critically recognised genre, focuses on the parallel tensions between the comedian's character conforming to the society represented in the film's narrative and the comedian's pre-established star persona conforming to the film's generic contract to provide comedy (1981: 3). Henry Jenkins (1992), in focusing on early sound comedy, begins to find the flaws in Seidman (defining the genre by criteria which really apply only to a specific historical period), yet Jenkins is in turn taken to task by Mark Winokur (1996) for neglecting what he sees as the overarching theme of ethnicity (as indicated by his title *American Laughter: Immigrants, Ethnicity, and 1930s Hollywood Film Comedy*). Ethnicity joins those recurrent academic frames which are the usual suspects in approaches to comedy (race, class and gender), since areas of conflict are also commonly areas for comedy.

We find that difference, while fundamental to humanity, has proved quite difficult for human cultures to negotiate. Complex and intelligent as human beings are, there appears to be a real difficulty in our assimilating the fact that others are not identical with ourselves. Where there is difference we subjectively define ourselves in relation to it, usually seeing ourselves in the best light by assigning negative characteristics, or at least inferior ones, to those who are different in whatever ways we deem to be important. As Eve Kosofsky Sedgwick points out: 'It is astonishing how few respectable conceptual tools we have for dealing with this self evident fact [of difference]. A tiny number of inconceivably coarse axes of categorization have been painstakingly inscribed in current critical and political thought: gender, race, class, nationality, sexual orientation are pretty much the available distinctions' (1990: 22). Contemporary critical approaches to comedy tend to highlight one or the other of these axes. For example, Gray (1994) and Rowe (1995) focus on gender, Winokur (1996) and Rappoport (2005) on ethnicity, and Beach (2002) on class. Choosing to focus on a range of these axes, rather than exclusively on one, we open ourselves to criticism from all those who come afterwards, though, as we have made clear, the expectations applied much depend on what each subsequent writer and critic aims to achieve. This is the point where we, if we wanted to, ought to start getting in some kicks at our predecessors. In the belief, however, that we are taking part in a noble enterprise, we claim to be standing on the shoulders of giants (though even this phrase may have originated as a joke), in fact several giants, at once.

Comedy texts, unlike criticism, do not have to be consistent in their approach, or in what they target and hit and therefore we haven't committed ourselves to any particular aspect of comedy in order to be free to choose the most productive approach to any given comedic text. Our attitude is that comedy is so heterogeneous, so diverse (often within the same text), that there is no single approach that can answer every circumstance (nor do we imply that foregoing writers believe this). It is simply wise to draw on a range of available approaches to explain different comedic phenomena in the most productive fashion possible and this is the approach we recommend. We don't expect that everyone will agree with our analyses, our choice of texts or this approach.

Theories of comedy

Abstract debate on the theory of comedy can be, as Gerald Mast acknowledged, 'a quicksand out of which many never climb' (1979: 3). Despite numerous important and illuminating contributions to understanding comedy, there is no one overarching theory of comedy which 'explains' comedy in all its heterogeneous diversity. We are with Andy Medhurst when he counsels us to reject the 'lure of the big C' and recognise the variety of intellectual paradigms that can be mobilised in any attempt to account for the complexities of comedy (2007: 10). We also heed Andrew Horton's considered view that 'No totalizing theory of comedy has proved successful' (1991: 2).

What we can say is that comedy has suffered from being taken *both* not seriously enough (in other words, not studied) *and* too seriously (that is, theorised about, but in ways that tend towards tedium). In the study of comedy there is something of a disjunction between those critical texts that focus on how humour works (for example, Freud's analysis of the mechanics of the joke) and those that focus on what appears to be at stake (that is, the content or subject of the comedy). Palmer, arguing in favour of his own approach, suggests that: 'To evoke values in the mode of humour is to evoke them in a special, unique way, a way which cannot be reduced to the serious presentation of the "same" material' (1987: 14–15). Medhurst argues, from a slightly different standpoint, that: 'Comedy is never just a question of content – questions of form, style, consumption, context and (often most crucial of all) performance must always be in play' (2007: 24). The complexity created for those studying comedy comes partly from the fact that: 'Humour is both a signifying process and a social process' (Palmer 1987: 204). That is, it is distinct from other genres but also embedded within wider culture. We have opted for a broad cultural focus while limiting (if that is the right term) ourselves to three media. The following comments attempt to position this book in relation to what we consider valuable – if sometimes contradictory and partial – theories of humour and comedy that have been advanced previously.

Though Aristotle argued that humour distinguished humankind from the beasts, Plato was fairly certain that comedy rotted thought, and his views were still current, among the educated classes, into the Renaissance and the early modern era (Morreall 1983: 85–9). If, as has been suggested, laughter is 'the enemy of social distinctions' (Stott 2005: 134), then, in fairly rigid, hierarchically structured societies, comedy clearly has subversive potential that needs careful policing. For Thomas Hobbes, writing in the early seventeenth century, laughter resided in a sense of superiority over others, such that we can laugh at their social inferiority. Though they emanate from a social structure long since gone, such notions of superiority, of scorn and disparagement, still carry a charge – where else does the comic potential of seeing someone slipping on a banana skin come from? Though much comedy relies on a sense of subversion, of undermining (if only briefly) treasured thoughts and beliefs, there is clearly a role for comedy in reinforcing views, values and attitudes, of utilising stereotypes and bolstering prejudices. If, as Andy Medhurst argues, 'Above all else, comedy is an invitation to belong' (2007: 19), it needs to be recognised that this sense of belonging is sometimes created by excluding others, which may explain why the British have their jokes about the Irish, the Americans their jokes about the Poles.

Politically situated explanations for humour ignore what many have seen as the ludicrous incongruities that are part and parcel of being human. For Henri Bergson, writing in 1900, 'the comic simply does not exist outside the pale of what is strictly *human*' (2008: 10). Faced with the eccentricities and foibles of human beings, laughter is a response, 'a sort of *social gesture*': human 'rigidity is the comic, and laughter is its corrective' (2008: 17). Though it is hard to take Bergson seriously once he asks 'What is there comic about a rubicund nose? And why does one laugh at a negro?' (2008: 25), his idea that laughter can arise only from an absence of emotion, that 'laughter is incompatible with emotion' (2008: 68), is interesting, as is his insistence on the social function of laughter and its reliance on the presence of others, as when he asserts that 'Our laughter is always the laughter of a group' (2008: 11). Bergson sees humour as springing from humanity's awareness of their helplessness in a crazy, machine-like world and his work does have considerable mileage in relation to silent, slapstick and physical comedy, as well as what Gehring (1996) terms 'Dark Comedy', where the world is often seen as inhospitable, antagonistic, strange (Stott 2005: 95).

If sociological and philosophical explanations of humour and comedy stress the extent to which human beings are not in charge of their world, the work of Freud and his followers questioned whether we are even in control of our own minds. In essence, Freud argued for a three-dimensional view of personality in which primitive, socially unacceptable *id* impulses are inhibited or censored by the moralistic *superego*, while the *ego* or conscious self mediates between them. In *Jokes and Their Relation to the Unconscious* (first published in 1905), he argues that all jokes and witty remarks relate directly or indirectly to some sort of socially unacceptable behaviour which is articulated in laughter. For Freud, most comedy and certainly most jokes centre on hostility and obscenity, on aggression and sex. Freud saw individuals in society as subject to various forms of necessary repression, involving us in the expenditure of psychic energy; a joke allows the feelings that are repressed to emerge into the open in a socially acceptable disguise. In this way, 'Jokes permit a brief holiday from inhibition and logic in order for them to be re-imposed with greater effectiveness' (Gray 1994: 29). They are 'little emissaries of the unconscious' (Stott, 2005: 11).

Freud allows us to make an important step. Our laughter is not consciously willed; it must come from part of us inaccessible to conscious thought. However, Freud's attempts to calibrate the psychic 'economy' of our response to jokes inhibits the development of this argument, and these aspects of his essay are regularly taken to task by commentators (Morreall 1983: 28–35; Palmer 1987: 35; Carey 2002). Though Freud did not set out to analyse a wide range of humour (only innocent wordplay and obscene jokes), his point about how humour accesses subconscious wishes is clearly a valuable one. His focus on release and relief, on the tension, arousal and release that accompany virtually all humour, is clearly relevant, especially when contentious topics such as sex, race, gender, religion and politics are being dealt with. Psychoanalytic theory allows us to make a distinction between 'Oedipal (accommodation, compromise, social integration) comedy and pre-Oedipal (wish fulfilment, dreams) comedy' (Horton 1991: 10). That distinction roughly equates to comedies interested in maintaining a link with narrative realism (affirmative comedies) and those comedies which favour the implausible and impossible (anarchistic comedies).

The notion of repression – whether social, political or psychological – has become central to our contemporary culture and this may explain the impact that Mikhail Bakhtin has had on recent attempts to explain comedy. Bakhtin has been invoked heavily since the mid-1980s because his concept of the carnivalesque, developed in relation to the works of the medieval writer Rabelais, seems useful in dealing with comedic excess (see Horton 1991: 12–14; Krutnik 2003: 13–16; Stott 2005: 32–9). The reversals of hierarchy and everyday order and the emphasis on the body, on food, drink, song, dance and sexuality in carnival certainly readily overlap with some forms of comedy. Carnival, like much popular comedy, offers a safety valve (or vent) for those at the bottom of the hierarchy and is nonetheless important for that, especially in its celebration of the universally human experience of the body. However, as other commentators have pointed out, carnival is a period of licensed transgression against the status quo rather than being genuinely subversive of authority. Moreover, Bakhtin's concern with sexuality is essentially with male sexuality, and his work does little to explain the abundance of mother-in-law jokes and the complete absence of father-in-law jokes. Nonetheless, Bakhtin's concept of the carnivalesque can be seen to combine Freud's idea of a temporary escape from the accepted order, even though, because of comedy's essential heterogeneity, it cannot account for all forms.

In different ways, Freud and Bakhtin suggest that, in the right conditions at the right time, the moment of laughter represents a willing, if temporary, suspension of normal mental processes, accepted mores, beliefs and values, whether these be moral, social or political. Given the right context, we are invited into a cognitive playground where anything goes, where we can transgress the conventional boundaries of taste, political correctness, morality, even reality itself. We acquiesce in a journey of exploration where there are few consequences since, and this is important, we are not being asked to abandon our moral values, political beliefs, deep-seated beliefs or even (dread the thought) our prejudices. We are asked to take a vacation, to imagine, to see things anew, rise above our thoughts, to stop taking everything so boringly seriously. As Rappaport points out, it was Erasmus who argued long ago in his *In Praise of Folly* (1509) that it is the impulsive, foolish, irresponsible thoughts and behaviours that make the practical realities of life bearable, and these are the stuff of comedy (Rappaport 2005: xiii).

This cognitive and affective clash between the world as it is and as it might be depends on our perceived sense of the ludicrous and the incongruous within a specific context. When two or more comments, characters, events or objects come into unexpected juxtaposition, the results can be jarring and, in the right context, frequently funny. Arthur Koestler (1949) explored this process in his concept of 'biosociation', where the juxtaposition of multiple 'independent and self-contained logical chains' creates a release of emotional tension resulting in laughter.

Jerry Palmer, who has made major contributions to the theory of comedy, especially with his *Logic of the Absurd* (1987), develops Koestler by positing the reciprocal relationship between plausible and implausible (absurd) explanations in gags – a kind of short circuit of logic – as the cause of laughter (1987: 70) Palmer uses a concise example from the film *Dr Strangelove* (1963) wherein Peter Sellers as President Merkin Muffley finds one of his generals and the Russian Ambassador struggling over a camera and is outraged: 'Gentlemen! You can't fight in here! This is the War Room!' Palmer explains: 'Both the plausibility and implausibility of this remark derive from the discourses that are fundamental to the structure of the plot. It is implausible because of the identification of "fight-war", plausible because war needs a high degree of organisation which must be conducted in a calm atmosphere' (1987: 190–1). The logic of the absurd is exactly what allows comic events to service simultaneously what others have called anarchistic and affirmative comedy narrative forms (1987: 143–9).

The comic effect that Palmer describes is, in fact, a double undermining from the space between the two explanations; a brief acknowledgement of the chasm that we have to leap across to continue the process of 'making sense'. This might seem frighteningly post-structuralist, but it also links back to psychoanalytical approaches because making sense, applying rules, is an imposition of 'grown-up' thinking over the untrammelled mind of childhood, still present in the adult subject but repressed from conscious thought in the *id*. Comedy might sometimes be seen as 'temporarily suspending the "rules" of adulthood and returning, albeit symbolically, to an earlier, pre-Oedipal state' (Horton 1991: 5). The activity of the *id* is routinely mastered by the rational adult mind, but the nature of comedy challenges that mental hegemony because comedy 'happens too fast for us to adjust to what is happening' (Morreall 1983: 48). The true laugh isn't consciously willed and one of humour's key elements is surprise, which is why jokes have 'punchlines' and comedians seek to 'knock audiences dead' (see Morreall 1983: 48–9). The key element of surprise creates hesitancy in the conscious mind (the *ego* – 'us') during which the unconscious mind can seize upon and apprehend other meanings and generate laughter. Explaining a joke, that is laying it out for the conscious intelligence, won't achieve anything like the same effect. Nonetheless, to do so occasionally might be instructive.

Here we return to one example briefly mentioned by Palmer (1987: 53–4) and discuss it in the manner that Horton (1991: 6–7) unpacks a Woody Allen joke, though, purposely, a little less neatly. The line is a short barb in the film *Horse Feathers* (1932) through which Groucho Marx indicates his irritation with a confederate: 'I'd horsewhip you if I had a horse.' Close analysis of this line puts it artificially into slow motion, even though the text in which it appears purposely gives us no time to do this. It is in fact a mere fragment, but how does it work as humour? Superficially, the line may be seen as two things: an expression of anger, and a knowing satire of a cliché of the angered aristocrat. These could be further complicated by the persona of the speaker and recipient (brothers playing father and son) and the situation of the delivery, but we will keep things simple for now (see Chapter 2). Our social conditioning tells us anger must be restrained; the tense used ('I would') already indicates the speaker has thought better of it, but it is the exposure of the reasoning behind the caveat ('if I had a horse') that creates the humour. The particular excuse we read off may be one of a non-exclusive range; the first is that the threat is immediately withdrawn because Groucho is too pusillanimous to actually offer any physical violence, thus the line diminishes his masculinity. A second reason might be that he thinks (very literally) that a horse and all the paraphernalia associated with it would be the only way to acquire the necessary equipment (a horsewhip) to carry out the threat, making this expression of anger impossible to him because it is dependent on wealth and class he doesn't have, another self-inflicted humiliation; a third excuse may be that the only thing holding him back is indeed the absence of a *horse* in the vicinity (rather than a horsewhip) with which he could whip the subject of his remark, which leads to either the impossible image of a man wielding a gramniverous quadruped or the implication that Groucho doesn't actually know what a horse or a horsewhipping is and that his use of language has exceeded his knowledge.

This may be a tortuous exposition of a single line and, of course, given the quick succession of gags, puns and one-liners that usually populate a comedy film (or television or radio programme) the chance to isolate one line is a luxury we don't get while viewing or listening. But, as Horton and Palmer indicate, given the correct climate or context (this is Groucho speaking in a Marx Brothers movie), we only need to perceive a pair of plausible and implausible readings to make the line effectively humorous. We've tried to indicate there is a wider range of possibilities open to us, whichever combination we might have used during viewing, without limiting the reading to a single meaning or pair of opposed meanings. We hope to have shown that this is also a line that may engage us in thinking about versions of social restraint, masculinity, class and the relationship between language and logic. In short, analysing one piece of verbal humour (reduced and simplified almost to a piece of text) has immediately plugged us in to a number of crucial issues. Such detailed analysis will clearly not be possible throughout. What we need to do now is to explain how the book will proceed.

The structure of this book

The focus, parameters and methodological approach of the book have been outlined above in this Introduction. We have argued that, though no single theory can possibly begin to explain the diversity and heterogeneity of comedy, there are some ideas and concepts that are particularly useful as we begin to explore comedy in our chosen media forms. A basic glossary of terminology for dealing with comedy concludes the Introduction.

The chapters that follow indicate the history and development of comedy in film, radio and television, consider the cultural functions of comedy and undertake close textual analyses of some comedy texts with a view to encouraging further work. We have split our ten chapters between two parts, and outline below the specific content and structure of these parts.

In Part I, we are concerned to look at how comedy works. In order to do this we turn our attention to the nature of comedy as manifested in specific media forms, from the exploitation of the non-visual in radio to the familiar, domesticated settings suited to television's small screen; from the silent cinema screen to the possibilities of CGI. We examine the historical, industrial and cultural contexts in which British and American comedy in film, radio and television developed (in that order). The chapters focus on certain genres rather than all sub-genres of comedy in these media and look at particular examples, evaluating specific criticism and a range of critical approaches to these forms.

Chapters 1 to 3 deal specifically with the development of comedy in film. The first chapter discusses silent comedy, including the classical comedian comedies of Charlie Chaplin, Harold Lloyd and Buster Keaton. The second chapter focuses comedy in the early sound period and the very different approaches to sound film of the Marx Brothers and Laurel and Hardy. The third chapter steps aside from these comedian comedies to follow the parallel 1930s development of the sound romantic comedy film. Across these three chapters considerations of genre, sub-genre and the dominant forms of comedy (slapstick, verbal humour) are highlighted with particular reference to the interaction between anarchistic and affirmative modes of comedy.

Chapters 4 and 5 on radio and television address comedy in broadcast media. We focus on the industrial context and practices that flow from and reflect different national attitudes to these media. Building on previous criticism of broadcast comedy, these chapters highlight the preferred comedic forms and formats of these media. In the distinctively different products from either side of the Atlantic across the two media there are, however, considerable continuities, such as the use of sketch comedy and its unique-to-broadcasting spin-off specialist form, the sitcom.

Having established some of the basic characteristics of comedy in these media as they developed over time, in Chapter 6 we discusses the disrespect with which comedy treats generic boundaries, looking in particular at comedy westerns, musical comedies and so-called mockumentaries. As the comic impetus finds its targets within the forms that surround and compete with it, the chapter discusses what this urge towards hybridising and self-reflexivity demands of its makers and audiences, and what it illustrates about the particularities of comedy.

Chapter 7 examines a special case in comedic form by taking a closer look at animation and the specific comedic modes developed by the early pioneers of animated comedy and sustained in the present by the computer-generated comedy blockbusters of recent years. Though not restricted to comedy, the history of animation on film and television shows it largely dominated by comedic forms, evolving in particularly surreal and self-reflexive ways.

All these chapters stress the importance of recognising formal, institutional and technological determinants that help shape comedy and raise issues about the transitory nature of much comedy, relating these to an understanding of the cultural dynamics of comedy's reception and consumption.

In Part II, the focus is on what comedy does, and we engage in more detail with the social functions of comedy and raise questions about the construction, transmission and contestation of cultural values by engaging with a few of Sedgwick's 'inconceivably coarse axes of categorization ... inscribed in current critical and political thought: gender, race, class, ... [and] sexual orientation' (1990: 22), though not in that order. In particular we look in more detail at the ways in which comedy texts engage in key social and cultural debates and form part of a culture's ongoing negotiation with fundamental issues in human life. Through a series of overlapping histories of comedy in film and/or television and radio we note the effects of comedy's engagement with these issues and the controversies it often causes. In particular we discuss ways in which issues of class and gender dictate the reputation of particular comedy texts and how comedy highlights issues of gender and race in ways that may be seen as liberating or divisive.

Chapter 8 deals with gender, sexuality and comedy, ranging from the depictions of femininity and masculinity in romantic comedy film to the representations offered of gay and lesbian characters across our chosen media. The chapter also highlights the opportunities comedy texts provide for queer readings of gender and sexuality simply by reason of their undermining the rigid categories of patriarchal discourse.

Chapter 9 considers taste as a criterion for evaluating comedy and the different standards invoked in relation to cultural capital, class, gender and postmodern irony. Studies of low British comedy and American gross-out comedy underpin work on specific examples which directly challenge standards of taste and cultural taboos.

Chapter 10 investigates race and ethnicity as issues for comedy, and evaluates various examples of screen and radio comedy which have picked their way through these cultural minefields. The chapter focuses on changes in television representations of race in Britain and on the representation of African-Americans in film and television, and explores why comedy is often the preferred form for raising these issues and how easily humour around race and ethnicity takes on an ambivalence that might be troubling as well as effective in producing laughter.

The book ends with a short conclusion that briefly considers the likely future of comedy, the impact on it of new technologies, where the frontiers of transgressive taste may lie, public nostalgia and affection for past comedy and the appetite for new forms of comedy. After that, we'll all need a lie down.

The Appendix is not for everyone.

Terminology

The following brief definitions are intended as a useful summary without providing a full justification or history of the terms. Steve Neale and Frank Krutnik's in-depth discussion in *Popular Film and Television Comedy* (1990: 1–82) has been a major source for the following.

Comedy: At its most basic a genre (in literature, theatre, film, radio or television) in which the narrative has a happy ending. As such laughter is not necessarily essential to a comedy. In film, television and radio the genre of comedy is usually assumed to entertain audiences by generating laughter. It doesn't, therefore, necessarily depend on narrative. Because the genre of 'comedy' is otherwise too broad to be critically useful, comedy is prone to hybridisation (e.g. comedy-drama, comedy-western, situation-comedy, comedy quiz).

Structure of comedy narrative: The sequence is usually Exposition, Complication, Resolution (Happy Ending); possibly extended with Further Complication before Final Resolution (Happy Ending). Other than the presence of the happy ending there is really nothing to mark this structure as comic.

Comic: Causing (or meaning to cause) laughter.

Comic motivation: Developments in comedy narrative tend to be less rigorously motivated than in other genres. Comedy conventions are flexible, and often laughter-generating comic devices work against coherent narrative development and verisimilitude.

Comic devices can be subdivided as follows: **Gag:** A joke or comic utterance (for Neale and Krutnik 1990: 51–2 the only type of gag is the visual gag defined below). **Visual gag:** From a pratfall to a visual pun. **Articulated or developed visual gag:** A sequence of visual gags. **Comic event:** Any of the above which is comic only by virtue of its narrative context.

Comic types: These might be sorted into one of the following: the joke-teller, the comedian (a particular comic persona), the stereotype, the fully rounded comic character.

Comic modes: Parody: A mode of comedy that targets the conventions of a pre-existing aesthetic form. This is not the same as a simple comedy hybrid because in a parody comedy dominates the partner genre. **Satire:** A mode of comedy that mocks or attacks social conventions. **Slapstick:** A physical mode of comedy that predominated in the silent period but is still with us in contemporary visual comedy (see Chapter 1). **Spoof:** A full-length parody (see Chapter 6).

Following up

☞ In each of the following chapters there will be several sections in this format and under this heading which will offer some suggestions for further exploration of the areas and issues discussed. No doubt you can think of other approaches that would be just as good, or better, to help you to get to grips with what really interests you about comedy. In this case just use the appearance of the 'Following up' sections as a reminder to do so. If you are studying comedy to write about it please refer to the Appendix at the end of the book for advice.

Recommended reading

Stephen Neale and Frank Krutnik, *Popular Film and Television Comedy*, London: Routledge, 1990.

Geoff King, *Film Comedy*, London: Wallflower, 2002.

PART I

Comedy forms

1

Silent film comedy

In 1954 the writer John Montgomery, having just seen Harold Lloyd's 1923 silent comedy *Safety Last* at a London cinema repertory club, proclaimed 'I have never seen anything so funny! The audience was in hysterics throughout' (Montgomery 1968: 268). Half a century later, it is difficult to imagine a contemporary audience having the same reaction. Although the work of Charlie Chaplin, Buster Keaton, Harold Lloyd and other silent film comedians has been made more accessible through DVD, for most people silent comedies have become unfashionable and incomprehensible artefacts from a distant and strange era, marked above all by the absence of audible spoken language which renders their aesthetic unacceptably 'difficult'. We might experience amused admiration of the clever antics on display, appreciate the witty intelligence of some of the comic material, but this is likely to be mixed with a degree of bemusement about exaggerated acting styles, discomfort about levels of physical abuse and annoyance at the ethnic and gender stereotypes on display. While revered as 'comedy greats' whose historical influence and significance is readily acknowledged, even the films of Chaplin, Keaton and Lloyd are more likely to be admired for their wit and visual audacity than for any ability to induce hysterical belly-laughs. The work of lesser-known talents such as Harry Langdon, Larry Semon, Mabel Normand and Ford Sterling seems even more remote from our contemporary comic sensibilities. Yet a consideration of silent film comedy raises important questions about the relationship between comedy and the cultural context in which it is produced, and about changing audience tastes and perceptions of what passes as funny.

Any attempt to understand silent film comedy fully is constrained by a number of factors. In spite of the greater accessibility of material on DVD, an enormous number of films have gone missing. As a result most critical writing about silent film comedy is constructed around those films and comedians that have survived. Archival research is helping us to 'recover' something of the historical and cultural context in which silent film comedy flourished, but much more needs to be done if we are to understand fully the modes, diversity and appeal of silent comedy for disparate cinema audiences. Moreover, a tendency to regard generic systems as synchronic and static rather than diachronic, subject to change and evolution, means that we often judge silent cinema through inappropriate criteria, often 'reading back' from contemporary notions of the comic in ways that do little justice to comedy forms, aesthetics and sensibilities that differ radically from our own, but which were popular in their own time. Add to this the alien, truncated experience of watching films with no spoken dialogue (often on a small screen), our unfamiliarity with having to read sometimes quite lengthy title cards and the fact that we are less adept at lip-reading than silent cinema audiences were, and it is easy to understand why even the greatest films from the silent comedy era can seem remote from what contemporary audiences expect from film comedy.

The history and evolution of silent film comedy from the mid-1890s to the coming of commercially viable synchronised sound cinema in the late 1920s mirrors changes within cinema itself during that period, changes which were evident not just in film production and aesthetics but in audience reception and consumption of films. From being a novelty whose lasting impact was still a matter of speculation, to becoming a medium of industrialised mass consumption, silent comedy no less than silent cinema as a whole underwent rapid transformation. This process was far from ordered and coherent, as competing companies attempted to discover comedians and comic modes that generated box-office success. However, it is possible to outline certain broad trends in the development of silent film comedy, trends that reflect changes in the development of the film industry and its relationship with audience taste and expectations, as well as broader historical and cultural changes. While recognising the diversity that characterised developments in silent film comedy, Peter Krämer (1988: 100–1) identifies six distinct phases in the development of American silent film comedy:

1. early 'trick' comedies that played with technical possibilities such as stop-motion and superimposition, but which were obsolete by 1908
2. 'slapstick' comedies and parodies of emerging contemporary cinematic genres produced by companies such as Keystone from 1912 onwards
3. social and situation comedies starring featured players such as John Bunny and Sidney Drew which, from 1912 onwards privileged characterisation rather than frenetic comic action
4. slapstick 'comedian comedies' such as Chaplin's early films at Keystone in 1914 and at Essanay in 1915 which emphasised the character and performance of the star, but still involved a high degree of physical action and knockabout
5. so-called classical 'comedian comedies' such as those starring Buster Keaton, Harold Lloyd and Chaplin's later films which paid much greater attention to integrating comic performance and persona into more structured dramatic patterns

6 more sophisticated social comedies of the late 1910s and early 1920s which dispensed with dominant comic personas in favour of intricate narrative construction, depth of characterisation and realistic situations and behaviour.

Early cinema and early film comedy

Like contemporary audiences at an IMAX screening, the audiences who flocked to see the Lumière brothers' Cinematograph in 1895 and similar shows went to experience novelty. They enjoyed the process of sitting together in a darkened space, caring little, certainly before they decided to go, about what types of films were being screened. What they saw at these and other early exhibitions of moving pictures in the 1890s and early 1900s were short actuality films, often shot in recognisable locations, military scenes, close-up 'facial' films and 'trick' films that exploited the mechanics of filmed projection, filmed stage acts featuring conjurors, dancers and gymnasts, and comedies, lots of comedies.

The early comedy shorts that have survived from this period, such as the Lumière brothers' own *L'Arroseur Arrosé* (aka *The Gardener and the Bad Boy*, 1895) appear at one level simple and unsophisticated. The Lumière catalogue described this 'domestic scene comedy' as 'showing a lawn with a gardener using a hose to sprinkle it. A bad boy steps on the hose, causing the water to squirt into the gardener's face. He drops the hose, runs after the boy, and gives him a sound thrashing.' However, as Charles Musser suggests, this and other early silent comedy films signal many of the formal, thematic and ideological issues that remain central to an understanding of contemporary film comedy (Musser 1994: 143). There is, arguably, a basic narrative, predicated on the relationship between cause and effect. This narrative is combined with and contains moments of physical excess and abuse, as the water squirts into the gardener's face. We, the audience, are to some extent implicated in the boy's determined act of transgression, unable and unwilling to warn the gardener of the boy's actions, but sharing in the process of retribution as the boy is chased and punished. The slapstick world of physical excess challenges, but is ultimately contained within, a wider moral world, as order and stability appear to be restored. *L'Arroseur Arrosé* inspired a genre that remained popular between 1896 and 1905; short, single-shot, films based around a single gag often featuring a 'bad boy' who is usually punished for his actions (Gunning 1995: 89). More importantly, *L'Arroseur Arrosé* is amenable to a range of social, political and psychoanalytical interpretive readings.

It is doubtful whether contemporary audiences entered into ruminations about the meaning of these early comedies, though they appeared to enjoy the moments of physical excess that were central to the films, moments that were imitated by different film-makers and different companies operating in different countries, often tailored to local audiences. The basic gag in

L'Arroseur Arrosé was copied by the British pioneer Birt Acres in his comedy *A Surrey Garden* (1896) and clearly influenced a series of early British comedy shorts made by James Williamson, including *Two Naughty Boys Teasing the Cobbler* (1898). The basic gag involving a fight with white flour and black soot in R.W. Paul's early British comedy *The Miller and the Sweep* (1897) is reused in his *Quarrelsome Neighbours* (1897). Biograph's *The Prodigal's Return* (1896), described as a 'laughing picture' in which a well-off gentleman returns 'to his home in a jolly condition and reveals his trouble when he attempts to find his way into bed' (Musser 1994: 157), sounds remarkably similar to R.W. Paul's *Two AM; Or, The Husband's Return* (1896) in which a drunk comes home and, despite his best efforts, inadvertently wakes his wife.

At a time when 'cinema', as we understand the term, did not exist, short films were exhibited at fairgrounds, travelling shows and other, often itinerant, sites that were already catering for a public eager for novelty and variety. The curiosity value of film was not confined to working-class audiences in the late 1890s, as suitable films such as travel shorts and news footage (both real and fabricated) were shown at respectable American venues such as Keith's Bijou, the Brooklyn Institute and their European equivalents (Musser 1994: 183–9). However, for poor, working-class and immigrant audiences across Europe and the United States, films needed to make an immediate and intelligible impact. Comedy films, particularly those with slapstick and visual gags centred on robust physicality, met this need. Originally referring to a light paddle made of two thin pieces of wood that made a loud noise when used to strike another comic or clown in pantomime, circus and other forms of 'low' comedy, slapstick became an important part of early silent comedy films.

American slapstick comedy, reliant on fast and furious physical activity, became associated with Mack Sennett's Keystone Company from 1912 onwards. Before that American audiences were supplied with imports and copies of European comedies, especially from Italy and France, where comedians such as Ferdinand Guillame and André Deed made comedies that exploited the ability of film to effect sudden transformations in time and space, challenging the accepted boundaries and physical logic of the material world. Known in France as Boireau, in Italy as Cretinni and for American audiences as Foolshead, Andre Deed and other comedians exploited the ability that silent film had to play easily to a range of international audiences. Many of these comedies relied on the seemingly universal appeal of film's special effects, on simple plots involving mistaken identities or simply on the chase. Perhaps the most important and certainly the most influential of these early European silent comedians was the Frenchman Max Linder (1883–1925), who began making films for Pathé in 1906. Though there are elements of physical slapstick in his films, Linder's films mark the development of that strand of early film comedies that rely on character and situation as much as physical excess. Initially unbilled, Linder's character Max was acknowledged from 1909 onwards in films such as *Max Takes a Bath*, *Max Is Jealous* and *Max's Mother-in-Law*. The importance of character and costume to Linder's success proved hugely influential when American film comedy began to challenge the dominance of European companies and comedians in the period just prior to the outbreak of the First World War. Max Linder's own move to America was more important as an indication of the growing power of Hollywood than for any success enjoyed by the films he made in America.

The emergence of American film comedy from 1912: Mack Sennett and Keystone

Comedy was an increasingly prominent element of film production across Europe prior to the outbreak of the First World War. In Britain, for example, the Ec-Ko Film Company was formed in 1912 and produced one slapstick comedy short a week. Billy Merson's Homeland Film Syndicate also produced a string of short comedies featuring British music hall talent. However, although the war in Europe was to cause immense damage to European film production capacity, the emergence of an increasingly powerful American film industry was evident even prior to 1914. A key figure in the development of this growth and in American film comedy was the Canadian-born Mack Sennett (1880–1960). Like the more recent 'dot com' boom of the late twentieth and early twenty-first centuries, from 1908 onwards a rash of new film companies started up and expanded to meet unprecedented audience demand for the new technology, increasingly being seen in purpose-built cinemas which were growing in number, size and luxuriousness. Sennett founded the Keystone Company in the summer of 1912, a subsidiary of the already successful New York Motion Picture Company owned by Adam Kessel and Charles O. Baumann. Between 1912 and 1932, Sennett, through various companies, produced over eleven hundred films, including the short silent comedies that characterised studio output in the late 1910s and early 1920s, an output that 'singularly influenced the direction and dimension of motion picture humour for over two decades' (Lahue 1971: 43).

In popular imagination Keystone remains best known for its Keystone Kops, frantic car chases and pie-throwing slapstick. In fact the contribution made by Sennett and the Keystone Company to the development of silent film comedy is more extensive and significant. In the first place, despite numerous experiments with early film sound, Sennett proved that a certain type of film comedy worked within the constraints and limit points of silent cinema, most notably the absence of audible dialogue, and worked in ways that appealed to contemporary cinema audiences. Influenced both by French film fantasy and by a more raucous American burlesque tradition, Sennett managed to combine the two in short two-reel comedy films (each reel lasting approximately ten minutes) that engaged with aspects of the lived experiences of emerging social and cultural modernity. Keystone's early ethnic comedies of 1912 and 1913 acknowledged the presence of Jewish and immigrant audiences, still struggling with English as a language, but having to deal with the exigencies of crowded urban and domestic life. Acknowledging the deprivations that audiences lived with, Keystone comedies celebrated the brutish vulgarities and injustices that were central to immigrant and urban working-class experience, and offered some form of carnivalesque retribution through their reiterative images of incompetent authority. At the same time Sennett was not slow in exploiting the commercial potential of female display through the increasing use of what officially became the Sennett 'Bathing Beauties' from 1917, even though the girls served little purpose as comic devices. In the same way, Keystone's 'Kid Komedies' series from 1913 onwards made unashamed use of the 'cute' appeal of child stars such as Paul Jacobs, whilst perpetuating the animosities between adults and malicious youngsters established with the 'bad boy' genre a decade earlier. In his highly unreliable memoirs, Sennett claimed that Keystone 'was a university of nonsense' but there is little doubting the success that the studio enjoyed (Sennett 1954: 140).

Sennett's significance also lay in the number of screen comedians who worked for him. As one commentator noted, looking at the cast lists of early Keystone comedies, 'it seems that virtually everyone who was anyone in the days of the silent film comedy had worked for Mack Sennett at one time or another' (Lahue 1971: 103). While most of these, such as Slim Summerville, Bobby Vernon, Charles Avery, along with numerous female comedians such as Louise Fazenda and Polly Moran, have been forgotten, others, including Mabel Normand, Roscoe Arbuckle, Ben Turpin, Edgar Kennedy and Charlie Chaplin, enjoyed more or less illustrious comedy careers with both Sennett and other companies. For many, notably Chaplin, Sennett's comedy formula, with its emphasis on pace, physical slapstick, reiterative visual gags and the inevitable climactic chaotic chase, proved too restrictive and 'Sennett invariably lost his people as they began to find themselves' (Kerr 1975: 70). Driven in part by his concern to resist the increasingly higher salaries demanded by players who could be readily identified by audiences, Sennett's ensemble-based comedy vehicles resisted the development of individual identification and talent, so that the byword amongst aspiring screen comedians became 'start with Sennett – get rich somewhere else' (Louvish 2003: 100).

Keystone's comic world was one of impossible physicalities, of fantastic biologies, where people are hit on the head with bricks and survive, are thrown down flights of stairs before scampering away, where tying a shoelace often involved being kicked on the backside, where, amongst others, Chaplin and Marie Dressler conduct their courtship by throwing bricks at each other. The sheer preponderance of successive visual gags has sometimes been seen as a weakness in Sennett's films, attracting criticism that they were 'long on gags and short on logic and story line' (Lahue 1971: 267). Arguably, such criticism not only misunderstands the nature of much silent film comedy but fails to account for the enduring popularity of slapstick well into the 1920s and beyond. While narrative cinema was developing in genres such as melodrama and the western, slapstick comedy gags were intended, as Donald Crafton argues, 'as a calculated rupture' (1995: 107), as moments of excess that disrupted and forestalled narrative. Though the ideological function that gags were able to undertake was increasingly threatened by film industry economics, manifest in the tendency towards increased narrative integration, it is possible to understand this distinctive phase of silent film comedy only by recognising narrative and slapstick as 'two distinct modes of cinema ... each driven by particular and historical contexts' (King 2002: 24).

Short comedies, in particular, were designed to be gag-driven and it was enough to establish a setting and situation in which the gags were to predominate. Though Sennett and Keystone excelled at such films and numerous other studios produced slapstick shorts, the demand for more 'culturally respectable' product was evident as early as 1912. John Bunny (1863–1915) is now the forgotten man of American silent film comedy, despite enjoying huge global success and earning a salary that matched US President Woodrow Wilson's (Gehring 1997: 37). Between 1910 and 1915 Bunny featured in over two hundred comedy shorts, most of which have not survived. A capable stage actor who also starred in a British three-part version of *Pickwick Papers* (1913), Bunny's Vitagraph domestic comedies, in which he was invariably at odds with a puritanical and domineering wife (often played by the diminutive Flora Finch), gave screen comedy a critical respectability, not least through their rejection of slapstick and physical violence as central comic mechanisms. Instead, Bunny relied on an understated acting style which expressed his frustration at his inability to pursue masculine activities that are frowned upon by his wife. In *A Cure for Pokeritus* (1912), for example, his love for gambling is frustrated by his wife's machinations that force him into a resigned form of domestic incarceration. At a time when women's suffrage and emancipation were major political issues, Bunny's comedies clearly keyed in to social anxieties centred on gender roles in ways that transcended some of the more basic comic appeal of slapstick. In much the same way, the popular Vitagraph films starring Mr and Mrs Sidney Drew were proof that there was a market for domestic film comedy in the early 1910s which relied on carefully performed, nuanced explorations of the comic potential inherent in 'respectable' married life. Like Bunny, Sidney Drew came from a 'legitimate' theatre background and his appearance in film comedy undoubtedly made silent film comedy more acceptable to middle-class audiences.

Following up: early silent comedies

☞ A lot of silent film comedies are now available on YouTube, though the viewing quality is often poor compared to how contemporary film audiences would have experienced them, and they may well be heavily edited or otherwise 'corrupted'. However, bearing this in mind, take a look at an example of an early comedy such as *L'Arroseur Arrosé* or *The Miller and the Sweep*, compare these with one of Sennett's Keystone Kops short films and consider the differences between them. Despite these differences, in what sense do the films share a reliance on visual gags and slapstick?

☞ Do you agree with Musser that these early films signal many of the formal, thematic and ideological issues central to contemporary comedy, or is King right when he asserts that slapstick and narrative in early films represent 'two distinct modes of cinema'?

☞ What are the limitations of slapstick and physical violence as comic mechanisms? By referring to specific examples, analyse the extent to which slapstick remains an element in contemporary film comedy.

The rise of the slapstick 'comedian comedies': Charlie Chaplin

Though the slapstick comedies produced by Keystone and others were criticised at the time and subsequently for what was perceived as their 'crude vulgarity', slapstick continued to be an important comic mode throughout the 1920s. However, improvements in technology resulted in better film stock and lengthier films, and the commercial drive to appeal to more affluent middle-class audiences, together with the development of narrative feature films in other genres, meant that accommodations needed to be made. Although slapstick comedy shorts continued to be popular with audiences as part of 'an evening's entertainment' (Koszarski 1994) along with newsreels, series, cartoons and a feature film, it became increasingly clear that, to avoid being marginalised commercially, film comedy would have to produce longer-length films. As a consequence, the disruptive, excessive moments provided by visual gags were increasingly required to relate in some manner to narrative plausibility. This inherent aesthetic and ideological tension between 'crude', logically incoherent slapstick gags and 'respectable', coherent and organised narrative found a formal solution in the rise of 'comedian comedies' that placed greater emphasis on performance through the presence of a star comedian. Prior to 1920 this development of comic personae took place within the short comedy film form rather than in feature films.

In Britain the most significant 'comedian comedies' starred Fred Evans in the 'Pimple' series of films produced between 1912 and 1918. Though Evans never created an entirely consistent costume for Pimple, the film titles, such as *Pimple's New Job* (1913), *Pimple Has One* (1915) and *Pimple's Uncle* (1915) clearly point to the central role played by the main comic character. Like Sennett's output, many of the Pimple films created comic effect through their parodies of contemporary film dramas and melodramas, such as *Pimple's Charge of the Light Brigade* (1914). Though their knockabout humour and emphasis on visual gags bear similarities with developments in American silent comedy of the same period, in many respects the Pimple films anticipated the absurdist tradition in British comedy evident later in the Goons and Monty Python. In America the central figure in the development of slapstick 'comedian comedies' was the British-born Charlie Chaplin (1889–1977).

Though not usually regarded as an innovator, Sennett had produced a feature-length comedy, *Tillie's Punctured Romance*, as early as 1914. Starring Marie Dressler in the title role and featuring Chaplin and Mabel Normand, the film was marketed as 'The Impossible Attained – A SIX REEL COMEDY'. A contemporary reviewer for the *Motion Picture News* saw the film as a 'masterpiece of the slapstick art' and as 'six thousand feet of undiluted joy' (Mitchell 1997: 259–60). Though the film has a clear narrative trajectory, much of the puncturing comes from successive visual gags performed by Chaplin, playing a decidedly unsavoury character cynically seeking a share of the millions that Tillie is about to inherit. Typical of the slapstick gags in the film are those that take place in the restaurant where Tillie, abandoned by Charlie, has taken a job as a waitress. When Charlie and Mabel, his altogether more attractive girlfriend, arrive in the restaurant for a meal, he has his chair pulled from beneath him and gets his ear pulled and face slapped as he flirts with an attractive waitress, before having a tray of food tipped all over him when confronted by the hapless Tillie. As he makes his exit amidst the ensuing bedlam, Charlie treads on the prostrate Tillie, who has fainted away at the shock of seeing him. A departing step on the stomach of a fallen adversary became one of the small defining trademarks of the tramp persona in Chaplin's two-reel comedies, a small gesture of triumph in a world where such triumphs are limited. Some comic meanderings and pratfalls on a park bench under the suspicious eye of a Keystone policeman occur before a return to the narrative announces the apparent death of Tillie's millionaire uncle, a cue for the cad to return to the restaurant where, slipping and sliding on the floor, he declares his 'love' for Tillie. Married and living in the palatial home, Tillie catches Charlie kissing Mabel and a frantic chase involving pie-throwing, gunshots and the incompetent Keystone Kops follows, as slapstick both ruptures and is clearly privileged over the plot. Interestingly, the film closes on a display of female solidarity as both Tillie and Mabel, friends united, reject the villainous 'city slicker' Charlie.

The thirty-four other pictures that Chaplin made for Keystone were all shorts. In spite of the success of *Tillie's Punctured Romance*, Sennett failed to capitalise on the success of feature-length comedy film and, indeed, on

Chaplin, who left Keystone for Essanay in 1915. Though his appearance in the film, dressed in over-sized boots and ill-fitting trousers that presaged the famous 'Tramp' costume, contributed enormously to Chaplin's rising fame and earning potential, neither he nor the studios he worked for returned to feature-length comedies until the 1920s. With the exception of some extended-length Mr and Mrs Sidney Drew comedies for Vitagraph, some adaptations of popular stage successes and feature-length character comedies starring Douglas Fairbanks, such as *Wild and Woolly* (1917) and *When the Clouds Roll By* (1920), star comedians developed their screen personas through comedy film shorts that retained a strong element of knockabout comic violence and visual gags.

The development of 'comedian comedy' was reliant on the construction of a consistent comic persona that was present in film after film (Riblet 1995). Though constrained by the short, two- and three-reel format, Chaplin was able to develop a screen persona that emerged more fully in his films for Essanay, including *The Tramp* (1915). Though he first appeared in a tramp costume in his second film for Keystone, *Kid Auto Races* (1914), he had previously appeared with 'a tall silk hat, a monocle and a "'way-down-East" droopy mustache' (Sennett 1954: 153) in *Making a Living* (1914), as the similarly well-dressed Lord Helpus in *Cruel, Cruel Love* (1914), in smart 'civvy' clothes in *Tango Tangles* (1914) and dressed as a woman in *A Busy Day*, in *The Masquerader* (both 1914) and in Essanay's *A Woman* (1915). In Essanay's *His New Job* (1915), Chaplin gets through several costume changes in a film studio, one of several reflexive films that have the emergent real-life film star playing someone struggling to find a place within the film business. This trajectory towards the development of a costume and screen persona that was appealing, memorable and that resonated with the times was not, as Chaplin often implied, natural, consistent or inevitable (Chaplin 1966: 145). As we have seen, Chaplin's character in *Tillie's Punctured Romance*, a cynical, misogynistic city slicker, was a deeply unsympathetic one, leading to rejection at the conclusion of the film. Chaplin's tramp costume accommodated the crude slapstick vulgarity that remained an element in his films even as late as *City Lights* (1931) (Paul 1991), but transformed him into a much more sympathetic character, both part of, and set apart from, mainstream society. In this he perhaps was able to represent the condition of millions of people, not just in America, but wherever the conditions of modernity were emerging. The shift from rural to urban existence and the alienating experience of working in factories and offices, the experience of poverty in the middle of apparent prosperity driven by powerful, uncaring, emergent corporations, the increase in the pace of life epitomised by developments in transportation and the media, the social and cultural shifts encapsulated by the notion of 'The Jazz Age', inform much of Chaplin's comedy. However, this development of what is sometimes referred to as an 'Everyman' figure was barely perceptible in Chaplin's films for Keystone;

as Sennett recalled, 'I did not see ... the subtleties and the pathos of the small, hard-pressed man in a dilemma' (Sennett 1954: 156).

This hesitant development of a consistent screen persona was reliant on Chaplin's growing, if still tentative, ability to motivate and justify knockabout physical comedy within the framework of a film's storyline, so that his comic gestures rooted in the slapstick tradition began to 'conform to an emotional reality' (Kerr 1975: 74). This is evident in Essanay's *The Bank* (1915), in which Chaplin plays a janitor who foils a bank robbery, but still fails to get the girl. Chaplin starts the film in tramp costume, but spends most of the film in his janitor's oversized coat that he keeps in the bank vaults. As with so many of Chaplin's comedies, not least *Work* (1915), one of his best films for Essanay which he wrote and directed, the comedy is rooted in the world of work, or at least the attempt to look for and sustain employment. Work, along with food, occupies a central place in his comedies, both of them rendered scarce and not to be taken for granted in a society riven by social injustice and inequality (Mellen 2006). In *The Bank* significant elements of knockabout physical comedy remain unmotivated, notably the rivalry with Charlie's fellow janitor. The blows to the head, swipes with a wet mop and kicks in the rear that Charlie delivers show little class solidarity or sympathy with a fellow worker who has done nothing to antagonise Charlie. True, the respectably attired middle-class bank executives are also on the receiving end of Charlie's slapstick violence, but it is not until the attempted robbery that the slapstick takes on understandable and justified motivation, as Charlie uses his violent skills to good effect. *The Bank* is important in revealing an element of pathos that was to become increasingly important in Chaplin comedies. Here, it centres on Charlie's mistaken belief that Edna, the bank typist (Edna Purviance), has bought him a tie as a birthday present, when it is actually intended for Charles, the middle-class, respectably attired bank cashier. The subsequent discovery of his mistake leads to what became trademark scenes of Chaplin pathos, as he fails to win the girl despite the heroics he has displayed and, in the process, comments on the class chasm that separates 'democratic' Americans.

The inconsistent, tentative progress towards both a consistent screen persona and the growing integration of slapstick comedy within a narrative framework is equally evident in the *A Woman*, produced by Essanay in July 1915 between *The Tramp* and *The Bank*. Dressed in the tramp costume, Charlie betrays a succession of mendacious and often malicious behaviours, using his cane as a dangerous weapon to rip women's skirts, knock hats off, trip people up, before leading the philandering, flirtatious father figure to the edge of a lake, where he promptly pushes both him and an interfering policeman into the water. Charlie and his victim meet up again back at the family home and old animosities are resumed. Following a lengthy knockabout sequence involving protruding hat-pins, squirting soda-siphons and slaps to several heads, Charlie loses his trousers and attempts to leave the house, much to the disgust of a passing Purity League crowd. In what looks as if it might be a useful plot strategem to make good his exit, Charlie dresses up as a woman. However, any intended plot motivation gets lost as the remaining ten minutes of the film are devoted to Chaplin hamming it in drag. The daughter (Edna Purviance) colludes in this, lending him a pair of her shoes and even persuading Chaplin to shave off his moustache, an unusual rupture of what became the Chaplin persona, a moment privileged in a series of close ups.

The complex politics of gendered identity were given considerable attention in silent film comedy, with comedians as diverse as Chaplin, Harry Langdon, Buster Keaton and Stan Laurel all continuing a music hall tradition of cross-dressing, a tradition that has continued via *Some Like it Hot* (1960) into contemporary comedies such as *Mrs Doubtfire* (1993) and *Big Momma's House* (2000) (see Chapter 8). Even rotund Oliver Hardy dressed like a young girl and posed in a bathing suit in a parody of Sennett's Bathing Beauties. The mutabilities of gender identity and challenges to concepts of masculine authority became pronounced in the 1920s, not least in the work of Laurel and Hardy, whose films 'present a series of experiments with different identities and roles, which are assumed by putting on and taking off the dress appropriate for each masquerade' (Sanders 1995: 2). Although Chaplin was less prone to abandon the tramp costume as his success grew, many of his films interrogate relations between the genders, though increasingly through the pathos that finds full expression in *City Lights* (1931).

Chaplin's silent comedies were concerned with social issues and subtle class divisions that impact on his characters. More than love, romance and the possibilities of domestic bliss, his comedies foreground the importance of employment and economic survival in what is often portrayed as an affluent yet uncaring society. As Joan Mellen observes, 'social inequality is the premise of all the tramp films, with the tramp on the wrong side of the class divide' (2006: 10). These central themes are increasingly evident in the comedies produced for Mutual in 1916 and 1917, including *The Floorwalker*, *The Rink*, *The Pawnshop*, *The Immigrant* and *Easy Street*, which represent the epitome of the short-form slapstick comedian comedies.

In *The Rink* (1916), Chaplin's impressive roller-skating skills are given considerable prominence in the slapstick antics in the second half of the film, though the ending disappoints, as Charlie escapes his pursuers by hooking his cane on to a passing car. The earlier scenes in the restaurant where Charlie works as a waiter offer much clearer evidence of visual gags that are motivated by the film's context. One such gag centres on the arrival of Mrs Stout, a very large woman (actually played by the male actor Henry Bergman), clearly too large to fit into the restaurant chair; Chaplin breaks off first one then the other of the arms of the chair before helping her to sit at the table. In formal terms, the film makes use of the long takes that had come to characterise

Chaplin comedies, enabling an emphasis on the performance of the visual gags. *The Rink* also makes effective use of Chaplin's direct appeal to the viewer, eliciting sympathy for the downtrodden protagonist, though this is overplayed in the gag where Chaplin serves a live cat to a restaurant customer, his look to camera breaking down as Chaplin is unable to restrain a smile, effacing the distinction between actor and character.

Perhaps more than any other film, *Easy Street* (1917) epitomises the maturity of the two-reel slapstick comedian comedy. Though centred on the clowning antics of Chaplin, *Easy Street* foregrounds the social chaos that characterises the poor, immigrant urban experience, a violent world fuelled by alcohol, crime and drugs, beyond the control of the forces of the law, and where domestic violence goes unrestrained. The transformation of Easy Street from lawless, violent bedlam, dominated by the towering drunken bully (Eric Campbell), into an orderly, law-abiding community is matched by Charlie's own transformation from an unemployed derelict to compassionate policeman. His transformation is due less to the evangelising sermonising of the church mission than to the attention of the female mission worker (Edna Purviance). Flattered by her attention (lip-readers would have had no problems reading her plea to Charlie 'Won't you stay? Please stay', shot, like his reaction, in a close up), Charlie decides to reform, even going so far as returning the collection box he had intended to steal. He takes a job as a policeman and is given the notorious Easy Street as his beat. A previous sequence has revealed the brawling chaos that characterises life on the street and Charlie comes up against the bullying Eric Campbell. After some violent but futile attempts to subdue the bully, Charlie finally succeeds by anaesthetising him with a gas lamp, in what has become one of silent comedy's best known gags. Having earned the temporary respect of Easy Street's inhabitants, Charlie not only fails to stop the bully's wife from stealing food but actually steals more on her behalf. Helping Edna with her charity work in the street, Charlie expresses amazement that a frail-looking man has fathered so many children and awards him his policeman's badge in a gesture of admiration. Having broken free from the police station, the bully returns and dispatches Charlie into a cellar where a drug-crazy man is assaulting Edna, the mission girl. Accidentally sitting on a syringe Charlie, fired up by drugs, cleans the street of the bully and his henchmen. The film closes with the New Mission now dominating Easy Street, and its inhabitants, including the bully, transformed into respectable citizens who, walking past a sign reading Employment Agency, appear to face a brighter future. Charlie accompanies Edna into the Mission Hall, his personal transformation seemingly complete.

The gag about sitting on a sharp pin-like object reveals the ways in which Chaplin's comedy has changed. In *A Woman*, the gag about sitting on a hat-pin remains just that, a visual gag that, although repeated several times, goes nowhere. When Charlie sits on the syringe needle, there are narrative consequences. The visual gags and slapstick in *Easy Street* enjoy a more complex and arguably more comically productive relationship with a narrative in a film that carries a degree of social, political and ideological weight. This relationship was still lacking, for example, in the early slapstick shorts of Stan Laurel, such as *Oranges and Lemons* (1923), prior to the establishment of his partnership with Oliver Hardy in 1927.

Chaplin was to go on in the 1920s to meet the demand for longer, narratively more complex, comedy features, beginning with *The Kid* (1921) and then with films such as *The Gold Rush* (1925) and *The Circus* (1928) Chaplin's resistance to the introduction of synchronised sound in the late 1920s meant that later features including *City Lights* (1931) and *Modern Times* (1936) remained essentially 'silent' comedy films.

Following up: Charlie Chaplin

☞ How do you explain the emergence of 'comedian comedies' such as those centred on Chaplin in the late 1910s and early 1920s?

☞ By contrasting an early Chaplin film such as *Tillie's Punctured Romance* or *Cruel, Cruel Love* with the later *Easy Street*, analyse the development of Chaplin's comic persona and the ways in which knockabout physical comedy is increasingly motivated by what Kerr terms 'an emotional reality'. To what extent is *Easy Street* still reliant on visual gags and slapstick and how are these used in a comically productive relationship with the film's narrative?

In what sense did Chaplin's comic persona in his later films represent an 'Everyman' figure in tune with the emerging conditions of modernity and how did this contribute to Chaplin's success?

☞ What is it about Chaplin's comedy that accounts for his continuing status as perhaps the greatest of the silent comedians?

Whereas Chaplin's fame rests to some extent on his short silent comedies, both Buster Keaton and Harold Lloyd are best remembered for their longer feature films of the 1920s, despite the fact that both men had performed in numerous comedy shorts that made use of slapstick and physical knockabout.

The classical 'comedian comedies': Harold Lloyd

Harold Lloyd (1893–1971) started in films a year before Chaplin, in 1913. Like Chaplin, Harold Lloyd realised the importance of constructing a screen persona that was distinctive and which struck a chord with audiences, though it took Lloyd much longer to establish that persona. Lloyd's initial character 'Willie Work' soon gave way to 'Lonesome Luke'. Though this proved a relatively successful character in a succession of profitable Hal Roach two-reelers, Lloyd's indebtedness to Chaplin was apparent, not least in a film like *Lonesome Luke on Tin Can Alley* (1917), released a mere two months after Chaplin's *Easy Street*. Reliant on slapstick knockabout comedy, Lloyd proved less adept at it than Chaplin. However, over time Lloyd developed a persona that was to emerge fully in his 'glasses' character, a comic protagonist who thinks twice about engaging in physical conflict, preferring to exercise patience and outwit his rivals and enemies through intelligence. The adoption of the round horn-rimmed glasses helped create a screen persona who was, in Lloyd's own words, 'quiet, normal, boyish, clean, sympathetic, not impossible to romance' (MacCann 1993: 209). Lloyd's insistence on a character who could be taken as 'an average recognizable American youth' was one indication of the growing rejection of the frantic physical excess of 'low comedy' in the early 1920s. However, the adoption of the 'glasses' character did not mean a radical rupture from existing comic modes, as *Haunted Spooks* (1919) illustrates. This broken-backed twenty-two-minute short begins by establishing the plot in which the young heroine is set to inherit a mansion providing she and her husband live in the mansion for a year. Unfortunately she has no husband, only a Ford and a phonograph, those twin markers of American modernity. Harold, fresh from disappointment in romance, having, as a title card puts it, 'lost another one of the only girls I've ever loved', agrees to fill the void, exchanging the recognisable confines of affluent middle-class America for a gothic southern mansion. Determined to prevent the inheritance, the heroine's uncle fails in his attempt to convince them that the mansion is haunted and the newly married couple retire to a life of presumed wealth and happiness. Along the way Lloyd provides an extended sequence where he attempts suicide, the comedy residing in the reluctance of modernity, in the shape of trams, cars and public boating lakes, to conform to his desires. This is Lloyd at his best. Less successful are the jokes at the expense of Jewish and African-American ethnic minorities, particularly the 'haunting' sequence in the mansion where comic wit is replaced with humour based on racial stereotyping.

Lloyd's comedies worked best when they engaged with aspects of the fast-paced modernity that was coming to characterise American culture and society even when, as in *Safety Last* (1923), he offers an ironic comment on the drive for success. As a contemporary review of *Grandma's Boy* (1922) written by Robert Sherwood noted, Lloyd's 'bespectacled young comedian is an apostle of the American faith: he represents the personification of pep, spontaneity and determination' (MacCann 1993: 212). Utterly normal, a combination of aggression and innocence, vigour and virtue, Lloyd's character wins sympathy through the ways in which narrative events are structured, events which allow his pluck, self-confidence and determination to unfold before us, a true understated American hero. Though he was capable of stunning acts of physicality, Lloyd's comedy emanates from believable narratives which allow his innocent determination to shine through, even when playing potentially dislikeable rich characters in films such as *A Sailor-Made Man* (1921) and *For Heaven's Sake* (1926). In *The Freshman* (1925) Lloyd's innocent naivety is at its most extreme. His head filled with romantic, movie-inspired images of college life, Lloyd's 'Speedy' becomes the target of the college bully and butt of an elaborate conspiracy in which, far from being the college hero he imagines himself to be, he is the college joke. Confronted with the truth, implored to be himself, he overcomes everything to emerge as the last-minute hero, winning the college football game. The narrative constructs a complex position for the viewer; despite our enjoying the jokes at his expense, a sense of genuine sympathy for Lloyd emerges from narrative events.

Lloyd himself made the distinction between his one- and two-reel gag comedies and the feature-length character comedies of the 1920s. However, although these later films were successful in grounding comedy and character in more complex narratives, they still made use of, often stunning and thrilling, visual gags. *Safety Last*, perhaps Lloyd's best-known film, is slightly unusual amongst Lloyd's comedy features of the 1920s in that it is essentially a gag comedy, from its 'trick' beginning when it appears that the 'long journey' Harold is about to take is to his own execution right through to the climatic climb up the side of the high-rise department store where Harold is employed. In most of his feature-length comedies however, the gags remain subordinate to character, situation and the increasingly important central romantic relationships within the films. Nowhere is this more evident than in *The Kid Brother* (1927) with Lloyd playing opposite Jobyna Ralston in a comedy with a western setting. As the much-maligned youngest son of county sheriff Jim Hickory, Harold Hickory is relegated to doing the domestic chores while his two elder brothers undertake the traditional male roles. Harold mistakenly gives permission for a travelling medicine show to perform in town and is forced by his father to close it down. After a series of comic humiliations and the discovery that money entrusted to his father for the town's dam project has been stolen by the villainous showmen, Harold manages to recover the money just in time to prevent the sheriff from being hanged. He is now, his father declares, 'a real Hickory'. Though the film uses a number of visual gags, not least when Harold is washing the family laundry, or doing the dishes or when he threatens the villain with a stick which, unknown to Harold, has a snake attached to it, they arise directly from Lloyd's initially ineffectual, but ultimately virtuous, central character.

Lloyd became known as the 'king of daredevil comedy', a label that reflected his ability to combine visual gags and thrilling stunts within increasingly narrative-driven, character-centred, longer comedies, a shift which amounted to a rejection of what was increasingly seen as the 'low-comedy' associated with comedy shorts. Lloyd's incarnation as 'an average recognizable American youth' enabled a type of more sophisticated comedy in which character and situation absorb and integrate the gags. Lloyd's 'glasses' character, with his zealous capacity to succeed and his frenzied engagement with the trappings of modern society, clearly resonated with aspirant American culture in the 1920s. Sound cinema and the economic depression of the early 1930s marked an end to Lloyd's complex comic appeal to the American public.

Following up: Harold Lloyd

☞ To what extent and what ways does Harold Lloyd's comedy in *Safety Last* suggest a rejection of slapstick and physical excess in favour of narrative-based and character comedy? Looking at a later film such as *The Kid Brother*, examine the ways in which Lloyd's celebrated physicality is subordinated to, and integrated with, character and narrative.

☞ What is it that made Lloyd's particular style of comedy and his 'glasses' comic persona so suited to silent cinema of the 1920s?

The classical 'comedian comedies': Buster Keaton

Buster Keaton (1895–1966) appeared in what many regard as some of the greatest silent comedies ever produced and, though he called his 1960 autobiography 'My Wonderful World of Slapstick', the sophisticated visual gags in Keaton's films go far beyond the limitations of physical knockabout comedy. His ten feature-length comedy films, from *The Three Ages* (1920) to *Steamboat Bill Jr.* (1928), exhibit a degree of structural intricacy and comic density that surpasses even Chaplin and Lloyd. Like theirs, his visual gags are clearly motivated by narrative events and situation though, unlike them, Keaton never repeated gags in his films. Of all the silent comedians, Keaton shows the profoundest understanding of the medium of film and much of his comedy flows from this understanding. He was, in Walter Kerr's view, 'the most silent, as well as the most cinematic, of silent screen comedians' (1975: 117).

Following a family career in vaudeville, Keaton literally walked into film slapstick comedy in Roscoe 'Fatty' Arbuckle's *The Butcher Boy* (1917). As he walked through a doorway, Keaton was hit in the face with a large paper bag full of flour with enough force to knock him off his feet. Keaton's growing influence on Arbuckle is evident in the fourteen shorts they produced between 1917 and 1919, as he begins to explore the comic possibilities involved in cinematic geography. In *Backstage* (1919), for example, he appears to be walking up and down some steps, but when a backstage flat is removed, we see that he is actually just getting up and down on his knees as he hammers in some nails to the floor. This process of exploration continued in Keaton's nineteen independently produced shorts from 1920 to 1923. In these films, he developed his trademark deadpan face, having learnt through his experience in vaudeville that keeping an expressionless face as things happened to him, and around him, seemed to get even more laughs from the audience. As Gehring argues, Keaton's 'deadpan is a twentieth-century response against the absurdities of the modern world' (1997: 5). In *Sherlock, Jr.* (1924) Keaton, with only two dollars in his pocket, is unable to buy a three-dollar box of chocolates for his sweetheart. Sweeping up the rubbish outside the cinema where he works, he finds a dollar amongst the rubbish, but reluctantly gives it back to an attractive young woman who searches in the rubbish for the dollar she has lost. Even more reluctantly, he relinquishes one of his own dollars to an older woman who also claims to have lost it, and then offers his last dollar to a large man of threatening appearance. Surprisingly, he throws it back at a bemused Keaton, before proceeding to rummage through the rubbish to find his wallet that contains a wad of notes. Throughout the ups and downs of finding and losing the money, Keaton's face is entirely devoid of expression, though his frenzied re-examination of the rubbish pile in the fruitless search for any remaining money gives some clues to his emotional state.

The visual gags that saturate his films became ever more intricate, as Keaton engages with a material world that functions like a crazy machine, in what Gehring describes as 'a comic battle not with men but with their machines, or with the elements themselves' (1997: 4). The films become littered with 'near-miss' gags, delayed gags and chain reaction gags firmly motivated by plot events. In *The Goat* (1921), for example, the accidental photographing of Keaton behind bars works well as a visual gag in its own right, but is delayed and extended when, later in the film, his photograph appears on wanted posters and Keaton is pursued not just by policemen but by the father of an attractive girl he had defended earlier, a father who turns out to be a detective. Walter Kerr characterised this intricate looping of gag-based action as 'the Keaton Curve', in which, despite all his physical attempts to outwit an apparently unfeeling world, he is often delivered right back to where he started from (1975: 145). In *Sherlock, Jr.* Keaton uses the one dollar he has left from the rubbish pile to buy a cheap box of chocolates, but alters the price on the box from one to four dollars to impress 'The Girl' (Kathryn McGuire). His moment of vain dishonesty comes back to bite him, as the price on the box appears to implicate him in the theft of The Girl's father's watch.

Keaton's awareness of the qualities of film as a distinctive medium and of its comic possibilities matured considerably, finding its fullest expression in the feature-length comedies. As he wrote in his autobiography, 'the greatest thing to me about picturemaking was the way it automatically did away with the physical limitations of the theatre' (MacCann 1993: 161). Keaton's fascination with film is clearly evident in the MGM feature *The Cameraman* (1928). Many of the gags in Keaton's films refer to and arise out of the very medium he was working in, dependent on film's ability to manipulate time and space in ways that live performance cannot. In *Sherlock, Jr.* he daydreams in his job as a movie projectionist and ends up *inside* the film he is projecting. In an extended sequence that interrupts the film-within-the-film narrative, Keaton finds himself dislocated and exposed by a sequence of cuts that make his own actions both irrelevant and comic, as he peers over a precipice, is confronted by lions in a jungle, narrowly misses walking into the path of an oncoming express train, sits on a sand mound that becomes a rock surrounded by water, then goes to dive into the water but ends up in a snowdrift. The sequence uses the illusory capacity of film both to make us laugh and remind us that we are watching an impossible construction, but a construction that we are willing to be engaged with, to believe in, no matter how temporarily.

Though Daniel Moews (in MacCann 1993: 183–91) argues that all Keaton's films have a basic fantasy pattern of failing, sleeping, waking and winning, where the basic psychological dynamic is one of adolescent transformation, a move from youth to maturity, from being a novice in life to being an expert, Keaton did not, like Chaplin and Lloyd, rely on the construction of a uniform screen character. Instead he developed a range of characters, though his essential personality remained constant, as did the trademark deadpan expression, no matter what life and the elements threw at him. The gravity of his expression enabled a degree of dramatic gravity to surround him, rooting his comedy in a world which is at once realistic, serious and absurdly malicious. Nowhere is this more evident than in *The General* (1926), considered by many to be Keaton's finest film, even though it was one of the less successful commercially.

The underlying trope of transition from novice to expert is clearly evident in *The General*, where much of the comedy springs from Keaton's clash with a hostile material world, in this case two enormous American railroad engines. With the exception of Keaton and his girlfriend Annabelle Lee (Marion Mack), most of the rest of the cast are shown as two relatively anonymous masses, the Union and Confederate armies fighting the American Civil War (1861–65). Keaton plays Johnny Gray, a railroad engineer who has two loves in his life, Annabelle Lee and his train, The General. Unable to enlist in the Confederate Army at the outbreak of the war, Gray is rejected by Annabelle, who refuses to speak to him 'until he is in uniform', but when The General is stolen by Unionist spies he gives pursuit by hand-cart, bicycle and another train, The Texas, overcoming all the obstacles that the Union spies throw in his way. The chase involves a number of stunning gags, as when he removes one rail sleeper by throwing another with pin-point accuracy, and when, gathering some dirt by the wayside to stop the train's wheels slipping, he turns round to see that the train has gathered traction and gone. Fully engaged with chopping wood for the engine's boiler, he remains blissfully unaware of the massive troop movements that are going on around him, as a result of which he is now in enemy territory. He seeks refuge in a house, overhears the enemy plans and discovers that Annabelle has been kidnapped with the train. They escape and after what a title card calls, ironically, 'a refreshing night's sleep', manage to recapture The General, so now the pursuer becomes the pursued.

In a mirror image of events during the first half of the film, the two do everything they can to delay the pursuing Unionist train laden with soldiers, though at one point Annabelle's contribution involves sweeping the engine in an attempt to make it clean and homely. Desperate though they are for logs to fuel the engine, Annabelle rejects one log because it has a knot in it, instead handing over a diminutive – but to her view perfect – slim wooden chip. Exasperated, Keaton first shakes her and then kisses her, a wonderful comic metaphor for decades of cinematic misunderstandings between lovers. Still wearing his stolen Union uniform, he gets fired at by a Confederate soldier. Later, he foils a Union sniper when, as he waves his sword in the air, the blade flies off and kills the sniper. The film climaxes with a spectacular crash as the pursuing Union train attempts to cross a burning bridge and plunges into the river below. The Unionist advance is routed, not least because Johnny's inept attempt to fire a cannon results in the shot skying upwards, only to fall and burst a dam, cascading water on to the Union soldiers. Johnny, who can now list his occupation as 'soldier', is promoted to lieutenant and ends up in the arms of Annabelle.

The film's epic closing sequence is a homage both to the films of D.W. Griffith and to the epic spectacle that cinema, including silent comedy, was capable of. The film still has pratfalls, moments of slapstick, Keaton's deadpan reactions and, above all, stunning visual gags, but these are skilfully motivated by and integrated into the lengthy chase narrative. As David Robinson has pointed out, Keaton's physical gags, often stemming from his innocent interaction with a hostile material world, are extraordinary, but not unrealistic or impossible. For Robinson '[T]his is the crux of the paradox of Keaton's work. A practical man, he is the greatest realist among the comedians' (Robinson, 1973: 185). Part chase film, part war film, part epic, *The General* is a measure of the changes that silent film comedy had undergone by the mid-1920s.

Following up: Buster Keaton

☞ Examine the view that whilst Keaton's films are dependent on visual gags, they are always motivated by narrative events and situations. By looking at a sequence in *Sherlock Jr.*, explain what you understand by the notion of 'the Keaton Curve'.

☞ Keaton has been called the 'most silent as well as the most cinematic' of silent screen comedians'; by looking at sequences from either *Sherlock Jr.* or *Steamboat Bill Jr.*, explain why this view of Keaton's comedy might be justified. To what extent does Keaton's comedy rely less on a consistent character and more on an enduring screen personality?

☞ One of the opening title cards for *The General* says that 'in the mechanical world of today, [Keaton] moves like an inhabitant of another planet, gazing with a look of bewilderment at a nightmare reality'. To what extent is this a useful description of Keaton's comedy? Does *The General* deserve its reputation as being amongst the best cinema films of all time?

☞ Chaplin used sound only reluctantly in his later films and then only sparingly. Why do you think that silent comedy produced by Lloyd and Keaton largely failed to survive the introduction of sound cinema?

Silent slapstick and its rivals

As the careers of Laurel and Hardy show, slapstick and knockabout physical comedy continued throughout the 1920s and into the era of synchronised sound with sound comedy shorts remaining an important element of cinema programming throughout the 1930s. As the later films of Jerry Lewis, Norman Wisdom, Steve Martin, Jim Carrey and others remind us, slapstick has remained an important element of film comedy even if, as Neale and Krutnik argue, 'the authentic slapstick tradition' became 'hybridized, combined with other components, or else industrially and institutionally marginalized' (1990: 131). However, the impetus towards longer, narrative-orientated films inevitably affected film comedy in the 1920s, to the point where the comedy was generated less by the presence of a central comic figure or comedian than by the comedy inherent in the situation and narrative. Although silent cinema had never shied away from exploiting literary or dramatic material, as the numerous silent film versions of Shakespeare indicate, an increasing number of feature-length comedies of the 1920s looked towards comic material that already existed in short stories, novels and plays. Inter-title cards, used in Lloyd's films as written gags in their own right or to pass ironic comment on events, were now limited to complex narrative explication or to fill in the back-story. Though, as we have seen, more 'culturally respectable' short comedies had been pioneered by John Bunny and the Drews, the aspirations of more confident and technologically assured industry to attract a different, more affluent, audience demographic encouraged the development of feature-length comedies that dispensed with dominant comic personas in favour of intricate narrative construction, depth of characterisation and realistic situations and behaviour.

This discernible trend is perhaps most evident in the work of Ernst Lubitsch, a German actor and director who arrived in America in 1922. Though Lubitsch went on to make films across a range of genres, he became associated with what Theodore Huff termed 'social comedies' in films such as *The Marriage Circle* (1924), *Lady Windermere's Fan* (1925) and *So This Is Paris* (1926), all of them based on stage plays and all of them films that 'explored the serio-comic aspects of the marital estate' (Poague 1978: 19). Lubitsch developed the use of a range of cinematic devices such as the close up, camera movement and editing to convey comic wit, substituting a repertoire of visual techniques for disruptive title cards. Alongside other lesser directors such as James Cruze, Reginald Denny and Mal St Clair, who directed the 1928 version of *Gentlemen Prefer Blondes*, Lubitsch created visually nuanced comedies of manners which redefined sophisticated screen comedy and which were, in the opinion of Richard Koszarski, perhaps more influential in the overall development of film comedy than the work of Chaplin, Lloyd and Keaton (1994: 179). Such a judgement needs to be treated cautiously, though it does illustrate the rich diversity of silent film comedy and the extent to which film comedy beyond slapstick was an important component in the development of cinema during these early years.

Recommended reading

Lee Grieveson and Peter Krämer (eds), *The Silent Cinema Reader*, London: Routledge, 2003.

Walter Kerr, *The Silent Clowns*, New York: Knopf, 1975.

2

Early sound film comedy

The addition of synchronised sound to mainstream film between 1927 and 1930 required expensive changes in the technology of both production and exhibition, but the novelty of sound film brought box-office income on a scale that not only allowed the American industry to afford the rapid conversion of its studios and cinemas but also to make substantial profits in the early years of the Depression following the 1929 Wall Street Crash.

During the change over to sound production, studios had to make decisions about which types of film were going to be most enhanced by sound. *The Jazz Singer* (1927), a musical, launched a new genre entirely dependent on the new technology, but was sound necessary for all genres? Comedy was low on the list of priorities for conversion to sound partly because the sound-recording technology inhibited movement and partly because slapstick silent comedy was still doing good business. Nonetheless, once sound had become the norm, comedy could not remain an exception.

Sound film brought serious difficulties for the stars of silent comedy. Buster Keaton was essentially sold by his producer (through family connections) to MGM which handled him badly (for example trying to team him with Jimmy Durante) and fired him in 1933. Thereafter Keaton made a living as a gag man, thinking up slapstick bits for other comics, before making a very late comeback as a comic actor in the 1960s. Harold Lloyd's career also suffered and in 1934 he stopped making films, until a brief 1940s comeback. Charlie Chaplin, on the other hand, sustained his career by making only three, essentially dialogue-less, films in the 1930s.

In this time of rapid and tumultuous change Hollywood's comedy producers had two options: either their resident comedians were going to have to find ways of making their comedy work for sound (and this looked tricky) or the producers could raid radio and the stage, chequebooks in hand, to hire comic talent that already made a living with dialogue to replace them. In this chapter we focus in particular on the work of Laurel and Hardy, who moved successfully from silent to sound film comedy within Hollywood, and on the cinematic work of the Marx Brothers, who came to Hollywood via vaudeville and Broadway. It is significant that there are partnerships involved here; although the single star comedian could be successful in sound film, their success depended on their on-screen collaborators. While Hollywood had any number of accomplished players on contract to play key roles, they changed from film to film. Comedy teams locked very particular modes of physical *and* verbal interaction into their acts. The works of both the Marx Brothers and Laurel and Hardy continue to be available in the twenty-first century, indicating there are some exceptional (timeless?) qualities in their combined comedy. This chapter examines the dynamics of their verbal humour while focusing on the key early sound period.

Stage to sound

The move from stage performer to film performer was not an early 1930s innovation (Chaplin had done it in the 1910s); there was simply a new wave of performers able to make the shift at this time as sound became a feature of cinema. Aside from stage comedies in the professional theatre, putting comedians on stage was an industry in itself. In variety theatres, owners booked individual acts and incorporated them into the bill or programme. Vaudeville was a chain of such theatres whose name became synonymous with this industry. According to Jenkins (1992: 84), though acts ranged from acrobats to musicians and singers, comedians dominated the bills. Only huge headline stars would ever get more than twenty minutes on stage (63). Since performers travelled from theatre to theatre, having much in the way of scenery or props was an expensive liability (77), and so, too, were detailed scripts since performers needed to be adaptable to the differing requirements of different audiences (74–5). It was also in vaudeville performers' interests to have more than one string to their bow. W.C. Fields was initially a juggler who developed a character and a line of patter to go with it, and Will Rogers, the American humorist, became a wit while doing rope tricks with a lasso (69). The Warner Bros experimental short sound films of the 1920s often captured vaudeville acts but these were one-off appearances.

Successful sound-based vaudeville comedians, largely excluded from the cinema by its silence (Fields, exceptionally, had separate silent and sound film careers), took their chances and became the headliners of the musical revues that became popular on Broadway during the 1920s such as Ziegfield's *Follies* and George White's *Scandals*. These long-running stage shows were super-vaudeville with scenery that formed the respectable pinnacle of vaudeville achievement. Broadway revues were thus the logical place for the Hollywood studios to seek sound performance talent in the early 1930s. As Jenkins (1992: 85–95) shows, Hollywood's booming business allowed it to headhunt the stage comedy business's established headline stars. Similarly, in Britain, film producers sought out top-of-the-bill music hall performers.

Until sound cinema took off, some venues had variety or music hall acts interspersing film performances (or vice versa). Once cinemas were able to show variety's headline performers on screen the theatres struggled to compete. Though it wouldn't become clear until the mid-1930s, vaudeville was doomed. *Follow the Boys* (1944) dates the end around 1938, while in *The Cat and the Canary* (1939) Bob Hope's character – a radio performer – quips: 'These big empty houses don't scare me; I was in vaudeville.'

What sort of films followed these raids by Hollywood on Broadway? Initially so-called 'book musicals', screen versions of hot Broadway properties, were prominent. The first one to reach cinemas was the screen adaptation of the Marx Brothers' first Broadway vehicle, *The Cocoanuts*, in 1929. The Marx Brothers were a singing act who turned to musical comedy after famously (anecdotally) being upstaged by a mule in Nacogdoches, Texas (see Louvish 1999: 66–8). It cost Paramount an impressive $100,000 to buy the rights (see Rosenberg and Silverstein 1970: 96 and Louvish 1999: 204). As the first all-sound comedy with music *Cocoanuts* became a substantial success. The film veteran Walter Wanger suggests that one reason for its good business was a boost given by repeat viewing from audiences who couldn't catch all the jokes the first time (Rosenberg and Silverstein 1970: 97). As this comment implies, there were differences between what a broad, national film audience was used to and what a seasoned Broadway audience could enjoy. Jenkins (1992: 153–84) suggests that there was real resistance among rural audiences to some aspects of the metropolitan performers' routines, mostly it seems to their cosmopolitan, ethnic and theatrical in-jokes. However, compared to later films, Groucho is relatively slow and deliberate in his delivery as if already wary of the potential problem.

After book musicals were exhausted Hollywood demanded that script-writers develop original scripts for its new contract players. Routines that had kept an act in business for years in vaudeville were quickly used up by film and there was no time to test the new material in front of audiences. This led to distinct variability in the quality of both scripts and the resulting films. Jenkins (1992) describes these sound comedy films of the early 1930s as 'anarchistic'. In their rough and ready attempts to showcase performers used to working in short bursts with the single focus of making their audiences laugh, these films offend against the idea of the well-made film that was becoming current as Hollywood began to give itself awards for achievement (the Academy Awards began in 1927). The chief challenge of these anarchistic films (and indeed many later comedies) is their heterogeneity or incoherence according to a rather monolithically defined idea of classical Hollywood narrative (see Introduction).

We will examine the idea of the anarchistic film more fully by taking examples from the Marx Brothers films. In one sense, singling the Marx Brothers out duplicates their popular and critical recognition since the 1960s and inhibits our ability to see the bigger picture, to see their works in context and not as some exception. Even their most extraordinary work, *Duck Soup*, is only their version of other madcap Paramount productions such as *Million Dollar Legs* (1932), starring W.C. Fields. Jenkins's *What Made Pistachio Nuts? Early Sound Comedy and the Vaudeville Aesthetic* (1992) is the best text currently available to look at the wider context.

The Marx Brothers films

The Marx Brothers were four while at Paramount (until 1933) but three at MGM (from 1934), when Zeppo's removal left Groucho, Harpo and Chico. These three had always been the core of the act on film: 'The Marx Brothers took the very notion of the "comedy team" to its logical conclusion. They included various comedy styles within their act. In vaudeville they had accomplished this by having each brother represent a different ethnic group. In films, though, each brother represented a different type of comedy. Groucho became the master of wisecracking insult comedy. Chico focused on dialect humour and malapropisms. Harpo was the expert at sight gags and pantomime' (Epstein 2004: 109).

Groucho has painted-on black eyebrows and moustache and an exaggerated stooped walk. With a rapid, muttering delivery he unleashes a torrent of words: '[Groucho's] Marxism is, precisely, a long monologue, an aggressive saying, and acting, out loud of everything the ordinary, responsible, hypocritical adult finds it easier not to say, and then, in the end, not to think, so becoming alienated from his own [*sic*] heart' (Durgnat 1969: 151).

Harpo, dressed in a shabby coat and sometimes a dented top hat cannot, or will not, speak but communicates by exaggerated gestures and expressions, or by horns and other props. His honks and whistles react to the spoken word at a speed impossible in silent captions. His ability to produce and destroy objects is surreal and disconcerting: 'Harpo is the conductor of an aggressive malevolence latent in the inanimate universe' (Winokur 1996: 164). The early films also show him free of the societal rules that bind others: 'Harpo ... takes to a bicycle to [literally] pursue blondes in *Monkey Business*. Such moments suggest the clown's immediate responsiveness to bodily desire without regard to social custom or self-restraint' (Jenkins 1992: 227).

Chico has curly black hair under a peasant cap and a strong (fake) Italian accent which generates endless puns and misunderstandings. As Charles Musser says of Chico's character in *Animal Crackers*, his 'choice of an Italian persona is a refusal to assimilate' (1991: 69). A trickster of low cunning, Chico's role is much expanded in the absence of Zeppo, since he must mediate between the other two, but he is usually in alliance with Harpo and an antagonist of Groucho.

The Marx Brothers films offer us many examples of three kinds of foil common to anarchistic films, the dupe, the killjoy and the counterfeit. The consistency of the foils' comic identities is quite strong. The dupe is the person trapped into conventional patterns of thought and who believes they have to act a certain way. The most consistent foil for Groucho is Margaret Dumont who invariably plays wealthy high-society matrons who are not only society's privileged dupes but are sponged upon by Groucho's characters and their rivals. Dumont's affliction, reminiscent of Sancho Panza, means that she only hears what she thinks she ought to hear most of the time in her (non-) duels with Groucho. The killjoys, by contrast, are humourless and often threatening characters: Edgar Kennedy in *Duck Soup* for example, the police in *Animal Crackers* or the bullies in the later films, who require a physical response and a slapstick comeuppance. The third type of foil is the counterfeit, the fake whose respectability is unearned (unlike the standard Dumont character). Examples include Trentino in *Duck Soup* and Chandler in *Animal Crackers*. The existence of all of these types is, as Jenkins (1992: 235) suggests, implicitly a critique of the society that produces such people. The brothers' reaction to all their foils is essentially aggressive: they attack, physically or verbally, everyone who does not acknowledge their own identity is fake, false or spurious (see Winokur 1996: 131), and overall: 'The transparency of their roguery (to us) helps blow the gaff and show that, from the point of view of mental freedom, respectability is dishonesty' (Durgnat 1969: 151).

The Marx Brothers' excessive and unrealistic type of humour is defined by Jenkins as 'clown comedy' which he opposes to the more affirmative 'comedian comedy': 'The comedian's comedy stems from mistakes arising from efforts to conform to social norms, the clown's comedy from disruptions and transgressions arising from a desire or a compulsion to break free of restraint' (Jenkins 1992: 236).

Using Jenkins's list of criteria for evaluating comedy performance and coherence in film (see Introduction), we find that in the Marx Brothers' films the emphasis is usually on gags over narrative. The character roles are ciphers for the star personae and the brothers perform them under sufferance at Paramount, though much more consistently at MGM. The ensemble consistency is split between the Marxes and the rest of the cast who labour under the disadvantage of believing they are living in a much more realistic world. The Marxes, Groucho in particular, are conscious that there is an audience, even if it is merely the ghost of their stage audiences. In fact the brothers toured with several of their shows to get a measure of how their material played across country before filming.

In placing all their work together, however, we must beware of imputing authorship of these films to the Marxes without acknowledging the numerous elisions involved. There are so many people involved in making any film that not everyone gets the credit they deserve and, in a limited amount of space, it is nearly impossible not to reproduce earlier elisions. Numerous writers contributed to their scripts, credited and uncredited (see Louvish 1999 for details). It may be difficult to believe that their Hollywood directors were able to demand that lines were delivered in certain ways or entirely to suppress ad-libs (not the same as improvisation), but films *are* a collaborative process. However, where credit for the Marx Brothers films is shared it is often to blame, rather than praise, the collaborators. James Groch (1990) suggests that 'If there has been a single distinctive feature of criticism about the Marx Brothers, it is the tendency to reify Marx Brothers' comedy as something separate from and more significant than Marx Brothers' comedies' (Groch 1990: 31). He argues that this is because we, illegitimately, cast the Marx Brothers as non-cinematic auteurs (authors) of their work. Groch makes this claim without explaining exactly why we succumb to this impetus but it seems that the Marxes' comic mode, which exploits literalness, evasion, surrealism and which challenges propriety, extends its disruptive influence to the cinematic frame which is therefore rendered pedestrian and restrictive. As a result, the Marxes, as apparent 'authors' of the chaos that the film struggles to accommodate, assume a position narratorially superior to the text in which they appear.

The feeling that the gears don't mesh between the brothers and their vehicles is widely shared. Leonard Maltin argues that: 'The crime is that the Marxes weren't allowed to function at full steam in more than a handful of pictures' (1985: 102). Certainly, whenever the films divert to narrative exposition we, the twenty-first-century audience, may bridle: 'We begin to become disappointed with any part of the film that does not provide us with immediate gratification, any part of the film that does not include the Marx Brothers. We become surprised at their absence rather than at their presence' (Winokur 1996: 170). This is essentially a rejection of any aspects of affirmative comedy that appear in a Marx Brothers vehicle, though it may have been much less of a problem for these films' original audiences.

Eyles notes these effects in the following way:

> It is sometimes suggested that the Marxes' work is 'uncinematic', that they fail to use the possibilities of the medium. This is to miss the point: the Marxes set the pace, and the camera's function is merely to catch their actions as unobtrusively as possible, not to restrict their freedom. The humour belongs to the Marxes and is best left unpolished by the finer tricks of style. (1969: 9)

In other words, they are the authors of the comedy but *not* the film. The ultimate expression of this line of argument would be to blame the films for not being vaudeville performances! To a certain extent this is supported by the films themselves, especially the earlier ones which are clearly unashamed of their stage origins and in which filming takes on a merely documentary function, becoming a barrier as much as a window on to the performances. It is worth remembering that, although Hollywood paid good money, the cinema was not quite so obviously the dominant industry that it became and was in the process of learning sound comedy from its prime live exponents. The Marxes' stage background brings a particular inflection to their comedy and its performative coherence. This certainly contributes to our difficulties in reading, from a historical distance, the unresolved struggle between the anarchistic style in early sound film and the more coherent 'classical Hollywood' style that had been developed in the silent period.

For detailed analysis we restrict ourselves to discussing *Animal Crackers* (1930), the team's second sound film from a Broadway show, particularly focusing on examples of verbal humour.

Following up: early sound comedy

☞ Analyse three scenes or sequences from early sound comedy feature films and consider them against Jenkins's criteria for coherence in narrative comedy laid out in our Introduction (p. 7). How anarchistic is the comedy of the early sound period?

☞ The received wisdom suggests that, the later in the 1930s a film was made, the more affirmative and less anarchistic the comedy, but is this supported by examples?

☞ How much difference does close analysis show between the four Marx Brothers' Paramount films and the three brothers' films for MGM? By examining work by other performers, consider the extent to which the Marxes form a special case.

The Marx Brothers' verbal humour

'I'll go further than that – I'll get off at the depot!' (Captain Spaulding).

The Marx Brothers' verbal comedy springs from interaction, from what ought to be realistic conversations but aren't. When they get together, language ceases to work normally. There are a number of routines that are known by the names of their central or capping pun such as 'Why a duck?' (*Cocoanuts*) and 'Sanity Clause' (*A Night at the Opera*). But their subversion of normal speech can be seen in any number of short excerpts. Take these lines about a power cut from *Animal Crackers*:

Mrs Rittenhouse: The storm. It's put the lights out and you can't see your hand before your face.
Groucho: Well, you wouldn't get much enjoyment out of that.

Groucho's line implies that the power cut distresses Mrs Rittenhouse because it prevents her guests engaging in this activity, a literalness that either means she idiotically believes people do look at their hands in front of their faces on a regular basis or that he idiotically doesn't recognise the clichéd phrase. At the same time Groucho mitigates her complaint (what he says is reassuring, despite being nonsense) and is clearly bristling with ideas about where his hand might more enjoyably go in the dark. The fact that Mrs Rittenhouse doesn't get it is a key part of the humour and allows all sorts of suggestive material to be slipped past the censor and offered to the audience. When Captain Spaulding decides to take a hand in detecting the crime, Mrs Rittenhouse says: 'Captain, I don't want you to worry. I don't want anything to interfere with your weekend.' He responds with mounting outrage: 'Nothing ever interferes with my weak end and I'll thank you not to get personal Mrs Rittenhouse ... A more dastardly crack I've never heard.' She is mystified as to how she has offended him but the audience are left to ponder what the puns imply about their relationship.

The chief victim of Groucho's invective in *Animal Crackers* is, however, Roscoe W. Chandler, the impresario identified by Chico and Harpo as really being Abie Kabibble, the fish man from Czechoslovakia. During his encounter with them Chandler manages to avoid exposure though he does have his cash, tie, hanky, garters and birthmark stolen. Afterwards, a relieved Chandler tries to cosy up to the guest of honour even though he should beware of a conversation that begins 'I've heard about you for a great many years Mr Chandler and I'm getting pretty darn sick of it.' Ordinary small talk is rapidly reduced to nonsense and insult. Groucho introduces himself as Captain Jeffrey T. Spaulding and adds: 'I bet you don't know what the "T" stands for.' When Chandler guesses 'Thomas?' Groucho snaps back 'No, Edgar. You were close though, ... and you still are, I'll bet.' The word 'close' is exploited to expose the meaning of 'near to being right' (though, if the answer is Edgar, Thomas isn't close) and in the meaning of 'close' as atmospherically 'humid' implying that humidity is a constant problem for the butt of the joke. What seems like ordinary phatic communication becomes an attack on a victim usually too dense or too flustered to notice, expressing agreement and confusion alternately, while Groucho's virtual monologue veers back and forth, towards and away from sense, with each additional phrase.

> *Groucho:* Tell me, Mr Chandler, where are you planning on putting up your new Opera House?
> *Chandler:* Oh, I thought I should like to put it somewhere near Central Park.
> *Groucho:* I see; why don't you put it right in Central Park?
> *Chandler:* Could we do that?
> *Groucho:* Sure – Do it at night when no one's looking. Why don't you put it in the reservoir and get the whole thing over with. Of course, that might interfere with the water supply, but, after all, we must remember that art is art. Still, on the other hand, water is water, isn't it, and east is east and west is west and if you take cranberries and stew them like applesauce they taste much more like prunes than rhubarb does ... Now ... er, now you tell me what you know.

Groucho appears solicitous of Chandler's cultural largesse but ultimately seems to understand Chandler's opera house as a small, temporary operation (such as a fish stall) doomed to failure as a public health hazard. 'Art is art' appears to offer an olive branch but its meaninglessness is emphasised by a sequence of similar statements that turn sentence structure, conversational logic and social communication on their heads.

Although this tirade may seem random, it is motivated; just as Chandler doesn't want his counterfeit background revealed, Spaulding is concealing (poorly) the fact that he is no explorer and has never been to Africa. When Chandler gets a handle on the conversation Spaulding immediately says 'I withdraw the question.' This refusal to give Chandler a chance is a repeated device. At one point Groucho offers a barrage of questions: 'What do you think of the traffic problem? What do you think of the marriage problem? What do you think of at night when you go to bed? – You beast!' When Chandler tries to explain himself Groucho cops out with 'I'd rather not discuss it with you any further; you see there are children present'. With a gesture of his cigar, Groucho makes it clear that he means the heterogeneous cinema audience. Here he implies Chandler may well say something inappropriate, in keeping with the last insult, but does so with the irony that he, Groucho, brought it up. Groucho shows an awareness of the audience that Chandler isn't granted. This awareness is at least as baffling as his quicksilver changes of tone with Chandler. At first Groucho defends the audience from Chandler's dirty mind, suggesting he believes in their innocence. Later, the audience-directed line 'Well, all the jokes can't be good. You've got to expect that once in a while' implies that the audience are experienced in comedy, that most of the jokes are good and that this is itself a joke.

Animal Crackers pushes the possibilities of verbal comedy and takes risks in that Groucho's mode of comedy on film is an extension of his stage performances. When the actor playing Chandler mixes up their names, Groucho highlights rather than ignores the blunder before asking 'Can I get a look at a programme? I might be the *News Weekly* for all he knows, or coming next week.' This comes off as a practised piece of stage improvisation that ignores its cinematic circumstances; an example of Marx Brothers' comedy emphatically resisting integration into the cinematic reality. Groucho's addressing the cinema audience appears (impossibly) to work. Jenkins suggests that: 'Paradoxically, such devices increase the sense of spontaneity and immediacy, allowing screen performances to substitute more fully for live stage appearances but they also direct attention upon the temporal and spatial gap between performance and reception' (1992: 137). For Winokur: 'Eye contact between actor and camera, or between audience and screen, replaces eye contact between humans. Still, the effect is startling, as if it were an address to an authentic audience, as if we were real [to the performers]' (1996: 145). Despite being scripted, directed and edited, the material feels improvised, and feels as if a live performance has been captured or even is being captured. Because this happens only in scenes with the brothers, the other scenes seem flat and lifeless impositions by comparison, though, in fact, they are the background without which the Marxian foreground cannot work (see Jenkins 1992: 107). Their films are heterogeneous vehicles of entertainment rather than packaged narratives (Jenkins 1992: 106). Very far from being stories well told, their films reject the novel and the literary stage as models for cinema and revel in their vaudeville roots (see Jenkins 1992: 5). In four words, performance triumphs over narrative.

This is key to our strong and enduring reactions to the Marx Brothers' films as recorded in the criticism we have noted previously. The main strength across the Marx Brothers' body of work is the consistency of their comic identities. This may seem contradictory. Jenkins emphasises the instability of characterisation but the dominance of star over character is the key here. As Jenkins says of the comedy team Wheeler and Woolsey's *Diplomaniacs*, 'our point of identification is not the characters but the performers' (1992: 205).

An increased subservience to the narrative in the later MGM films is only really a minor change. The brothers are still what they were at the start of the films and must be accepted or rejected as such, which is true as much of *The Cocoanuts* as of *Night at the Opera*. No matter how violently they overthrow pomposity, propriety and even sanity (anything that may be lumped in with mendacious old hierarchies such as class or money or officialdom), by collaborating with the younger generation the brothers show that their hearts are in the right place (see Jenkins 1992: 238). *Duck Soup* is the exception in that there is none of this affirmation: 'the power of its justly famous conclusion is that it pushes the brothers outside of narrative, essentially outside of causality and continuity, with no hope of assimilating them back again' (1992: 241). This is a particular achievement and the one largely responsible for lifting them above the anarchistic comedians who were their contemporaries.

The sustained focus of their comedy is on a dynamic rejection of logic and accepted codes, whether these be verbal, narrative, filmic or societal. Rather than this appearing gratuitous or opportunistic, the audience understand that the compulsive nature of the Marx Brothers' star personae means they have no choice but to reject order and propriety in any form. Although the team's ability to apply their comedy of disorder to all levels of the narrative diminishes in the later films, audiences still recognise the anarchistic impulses that drive the Marx Brothers and, equally, that the consequences of such impulses being given free rein is not to be seriously contemplated.

Following up: Marx Brothers comedy

☞ Taking examples from specific films, consider who comes out on top in Marx Brothers films. Are the brothers equally successful in overcoming the situations they find themselves in? To what extent do the brothers share a language with the other characters? Do linguistic differences contribute to – or merely indicate – the comedians' difficult relationship with conventional society?

Silent to sound

Of the comedy teams working in Hollywood in the early sound period, Stan Laurel (1890–1965) and Oliver Hardy (1892–1957) are, with justification, the most fondly remembered. Teamed from 1927, initially in silent films, after long separate careers they moved to sound shorts and sound features and worked throughout most of the 1930s, making only a few lacklustre features in the 1940s before ill-health got the better of them. Recognised around the world, under a variety of names, one fat, one thin, and usually both bowler-hatted, they were enormously successful. Although their work was allowed to drift into obscurity in the 1950s several of their silent films were excerpted in Robert Youngson's successful archive compilation film *The Golden Age of Comedy* (1958). Becoming increasingly prominent in the Youngson sequels they became the titular stars in 1964 with *Laurel and Hardy's Laughing Twenties* and for three subsequent compilations. Their sound films and short films were later released to television, gaining new audiences. Even without this surge of interest it would still be incumbent upon us to ask how and why, in the late 1920s and early 1930s: 'Laurel and Hardy were the only silent screen comedy team to make the successful transition to sound film' (Epstein 2004: 99).

There appear to be three key factors in their successful transition from silent to sound film. The first is the environment and conditions in which Laurel and Hardy worked. They were separately contracted to Hal Roach studios which, in the early sound period, was primarily involved in the production of short comedy films. There were a number of other comics on the lot whose experience, ideas and expertise could be used on both sides of the camera. These colleagues also provided both a collaborative and a competitive environment in which they could jointly build upon the successes of Chaplin, Keaton and Lloyd in a short, inexpensive format. The nature of the studio meant that the team, in practice mainly Laurel, generally had good creative control of their work. This allowed them to draw additionally on their own long experience in the business (and in Laurel's case on his family's British music hall background).

The second key factor is that their speaking voices matched the screen personas that they had already created: 'their voices, the courtly Georgian tenor from Hardy and the light Lancastrian accent from Laurel with its emphasis of the first syllable of a word, were perfect for their characters' (Epstein 2004: 99). While it is interesting to note their attempts to package their established slapstick and physical comedy routines for audiences in other languages (see for example *Night Owls* and its Spanish version, *Ladrones*, made side by side in 1930), linguistic dexterity is not their great strength. They did not develop a sideline in radio comedy as (two of) the Marx brothers did. Yet many of their lines and their catchphrases ('Here's another nice mess you've gotten us into') are eminently repeatable.

The third key factor in the transition is that sound in Laurel and Hardy films is expressly designed to complement the visuals. Although a considerable amount of music was retro-fitted to their short films at various points, they quickly found the cuckoo song theme and other musical accompaniments that perfectly set the tone for their comedy. One of the team's first sound shorts, *Perfect Day* (1929), simply uses repeated choruses of goodbyes from the neighbours to mock Stan and Ollie's inability to actually set out on their picnic. As Durgnat suggests: 'the mere presence of dialogue quickened a tendency towards realism' (1969: 118). Compared to earlier purveyors of slapstick, their mature style is slower and more deliberate and the gags, however manic and violent they become, are always motivated.

Despite the fact that there are surreal elements in several films, it is the embedded realism that is key to their long-lived appeal. Epstein suggests that, in their team, it was reality that 'functioned as the straight man' (2004: 94). The straight man in a comedy team is often a dominant interpreter figure better able to deal with reality and who feeds lines to the comedian. While Hardy fills this role to a large extent, Epstein's point reveals that ordinary reality is alien and unmanageable for *both* members of this team. Their characters' incompetence is childlike, tapping into all of our experiences as children when the world refused to conform to our expectations. Our tendency is to (superficially) forget these experiences and to deny the knowledge that 'The world really isn't as manageable and understandable as we, as adults, try to pretend it is' (Kaminsky 1985: 163). Stripping away this adult pretence, Stan and Ollie act as if they were children, but children at different stages of development. Epstein suggests that 'Ollie played a somewhat older child, a child who knew there is an outside reality but wanted it to correspond to his visions and expectations' (2004: 90). Stan is thus, superficially, the more childlike and helpless: 'Stan cannot function in the real world, but his otherworldliness (which is magical) protects him, always to Ollie's dismay. It is a gift Ollie would like; but, because he is too much tied to human weakness and his hopes for adulthood, he is beyond it' (Kaminsky 1985: 162–3). For example, at the end of *Busy Bodies*, when their car is sawn in two Ollie understands they are ruined but Stan finds solace in the fact that their record-player is still working.

Yet Ollie does have a sort of magic too, though it is clearly no protection. His numerous looks at the camera are not (generally) granted to any other characters. They are more eloquent than any speech and though developed in silent films they (necessarily) stay silent in the sound films. Steve Seidman states that 'the camera looks suggest an extra-fictional intelligence while at the same time perpetuating the pair's fictional stupidity, since appeals to the camera can never be answered' (1979: 60). While this is literally true, it limits our understanding of the effectiveness of the device. Ollie does not look at the camera: he looks at us. Though the connection is demonstrably not eye-contact, it functions *as if* it were in a way that telescopes time and place as efficiently as first-person literature does or that live television recorded two years ago still says 'And tonight on ….' It may be that our suspension of disbelief is punctured by such acknowledgement of our presence, but we *are* present and nothing is more certain (philosophers may ponder whether Ollie looks when we aren't watching). It is true, as Seidman says, the looks are not effective communication: there's nothing we can do for Ollie, but they are an expression of how little Ollie can do, too. Frustration is built in to the device. Louvish calls it 'the melancholy gaze reflecting the orneriness of life' (2002: 207). We know Ollie is going to take a fall, another fall, another brick to the head or worse. Despite his awareness, despite our communication, there's nothing we can do to help him (one of his repeated verbal appeals to Stan is 'Why don't you do something to help me?'). His looks towards the camera are always nuanced expressions of exasperation: 'Can you believe this?' 'Why me?' 'How could I have been expected to forsee that happening?' 'Is there anything else that could possibly go wrong?' (These looks to camera may even possess an extra metatextual element through which we might see Oliver Hardy, actor, questioning what he is being made to go through in the name of comedy.) They are also often part of a slow-burn build-up to the point where Ollie will attempt some violent retribution and get into further trouble. Louvish (2002: 215) tries to sum up our relationship to Ollie and its peculiar intimacy. I don't think it is the case, as Louvish asserts, that we always laugh with Ollie rather than at him, but there is certainly a sense of recognition: 'He gazes at us, because he knows we all share his frustration. Life should surely be better than this … We know he understands us as well, or better, than we understand him, and he represents our own follies, and our hopes.' Ultimately, it may be Ollie's faltering awareness of being observed by an audience that prompts him to peer out of the distinctly uncooperative (or ornery) world he has not yet mastered but remains trapped inside. The critique of society offered in Laurel and Hardy is much more gentle than in anarchistic comedies, but it is still there. It is not angry but anxious: doesn't society expect too much of us?

Laurel and Hardy's verbal humour

Analysis of the opening section of *Beau Hunks* (1931) will show how Laurel and Hardy's humour works. Although the film goes on to be a parody of *Beau Geste* it begins in a domestic American setting. Several of the early lines will be referenced in the French Foreign Legion scenes and are carefully set up here. The film begins by immediately using the team's sound talent with Ollie singing (very well) a love song at the piano while Stan cuts an advert for fertiliser out of the newspaper and inadvertently cuts through a seat cover exposing a spring that will be used in the slapstick climax to the scene. When Ollie has finished his song he looks at the audience and sighs. As the following exchange goes on, the camera cuts from speaker to speaker, with deviations from this noted in the transcript:

Stan: What are you getting so mushy about?
Ollie: Well, I'm glad you asked me, I couldn't keep it from you much longer.
Stan: What?
Ollie: Life's biggest moment: I'm going to be married.
Stan: Who to?
Ollie: Why to a woman, of course, did you ever hear of anybody marrying a man?
Stan: Sure.
Ollie: [Glances at the audience] Who?
Stan: My sister.
Ollie: This is no time for levity. [Assertive nod]
Stan: [Nods then looks puzzled and fails to speak]
Ollie: She's the sweetest girl you ever saw: well read, travelled all over the world, loved by everyone, and she's mine all mine. [Twiddles tie and beams] Well, what do you think of her?
Stan: What does levity mean?
Ollie: [Looks at audience] Levity is a synonomym. [CUT to a blank Stan] You know what a synononmym is ... [CUT to another blank look from Stan] A synononmym is cinnamon ...
Stan: [Appears about to object when there is a knock at the door. Stan picks up the phone] Hello?
Ollie: What are you doing?
Stan: Someone's knocking on the 'phone.
Ollie: That's levity.
Stan: [Looks at the receiver] Hello Mr Levity.
[Another knock at the door]
Ollie: Go to the door! [Aside] 'Hello, Mr Levity,' mm! [Glancing at the audience].

After trying to put the telephone receiver into his pocket Stan finally answers the door and is startled by the messenger delivering a telegram for Ollie. Having taken the telegram Stan says: 'Thank you Mr Levity.' The telegram is from Ollie's fiancée, ending their relationship. Disappointed in love, Ollie wants to do the appropriate thing, and makes the ridiculous romantic gesture of joining the French Foreign Legion but, never quite able to get these things right, he spoils it by dragging his buddy along to 'help him forget'.

2 Oliver Hardy's eloquent looks to camera involve the audience. Example taken from the opening sequence of *Beau Hunks* (1931).

There are three sources of comedy in this opening scene. The first is Ollie's ridiculously self-centred infatuation (his fiancée, Jeanie, is seen in photographs to be the contemporary sex symbol Jean Harlow). The second is the slapstick which brings the scene to a climax when Ollie, chair spring attached to his bottom, falls over and bounces on to the piano, smashing it. The third source is Laurel's idiocy. Stan can't seem to react correctly to anything but this is far from all one-way traffic: at times his logic ('My sister') is actually better than Ollie's. Furthermore at 'synonomym' Ollie has clearly overstepped the limits of his own understanding of language. Yet the problems of his explaining the concept of 'levity' are increased because, for Stan, it could literally mean anything or anyone, such as a person on the phone or the messenger. The pair's similarity to children playing at being adults but unable to dictate the terms of the game is striking. On the day I was writing this I (Glyn) put a crumpet on a plate for my four-year-old daughter and told her 'You can put the butter on yourself'. Her immediate outraged response – 'But I don't want butter on me' – illustrates the arbitrary insanity adults are capable of, when taken literally.

Ollie has a superficial verbal and physical mastery of the world but it is always being challenged by Stan's questioning. The fact is he has no idea why things are the way they are or why people say the things they do. The physical world and language are both full of surprises. In his dialogues with his military superiors later in *Beau Hunks*, Ollie shows awareness of a great range of titles but can never find the right one and stick with it. Ollie thinks he knows how to act, thinks he knows what he means, but is often disappointed though 'never losing sight of his essential dignity' (Louvish 2002: 215). The fact that Ollie is in charge is, Louvish (2002: 296) suggests, an 'exposure of the often arbitrary nature of the adult presumption of authority'. Our experience of this, from our childhood, stands us in good stead here. Ollie is inclined to get tough unnecessarily and inappropriately when his dignity (i.e. adulthood) is offended or to insist upon maintaining that dignity when most would give up. In *Going Bye Bye* (1934) he is compelled to pause a telephone call with the words 'Pardon me, my ear is full of milk'.

Stan, by contrast, knows nothing and is all questions. In *Come Clean* (1931) Ollie and Stan see a woman throwing herself into a river. Trying to do something to help, Ollie tells Stan: 'She's committing suicide!' Stan's response is 'Why?' It's a great question, just not the right moment. With Stan it never is. As the opening sequence of *Beau Hunks* makes clear, his mind sticks to one thing at a time, struggles to recognise cause and effect, misunderstands appropriate contexts and, though he can sometimes articulate a brilliant (or at least sound) idea, he can do so only once. In another life he is a genius (see *Chumps at Oxford* 1940), but in this one mostly not:

> Life, for on-screen Stan is an endless variety show of events and activities that cannot be fathomed: motivations that cannot be understood, … utensils and tools whose function is wholly mysterious, and social structures, such as employment, finances or marriage, which have rules that are utterly occult and meaningless, and can be survived only moment by moment. (Louvish 2002: 238)

In the opening sequence from *Beau Hunks*, Stan's body control is somewhat automatised. It repeats movements unbidden, acts without specific instructions, slips the leash. On the positive side he is satisfied with less, thinks outside channels, and is not restricted by considerations of reality. Occasionally he even has that magic ability to 'make reality fit his deepest fantasies' (Louvish 2002: 352). This can be seen especially effectively in *Way Out West* (1937) where Stan can flick and light his thumb as if it were a cigarette lighter. Ollie dismisses this talent but secretly attempts to reproduce this ability (if Stan can do it, surely he can). When it finally works, Ollie panics because he is conscious of the reality: that his thumb is on fire.

Evaluating the performance coherence in *Beau Hunks* we find that there are gags that don't advance the narrative (falling on to the piano) and gags which impede it (Stan's difficulties in reading the telegram) but the emphasis is shared between narrative and gags. The characters and the star personae are very close (they have the same names) which makes them fit, and the performances are quite coherent. In terms of ensemble consistency in the film, the most wildly over the top performance is the pantomime villainous Arab of the final sequence. Awareness of the audience is restricted to Ollie's character in a very particular way, as we have discussed.

Laurel and Hardy comedies are not anarchistic. Whatever social class their characters inhabit, the pair always want to do the right thing, to obey social convention, though they often aren't equipped to succeed in that aim. But their best works are not affirmative either: the films do not, as a rule, feature romances for the team or for additional characters. The consequences of their actions, and the stakes, are serious. The destroyed small businesses, homes and property are seldom softened; poverty often beckons when it is not already a given of the characters' situation. There is never a Mrs Rittenhouse to foot the bill though there is often a fuming wife to answer to. The underlying drama being played out here is one all of us have experience of, the story of children attempting to attain adulthood. Like the possibility of romantic failure invoked by the romantic comedy (see Chapter 3), the failure to achieve adulthood is ultimately not pleasant to contemplate, but Laurel and Hardy at once reassure us we can do better than they can and offer comfort by showing us that our lingering childhood experience of the mysterious, harsh and unfair world of adult rules is still shared by others. In that common ground, between empathy and superiority, lies great humour. Perhaps a further ingredient in the affection in which their team is held by those who know their work is that these representatives of our childish struggles to master the world never have to struggle alone; implying that there will always be someone – friend, sibling, parent – with us no matter what our failings, or theirs.

Following up: Laurel and Hardy's humour

☞ Taking examples from short films, consider the extent to which Laurel and Hardy's difficulties with the world are established by their difficulties with verbal communication. How successful are Laurel and Hardy in winning their battles? How much of their narrative success or failure is determined by the dynamics of the relationship between Stan and Ollie? How are audiences meant to read the negative outcomes for them at the end of many of their short films (e.g. *Towed in A Hole, Going Bye Bye, Busy Bodies*)?

Comedians for the early sound period

Where the Marx Brothers set out to ridicule and subvert the adult world of propriety, Laurel and Hardy struggle to master it. Neither team can conform to it. The combinations of verbal comedy and slapstick that these teams generate draw on expertise in the field. In both cases conversation cannot proceed as it should, which forms an exact parallel to the characters' relationship to society. Groucho refuses the dictates of polite and logical dialogue, Chico misunderstands common usage through both ignorance and deviousness, Harpo simply refuses speech itself. Stan and Ollie do their best but, despite some superficial articulacy, neither can actually hold up his end of any dialogue without revealing his inadequacies to anyone he interacts with. Speech reveals everything. The lack of success of silent comedians in sound film appears, in the end, to be a result of the fact that speaking was simply redundant for their characters. For other comedians sound completed their characters and revealed their true natures, and all the most successful film comedians over the next half century would be marked by distinctive appearance and voice.

A British example

Will Hay was a star of British music hall and radio before he ventured into film (see Rinaldi 2009). Hay's first films in the early 1930s conciously avoided recreating his successful schoolmaster routines, but by the middle of the decade he had successfully debuted that character on film (*Boys Will Be Boys* 1935) and was looking to branch out. The chief characteristics of Hay's comic persona, effective on stage, radio and film, were pomposity, 'crass incompetence and superb bluffing' (Eyles 1969: 9). In the best of Will Hay's films for Gainsborough Pictures (1935–39), he was teamed with Moore Marriott and Graham Moffatt and their films together form 'the high point of music-hall derived British comedies' (Sutton 2000: 131). David Sutton states: 'Moffatt's petulant fat-boy ... and Marriott's toothless, shrill-voiced old repobate were the perfect complements to Hay's persona, the only characters who could conceivably be even more venal, dishonest, ignorant and workshy than Hay himself' (2000: 132). Our brief example, *Ask a Policeman* (1939), vies with its close relations *Oh Mr Porter!* (1937) and *Where's That Fire?* (1939) to be recognised as the best of the sequence.

Ask a Policeman has Hay, Moffatt and Marriott as the 'protectors' of Turnbotham Round, 'the village with no crime', and recognition of their dishonesty begins in the first scene when we are shown that they supplement their income by poaching. Before long they are fighting over the cash in the

3 Will Hay as schoolmaster. In all of his best roles, his authority is nominal, spurious and easily undermined.

police outing fund, and have knocked out the Chief Constable and smashed up his car with truncheons before driving it through a shopfront. There is considerable subversive energy in this and their other films. Though the trio defeat the smugglers' plot this is not before they've been successfully incriminated and handcuffed together for the last twenty minutes of the film. When the Chief Constable refuses to believe their account Hay knocks him down again and they run for it, reaching breakneck speed around Brooklands racetrack, showing them to be impossible to recoup for honesty, normality and realism.

What makes their verbal comedy particularly distinctive is the disharmony of their cracked voices bickering at speed (under Marcel Varnel's direction) with 'an escalating absurd logic' and engaged in a 'relentless deconstruction of common sense, while never letting these attractions completely derail the narrative from its linear movement' (Sutton 2000: 128, 131). The brief example following (it takes all of fifteen seconds) comes after the trio realise they will need to find some crime in the village in order to justify their existence:

> *Dudfoot [Hay]:* Hey, there's an idea: restricted area – we'll set a speed trap. Lumme, we'll give 'em arrests: we'll stop everything. Hey, where's my stopwatch Albert?
> *Albert [Moffatt]:* I gave it to Harbottle.
> *Harbottle [Marriott]:* Yes, I had it, but ... er ... I boiled it.
> *Dudfoot:* You what?
> *Harbottle:* You see I had the egg in one hand and the stopwatch in the other and I put the wrong one in.
> *Dudfoot:* You would! (*Rushing to leave*) Well, you better bring the egg.
> *Harbottle:* What shall I do with that?
> *Dudfoot:* Suck it and see!

Refusing to be held up by the idiocy of his confederates, Hay rolls with the illogic. If the watch has changed places with the egg, maybe the egg can replace the stopwatch.

Films such as *Ask a Policeman* show how the first decade of sound film comedy established the basis for British slapstick of the 1950s, the institutional *Carry On* comedies of the early 1960s, and the surrealism of some Britain's best radio and television programmes.

Following up: comedy teams

☞ Watch films starring Will Hay and confederates, the Crazy Gang or, in America, Wheeler and Woolsey, Olsen and Johnson or the Three Stooges. How much of their narrative success or failure is determined by the internal dynamics of the team? To what extent does the interplay of such teams (and others such as the Marx Brothers and Laurel and Hardy) mark out the limits for subsequent comic teams in film, radio and television?

Recommended reading

Henry Jenkins, *What Made Pistachio Nuts?: Early Sound Comedy and the Vaudeville Aesthetic*, New York: Columbia University Press, 1992.

David Sutton, *A Chorus of Raspberries: British Film Comedy 1929–1939*, Exeter: University of Exeter Press, 2000.

3

The romantic comedy film

In chapter 1 we dealt primarily with solo male film comedians and in Chapter2 we discussed male film comedy teams. Identifying such star vehicles as a sub-genre of the comedy film, Steve Seidman named it 'comedian comedy' (1979, 1981, 2003). Such films, Stuart Kaminsky argues, are about 'the human struggle to attain a satisfying role in society', a topic that is 'difficult – maybe even impossible – for us to face and deal with unless ... in comic form' (1985: 137). The comedy pair or team dynamic is inherently more anarchistic than the single comedian form of comedian comedy because it shows alternative versions (i.e. at least two) of the individual struggling with the demands of society, and its comedians are less likely to achieve successful integration than the individual comic because the option to maintain their own relationship continues.

The female version of the comedian comedy, however, appears to be almost non-existent (Jenkins 1992 points out a few early exceptions). Female stars' negotiations with femininity are often conducted through the romantic comedy genre which historically (and in the present) provides the prime comedic focus on the performance of femininity. The basic structure of this sub-genre of comedy as illustrated by examples from the 1930s is the focus of this chapter. Further examples from the second half of the twentieth century will be discussed later in the book (see Chapter 8).

The romantic comedy film was established in recognisable form before the early sound period (see Musser 1995). However, just as sound film unleashed an influx of new comedians to supply verbal comedy and required silent film comedians to adapt, the new technology of the 1930s renewed and transformed the romantic comedy film into one of Hollywood's staple forms. In some linear narratives of the history of film comedy, the romantic comedy arrives in the mid-1930s to supersede the anarchic, vaudeville-inflected sound comedy of the early 1930s after the enforcement of the Production (or Hays) Code by the Production Code Administration in 1934. As ever, the actual history is less clear-cut than that. The film industry did not stop making other sorts of comedy film in favour of romantic comedies though there was a temporary shift in dominance. The romantic comedies of the 1930s (and early 1940s), often called screwball romantic comedies, drew heavily on the madcap slapstick and crazy verbal humour of the early 1930s films but focused their comedy on the archetypical Hollywood romance narrative: Boy meets Girl, Boy loses Girl, Boy gets Girl, a sequence clearly indicating the passive female and active male of classical Hollywood, which was already in place when the sound romantic comedy arrived. The formation of a couple (or, in what Stanley Cavell (1981) calls 'comedies of remarriage', the couple achieving harmonious co-existence) resolves all difficulties, fulfilling the basic 'happy ending' of the genre, and the comedy (in terms of both narrative and humour) tends to leave its protagonists at this point.

The establishment of a romantic couple is not simply a twentieth-century phenomenon; the genre continues a long tradition. Romantic comedy can be associated with certain Ancient Greek plays (such as Aristophanes' *The Acharnians*) and Shakespearian comedies as 'New Comedy'; that is, narratives which are about younger people circumventing parental restrictions and finding partners to suit themselves (see Frye 1990: 44). New Comedy is not about escaping from, or rejecting, society *per se* but about being able to become independent, decision-making members of that society, for its ultimate benefit. It is a comedy of renewal and tends to be much more narratively coherent than so-called Old Comedy, the comedy of clowns and buffoons. In film the contrast is between comedian comedies (see previous chapters) and romantic comedy. In Jenkins's (1992) terms, while the comedian comedy tends to be more anarchistic than affirmative, romantic comedy is more affirmative than anarchistic, though we must be careful not to see the two as mutually exclusive. The danger is that such categorisations fail to acknowledge that '[t]he comic perspective is a crucial component' of romantic comedy and imply it is a sub-genre which uses comedy as 'sugar coating that helps us swallow the pill' of its repetitive romantic narrative structure (Deleyto 2009: 18, 20).

The most noticeable difference between traditional New Comedy and film 'romantic comedy' is a reduction in the number of different character roles required. The romantic couples in New Comedy (however many) were traditionally supported by comedians or more broadly comic characters (e.g. Bottom in *A Midsummer's Night Dream*) while their own problems tended to be treated as more serious, more dramatic. Early film comedies initially followed this model, though the tendency was to focus on the comedians rather than the couple (think of the short shrift given to the young lovers in the Marx Brothers' *Animal Crackers*). However, in cinema's version of New Comedy (i.e. romantic comedy), the comedian roles are not absent, rather they have been subsumed into the leads. Film comedy is not entirely responsible for the successful innovations; it does not develop in a vacuum and in this instance stage comedy (for example, Noël Coward's *Private Lives* (1931)) was an important influence that remains under-recognised. It is also clear that

Hollywood wasn't entirely sure how it had improved on this venerable tradition. The *It Happened One Night* director Frank Capra quoted collaborator Myles Connelly (cited in Siegel 1994: 146), noting the comedian role being absorbed into the male lead alone. This might be true of the later works of Chaplin, Keaton and Lloyd, but with regard to the 1930s romantic comedy it is a misreading presumably based on the prejudice that women cannot be both attractive (as the lead in romantic comedy is usually tasked with being) and funny. In successful romantic comedy films the comic duties are actually shared out (see Kendall 2002) and one of the genre's key elements is that it presents a dual address – male *and* female – to its audiences. This relative equality increased the genre's appeal to classical Hollywood's mainly female audiences, and was one of the reasons for its initial box-office success once it was configured in this way. The dual address also allows these films to retain their appeal: 'One of the great attractions of the screwball genre is its binary system: in its universe, women are on equal footing with men' (Sikov 1989: 10–12). Thus the fundamental 1930s screwball romantic comedy shows faith in companionship (which contains sexual compatibility) between equally matched but different partners.

The function of New Comedy is not to position youth and sexual difference above generational gender power (i.e. ongoing patriarchy), but to acknowledge during its narratives the impediments such constructs make for younger people. The forces ranged against the couple are key elements of romantic comedies (there would be precious little to interest an audience in a narrative in which Boy meets Girl, the end). The general obstructions to romance hold true over time but the emphases of particular films (and film cycles) vary vastly, as we shall see. Dealing with difference is difficult, comprehending compatibility is a problem, establishing equality is awkward, but these must be symbolically overcome in the narrative (though various caveats may remain). Obstacles to a successful romantic outcome were (and are):

1 social conventions and larger, related, issues such as class, race and religion
2 parents, other relatives, friends (likely to overvalue one of the issues in 1, above)
3 personal psychology (the individual pasts of the ideal couple)
4 body and image (likely to be related to 3, above)
5 misunderstandings (illusory problems usually predicated on one or more of the above).

These problems are *not* necessarily overcome in life (and this is why we are interested in them). The films' happy endings are acknowledged escapism, and convince only as regards the individual cases of the characters portrayed without giving any real expectation that such resolutions will be mirrored for their audiences off-screen. If they did, the genre would not be so vast nor the problems so repeatable. In the 1930s films were produced at a truly industrial rate, with the bigger studios each making over fifty a year of which comedies formed a significant proportion. The rapidity of classical Hollywood film production meant that when couples 'worked' on screen it was to the particular studio's advantage if they could be reunited in a series, for example William Powell and Myrna Loy in *The Thin Man* series (see Glitre 2006: 65–87). When pairings did not work, the same stars would be back often in mere weeks with new romantic partners. Comedy, and its throwaway quality, makes individual films more easily assimilable for audiences as examples, rather than definitive versions or paragons of romance.

We will now summarise how the genre of romantic comedy developed through the first decade of sound film with three selected examples illustrating the industrial background, the relationship of film to self-regulation and critical reactions.

Behind the curtain of decency: *It Happened One Night* (1934)

It Happened One Night achieved stratospheric box-office success over other significant romantic comedies in that year (*The Twentieth Century*, *She Done Him Wrong*) and can be seen to initiate the genre in sound film properly. Its impact was, however, unexpected.

Coming from lowly Columbia studios, *It Happened One Night* was not one of the big productions of 1934. For its ambitious director, Frank Capra, it was a project between films he thought of as more significant for his career. The male lead, Clark Gable, an up-and-coming star at MGM, was being disciplined (for asking for a raise) by being sent to an inferior studio. The chance to work with him tempted Claudette Colbert, star of *Sign of the Cross* (1933) and *Cleopatra* (1934), two big Cecil B. DeMille pictures at Paramount, to use up her vacation on this contemporary-set picture for $50,000 (a sixth of the film's budget) and top billing. Though the basic plot was taken from a short story set on a bus, Harry Cohn, president of Columbia Pictures, knew that previous pictures with such a setting had failed and had the title changed from 'Night Bus'. No one expected much from *It Happened One Night*, and the pace at which films were then made meant that they were all on to other projects by the time it was released, yet most critics and audiences loved it and the film made a clean sweep of the Academy Awards with one each for the leads, director, screenwriter (Robert Riskin) and the film itself, an extremely unusual achievement for a comedy in any era. In the aftermath Gable got his salary trebled at MGM, Colbert rose to the top of the heap at Paramount, Capra became an important director and Columbia became a much more important studio.

A further obstacle to the film's success, beyond its modest expectations, was that the Production Code, written in 1930, was fully enforced in 1934 owing to increased criticism of Hollywood's purported influence on morality, in the context of a national crime wave that was one of the effects of the Depression. The influence of films on the society that produces them is, periodically, a major concern for those who claim to be society's moral arbiters and the Code's central concerns are the moral standards of audiences:

> *General Principles*
>
> 1. No picture shall be produced which will lower the moral standards of those who see it. Hence the sympathy of the audience shall never be thrown to the side of crime, wrong-doing, evil or sin.
> 2. Correct standards of life, subject only to the requirements of drama and entertainment, shall be presented.
> 3. Law, natural or human, shall not be ridiculed, nor shall sympathy be created for its violation.
>
> *Particular Applications*
>
> II. SEX
>
> The sanctity of the institution of marriage and the home shall be upheld. Pictures shall not infer that low forms of sex relationship are the accepted or common thing.
>
> 1. *Adultery* ... 2. *Scenes of passion* ... 3. *Seduction or Rape* ... 4. *Sex Perversion* ... 5. *White slavery* ... 6. *Miscegenation* ... 7. *Sex Hygiene* ... 8. *Scenes of actual child birth* ... 9. *Children's sex organs* .... (See Belton 1999: 135–49)

In addition to the above, the Code also contained prohibitions against vulgarity, obscenity and profanity and restrictions on costume, dances and locations that could be included. Its concerns imply that cinema is a medium inclined towards lust and sin with an easily led audience at its mercy.

Initially 1930s filmmakers responded to the threat of censorship by moving the passion of drama to the potentially less contentious ground of comedy, where a lack of seriousness might defuse issues. Without confronting or explicitly rejecting the Code writers, directors and filmmakers were not about to simply toe the line. For their own amusement and to engage with a more active audience than the Code conceived, they began to smuggle material in, to obey the Code literally but also to engage knowing audiences with subtle double entendres and innuendo in order to convey more up-to-date attitudes to sex and marriage through the medium of film. The presence of censorship was also instrumental in making obstacles to romance take the place of the negative consequences of romance ('fallen women', the feud, adultery).

The narrative of *It Happened One Night* has Gable as out-of-work journalist Peter Warne helping Colbert as heiress Ellie Andrews escape her controlling tycoon father to return to the man she has married but been snatched away from, the celebrity aviator King Westley. It is important that this isn't a real marriage and that it will be legally and practically annulled during the story (Cavell 1981 stretches the point to make this a comedy of remarriage). The true couple meet on a bus. Peter realises who Ellie is and figures he can resurrect his career by telling her story exclusively. If she won't play along he will tell her father where she is and ruin her escape. The couple are thus tied together, hampered by a lack of money, travelling by the lower-class means of a bus (both auto-gyro pilot Westley and Ellie's father have access to flight).

Examples of subversion of the Production Code's standards become apparent early on in the film. Having just been fired by his editor and having attempted to tell him what he thinks of him by telephone, Peter Warne gets on the bus back to New York. Too late to get a seat he notices the back seat occupied only by a stack of newspapers. He asks the driver (Ward Bond) to remove them, then impatiently does it himself, throwing them out of the window. This leads to an argument with the driver in which Warne explains why he won't sit on newspapers by telling the story of how he once sat on a copy in white trousers and 'no one in town bought a paper that day they just followed me around and read the news off the seat of my pants'. The driver replies 'Fresh guy, huh?' clearly getting the insult. The insult is that Gable refers him to the euphemistic 'seat of his pants', a point emphasised by the way his backside faces the audience through most of the scene as he ostensibly puts his bag on the overhead rack. While their argument continues (to comic victory for Warne) Ellie slips by and takes the empty seat. Warne then speaks to her, saying 'That upon which you sit is mine'. His bombastic drunkenness motivates the peculiar sentence construction but there is a clear second meaning in the statement that refers to Ellie's rear rather than the seat, and this is just as clearly behind her irritated 'I beg your pardon' response as the sense on which the scene proceeds. There is more in this vein when Ellie, putting her luggage up in the rack, stumbles and sits in Peter's lap. A comic line follows ('Next time you drop in bring your folks') but the couple's edgy glances at each other afterwards before the scene fades allow us to see that there will be a sexual subtext to all their subsequent dealings, whether we read it as conscious or subconscious. The Production Code forbade direct references to that part upon which we all sit but *It Happened One Night* is able to work around it through innuendo and double meanings that don't necessarily present themselves in the script (which would be all the PCA had to go on). The film is full of such set-ups that depend on the audience to fill in gaps. When the telegraph operator reads back Peter Warne's insulting telegram to his editor, her hesitation over his handwriting leaves us time to guess exactly what the editor is a tub of ('Mush. Mush,' Gable repeats, after a beat, as if surprised by any other suggestion). When the bus arrives at the rest stop the euphemism in that location's name is revealed by a passenger's unheard whisper to the cook ringing a bell to advertise his wares. The passenger is directed around the corner to what must surely be a toilet, something else the Production Code would deny filmmakers reference to but which the audience's attention can easily be directed to just for the entertainment of doing so. Of course, such minor points may not mean much to modern audiences but they do give us a perspective within which to view the key scenes in the film. The scenes we will now concentrate on are the three which feature Peter and Ellie sharing rooms.

On the first occasion, with the bus halted because of a washed-out bridge, the couple decide to spend the night in an auto camp (a primitive motel). Owing to lack of funds, Peter signs them in as man and wife (motels also have to keep up respectable appearances). In order to deflect accusations about his intentions towards Ellie he reveals to her that he is a journalist and interested in her story rather a man interested in her person (or that upon which she sits). Not only are there two single beds in the room, but Warne puts a blanket over a string he suspends across the centre of the room. He calls this barrier 'the Walls of Jericho', a biblical allusion familiar to religious revivalist 1930s America, and which sanctifies the makeshift arrangement to the extent Ellie soon learns to trust it. Yet the barrier, which satisfies the PCA, eroticises the scene. There to maintain decency between the characters it lets the audience see both sides, unimpeded. Not only does the camera linger on Ellie getting changed, but those moments we do not see are fetishistically portrayed by bumps against the blanket and her stockings and underwear draped over the top. Warne points them out and Ellie apologises and removes these signifiers of sensuality. As they settle down, having exchanged their mock-married goodnights, the camera focuses on light reflected in Ellie's eyes showing her still awake. There are a number of ways we might read this, from her being fearful about her situation but, perhaps, and it can only be perhaps, she is imagining what life would really be like as Mrs Peter Warne, with all that that would entail.

The morning after, Ellie tells Peter 'This is the first time I've really been alone with a man'. She reveals that her putative husband, Westley, was always surrounded by an entourage and, thus, just how little real experience she has. In the first half of the film Gable is the wordly-wise one, not a successful man but one knowing well enough how to look after their limited resources (Kendall 2002: 45). Ellie, working from a standing start, soon progresses though, for example, by joining in their masquerade as a white trash couple to fool her father's detectives. The turning point, however, is the famous hitch-hiking scene where Peter tries to thumb a ride and fails, after which Ellie stops traffic by showing her leg, so proving that 'the limb is mightier than the thumb'. The humour comes from the deflation of Warne's knowledge and the dramatic effect of Ellie bringing her talents to bear. Sex trumps abstract knowledge every time. Though the strength of reaction to a stocking-top is still funny today it is perhaps comic in different ways (as we have suggested in the Introduction, time affects humour). The stocking (and the leg which it emphasises) offer the driver the prospect of sex, a prospect he cannot possibly acknowledge once he has stopped, especially when another man is also present. Yet Warne is grumpy afterwards and the driver is ultimately punished: when he later attempts to drive away with their luggage Warne chases him, and comes back bruised having regained the luggage and won the car (an apparent theft that didn't trouble the PCA).

It isn't long afterwards that Ellie prevails on Peter to stop at a second motel, three hours from New York, against his better judgement. She does so because she enjoys spending time with him. He, however, makes clear that as soon as they reach the end of the journey they will no longer see each other because she is a married woman. This makes the second version of the Walls of Jericho scene a much more sombre affair. We see the blanket from the side, not the end, now, Ellie apparently addressing questions to it, or in a three-quarter view which gives it the appearance of a square block between the characters. She asks him if he's ever been in love and he replies: 'Sure, I've thought about it. Who hasn't? ... if I could just meet the right sort of girl. Aww, where are you gonna find her? Somebody that's real, somebody that's alive.' The audience, of course, have a good idea that she is the person on the other side of the blanket and may even suspect that perhaps, deep within himself, Peter Warne knows it too; his conscious mind just hasn't caught up. When he wants to go to a Pacific Island with a girl who would jump in the surf with him and love it as much as he did we may remember Ellie diving into the sea to escape her father's yacht and outswimming his boatbound employees.

As Peter continues in the same vein, poetic but natural, Ellie appears suddenly, surprisingly, around the end of the curtain, dewy-eyed. But the couple cannot get together at this point and Peter insists she goes back to her bed, on the other side of the blanket. It is not until she has sobbed herself to sleep that he finally realises the significance of their conversation and leaves to get money by selling *their* story. The blanket clearly forms a barrier to full communication. The motel proprietors see him go and assume the worst (that the unmarried or duplicitously married woman has been used and discarded). Ellie is forced to contact Westley and her father who retrieve her before Warne can get back.

The final Walls of Jericho scene plays out off-screen as the final scene of the film. From a discreet distance we see the cabin where the reunited couple are honeymooning. They are doing something peculiar according to the rustic proprietor; stringing up a rope and a blanket between them (despite showing him their marriage licence!). They have also sent him to the store for a toy trumpet which he has delivered presumably along with the telegram from Mr Andrews dictated in the preceding scene, which simply says 'Let 'em topple', indicating that a legal annulment of Ellie's marriage to Westley has been obtained. As the trumpet blows, the lights in the cabin go out, the soundtrack picks up on the fanfare and the film thus ends elegantly as the Walls of Jericho tumble. We haven't heard the voices of the leads since they were absolutely at odds during preparations for Ellie's 'proper' wedding to Westley. Warne replied to her invitation to stay with 'I would – but I've got a weak stomach' and, as her father tried to plead Warne's case, Ellie stated 'I never want to hear about him again'. In resolving and concluding their relationship from this point the film seems to know the genre conventions it is shaping backwards and gives us only what we need. The ending, with the blanket finally falling, means the couple can have sex. Ellie's first marriage is a thin barrier, like the Production Code, formidable from certain angles but actually easy to get around. The romantic comedy is, in essence, preparation for sex: a form of narrative foreplay. And yet the audience are fully satisfied with the way this film is put together. Its playfulness in dealing with the contemporary problem of whether or not such a narrative could even be told under the strictures of the Production Code is balanced with what Rowe notes is the melodramatic possibility of the central couple not getting together (1995: 110).

Critical readings of *It Happened One Night*

It Happened One Night is an important and significant film which still holds considerable charm today (Pauline Kael cited in Harvey 1998: 110). It is also widely available and numerous commentators have dealt with it in varying degrees of depth. What have they been able to say about it? It is unfair to reduce complex approaches to single meanings but it is possible to indicate the particular emphases of the various studies. Several scholars (Beach 2002; King 2002; Lent 1995; Mellen 1978; Polan 1991; Rowe 1995) point out the significance of class conflict and its resolution in the film in its historical context of the white Anglo-Saxon protestant elite being blamed for the Depression by those suffering most from it. Kendall (2002) even goes so far as to suggest it is Capra's intent to rehabilitate the elite (such as film directors) in the affections of the masses. Some commentators (Karnick and Jenkins 1995; Siegel and Siegel 1994) emphasise the importance of the film as inaugurating a new cinematic genre (if not romantic comedy then screwball romantic comedy). Others (Musser 1995, in particular, but also Cavell 1981; Polan 1991 and Lent 1995) take a longer view, fitting the film into an ongoing dialogue between Hollywood and American culture about marriage, taking in the increasing possibility of divorce (very rare outside the elite in the 1920s), and the new emphasis within the institution of marriage away from property and ownership and towards compatibility and companionship. Others (most of those cited above but also Harvey 1998 and Sikov 1989) tend to point to the film's sex appeal within the broader context of the genre. As we have already suggested, the romantic comedy genre tends towards a dual address. Both Kendall (2002) and Rowe (1995) are right to argue that Gable's character has to change, too, for the relationship to work. Seeing the film as a contribution to the development of masculinity is easy enough if we bear in mind the apocryphal story that, when Gable's demonstration of male undressing in the first Walls of Jericho scene showed that he did not wear a vest, manufacturers saw their profits slump as thousands of American men stopped buying undershirts.

Certainly his character is the inheritor of the old patriarchal power, approved of by Mr Andrews, but his rejection of money (a $10,000 reward) and fame (describing Westley as 'the pill of the century') and the decision to go honeymooning modestly in Michigan on his money shows he has his own values.

We have focused on the blanket as a metaphor for censorship (agreeing with Cavell 1981: 80–3). Rowe (1995: 128) suggests it is an insistent emblem of Ellie's virginity (i.e. the hymen). We prefer that the fall of the blanket represents entering the adult world beyond other people's regulation. Rowe (132) understands Gable's dialogue in the second Jericho scene (quoted above) to supply Warne with a failed romance in his past that supports her argument about the contrast of innocence and experience, but his planning might equally have been without a specific person in mind. Nevertheless, while it could be claimed that Warne, as written, was inexperienced, the point is that it seems impossible to read the character portrayed by Gable as inexperienced. The same may also be true of Colbert, whose naive innocence comes from someone also capable of playing Cleopatra. There is simply a depth to both characters on screen that isn't in the script but in the players and this is the film's enduring strength.

All the critical emphases noted above, including our own, depend on the equality of the central couple whether as carriers of class conflict, as demonstrators of companionable marriage or as performers of code-sanctioned sexuality. If there was an imbalance between the central characters, through a mismatch of style, chemistry, appeal or power of action in the narrative, such arguments would not work. The surviving potency of this film depends, however, not just on the balance of the central couple but on the fact that such balance means it can still be funny and be read a number of ways.

It is possible to object to the enforced heterosexual and marital solutions to the problems of gaining personal happiness offered by films of this genre. It is, among the available readings, possible to make a feminist reading of *It Happened One Night* which figures it entirely negatively as essentially thwarting Ellie Andrews's independence as she struggles to free herself from her father, but ultimately ends up with a man her father approves of who expresses the view that she needs a husband who will 'take a sock at her every day whether she deserves it or not'. The only other potential husband offered is the easily bought-off Westley, whose compatibility, evidenced only by the feeble embrace he gives her while driving away from the motel in her father's limousine indicates he is more interested in her father's money than in her. This possible reading of *It Happened One Night* would, however, largely ignore the contemporary reality for most women in the 1930s; companionate marriage is actually an advance on what existed before (see Lent 1995; Glitre 2006: 15). Films like *It Happened One Night* buck repression, meaning the established views that hold young people back. In *It Happened One Night* the objections of Ellie's father to her first choice and the social conventions that have kept her too cosseted to be able to make a better choice are the initial blocks, but the standards of Peter Warne also have a blocking function (propriety and financial independence) as does his inability to see beyond his immediate task in gaining exclusive rights to Ellie's story. Both characters learn during the course of the film and thus justify the sub-genre's dual address as well as its significant engagement with social conventions and class. The film's narrative plausibly sets these obstacles up and knocks them down, like the walls of Jericho, at the appropriate moment, simultaneously pleasing sophisticated and unsophisticated film audiences alike.

Following up: *It Happened One Night*

☞ Consider how the dual address of romantic comedy – the appeal to both male and female audience members – is established in *It Happened One Night*.

☞ Were the strictures of the Production Code limiting or productive for filmmakers?

☞ What aspects of the wealth of published analyses and interpretations of *It Happened One Night* make most sense from (1) an historical perspective; (2) today's perspective?

The anarchistic and affirmative poles of romantic comedy: *Bringing Up Baby* (1938) and *The Philadelphia Story* (1941)

When dealing critically with the romantic comedy genre it is unhelpful to 'obscure the importance of humour' or to decide beforehand that all films in it will 'always say the same thing' (Deleyto 2009: 24, 25). In particular, we must not allow the fact that romantic comedy is a sub-genre of comedy more driven by narrative than comedian comedy to prompt us to think of them as opposites, with romantic comedy as affirmative and relatively conservative and comedian comedies as wholly anarchistic and subversive. The importance of the humour in romantic comedy, and the range of positions it offers on the anarchistic to affirmative continuum, can be illustrated by drawing on two examples from the end of the sound romantic comedy's first decade, which share the same stars: *Bringing Up Baby* and *The Philadelphia Story*.

Bringing up Baby, perhaps now regarded as the epitome of the screwball romantic comedy, stars Cary Grant as engaged palaeontologist David Huxley and Katharine Hepburn as a wealthy socialite, Susan Vance, whose accidental meeting sparks a frenetic narrative (exceeded in rapidity only by *His Girl Friday* (1940)). The film contains plenty of slapstick and a madcap plot in which there are identical leopards (one a killer and one rendered docile by the song 'I can't give you anything but love, baby'). It soon becomes clear that the couple are attracted to each other; she consciously trying to overcome his inhibitions and plans (such as marriage to the prim Miss Swallow); his – less conscious – desires revealed by his inability to get shot of this exasperating woman who is turning his life upside-down. As in *It Happened One Night*, the woman is connected to wealth that the man doesn't have, but can help him get, though in this case it is the woman who educates the man (Grant's knowledge is purely academic). The stars bring a sexual charge to the material, whether it is Hepburn in her ripped dress or Grant in her flouncy dressing gown, but there is very little conventional romance. In their wilderness leopard hunt Susan breaks David's spectacles, implying that he has been looking at things all wrong, and a kiss is threatened though it isn't delivered until the end of the film when he eventually gives up his career (his dinosaur skeleton comes crashing down) to be with her and to embrace the chaos which that entails. This is a narrative which encourages commentators to write about romance being displaced into comic actions (see Glitre 2006: 27) and the sexual angle does indeed seem subsumed into other things which are quite blatantly open to Freudian readings (these are not anachronistic – there is a comic psychologist in the film whose heavily accented burblings ridicule the currently fashionable concept of trauma). For example Susan is associated with the contrary but relatively tractable leopard, Baby, but the realisation that she has dragged its dangerous double into the police station causes her to panic (and inadvertently express her love for David out loud). This comes after she has acted the gangster's moll (the dangerous woman) to gain her freedom from the cells. This sequence of narrative events might be seen to illustrate Susan's desire, manipulated by her for effect on others, becoming less and less controllable until she has unwittingly become as 'dangerous' as the man-eating leopard. The tuneless renditions of 'I can't give you anything but love' that she insists David sing to calm the leopard's mating calls aren't always going to be enough to tame this feline. David faints, having managed to rescue the situation by containing the other leopard. David, however, is associated with the much more domesticated pet dog (Asta) who is also fascinated with bones. The lost bone (an intercostal clavicle) represents his lost phallus and is a 'more or less blatant and continuous *double entendre*' (Cavell 1981: 116; see also Babington and Evans 1989: 8; Rowe 1995: 150; McDonald 2007: 27). The cat couldn't care less about the bone though: it wants to hear the song. This is as good a representation of differing male/female goals (respectively tangible/intangible) in romantic transactions as cinema has given us. The resolution of the film, however, makes clear that ultimately what Susan seeks is tangible: David (whose bone she returns) – and that what his life lacked was intangible: excitement (which Susan provides). In the way of their realising this lie social conventions, economics, common sense, logic, propriety, personal psychology (plus psychologists and psychology *per se*) and patriarchal law and order (the sheriff). All of these obstacles needs to be shoved out of the way to bring this couple together or, using the film's symbolic euphemisms, to let the bone see the leopard.

Bringing up Baby was unsuccessful at the time it was released and seen to go too far (see Rowe 1995: 152–3). This reaction undoubtedly has something to do with the abandon with which the film makes everything irrelevant besides the search for love and how little the patriarchal order gets a look in; its fossilised version of masculinity is represented by the collapsing dinosaur skeleton (Babington and Evans 1989: 43; Rowe 1995: 146; Glitre 2006: 61). *Bringing Up Baby*'s anarchistic disdain for conventional romance elements (kissing, marriage) partly comes of its focus on uniting two otherworldly characters who are extremely well suited, though both lack the down-to-earth charm of Gable and Colbert reduced to eating raw carrots. Grant throws himself into the film confident enough in his masculinity to endure all manner of humiliations but Katherine Hepburn's tribulations are instructive. Her spirited portrayal of independent woman (one reason for the film's great appeal today) was unfairly added to her perceived culpability in a string of flops that helped her become regarded as 'box-office poison' by exhibitors at the time.

Hepburn escaped this 'box-office poison' tag by being a success on Broadway (again the stage is significant) and holding the film rights to the vehicle for her success, Philip Barry's hit play *The Philadelphia Story*. Despite these shrewd off-screen moves the entertaining film version (1941) serves the perceived need to humanise Hepburn's aloof, aristocratic persona and retrieve her for the patriarchy or, to put it another way, to make her more acceptable to the mainstream. Her character, Tracy, has ultimately to return to her first husband C.K. Dexter Haven (Cary Grant) whom she had formerly eloped with but eventually drove to drink through her virginal statue/goddess personality. Though Tracy starts the film with a fiancé, Kittredge (John Howard), who worships her as she is and doesn't want her to change, she is brought down to earth by realising how most others see her, particularly the writer-turned-journalist Mike Conner (James Stewart, winning an Oscar). The most bizarre element in returning her to the patriarchal fold is her submission to her father (John Halliday), a philanderer whose excuse is a lack of daughterly love. Rowe (1995: 112) is able to explain this as an Oedipally necessary rejection of the mother. Tracy's drunken flirtation with Mike leads Kittredge to assume the worst and so prove his small-mindedness (and, incidentally, overturn the journalist's inverted snobbery), but when Mike offers to fill the role of groom he is quickly rebuffed. The female staff photographer (Ruth Hussey), really a painter and a genuine divorcee, is Mike's soulmate and is there to cushion his fall as Hepburn's and Grant's characters go down the aisle (as they did not before) to be properly married. *The Philadelphia Story* is a comedy of remarriage in which Hepburn's character is still privileged but is brought down to earth by exposure to everyday honest Americans – again exemplified by a journalist – and thus realises her folly, avoids the wrong partner and rediscovers the right one. With the father restored and the feminine subdued, the narrative of *The Philadelphia Story* clearly serves a conservative agenda, but to what degree is its meaning to be defined by the narrative end rather than the possibilities within? While *Bringing Up Baby* focuses to the exclusion of much else on the psychologies of its protagonists and their readiness for romance, *The Philadelphia Story* keys in to the social implications. While its ending clearly is conservative, of the two films it is the one to engage with a range of social positions and antagonisms and at least flirt with class-crossing romance.

The romantic comedy films of the 1940s overall showed a diminishing interest in the rich and privileged of American society, so often prominent on one side or the other of many 1930s romantic comedies, and an increase in focus on career-minded women (see Glitre 2006). The early 1940s also offer the apotheosis of the screwball form in the Preston Sturges romantic comedies *The Lady Eve* (1941) and *The Palm Beach Story* (1942). In Sturges's subsequent comedies *Sullivan's Travels* (1942) and *The Miracle of Morgan's Creek* (1944) the emphasis is on marriages of convenience until his *Unfaithfully Yours* (1948) offers the darkest comedy of remarriage possible. In Chapter 8 we will pick up on the history of the romantic comedy film but we conclude this chapter by focusing on the narrative outcomes associated with this genre.

Following up: the first decade of sound romantic comedy

☞ How do the romantic comedies of the 1930s negotiate the discrepancy between their (and their audiences') interest in sex and the Production Code's interest in restricting any suggestion of it?

☞ To what extent are the romantic comedies of the 1930s about things other than romance?

☞ What particular comedic qualities does Cary Grant bring to his roles in the run of romantic comedies that includes *The Awful Truth*, *Bringing Up Baby* and *His Girl Friday*?

Romantic comedy ending

In terms of relative attention and time on screen given to female characters the romantic comedy as established in the 1930s remains attractive to female audiences. Consequently this sub-genre is seen as feminised, though this is far from making it a feminist genre (see Carson 1994). By early twenty-first-century standards it is certainly possible to see examples of the romantic comedy from the first decades of sound cinema peddling repressive messages and to see contemporary examples as being equally conservative in their values. Western, and indeed all commercial cinema internationally, privileges and promotes heterosexuality with romantic comedy in particular naturalising gender ideology and the cultural myths around it. However, it would be wrong to imagine that such bias is timeless or that the romantic comedy genre ignores 'the hard evidence [contradicting this message] found in contemporary western societies where heterosexual monogamy is in permanent crisis and has become only one option among many others' (Deleyto 2009: 25). We will revisit romantic comedy as a participant in cultural discourses about gender (in Chapter 8), but here we examine the idea that the romantic comedy promotes the institution of marriage.

Marriage from its inception as an institution, although ostensibly about the joining together of man and wife, has essentially been a property transaction between men. This is revealed in the traditional trappings of western marriage such as the father of the bride walking his daughter down the aisle and handing her over to another man, to only men speaking formally at the traditional wedding reception, etc. In other words, marriage is a procedure for preventing independent female activity, with particular regard to sex. Traditional patriarchy is prepared to license female sexuality only to the extent that it attracts men towards marriage: female sexuality that doesn't is stigmatised. The task of the husband is ultimately to prevent and put an end to independent female sexuality. However, despite often ending in marriage, the romantic comedy does not primarily exist to boost the institution, and too much concentration on the conservative nature of the genre underplays the renewal at its core: 'It is not enough to claim that The End is the meaning – that, simply by ending in the union of the heterosexual couple, romantic comedy is about the traditional institution of patriarchal society and must be inherently conservative. The context of The End must be taken into account' (Glitre 2006: 17). Rather than simply delivering its characters into the traditional, patriarchally acceptable marriage, romantic comedies question the version of the process that applies at any given time. Successful romantic comedy almost always illustrates progressive attitudes, even if it doesn't insist upon them or suggests they might be too progressive. This is a good example of the relationship of cinema to culture which is one of simultaneous reflection, refraction and formation. The reason why the key historical institution of human sexuality is so regularly bound to comedy is because of the seriousness of what is at stake: the difficulties of human sexuality, of bringing two conscious, independent humans equitably together. As Molly Haskell has argued, the concerns of the romantic comedy genre of the 1930s were far from entirely frivolous:

> The mating games played within their frames were testimonials to the fact that the choice of partner – the most important choice most people ever make – is nothing less than earth-shaking, an assertion of one's deepest instincts and destiny through love, a leap of faith into the void. (Haskell 1989: 10)

Romantic comedies reflect the social and psychological pressures current at the time they were made. They reveal contemporary attitudes to gender, sexuality and identity. They show us different levels of personal independence versus social conformity, individuality versus compatibility, sexual innocence versus sexual knowledge and, almost invariably, have something to say about class, money and status. But, in the end, they tend to hedge their bets towards the tried, tested and safe (marriage) even if, during the course of the narrative, they may have conveyed a striking ambivalence about such outcomes.

We cannot understand entries in this sub-genre of comedy without close examination. Romantic comedy is far too convenient a label that sometimes seems to allow critics to disregard other generic elements in the mix and to underestimate the inclusion of comedy. We will find romantic comedy a key aspect of generic hybridisation in film (see Chapter 6) since, as Deleyto (2009) implies, romantic comedy is a flavour that goes with (almost) anything.

Following up: the romantic comedy genre

☞ Using specific examples of romantic comedies, is it possible to support an argument that this sub-genre is largely affirmative rather than anarchistic in its humour?

☞ Take any romantic comedy film and analyse the obstacles to the couple getting together or staying together. The list on page 67 may be useful. How seriously are we meant to take these obstacles? Repeat the process for a film made in a different decade (see also Chapter 8). How much (or how little) have the concerns of the genre changed over time?

Recommended reading

Kathrina Glitre, *Hollywood Romantic Comedy: States of the Union 1934–65*, Manchester: Manchester University Press, 2006.

Celestine Deleyto, *The Secret Life of Romantic Comedy*, Manchester: Manchester University Press, 2009.

4

Radio comedy

Just as silent film comedy developed in ways which overcame the absence of speech and other aural effects, radio comedy developed techniques which circumvented the medium's lack of pictures and which emphasised its own distinctive codes and conventions. Whereas silent film comedians relied on visual comedy, radio comedians and their scriptwriters explored the potential of speech, sounds and silence to generate humour and laughter in ways that made the absence of pictures irrelevant.

Considered by some as 'the most important electronic invention of the [twentieth] century' (Douglas 1999: 9), the conventional view of radio often stresses its limitations, since it is essentially 'a blind medium' (Crisell 1986: 3). Yet because radio, more than any other medium, requires an active use of imagination, it can roam in spaces which are essentially polymorphic, a factor which goes to the essence of radio as a medium and to the distinctive nature of its comedy. As Michele Hilmes has noted:

> In a society based on visual cues, where appearances superseded almost every other social indicator, radio's ability to escape visual over-determination had the potential to set off a riot of social signifiers – indeed, this is one of radio's most fascinating attributes. (Hilmes 1997: 20)

Though radio might appear ill equipped to deal with comedy, lacking the visual dimension of live performance, film and television, and often listened to by the solitary listener who is psychologically less inclined to laugh than an individual in a group, the ability of radio to construct a playground for the imagination has enabled comedy to become and continue to be an important part of radio programming. Unlike film and television, radio requires its audience to actively fill in the visual. Using imagination in this way makes listening to radio an active process. The sheer work involved in listening, particularly to talk radio, can result in the formation of a deeply personal and private bond with the radio programme, and this may explain why, as Andrew Crisell claims, 'comedy has not only been hugely successful on the radio, but also achieved its success in a wide variety of forms' (1986: 157).

Though, like film, radio was founded on late nineteenth-century technology, it emerged as a developed medium only in the 1920s. Initially the provenance of enthusiastic, mostly male amateurs, radio developed in very different ways in the United States and Britain. Though the technology was similar, the different ways in which it was exploited and structured reflected distinctive cultural, political and ideological differences between the two countries. In America, despite some opposition from education and religious groups as well as some progressive politicians, radio rapidly became commercialised, with programmes paid for and indeed run by advertising agencies and sponsors (Smulyan 1994). Although the National Broadcasting Company (NBC) and the Columbia Broadcasting System (CBS) were established as country-wide networks in the late 1920s and were charged with maintaining and upholding 'cultural standards', by the mid-1930s radio programming and scheduling in America were dominated by powerful advertising agencies such as the J. Walter Thompson Company. This commercialisation of radio not only gave businesses, as one corporate executive put it, 'a latchkey to nearly every home in the United States' (Smulyan 1994: 86), it had a profound effect on the commissioning, scheduling, timing and content of radio programmes. By 1930 Thompson's Radio Department had originated over thirty programmes, amounting to sixty hours' broadcasting a week (Hilmes 1997: 116). Radio programmes that failed to attract big enough audiences to satisfy sponsors and advertisers were removed. Those that proved popular provided increasingly huge salaries for radio personalities including, from the early 1930s until the advent of television in the 1950s, radio comedians.

The situation in Britain was markedly different. Although a commercial consortium of wireless set manufacturers founded the British Broadcasting Company in 1922, a combination of financial difficulties, government concern and an emergent set of attitudes which stressed broadcasting's moral and cultural responsibilities, led to the establishment of the publicly funded but quasi-autonomous British Broadcasting Corporation in 1927, paid for by licence fee money (Briggs 1961, 1965). A commitment to public service rather than commercial exploitation, enshrined in legislation and made flesh by the BBC's domineering first Director-General John (later Lord) Reith, meant that British radio programmes valued information and education above entertainment. Though jazz bands and 'sketches by humorists' such as 'Our Lizzie' (Helena Millais), 'Wireless Willie' (Willie Rouse) and John Henry did feature in programming from 1922 onwards, much of the BBC's early output was designed to be 'uplifting' and informative, with classical music, light music and talks and discussions dominating. Though comedians such as Will Hay and 'cross-talk' duo Clapham and Dwyer were broadcast in live relays from variety theatres and music halls in the 1920s, comedy talent with suitable material for radio was scarce before the creation of a separate 'revue and vaudeville' section in the BBC in 1930.

Early radio comedy: The influence of vaudeville and music hall

If, in the words of one NBC executive in the late 1930s, American radio gave 'the radio audience what they apparently like to listen to', whereas the BBC gave audiences what they 'think they ought to have' (Hilmes 1997: 126), comedians in both countries initially struggled to come to terms with the new medium. Though Eddie Cantor had first appeared on WJZ in Newark as early as 1921, radio stations could not match the salaries that comedians and variety artists were earning in vaudeville. Moreover, many vaudevillians who tried radio found it an uncomfortable experience, with no audience to react to and with no visual props and gestures to help their act. Slapstick antics that were funny on the vaudeville stage simply did not work on radio. The most successful radio acts in the 1920s were 'music and comedy patter' acts, such as Billy Jones and Ernie Hare, the so-called 'Happiness Boys'. Sponsored by the Happiness Candy Company, Jones and Hare first broadcast on New York station WEAF in August 1923 and then from 1927 on the NBC national network. The first regular comedy show on radio, their harmony singing and comic patter were structured around regular opening and closing theme songs and a series of jokes that often satirised the inadequacies of early radio broadcasting. Significantly, the pair were amongst the first to tailor their material specifically for radio, not pausing, for example, after a gag in ways in which performers in front of a live audience usually did. In Britain the BBC acknowledged that 'the circumstances of a wireless studio are particularly suited to cross-talk between two comedians' (BBC 1932: 193); music hall and variety comedy duos such as Clapham and Dwyer, Claude Hulbert and Enid Trevor, and Doris and Elsie Waters were popular in the late 1920s.

By 1929 a third of American homes had a radio. As the popularity of radio grew, well-known recording stars and vaudeville artists were in increasing demand, appearing in shows such as Rudy Vallee's *The Fleischmann Hour* from 1929 and Eddie Cantor's long-running *Chase and Sanborn Hour* which premiered in September 1931. Even so, many of these artists were slow to adapt to the demands of radio comedy. Broadcast live in front of studio audiences who were initially requested to remain silent, Cantor stumbled across the idea of having the live audience laugh. However, as much of what they laughed at was the physical and visual aspects of his act, such as the costumes he wore, his slapstick routines and visual gags, this left the radio audience listening at home wondering why the studio audience were laughing. In the same way the hugely successful vaudeville comedian Ed Wynn enjoyed some success on radio in his NBC network programme *The Fire Chief* between 1932 and 1935. Wynn's clever wordplay and puns worked well on radio, but too much of his act relied on zany costume and visual antics which were missed by listeners. Both Cantor and Wynn introduced important innovations in radio comedy, such as the use of an announcer who played the straight man and acted as a comic foil, but their training in live vaudeville performance militated against ready adaptation to the demands of radio comedy. As Susan Smulyan notes, 'the performers who relied on word play and situation comedy lasted longer on radio than those who appeared in funny hats' (Smulyan 1994: 121). Cantor went on to star in a number of Hollywood vehicles including *Whoopee!* (1930) and *Roman Scandals* (1933), films that exploited the visual elements of his comic persona.

Others were quicker to realise the distinctive nature of radio as a medium, its reliance on the importance of words and tone of voice, reinforced by sound effects and music. Though he later complained about the voracious, never-ending appetite that radio had for new comedy material, the influential American comedian Fred Allen, whose career on radio began in 1932, saw radio as a 'theatre of the mind', arguing that radio is:

> meant for people at home. Give 'em the right sound effects and music, and their imaginations will work for you ... a fly crawling up the Empire State building, scenes in outer space or under the sea. These are things that radio can do best – better than the movies. (Wertheim 1979: 162)

Radio's ability to circumvent the confines of visual anchorage was behind the success of NBC's *Quaker Early Birds Program* in the late 1920s. Featuring Gene Carroll and Glenn Rowell, the show was a daily fifteen-minute situation comedy which based its jokes on character and voice, with Carroll playing the part of Lena, a female boarding house owner. This ability of radio to facilitate vocal cross-dressing was extended to other areas of aural illusion, most notably in the long-running and influential comedy series *Amos'n'Andy*. Featuring two white performers, Freeman Gosden and Charles Correll, *Amos'n'Andy* followed the comic exploits of two fictitious African-Americans who migrated, as did millions of real African-Americans during the 1920s, from the rural south to the northern cities. The daily programme had started life as *Sam'n'Henry* on WGN in Chicago in 1926, but was picked up and renamed *Amos'n'Andy* by NBC in 1929. Rooted firmly in the minstrel show and blackface comedy tradition, the show's source of humour was, as Michelle Hilmes puts it, 'the theme of cultural incompetence' (Hilmes 1997: 89) as the two displaced protagonists struggled to survive against a backcloth of economic depression and the problems of racial segregation. Though visual slapstick had been an important part of vaudeville, so too was what Susan Douglas terms 'linguistic slapstick', an emphasis on word-play, puns, jokes and punch lines. *Amos'n'Andy* relied heavily on this linguistic slapstick, on the 'mangling of conventional English, the incessant malapropisms, inadvertent puns and total misunderstanding of regular terms and phrases' (Douglas 1999: 106). When Andy remarked that 'de stock market crashed', the next question was 'Anybody git hurt?' Though not without its critics, *Amos'n'Andy* was the most popular show on radio from 1930 to 1932, with an estimated forty million listeners tuned in daily, adjusting their daily routines around the broadcast. The popularity of the show between 1929 and 1935 was such that some cinemas interrupted the film so that the audience could listen to the show on a radio placed by the screen (Wertheim 1979: 48). Less controversially, but only slightly less successfully, social ventriloquism was at the centre of *Lum and Abner* in which, from 1931, creators Chester Lauck and Norris Goff played two rural 'hillbilly' characters whose misunderstandings and social scrapes in the fictional backwoods town of Pine Ridge formed the basis of the comedy.

Recognition of the supremacy of the spoken word was an important element in the popularity of Will Rogers, the 'cowboy humorist' who began broadcasting on American radio in 1922. In front of a studio audience, Rogers spun out wisecracking monologues about all aspects of contemporary American life, including sport, politics and Mother's Day. His carefully timed delivery was a matrix of common-sense aphorisms, metaphors, similies, proverbs and puns. Siding with the rural 'ordinary folk' against the big-city politicians and businessmen, Rogers spoke with a south-western drawl and adopted a homely colloquial speaking style full of 'hot dog's and 'kinder', 'sorter', 'woulda' and 'coulda's that placed him firmly within the tradition of rural and frontier humorists. His satirical wisecracks at institutional America, as when he joked that 'with Congress, every time they make a joke, it's a law ... And every time they make a law, it's a joke', meant that he appealed to 'the old agrarian values of neighborliness and self-reliance' at a time when many Americans felt that such values were threatened (Wertheim 1979: 73). During the Depression years of the early 1930s, Rogers appealed to ordinary listeners frustrated and bewildered by events, as when he joked that 'we are the first nation in the history of the world to go to the poorhouse in an automobile'.

Following up: radio comedy

☞ How does radio exploit the fact it is not a visual medium in the ways that film and television are? Using examples from radio comedy programmes consider in what sense and in what ways radio could be said to require 'an active use of the imagination'.

☞ Radio in America and Britain developed in radically different ways. What were the main differences and in what ways can these still be said to influence radio today, particularly with regard to comedy broadcasting?

☞ What do you consider to be the main 'building blocks' of radio as a medium, and how were these used in early radio shows for comedic purposes?

☞ What enabled some music hall and vaudeville stars to make a successful career in radio when others failed?

American new radio comedy of the 1930s

Early radio comedy in Britain and America had relied on performers from vaudeville and music hall, not all of whom came to terms entirely with the demands of the new medium. By the early 1930s, however, a number of comedians emerged who realised the enormous power of radio to create distinctly different comedy. In America this 'new radio comedy' was based much more on character and situation rather than cross-talk jokes and puns that had become increasingly seen as 'corny'. One of the central figures in the development of this new radio comedy in America was Jack Benny.

Though Benny had begun in vaudeville in 1912 honing musical comedy sketches around the comic use of his considerable talent on the violin, he was increasingly attracted to comedy. By the 1920s the violin was being used only as a prop for his comedy monologues, a format that was to carry over into his radio shows. Though rejecting the rather crude 'ethnic humour' common in vaudeville, especially amongst Jewish performers, Benny told jokes that centred on stinginess. He was not above telling 'cheap Scotsmen' jokes that were fashionable during the 1920s, such as the one that asked 'what is the difference between a Scotsman and a coconut?', the answer being that 'you can get a drink out of a coconut'. When his first radio show *The Canada Dry Ginger Ale Show*, was cancelled by the sponsors in 1933, Benny moved away from his over-reliant use of corny vaudeville gags and began to develop comedy that centred on deprecating the radio persona he was constructing. In the series sponsored by General Motors from 1934, the character that Benny developed on radio was a self-opinionated, egotistic, vain braggart whose over-inflated sense of his worth and his talents, especially on the violin, became the butt of the jokes made at his expense by other members of the show's permanent cast.

In both the 1934 *Chevrolet* programme and the later *Jell-O Program* sponsored by General Foods from late 1934, Benny encouraged the team of writers he employed to develop these jokes at the expense of his radio persona, especially his increasing reputation for penny-pinching. Benny's attempts to borrow money from the cast became a regular running gag, as did his inexpensive gifts to the 'gang' on successive Christmas editions of the show. The degree to which Benny had mastered radio comedy was exemplified in a sketch in the late 1940s where he was held up at gun-point and asked to choose between his wallet or his life; a pregnant, silent pause was slowly filled with the sound of audience laughter, as they realised that Benny was, as he finally interrupted the silence to say, 'thinking it over'. Benny's *Jell-O Program* was not without its controversy, especially around Eddie 'Rochester' Anderson who first appeared on the show in March 1937, the first regular black performer on radio. However, the family of regular characters and Benny's central radio personality as a vain, egotistical and tight-fisted boss proved a hugely successful comic formula that persisted into the 1950s and was enormously influential on subsequent radio comedy. As Wertheim states, 'largely due to Benny's success, character comedy replaced vaudeville buffoonery as the dominant comedic form on the airwaves by 1937' (1979: 156).

The success enjoyed by Jack Benny was replicated in other, equally popular, American radio comedy shows in the 1930s. Fred Allen began his radio career in 1932 in a show that eventually became *Town Hall Tonight*, running from 1935 until 1940. Like Benny, Allen relished working in radio and created a brand of acerbic comedy based on his mastery of 'linguistic slapstick' which addressed the listeners in their homes rather than playing to the studio audience. Like Benny, Allen traded comic dialogue with a regular supporting cast in a series of sketches based around a fictional town hall, the hub of a varied and disparate community. Allen developed a reputation as a literate and highly intelligent comedian, and some of his skits at the expense of politicians and other pillars of the community sometimes led to conflict with the programme sponsors, as when he cracked the joke that 'if all the politicians in the world were laid end to end they would still be lying'. The ability of his regular supporting cast to play up to eight different characters in a sketch, the lavish use of sound effects to enhance the comedy, together with hard satirical edge that Allen brought to his jokes, consistently attracted some of American radio's biggest audiences. Again, like Jack Benny, Allen introduced an element of self-reflexive intertextuality within his programme, often commenting on the nature of radio and its power and influence, culminating in the running on-air comic mock feud between Benny and himself, the two trading exaggerated insults about each other's programmes and personas, such as when Allen joked that Benny was so tight that 'you not only got the first dollar you ever earned, you've got the guy's right arm that handed it to you'. Benny lambasted Allen's appearance, joking that 'with those bags under his eyes his face looks like an old pair of pants with the pockets inside out'.

The success of both Benny and Allen lay in their understanding and use of radio's distinctive qualities. Their dexterity with words and their ability to construct comic personas and situations that became embedded in listeners' imaginations was matched by other hugely popular American radio shows of the 1930s and 1940s. After separate careers in vaudeville, the husband and wife team George Burns and Gracie Allen first broadcast on radio in London in 1931, and appeared on their own American radio show in 1932. Sharing the bill with Guy Lombardo and the Royal Canadians, the thirty-minute show combined music and comedy, the centre of which was the scatterbrain personality of Gracie and her insistent misunderstanding of basic vocabulary, such as confusing wizard, blizzard and lizard in extended repartee with the long-suffering Burns. In this comedy of marital sparring, Gracie was often allowed to get the upper hand, as when George, commenting that she 'ought to live in the home for the feeble minded', is told by her that she would 'love to be your house guest sometime'. By the late 1930s their show was increasingly reliant on the format of domestic situation comedy, a format that was also the key to the success of other husband and wife comedy programmes, including *Easy Aces* with Jane and Goodman Ace, and *Fibber McGee and Molly* starring Jim and Marion Jordan, both of them remaining popular into the 1940s. The setting for *Easy Aces* was the home of a married, prosperous white couple, the comedy stemming from the scatterbrain scrapes that stay-at-home Jane was constantly getting into, mixed with a steady flow of comic but barbed malapropisms such as 'we're all cremated equal'. *Fibber McGee and Molly*, dating from 1935, was also a situation comedy. Based on a different situation each week, the central characters were the bragging, bungling, accident-prone husband Fibber and his long-suffering wife Molly, supported by a regular cast of memorable and idiosyncratic comedy characters living in the fictional town of Wistful Vista. Though much of the comedy stemmed from the deflation of tall tales told by Fibber, catchphrases and running gags were also important, to the point where the anticipation of the joke became as important as the joke itself. The show made excellent use of sound effects, not least with Fibber's closet, full of jumble and gadgets that spilled out every time the door was opened. The show lasted until the early 1950s and became 'an institution that upheld national morale' during the Depression of the 1930s and during the Second World War (Wertheim 1979: 239).

British radio comedy of the 1930s and 1940s

The emphasis on education, information and 'cultural uplift' meant that radio comedy on the BBC developed more slowly than it did in America. Though some music hall comedians and concert party artists did appear on radio in the 1920s, it was not until the mid-1930s, when faced with growing competition from Radio Luxembourg and other populist foreign radio stations broadcasting in English, that the BBC gave regular airtime to comedy. The influence of American radio comedy was evident as early as the 1930 Billy Bennett show *Dark Subjects* which featured 'Alexander and Mose' in a spoof 'black-face' cross-talk act. Following *Myrtle and Bertie* which featured Claude Hulbert in 1935, the Western Brothers' *Cad's College* in 1938, and the longer-running situation comedy series *Mr Muddlecombe* starring Robb Wilton which began in 1937 and continued in slightly altered form throughout the war years and into the early 1950s, the most significant radio comedy was *Band Waggon* featuring Arthur Askey and Richard Murdoch. Though it ran only for three series in 1938–39, its impact on listeners 'altered the nature of radio comedy irrevocably' (Foster and Furst 1996: 17). Alongside regular talent and guest spots, dance music and songs, Askey and Murdoch swapped jokes in their fictitious flat above Broadcasting House. Apart from the highly effective use of sound effects, the comedy was rendered memorable by the regular use of numerous catchphrases such as 'I thang yew', 'hello playmates' and 'doesn't it make you want to spit', many of them taken up in everyday use. Indebted as it was to some of the American pioneers, *Band Waggon* clearly indicated that the British audience appreciated radio comedy and ensured its place in the broadcasting schedules. Though BBC shows starring well known British artists such as George Formby (*A Lancashire Lad in London* 1938), Charles Penrose, the 'Laughing Policeman' (*The Pig and Whistle* 1938–44), and Billy Bennett (*Almost An Academy* 1939) attempted to keep audiences away from a growing number of radio comedy shows on Radio Luxembourg and Radio Normandie, it was the long-running series *Danger! – Men at Work* and especially *It's That Man Again* (quickly known as *ITMA*) that ushered in what became the golden age of British radio comedy in the 1940s, 1950s and 1960s.

Danger! – Men at Work (1939–47) represented a break from the soporific comedy that still characterised much British music-hall-inspired radio comedy. Essentially a situation comedy, the show was set around the attempts of the formidable landlady and comic foil Anaesthesia Ponsonby to keep the Hotel Mimoar running with the help of the 'men at work' sent by an employment agency. Though such jokes as 'I've never been so insulted in my life' – 'You should get out more' now appear clichéd, they were delivered at a furious pace in ways that broke the mould: as Foster and Furst comment, 'surreal, innovative and inspired, the show was ground-breaking in its use of sound effects and insult comedy' (Foster and Furst 1996: 25). Like most comedy shows, the comedy was interlaced with musical interludes, in this case from Billy Ternent and the BBC Dance Orchestra, though on one occasion even these failed to prevent a live transmission from ending ten minutes early, such was the pace of the programme.

Perhaps the most successful British radio comedy show ever, *It's That Man Again* (*ITMA*) ran for twelve series between 1939 and 1949, attracted a listening audience in excess of twenty million and, in 1942, became the first radio show to be chosen for a Royal Command Performance. Scripted by Ted Kavanagh and centred on established comedian Tommy Handley, 'a born radio comedian who by a lucky chance was in at the birth of radio' (Kavanagh 1949: 70), *ITMA* underwent some significant changes throughout its series, but what characterised much of its comedy and accounted for its popularity was its consistent, often irreverent, topicality. Held together by Handley's quick-fire delivery, the jokes came thick and fast, one every eleven seconds on one count. Usually playing a pompous but incompetent minor official, Handley was constantly interrupted by a series of zany, faintly exotic characters, each with their own catchphrase, such as Mrs Mopp and her 'Can I do you now sir?' and morose Mona Lott with her 'It's being so cheerful as keeps me going!' Unafraid to lampoon and spoof hallowed British traditions, *ITMA* even made fun of British government wartime restrictions as the Minister of Aggravation and the Office of Twerps even confiscate their own offices. Using radio's 'invisibility' to the full, the show was peopled by a succession of vocally improbable characters, including Funf the German spy, voiced by Jack Train, the character actor described as 'twenty-five voices under one hat'.

As much as Jack Benny and Fred Allen on American radio, *ITMA* succeeded by playing to the unique strengths of the medium. Scriptwriter Kavanagh clearly understood the special demands of radio comedy:

> My own idea of radio-writing was an obvious one – it was to use sound for all it was worth, the sound of different voices and accents, the use of catchphrases, the impact of funny sounds in words, of grotesque effects to give atmosphere – every device to create the illusion of rather crazy or inverted reality. (Kavanagh 1949: 107)

Anticipating an important trend of more recent decades, attempts were made to translate *ITMA* into visual form, first as a film and then as a television programme, but both lacked the impact of the radio version. As the producer Francis Worsley insisted:

> sound radio, being different from every other entertainment medium, compels the listener to form his or her own mental images of the characters he [*sic*] hears ... It is one of the most appealing qualities of radio that we build up a world peopled with creations of our own. (Worsley 1949: 69)

The sudden, unexpected death of Handley brought the series to an end in 1949. Though the topicality of much of its comedy is lost to contemporary ears and its ethnic and gender stereotyping is now embarrassing, *ITMA* remains an outstanding example of radio comedy at its best and served to usher in the golden age of British radio comedy.

Following up: early British and American radio comedies

☞ Though the full radio shows are available on CD, extracts from early British and American radio shows are available on YouTube. By listening to extracts from the British *ITMA* show and *The Jack Benny Jell-O Program*, analyse the key differences between the two programmes. Though these differences reveal the ways in which British and American radio developed, they do share certain things in common. Analyse the ways in which the shows make use of radio's formal elements to produce comic effects. To what extent are the jokes and gags in the programmes dependent on the personas of the leading comics, Handley and Benny? Do the topical references and the ethnic and gender stereotyping render the comedy ineffective to our contemporary taste, or is some of the comedy still funny?

The golden age of British radio comedy 1940s to 1960s

While American radio comedy was increasingly influenced and perhaps diminished by Hollywood and the rapid development of television from the late 1940s, British radio comedy thrived throughout the 1950s and 1960s. Though the BBC public service remit remained paramount, the end of Reith's tenure as Director General in 1938, the chastening experiences of wartime broadcasting and the growing influence of American popular culture ensured that variety and light entertainment, including comedy, were well represented in BBC radio programming. *Band Waggon* and *ITMA* had showed that scriptwriters and performers had mastered the specific demands of the medium, and that radio comedy was capable of appealing to huge audiences by resonating with the contemporary cultural climate. Radio comedy attracted established artists as well as a new generation of comedians that emerged during and after the war years. New and existing talent was paraded before listeners in programmes such as *Variety Bandbox*, which ran from 1944 to 1953. Old-fashioned in format, the show gave first exposure to comedians such as Dick Emery, Tony Hancock, Bob Monkhouse, Frankie Howerd and Benny Hill.

Though a number of other BBC radio comedy shows featured existing talent such as Will Hay, Elsie and Doris Waters, Arthur Lucan, and Jimmy Jewel and Ben Warriss, it was *Take It From Here*, running from 1948 until 1960 and scripted by Frank Muir and Dennis Norden, that 'began to change the route of radio comedy' (Parker 1977: 120). Featuring 'Professor' Jimmy Edwards and Australians Dick Bentley and Joy Nichols, the programme included satirical sketches and parodies of films that involved a rich vein of absurdity. Already successful, the show reached new heights in popularity with the introduction in 1950 of 'The Glums', a comic portrayal of a dysfunctional family headed by a boozy, belligerent and overbearing Mr Glum (Edwards), his timid, ineffectual wife who never actually spoke but was limited to 'noises off', their dim-witted son Ron (Bentley) and his fiancée Eth (June Whitfield) enduring an apparently interminable engagement to a man devoid of initiative, emotion, almost of masculinity itself. Framed by a device in which Mr Glum recounted the latest hapless episode in family life to the landlord of his local public house, this extraordinary situation comedy segment clearly struck a chord with the listening public, not least the frustrating sense that domestic aspirations and 'normal' sexual relationships between the two young people were to be delayed indefinitely by the overbearing material and cultural restrictions which were central aspects of life for many people in postwar Britain.

Though less of a formal departure from existing radio comedies, *Ray's a Laugh* (1949–61) featuring Ted Ray owed much of its success not just to his professional skill as a radio performer but to the fact that the comedy was again rooted in recognisable everyday life, such as working in a factory. The show benefited from the huge array of different comic character voices provided by newcomers Peter Sellers and Kenneth Connor. A more unlikely success was *Educating Archie* (1950–59). Though Edgar Bergen had set a precedent with Charlie McCarthy in America, a radio comedy based on ventriloquist Peter Brough's attempts to 'educate' his dummy Archie Andrews was an unusual winner of the 1950 *Daily Mail*'s Variety Award. The logical redundancy of ventriloquism on the radio was thwarted by Peter Brough's consistent vocal characterisation that clearly differentiated his own, often ill-tempered, exasperation from the impudent charm exuded by Archie. Brilliantly scripted by Eric Sykes, the show's success was in part dependent on the numerous supporting cast members, including Tony Hancock, Max Bygraves, Hattie Jacques, Beryl Reid, Harry Secombe and a teenage Julie Andrews, as well as what Sykes calls the 'spectacular sound effects' achieved during the programmes (Sykes 2005: 238). Popular with young and old listeners alike, Archie's impudent and often subversive disregard for those in authority offered an intriguing foretaste of 'youth rebellion' that became a distinctive element of 1950s cultural life.

The relatively slow development of television in Britain meant that radio remained the primary source of domestic entertainment throughout the 1950s. Radio comedy proved extraordinarily popular with the listening public throughout the decade and developed the careers of many comedians, some of whom enjoyed successful television careers in the 1960s and beyond. Al Read, Jimmy Clitheroe, Frankie Howerd, Eric Barker, Ken Dodd, and Morecambe and Wise were amongst the many to feature in radio comedy in the 1950s and beyond. However, the two most significant developments in radio comedy centred on an outstanding comic performer, Tony Hancock, and on some young comedians who collectively became known as The Goons.

Written by Spike Milligan, Larry Stephens and Eric Sykes and featuring Milligan, Peter Sellers, Harry Secombe and, in the first series, Michael Bentine, *The Goon Show* (1951–60), described by one contemporary reviewer as 'pure radio' (Briggs 1979: 719), was perhaps the most original and innovative radio show ever. Along with later British radio shows such as *I'm Sorry I'll Read That Again* (1964–68) and *Round the Horne* (1965–68), *The Goon Show* is a fine example of what Crisell terms 'radiogenic comedy' (1986: 163). Originally titled *The Crazy People*, the show was a sustained, absurdist, erratic and surreal exploration of the unfettered limits of the radio medium itself, of the ways in which words and sounds can be used simultaneously both to represent and to subvert representation, of radio's ability to circumvent time, space and other physical laws. Following some early episodes which were essentially sketch-based comedy, the show developed a format centred on single-episode narratives in which regular characters such as Neddie Seagoon, Major Bloodnok, Eccles and Count Jim Moriarty were voiced by Sellers, Milligan and Secombe, though these characters often played other 'characters' within each new story. As Roger Wilmut points out, the show operated at three levels, the actors themselves, their basic stock characters and the roles they adopted in individual episodes, many of which, such as 'Drums Along the Mersey' and 'Ill Met by Goonlight' parodied other entertainment forms and texts (Wilmut 1976). The recurrent, comforting presence of these characters enabled listeners to cope with the surreal excesses on which much of the comedy was based, so that even intrinsically unfunny catchphrases such as 'he's fallen in the water' raised howls of laughter from the studio audience when worked into narrative events.

Reliant on radio's armoury of words, silence and sound effects, *The Goon Show* consistently exploited the instability of constructed aural representations, freed from visual anchorage, for comic effect, as in the episode from series 8, 'The Evils of Bushey Spon':

> *Idiot:* I've got the pencil.
> *Seagoon:* That's a steamroller.
> *Idiot:* Is it? I'll kill that blasted store keeper!

Importantly, the show went beyond an acceptance of the supposed 'limitations' of the medium, often making the formal elements of radio part of the self-reflexive joke, as when in the episode 'Napoleon's Piano' broadcast on 11 October 1955 the characters step aside from narrative events to comment on the process of producing sound effects:

> *Seagoon:* I was at the address and with the aid of a piece of iron and a lump of wood, I made this sound:
> *FX:* [Knocks five times on door]
> *Moriarty:* When I heard the sound I ran downstairs, and with the aid of a doorknob and two hinges I made this sound:
> *FX:* [Door handle turns, door creaks open]

Though some of the comedy was more laboured, it still playfully emphasised the polysemic nature of words as signs, as this exchange from 'The Spanish Suitcase' (series 5 1954–55) suggests:

> *Seagoon:* Do you think they suspect him?
> *Moriarty:* That's difficult to say.
> *Seagoon:* Do – you – think – they – suspect – him. Hmm, it is a bit difficult to say.

As with so much radio comedy, vocal performance was central to the effect and success of *The Goon Show*, as Milligan and Sellers in particular proved consistently adept at voicing a range of characters, some of whom such as Eccles and Bluebottle, along with their catchphrases, entered daily life in Britain.

Following up: *The Goon Show*

☞ The significance and enduring popularity of *The Goon Show* is evident from its continuing availability, whether on CD, on YouTube, or (in Britain at least) on Radio Four Extra which carries regular repeats. Why do you think that some commentators have referred to *The Goon Show* as 'pure radio'? How important was the development of regular characters and in what ways did they contribute to the comic effectiveness of the programmes? Through a close examination of a sequence from any *Goon Show* episode, explore what you understand by the notion that language on radio, 'freed from visual anchorage', is used to produce comedy. In what other ways does *The Goon Show* manipulate the medium of radio for comic effect?

Though *The Goon Show* illustrated the comic potential of radio's distinctive appeal to the imagination and its consequent liberation from the constraints of naturalism which can impede visual comedy, and despite the apparent timelessness of its surreal humour and the continuing high regard in which it is held, elements of the show remained rooted in its historical context. It would be possible, for example, to analyse the extent to which its comedy and content reflect, albeit in an indirect manner, Britain's declining role as an imperial power. Certainly, as one comic punch line – 'two wongs don't make a white' – from the episode 'Shangri-La Again' (1955) suggests, the humour was not always immune from racist overtones. Though some attempts were made to present the Goons in visual form, such as BBC Television's 1963–64 animated puppet series *The Telegoons*, their radiogenic comedy remained resistant to such visual transformations. This was not the case with the other most successful BBC radio comedy of the 1950s, *Hancock's Half Hour* (1954–59).

Scripted by Ray Galton and Alan Simpson, *Hancock's Half Hour* took character-driven situation comedy on radio to a new level. At the centre of each

4 In Tony Hancock's most successful period his radio sitcom, *Hancock's Half Hour,* ran alongside an even more popular television version.

episode was Hancock, a gullible, irrascible egotist with unrealisable aspirations based on his snobbish middle-class disdain for most aspects of contemporary British social and cultural life, arguably 'the greatest comic creation of the post-war years' (Foster and Furst 1996: 187). The distinctiveness of the programme was, as the producer Dennis Main Wilson argued, in its desire to present a 'satire on real life today' (Webber 2004: 69). In contrast to the hectic disdain for time, place and reality essential to Goon comedy, Hancock became increasingly rooted in the uncomfortable and restrictive suburban domesticity of 23 Railway Cuttings, East Cheam. Goaded, cajoled and sometimes supported by other regular characters played by Bill Kerr, Sid James, Kenneth Williams and Hattie Jacques, Hancock is often duped into going along with some illicit or downright unlawful venture. He is often a victim of his class snobbery and his cultural aspirations are usually demolished, as when the scarce tickets for the Bolshoi Ballet that Sid James offers turn out to be tickets to watch a football match, at that time essentially a working-class activity. In contrast to much American comedy, the humour in *Hancock's Half Hour* was based on 'poverty, failure and unsuccessful people' according to scriptwriter Simpson (Webber 2004: 102).

Although the radio series continued until 1959, *Hancock's Half Hour* moved in 1956 to television where its popularity matched and exceeded the success of the radio show (see Chapter 5). Inevitably, the shift to television led to a greater emphasis on visual aspects of Hancock's performance, to more realistic scripts and to a reduction in the number of speaking characters since, as Simpson realised, 'you didn't need as much happening as on the radio' (Webber 2004: 75). Though something was gained, the ability of radio to appeal to the imagination and the resultant freedom to make eclectic use of time, place and characterisation was lost. However, as American comedians had discovered a few years earlier, the growing power of television meant that, by the late 1950s and early 1960s, 'it wasn't an option to stick to radio, otherwise – and quite unfairly – performers were classified as second-rate comics' (Webber 2004:78).

Radio comedy, television and the internet

Television seriously damaged radio comedy, as many comedians migrated to the new medium. In America the displacement of radio listening by television viewing happened earlier and was far more extensive. By 1950 American radio comedy was reliant on comedy series that had been on air for ten years and more. Established comedians drifted to more lucrative contracts in television, as did advertising revenues and sponsorship, and radio comedy suffered as a result. Stan Freberg briefly offered parodies of popular songs and musicians in the mid-1950s. Bob Elliott and Ray Goulding, first on local and then on network radio, offered satire on American institutions and customs from the 1950s until the 1970s, but they were exceptions to a trend that saw radio increasingly dominated by talk and music. This in part reflected changing cultural tastes as well as the emerging power of television to take audiences away from radio.

In Britain television's impact on radio comedy was less radical and immediate, and a number of BBC programmes such as *Beyond Our Ken* (1958–64) and *The Clitheroe Kid* (1958–72) continued to attract large audiences. Even the safe situation comedy *The Navy Lark* remained on the air for eighteen years between 1959 and 1977, and introduced listeners to Ronnie Barker who was later to enjoy considerable television success. Like *The Men from the Ministry* (1962–77), *The Navy Lark*'s self-deprecating comedy at the expense of institutionalised bureaucracy and its failings clearly struck a chord with listeners. Despite the increasing ability of television to entice established British comedy talent, BBC radio proved capable of innovative comedy in programmes such as *I'm Sorry, I'll Read That Again* (1964–68) and *Round the Horne* (1965–68), two programmes that had a strong sense of 'controlled anarchy' about them (Foster and Furst 1996: 237). Drawing upon a new generation of Oxbridge graduate comedians, *ISIRTA* lampooned elements of contemporary British culture, including the BBC through its fictitious 'Radio Prune', as well as reflecting changing attitudes to sex and gender.

Round the Horne, created by Barry Took and Marty Feldman, was broadcast for a total of sixty-six episodes between 1965 and 1968. Although a child of its time, *Round the Horne* remains classic radio comedy. With a string of characters performed by the ensemble cast of Kenneth Horne, Betty Marsden, Hugh Paddick, Kenneth Williams, and Bill Pertwee (series 1–3), the show was strong on parody, exploited surreal humour, was laced with catchphrases and replete with double entendres and sexual innuendo. Music was provided by the Fraser Hayes Four, who were often ushered in with improbable introductions. The programme opened either with answers to questions that had supposedly been posed the week before (they hadn't) or with some inconsequential surreal announcement about forthcoming events, such as 'coat a sheep in raspberry jam week'. Like *The Goon Show*, *Round the Horne* was self-reflexive, alluding to the processes of making a radio programme through the use of sound effects, or by announcer Douglas Smith bemoaning the lot of a poorly paid BBC radio announcer. In another episode, told that 'disaster is staring us in the face', Horne replies 'Yes I know. I've read the rest of this lousy sketch.'

Before the decriminalisation of homosexuality in England and Wales in 1967, the programme caused considerable controversy with its camp characters Julian and Sandy whose encoded conversations left few in doubt as to their sexual orientation. As two solicitors whose advice is sought by Kenneth Horne who has 'erred', Sandy (Kenneth Williams) replies that 'Well, we've all erred ducky. I mean it's common knowledge, en it Jule?' Jule (Hugh Paddick) tells Horne that 'We've got a criminal practice that takes up most of our time' (Took 1998: 12). Objections were made to J. Peasmold Gruntfuttock, here announcing his abdication as self-appointed King of Peasmoldia in anti-monarchist mockery:

> Yes I have abdicated off the throne. You see the voices did speak to me and they did say 'Gruntfuttock, my child, my lamb, arise now, lay down your orb and sceptre and abdicate off out of it – and while you're out get the Racing Pink and see what won the three-thirty. (Took 1998: 19)

The BBC hierarchy, aware of complaints, warned the programme to 'watch its step' and 'keep itself within reasonable bounds', but the programme merely attacked 'that much-abused but nevertheless essential department, the BBC censors, whose job it is to force out hidden dirt'. This is the way they did it:

> *Horne* (as BBC censor): Gentlemen, simmer down. There's too much filth going out on the air –it's our job to stop it. Only this morning I heard a reference to a lady's ankle.
> *All:* Depravity! Lewdness! It's Sodom and Gomorrah all over again.
> *Pertwee:* Yesterday Mrs Dale said she had a ladder in her stocking. Where is it leading to?

Objecting to 'suggestive' programme titles, they pick on a then current and very innocent radio favourite, *Have a Go with Wilfred Pickles*, because it has a suggestion of vinegar and:

> *Marsden:* ... as everyone knows, vinegar is alcoholic – and we know what alcohol leads to.
> *Williams* (getting worked up): Screaming and carrying on and tearing their clothes off. (Pause and then calmly) At least that's what always happens in my case.

The answer is to get to change the programme title to something healthy, like 'Have a Go with a Grated Carrot'. Enough said.

Following up: *Round the Horne*

☞ After listening to one or more episodes of *Round the Horne*, analyse the extent to which you think radio comedy can have a serious role in engaging with moral and ethical issues. How is this achieved in *Round the Horne* without the programme losing its comic effects?

☞ Taking examples from this and other radio comedy programmes that you have listened to, explain what you understand by the terms 'radio-genic comedy' and 'linguistic slapstick'?

The 1970s were relatively lean years for British radio comedy but, by the late 1980s, an increasing number of sitcoms, sketch shows and comedy panel games that started life on radio transferred to the small screen, by this time liberated from the restrictions that had characterised live television in the 1950s and early 1960s. Simon Brett's amiable middle-class sitcom *After Henry*, which was first broadcast on radio in 1985 and transferred to television in 1988, heralded a new and highly productive relationship between BBC radio and television. Inevitably, adaptations were needed, but radio formats were successfully remodelled for television as with sketch-based parodies such as *On the Hour* (successfully transferred to television as *The Day Today*) and *Knowing Me Knowing You* with Steve Coogan. Radio's *The News Quiz* was adapted to become the long-running television panel quiz as *Have I Got News for You*. The convergence between the two media has, in recent years, produced some major comedy triumphs for the BBC; *The League of Gentlemen*, *Little Britain*, *Goodness Gracious Me* and *Dead Ringers* all began life as radio comedy shows. Though radio comedy can sometimes be seen as the testing ground for 'something better', the success of this strategy has ensured that the BBC continues to support innovative radio comedy, primarily on nationally broadcast Radio 4 but also on digital radio channels such as Radio 4 Extra. Though radio comedy is often now written with an eye on a transfer to television, some current BBC comedy shows such as *Down the Line*, a spoof radio phone-in, essentially draw on radio's unique qualities, including the ability of comedians Paul Whitehouse and Charlie Higson to vocalise a huge range of different characters. In the same way, Marcus Brigstocke's bumbling, naive private-educated comic creation was able to stumble through locations including China, Bolivia and the Artic in *Giles Wemmbley Hogg Goes Off* (2002–6), courtesy of radio's ability to construct soundscapes cheaply and effectively. Though radio comedy in Britain no longer broadcasts to huge audiences, it remains a vibrant and inventive presence in the British media landscape.

If the BBC's continuing commitment to maintaining and developing radio comedy on mainstream radio stations is evident in current programming, the commercialisation and increasing fragmentation of American broadcasting, together with changes brought about by the internet, has produced different results. Though personality-driven shows such as that hosted by Howard Stern have redefined conceptions of what is considered funny, radio comedy remains alive and well on National Public Radio (NPR) as well as local and internet radio channels. NPR operates as a not-for-profit programme distributor for comedy shows such as *Car Talk* with Tom and Ray Magliozzi and *Wait, Wait ... Don't Tell Me!* a comedy news quiz show and, from Minnesota Public Radio, Garrison Keillor's cult show *A Prairie Home Companion*. Stand-up and classic comedy can be heard on satellite radio stations such as Sirius, which has three dedicated comedy channels, as well as on myriad local radio stations.

The boom in internet provision and the relative ease with which audio material can be streamed has lead to significant developments in radio listening, including radio comedy. New sites are available on-air via digital radio and television as well as on-line, though at the moment licensing laws restrict this on-line access to the UK. However, it is clear that internet streaming of audio material is proving a powerful addition to conventional radio listening, something that a growing resurgence in radio comedy will both benefit from and contribute to.

Following up: radio comedy, television and the internet

☞ A significant number of radio comedies have migrated to television. Taking one or more examples of comedy programmes that began on radio and then transferred to television, analyse the key differences between the radio version and the television version.

☞ How successful has the internet been in providing access to classic radio comedy and promoting new radio comedy?

Recommended reading

Andy Foster and Steve Furst, *Radio Comedy 1938–1968: A Guide to 30 Years of Wonderful Wireless*, London: Virgin, 1996.

Christopher H. Sterling and Cary O'Dell, *The Concise Encyclopedia of American Radio*, London: Routledge, 2009.

Arthur Frank Wertheim, *Radio Comedy*, New York: Oxford University Press, 1979.

5

Television comedy

Comedy, in a variety of guises, has been a staple of television broadcasting from its industrial beginnings and is thus far too broad a topic to treat fully in one chapter. Our focus here will primarily be on the situation comedy, the most clear-cut and, for exactly this reason, the most studied sub-genre of television comedy.

Radio, the first broadcast medium (see previous chapter), has been and still is hugely influential on the development of television, especially in terms of supplying talent and formats. Television, however, is an aural and visual medium, like film, but film and television comedy are far from being identical. Though film comedies are regularly broadcast on television, the comedies that television makes for itself are very much more tailored to the characteristic strengths and weaknesses of the medium. While we cannot discuss all television comedy forms in detail, it is worth emphasising how ubiquitous comedy is in television and worth considering what it is about the medium that makes it deliver comedy – or attempt to – so often. Its characteristics, including image size and quality, domestic setting for consumption and the possibility of live broadcast, are discussed below.

The television picture is usually smaller and less detailed than a cinema image and, because of this, television images have traditionally favoured medium and close up shots, emphasising facial expressions. Television comedy in particular loves the comic reaction shot. While technological advances, such as ever-larger flat screen televisions with increased definition, diminish the distance between television and film, the increased use of smaller screens in new media (phones etc.) for downloads only supports television production conventions against those of the cinema.

Unlike cinema, television is generally viewed in a domestic setting, and Mills suggests: 'The domesticity of television remains one of its principal features' (2009: 19). The result is that a very specific relationship is created; the television is one of the family, almost, as we see its performers close up. However, this domesticity means that television is a medium that can't guarantee the attention of its audience (see Ellis 1982: 128 and Marc 1997:

132). In order to combat domestic distractions, television programming has developed a strategy of segmentation, each new segment making the effort to engage anew the audience whose attention may have wandered (see Nelson 1997). In comedic texts this strategy is supported by stings (short excerpts of music which both link and separate sequences) and the use of laugh tracks which try and cue the home audience to accept that what is on screen is funny by accompanying it with the sound of other people laughing. *You've Been Framed* (1990–), a home video compilation show, for several years framed the clip sequences with an in-studio presenter and a studio audience assembled to watch them and justify the laughter on the soundtrack. The elaborate 'live audience' set-up ensures that domestic audiences 'are primed to laugh' (Mills 2009: 92). Once properly primed, an audience will laugh at just about anything.

Creating a microcosmic in-show audience through the use of the laugh track speaks of the theatrical origins of most forms of television comedy. Television as a broadcast medium is presented to us as occurring 'now', 'here', 'tonight', in other words with what Ellis calls a 'rhetoric of liveness' (2000: 33). For genuine live broadcasts and news this is a guarantee of authenticity, yet the laugh track in comedy programmes – it is standard sitcom practice – signals the quotation marks around the 'live' nature of the experience (Mills 2005: 50). The laugh track is both a cue to individual viewers and a way of placing those viewers in a larger regional or national audience. Mills notes the way in which comedy can 'bind groups together at the moment of consumption' (2005: 142).

The fact that broadcasters do not ultimately know their audience or their sensibilities makes television a relatively conservative medium. This varies in only a few instances. These occur where the broadcasters (who are held responsible for what they broadcast) have control of what time of day the material will be seen (Britain's nine o'clock 'watershed' after which children are expected not to be viewing), where the broadcaster has a remit to produce challenging material (for example, Channel Four) or where the audience *is* a known quantity (as in US subscription cable channels such as HBO).

Following up: television comedy

☞ From outright comedies to many 'And finally' items on news reports, television is wedded to the use of humour. Why?

☞ What does television comedy share with radio comedy?

☞ How is television comedy different from film comedy?

☞ What techniques does television comedy use to engage its audience?

The general conservatism of the television medium has been damaging to its critical credibility, and television's availability and appeal to the mainstream have further contributed to its low critical status: familiarity breeds contempt. Television is therefore seen as 'a low cultural form' (Mills 2005: 153) and 'critical discourse ... equates "popular" with "poor quality"' (Mills 2009: 64). Paul Attallah suggests that 'television and everything connected to it is seen as unworthy' (2003: 93). This critical hostility can be seen at many levels, from Theodor Adorno's critique of the mass media as essentially a sedative of its consumers' intelligence, 'a means of fettering consciousness' (1999: 37), to the band Rage Against the Machine's description of television as 'the in-house drive-by' in 'Bullet in the Head' (1992). Comedy, a major element of television seen as both popular and consolatory, is particularly questionable.

A recurrent element in the critical devaluation of broadcast media is that they are generally received regularly rather than as a one-off artistic experiences. There are plenty of exceptions, but broadcast media have a schedule to fill each week and seek to generate an ongoing relationship with their audiences. In comedy shows this means that regular viewers get to know the recurrent characters' foibles. The task of programme makers is to reward these long-term fans while not alienating casual viewers (in other words, giving them multiple chances to become fans). Thus a repeatable format is important to the industry, but such formats provoke particular criticism. For example, David Grote argues: 'No television comedy series begins each episode with "in our last episode ..." because it does not matter what happened in the last one' (1983: 63). While this is often true, repetition is not, however, proof that television is corrupter of the masses or invariably seeks the lowest common denominator. Television products need evaluating and understanding within the industrial context of their medium.

The television industry: British and American models of the sitcom

The separate historical contexts of the development of television in Britain and the United States have given rise to substantially different outlooks that have impacted on the ways in which comedy programmes are produced. In Britain the British Broadcasting Corporation continued its radio monopoly into television as a quasi-state organ providing a public service for the price of a licence fee. In America independent business concerns were relied on to provide commercial television to consumers by delivering the attention of those consumers to advertisers and sponsors. When the British system was seen to be too limited (by 1955) a licensed commercial channel (ITV) with regional franchises was allowed, but even then (partly in fear of possible 'Americanising' effects) commercial television in Britain was tightly constrained by the public service ethos, with sponsorship not allowed (until 1988) and advert breaks to be clearly labelled and restricted to six minutes in an hour in 1954 (Crisell

1997:91) and up to twelve minutes per hour currently. Additional channels were gradually added to terrestrial television, BBC2 in 1964, Channel Four in 1982, Channel 5 in 1997, with satellite competition from Sky since 1989.

In the United States the commercial broadcast networks established through radio (ABC, CBS and NBC) dominated until the 1980s. Fox, competing from 1986, made its programming distinctive through the animated comedy *The Simpsons* (see Chapter 7) and other shows and achieved mainstream status by outbidding its rivals for rights to the NFL (American Football) in 1994. Cable television has also become significant with subscription channel HBO, developing slowly since 1974, now leading the way and making an impact with its distinctive programming independent of interruptions by advertisements and network regulations.

American programmes are generally made to run in seasons, and each season is usually from twenty-four to twenty-six episodes in length whereas British comedy series have traditionally been commissioned in batches of six. If an American sitcom does not succeed – with success measured in terms of audience ratings – its production will cease, but if it does succeed it will usually be re-commissioned annually for as long as its popularity lasts. This means that the reliability of date designations for the production of a show varies considerably across the Atlantic. A designation of (1998–2002) for an American show refers to back-to-back seasons throughout that period. By contrast, even highly popular British comedies may be made irregularly when the writers have scripts and the performers can be reassembled. *Open All Hours*, for example, after a 1973 pilot, was made in four series in 1976, 1981, 1982 and 1985. Rather than render the full complexities of British productions in their entirety, we rely on interested readers to consult Lewisohn (2003b and subsequent editions).

British television comedy products are often writer-led, with pairs of writers or single authors being responsible for the entirety of a show's run (Mills 2005: 55). The British approach validates the writer or writers who can then sustain long careers working in television comedy, especially the sitcom. There are significant individual writers including Johnny Speight, Roy Clarke, John Sullivan, David Renwick and Victoria Wood, but the situation comedy seems to favour the pair of writers who can spark ideas off one another. Examples of this would be Ray Galton and Alan Simpson, Jimmy Croft and David Perry, Dick Clement and Ian La Frenais, John Cleese and Connie Booth, Richard Curtis and Ben Elton, Laurence Marks and Maurice Gran, Graham Linehan and Arthur Mathews, Ricky Gervais and Stephen Merchant. The emphasis on authored scripts means that British sitcoms tend to be quite distinct from one another and, even with two writers, British sitcoms usually have a limited run, often no more than two series (twelve episodes), half a single American season. Certainly, British sitcom authors are under less pressure to repeat or extend a premise *ad nauseam*.

By contrast, the American system of team-writing comedy tends to make American sitcoms more homogeneous, partly though producing a greater density of jokes. This system diminishes the status (though not the pay) of the writers and means that the average American sitcom is more slick and polished than the British equivalent, though no amount of professionalism can guarantee a ratings success. During a season's production American writers are required to react to what is working best for audiences while British writers, if re-commissioned, get more time to evaluate what worked and what didn't work in their previous series. On the other hand, the length and number of American shows (two to five seasons are required to get into profitable syndication) may mean that series are less stable over time, especially where there are changes of acting personnel (see, for example, Doty 2003: 204–8 on *Designing Women* (1986–93)). In the face of such changes Jane Feuer asserts that 'US sitcoms usually reveal their ideological frames much more clearly in the first season than in ensuing ones, and in studying the family sitcom, we often make generalisations based on the first season of the show's run' (2001: 70). This is clearly pragmatic, but also somewhat dangerous as, especially in the common production circumstances of a British series, it may take more than one series for the sitcom to hit its stride and find its most effective sources of comedy.

Despite the differences between the national industries, since the mid-1950s there has been traffic in programmes across the Atlantic. American comedy programmes, mainly sitcoms, have been accepted in the UK, though they have never looked like dislodging the indigenous forms as they have done in many other markets. The sitcom is largely 'a curiously Anglo-American form' (Mills 2005: 60). While British drama has occasionally made an impact on American screens (for example *The Forsyte Saga* in 1967 and *Upstairs Downstairs* in 1973), British comedy has almost invariably been remade for American audiences. Only in the 1990s with increased access to varied channels (and indeed BBC America) have American audiences had sustained access to British comedies resulting in a wave of interest in 'the Britcom' (sixty shows in the 1990s according to Berman 1999: xv).

It is difficult to attribute a single reason to the (albeit limited) American take-up of Britcoms. Part of the appeal may simply be the variety of pacing: 'Americans like jokes. In fact, we don't really have sit-coms – we have joke coms', suggests Gregory Koseluk, whereas British sitcoms by contrast 'have no jokes at all and are, instead, twenty five minutes of exposition and building circumstances that lead to one final big laugh' (2000: 1; see also Mills 2009: 57). In some ways Koseluk's point is a product of a relatively thin diet of Britcoms available in America. It characterises certain 1970s sitcoms with a slapstick payoff, for example *Some Mothers Do 'Ave 'Em* (1973–78) and many episodes of *Last of the Summer Wine*. On the other hand, rather than appealing to US audiences as quaint and cosy, British sitcoms might also appear to be diverse and perverse. Another commentator on the Britcom (Berman 1999:

xv) contrasts the generic predictability of the US sitcom with British versions that 'defy neat categorization. The sitcom rules are often challenged, rewritten or thrown out. Boundaries are tested and pushed, and the sitcom form itself is sometimes stretched in innovative ways almost unknown to American audiences.' If judging how British sitcoms appear in America is difficult (see Mills 2009: 106–13), we must also remember that making judgements on the American sitcom in Britain takes them out of their original context and that the few shows that cross the Atlantic to Britain are only the healthiest swimmers. After this note of trans-Atlantic caution, it nonetheless becomes necessary to focus on the specifics of situation comedy.

Following up: different approaches to television comedy

☞ While films are almost always made with an international audience in mind, television comedy must succeed locally to be viable. Watch episodes of British and American sitcoms made at roughly the same time and assess the ways in which the humour they offer differs. Are the practical differences in format, writing and production process more or less significant than differences between British and American culture and outlook?

Sitcoms

The situation comedy is the predominant comedic form in television, being the favourite television genre in the USA and second favourite in the UK (see Mills 2005: 57, 54). Grote (1983: 131) makes the point that even the most successful films at box office would be cancelled for low audience figures if they were sitcoms appearing on television. Though Grote's point is less true today, owing to an overall diminishment and splitting of television audiences with greater access to choice in their viewing, it indicates the impressive reach of the sitcom form at its peak.

The sitcom developed out of the variety sketch adapted to the regular broadcasting of radio to become the most efficient form for delivering comedy within television: 'the sitcom is the result of the interplay between the comic impetus of all comedy and the specifics of television' (Mills 2009: 23). In other words, we must not forget the 'television-ness of sitcom' (13).

The television sitcom is a series form conventionally thirty minutes long on the BBC, twenty-four minutes long on ITV and in American primetime twenty-two minutes long. Usually sitcom production is studio-bound with British examples more likely to escape, partly or wholly, than American ones. In order to make the shows efficiently in a studio environment and allow the editors material to work with, three cameras are regularly used, the so-called three-headed monster, shooting the scene thrice simultaneously: one covering the whole, one focused on the speaker and one on whoever is reacting to them. This quickly became the standard form for shooting the sitcom, allowing the performers to play off an audience and, to some extent, keep the comedy flowing.

In terms of construction, sitcoms might be designed around a star, a double act or a team, or have a carefully constructed ensemble cast. In each case the nature of the performances is particular: 'For comic performance to offer pleasure it must demonstrate the abilities of the person performing far more obviously than non-comic forms do' (Mills 2005: 70). This is a key characteristic of the genre. Though the sitcom is narrative television, and thus a form of drama, the 'realism' of the sitcom is markedly different from the realism of other television genres: 'the sitcom's artificiality marks it out as different to the majority of the medium's fiction' (2005: 75). But the level of artificiality varies from sitcom to sitcom. Terry Lovell argues that '[t]he stronger the referencing of social reality, the less "subversive" sitcoms tend to be' (1982: 30). This has the ring of truth but it is a very difficult point to prove given the general artificiality of the genre's storytelling. It is possible for drama to reference social reality and be comic and subversive as in *The Boys from the Blackstuff* (1982) (see King 2002: 196), and it is also possible for a sitcom to subvert the conventions of its genre and approach social reality (*The Office*) (see Chapter 6). Noting the sitcom's artificiality as well as its realism shows us how the genre is poised between straight drama and anarchistic types of comedy that reject narrative coherence (e.g. the sketch show). Both at the level of performance and at the level of narrative, the sitcom can flirt with the artificiality of its constraints if only to embed them within a realistic, plausible, socially recognisable frame.

The use of stereotypes, key to both the variety sketch and the sitcom's easy consumability, is significant here. Feuer points out that on the one hand 'flat characters [such as stereotypes] are more politically progressive because they take us away from our identification with the characters' or, in other words, we can laugh at them. However, on the other hand, a rounder and more complex character allows us to laugh with them and, furthermore; 'character development is ... a quality prized by the upscale audience which tends to have a more literary standard of value' (1992: 154). This is another way of putting Lovell's point that realism in the presentation of social reality conveys conservatism.

The sitcom is often characterised by 'a repetitive form' (Bazalgette, Cook and Medhurst 1985: 4) and each episode may be reduced to a very basic plot of equilibrium, followed by disequilibrium and then a return to equilibrium in the fictional world. The remarkable stability of the form can be seen in Marc's summary of episodes of hit series from 1950s to the 1980s (1997: 190–1), and the 'ritual mechanism' (191) as he puts it: 'Episode = Familiar Status – Ritual error made – Ritual lesson learned – Familiar Status Quo' (190). Formularisation often makes individual sitcom episodes nearly indistinguishable from one another so that the situation is the same week in, week out, without narrative development: 'The principle fundamental situation of the situation comedy is that things do not change. No new society occurs at the end' (Grote 1983: 105).

This critical discussion reminds us of television's low critical status: 'running throughout analysis of the sitcom is the critique that it is hegemonic and conservative' (Mills 2009: 30. See also Cook 1982: 2). Paul Attallah is particularly sharp here in recognising that this conservatism is just the sitcom's version of generic plotting: 'Genres ... are specific ways in which equilibrium is conceived, disrupted and replaced.' The key thing to consider should be: 'what is the nature of the original equilibrium'? (2003: 104). Attallah goes on to explain that what is significant in sitcoms is not plot but discourse: 'The ideal situation ... is one that is both open and closed at the same time: open to outsiders or to other discursive hierarchies but closed to experience or to the modification of discursive hierarchies' (2003: 107). As narratives, most sitcoms deliver nothing subversive, but they may mark areas of social tension by including, albeit without narrative consequence, other discourses.

Academic analysis of sitcoms tends to separate elements for particular attention. Jane Feuer (1992) notes a split between aesthetic and ritual or ideological critiques. Attallah splits the ritual or ideological critique into industrial, historical and social science approaches (2003: 97). For critics wishing to talk about a particular nation, the sitcom appears to be a barometer of culture, and Mills suggests that some US surveys 'see the genre as serving little purpose other than reflecting attitudinal developments in American Society' (2005: 102). When expectations of social progressiveness are applied to comedy products (as in Hamamoto 1989, for example) it produces analyses that imply something has gone wrong, that commercial mass media ought not to be like this. Such critiques almost write themselves since it is clear that commercially produced comedies can never fulfil the radical potential that is attributed to comic undermining of cultural institutions (such as patriarchy, race and class). Nevertheless, in using cultural institutions as the sources of social comedy 'situation comedies mobilize a discourse on class' (Attallah 2003: 110). This is not to claim class as the defining 'essence' of the sitcom, or the only source of humour, but we do suggest class is fundamentally present in both British *and* American situation comedies. How class determines taste is addressed in Chapter 9.

Taking an aesthetic approach to the genre it becomes possible to focus in on the specific ways the sitcom delivers what Cook calls 'social comedy' (1982: 17) but this needs to be contextualised rather than become a quest to find some sort of generic essence, pre-defined by the examples already selected. Mills attempts to resolve the division between aesthetic approaches that focus on the comedy, such as his own, and those which privilege narrative content: 'The pleasures of sitcom oscillate between those of comic moments and those of narrative development, with both of these aspects partly reliant on one another for their effects' (2005: 139). In other words neither the comedy nor its narrative construction should form the only focus of critical engagement with the sitcom.

In order to discuss a range of the targets and sources of humour in this vast genre we will approach it in three stages; firstly by further identifying the sitcom's dominant tropes, secondly by general historical survey and thirdly by noting strands which may be significant locally, nationally and generically over longer time spans.

Following up: sitcom form

☞ To what extent is the predictable and repetitive form of the sitcom responsible for its success? In what ways have these features compromised its critical status?

☞ To what extent does looking critically at television comedy change our expectations of it? Are we looking for evidence of cultural attitudes or for the ways in which comedy can be delivered in terms of writing, timing and performance?

Basic situations: domestic and workplace

In 2003 the BBC ran an on-line poll for the best (UK-produced) sitcom and supported it in 2004 with ten programmes advocating each of the top ten shows for the overall title (see www.bbc.co.uk/sitcom/winner.shtml). In terms of capturing the British scene the poll has several limitations: it clearly favours BBC sitcoms (no ITV shows appear in the top 25), it allows only the votes of those with internet access, and the timing favours contemporary, or regularly repeated, sitcoms. The poll does, however, select for us one hundred examples of British sitcoms out of the hundreds more that have been quickly forgotten. These examples have been remembered for one reason or another. What can we say about the genre using these examples?

By rough categorisation, the dominant sub-genre is the domestic sitcom, which accounts for about half of the entries. By 'domestic' we mean set in a living space or home environment whether the persons inhabiting it are friends or family, or perhaps families and surrogate families (see Mills 2005: 44). Examples of the domestic sitcom might thus include *The Good Life*, *The Young Ones* and *Only Fools and Horses* (the poll's overall winner). American examples of this genre would include *I Love Lucy*, *Friends* and *Two and a Half Men*. Nuclear family sitcoms (i.e. mother, father and children) are simply a sub-genre of the domestic sitcom that accounts for no more than a third of the domestic sitcom subtotal. The family domestic sitcom is nevertheless perhaps the default setting for the form: 'the sitcom, the living room in the living room, the mirror of family life, the barometer of the normal thing' (Marc 1997: 105).

It is important to remember that the traditional sitcom is the background against which innovation in the genre occurs.

The Royle Family (1998–2000) written by Caroline Aherne and Craig Cash has perhaps taken this to its natural conclusion by focusing for the vast majority of its running time on the eponymous northern, working-class family in front of the television: 'Never had the form of a programme so closely resembled the circumstances of its consumption' (Walters 2005: 104). Recognition of the situation was strong for most middle- and working-class British viewers but few ever identified themselves in this mirror, only someone they knew. *The Royle Family* is, however, the highest rating example of its type at number nineteen in the 100. Other examples of British family sitcoms, including *'Til Death Us Do Part*, *Butterflies* (1978–83) and *My Family*, ranked lower. The numerous successful American examples of the nuclear family sitcom, such as *Father Knows Best*, *The Cosby Show* and *Family Ties*, point to a higher level of popularity among American viewers (especially in politically conservative periods). Attallah claims that 'the family is probably the dominant metaphor for all North American television' (2003: 107) but the industrial emphasis on repetition and maintaining a successful format may equally be the governing concern.

Next most significant, after the domestic sitcom, is the workplace sitcom, which accounts for about a third of the situations used in the sitcoms included in the poll. Workplace sitcoms include *Open All Hours*, *dinnerladies* and *The Office*. American workplace sitcoms exist, *Taxi* for example, but far more often the tendency is to mix areas of works and relaxation as in tavern-centred comedies like *Archie Bunker's Place* and *Cheers*. In fact many American sitcoms keep both options open as, for example, with *The Dick Van Dyke Show*, centred at the family home but spending time at the office (see Marc 1997: 83–4) or the newsroom-set *Mary Tyler Moore Show*, also including a home situation. We can also compare the way *Frasier* pitches the central character's domestic set-up and his workplace (not a straightforward psychiatric practice but a radio show which plays things out in front of the public). The difficulty of keeping these designations separate can be seen in many excellent sitcoms. *Fawlty Towers* is workplace-set but the hotel is also background to scenes of Basil and Sybil's disastrous domesticity. The same goes for the kitchen of Tom and Barbara Good in *The Good Life*, very much in contrast to the purely domestic interior of their neighbour Margot Leadbetter (in which they are often paused in the hallway to be 'decontaminated' from the signs of manual labour). In fact the shift of emphasis from work to home (to be self-sufficient without earning a wage) is the focus of the show.

There are ways of seeing workplace comedies as opened-out versions of the family comedy in which the same premium is attached to maintaining the group come what may (see Hilmes 2003: 216–17). John Hartley ties workplace comedy to 'sexual chemistry rather than occupational specificity' and ends up with a large group of hybrids with his other main category of sitcom: 'family' (2001: 66–7). Ultimately, it's worth maintaining the distinction between domestic-based and workplace-based sitcoms, given the importance of the workplace and workplace-based relationships in our lives, but, however distinct our categories, fitting texts into narrower generic definitions is an exercise in herding cats. We will discuss comedy's effects on genres in Chapter 6 and attempt to corral some viable smaller sub-genres of the sitcom after the following section.

A brief survey of the history of the situation comedy

As we have seen, the sitcom is an outcome of the variety sketch adapted to the regular broadcasting of radio. Marc (2005) shows that early American manifestations are not quite true sitcoms, mainly being based on ethnic dialect humour. Early television came closer to the sitcom we know with what Marc calls 'variety sitcoms' in which the characters are the entertainers themselves in domestic surroundings as in *The Burns and Allen Show* (1950–58) and *The Jack Benny Program* (1950–65). The link to the variety sketch show can also be seen when we learn that one of the most famous American sitcoms of the 1950s, *The Honeymooners* (1955–56), was originally part of Jackie Gleason's hour-long variety show subsequently extracted and syndicated. In all these early examples there is an element of blurred demarcation between the stars and their fictional counterparts as they are 'biographically linked' (Mellencamp 2003: 49). Virginia Wright Wexman argues that this feeds on the 'continuum that exists between actor and role in the realm of TV entertainment' and that because 'television promotes an aesthetic of realism ... TV characters strike us as being just like the actors who play them' (2003: 56). Gleason was able to show a range of characters in his variety show rather than be restricted to the argumentative bus driver, Ralph Kramden, as he was in *The Honeymooners*. It meant that this performance could go further and is one of the reasons that the show was able to push the boundaries of the time.

Father Knows Best (1954–59), losing the question mark it had while it was a radio show, has become an exemplar of the 1950s sitcom. It portrays a vision of WASP suburbia, as opposed to the suppressed vaudeville ethnicity of the variety sitcoms or the urban stresses of *The Honeymooners*. Focused on family life, *Father Knows Best* was praised for showing its viewers how to deal with problems (see Haralovich 2003: 73–4) and the ultimate logic of this role was an unbroadcast special using Cold War propaganda to promote US bonds (see Marc 1997: 53–4). Shown again in the cable era, *Father Knows Best* is among the period sitcoms that have been repeated in a number of different formats with added mockery or reverent nostalgia (see Collins 1992: 334). *The Simpsons* pays homage to it by using the same (relatively common) town name of Springfield. As Mick Bowes suggests: 'viewed nostalgically, the world seems safe, funny, or even innocent. But as always, we read the past through the assumptions of the present' (1990: 138). The film comedy *Pleasantville* (1998) shows us the nostalgia in our relationships to sitcoms of the past alongside what their representations repress.

The best-known American sitcom of the 1950s, *I Love Lucy* (1951–57), exploited the relationship of star to character most effectively with Lucille Ball playing opposite her husband Desi Arnaz (see Landay 2005: 90). When the focus of the television world was New York (drawing together Broadway and Madison Avenue, centres of stage acting and the advertising industry) the couple preferred to stay in California and recorded their shows on film rather than perform them live. Because they had to pay the costs of filming, the rights reverted to them after the show had been broadcast twice by the network and they were made wealthy by the show's ongoing repeatability. The reason for *I Love Lucy*'s appeal today is related to the ambivalence of comedy within the sitcom, what it opens up rather than what it shuts down and the 'timeless' slapstick performances of its female star. Mellencamp points out that though 'Lucy's plots for ambition and fame *narratively* failed ... *performatively* they succeeded' and that 'perhaps the supreme fiction of the program was that Lucy was not star material' (2003: 49). Unlike *Father Knows Best*, whose staid, homely messages of family unity may be ridiculed as easily as regarded with nostalgia, Lucille Ball as performer (and producer) has acquired feminist retro-cool in the way she resists 1950s male authority (see Marc 1997: 46). Britain's fourth channel showed this sitcom regularly in the early 1980s.

5 The Phil Silvers Show: Motor Pool Sgt Ernie Bilko (centre) tries to get rich in the army.

Landay suggests that *I Love Lucy*'s initial success was because it 'suggested the failure of the domestic ideal – based on the rigid gender roles portrayed in popular culture – to match up with people's real experiences of everyday life' (2005: 91) and that its 'continued appeal ... in reruns is not only due to comic brilliance, but also to how it offers contemporary audiences a fitting precursor to the women's movement of the 1960s and 1970s' (2005: 96).

A key American sitcom for British audiences is *The Phil Silvers Show* (aka *Sergeant Bilko*) (1955–59) which, though somewhat forgotten in the USA despite its three consecutive Emmy awards, was regularly repeated on UK television from its first broadcast in 1957 to the end of the century. It seems to have been an acceptable view of the GI, and perhaps of American society, for British audiences. Set on a peacetime American Army base (for Hamamoto (1989: 55) it naturalises a standing army) it featured Phil Silvers's best role as a scheming motor pool sergeant fleecing his shambolic platoon and fellow NCOs and manipulating his bumbling superior officer, Colonel Hall (Paul Ford), in the service of get-rich-quick schemes that never quite come off. Though an expert at surviving the scrapes he gets himself into, Bilko never makes the kind of wealth he aspires to. Written mainly by Nat Hiken (see Everitt 2000) and performed in New York even though by then much television production was moving to California, it has considerable zip, being driven by the pace of the dialogue and of Bilko's mind as anyone not doing his bidding fast enough is subjected to a burst of drill sergeant yelling. As episodes barrel along, cast and audience have to keep up and the show is enlivened by its rough edges, apparent ad-libs and a lot of specific (rather than canned) audience reaction on the laugh track.

Early British sitcoms had to compete with these slick American classics and did so by focusing on British obsessions and settings in ways that were at once slightly more real, in the sense of depicting the grim reality of mid-1950s Britain, and considerably more introspective. The work of Tony Hancock is particularly significant as he shifted from radio to television with *Hancock's Half Hour* (1956–60), written by Galton and Simpson and co-starring Sid James. It was not a regular sitcom, in that Hancock changed professions weekly and supporting cast recurred in different roles, and neither were the six shows of *Hancock* (1961), also written by Galton and Simpson, but without James, for which Hancock is best remembered. For example 'The Bedsitter' is a monologue and 'The Lift' takes place in a stuck elevator at the BBC. 'The Blood Donor' features several classic lines as Hancock begins to regret his volunteering: 'I don't mind giving a reasonable amount, but a pint! That's very nearly an armful!' This line alone reveals the pomposity and ignorance of the character at odds with his vision of himself as a sophisticated and manly do-gooder (see Goddard 1991).

Considering *Hancock* against *Father Knows Best* allows us to glimpse another difference in the modes of humour between UK and US examples of the genre: 'While American sitcom often invites the audience to laugh with characters, Britcom instead offers pleasure in laughing at them' (Mills 2005: 42). Alternatively, comparing *Bilko*, admittedly popular in the UK, and *Hancock* shows the nuances and complexities within Mills's US/UK opposition. Though Ernie Bilko and Anthony Hancock are clearly the articulate centres of the worlds depicted, they are strikingly different sources of humour. Bilko is a manipulator seizing every day and every dollar while Hancock is a victim better at bemoaning his fate than escaping it. In *Bilko* the central character makes things happen and is ultimately thwarted whereas Hancock is often beaten before he starts. The schemer role in *Hancock's Half Hour* belongs to Sidney James, while the central character shares similarities with the poorly equipped bumbler of *Bilko*, Captain Hall, all too susceptible to ideas of greater honour and all too fearful of a loss of status. Ultimately though, as we shall soon see, the distinction between laughing 'with' and 'at' is hard to maintain.

Cut loose by their star after *Hancock*, Galton and Simpson went on to write a second hugely successful sitcom: *Steptoe and Son* (1962–72). Beginning as a one-off episode of *Comedy Playhouse*, it became a successful series starring actors, not comedians, Harry H. Corbett and Wilfrid Brambell. Once again the central character (Corbett) was obsessed with class and raising his status, but his circumstances as a rag and bone man with an elderly dependent father (Brambell) were always to sabotage his efforts. The atmosphere of ever-thwarted aspiration turns their relationship quite poisonously hostile in some episodes, taking the sitcom into much darker territory than American shows would manage for some time.

Till Death Us Do Part (1966–75) written by Johnny Speight and starring Warren Mitchell as Alf Garnett offered another generationally riven family. Garnett accepted his working-class social position and took pride in it but constantly complained of the state of the country, the lack of respect he was held in by his family (Dandy Nichols and Una Stubbs) and his daughter's unemployed socialist partner (Anthony Booth). Xenophobic and racist, Garnett spouted his bigoted opinions loudly and ignorantly in a way that was meant to satirise them but did not necessarily do so for all members of the audience (see Chapter 10). In some ways, Wagg suggests, 'he is redeemed, like "Hancock", by pathos: he is invariably humiliated in arguments: he often becomes frustrated and close to tears and, as many viewers will have seen it, he did work for his living' (1998: 11). The programme's popularity was indicative that it could entertain both those who agreed with the satire and those who agreed with Garnett. Mills notes that this show turns on 'a long standing issue of comedy, of whether we laugh *with* or *at* something' but that in the absence of analysis of audience reactions 'it's problematic to always see the *with* and *at* dichotomy as mutually exclusive' (2005: 107). The ambivalence of this character's reception crystallises the particular problem of using stereotypes in the sitcom form and how they will be interpreted by audiences and critics. Garnett's use of stereotypes distances the viewer from those he stereotypes and draws us closer to the character's point of view. At best Speight's series offered a space for Britain to explore its attitudes towards the family, sexuality and race. Disguising a minefield as an arena of comic play at the time shows *Till Death Us Do Part* recognising the inadequacy of old discourses of British white male working-class masculinity even while it embodies them.

While British sitcoms were increasingly focused on class tensions, 1960s American sitcoms had a spell of using fantasy situations: such as *Bewitched* (1964–72), *I Dream of Jeannie* (1965–70), *The Munsters* (1964–66) and *The Addams Family* (1964–66). Marc dubs them 'magicoms' (1997: 107). In the latter two, families of monsters want to be left alone to continue their own versions of normality. In the former two, female characters with magical powers are taught *not* to value or use their powers. The husband in *Bewitched* is, Marc argues, an 'ideologically committed sexist' (1997: 112) who insists his wife Samantha (Elizabeth Montgomery) does the housework and business entertaining without her supernatural powers. His mother-in-law, Endora (Agnes Morehead), is mystified by her daughter's desire to conform to patriarchal normality (1997: 114). This situation is, of course, never resolved, as the husband's wishes for his domestic sphere are complied with, ostensibly reinforcing the idea of family patriarchy while actually illustrating the untenability of it (see Wells 1998: 193).

Flatter, more stereotyped characters were also present in the enormously successful *The Beverly Hillbillies* (1962–71), where the Clampett family are Ozark rednecks made spectacularly wealthy by oil, who become fish out of water in upscale California. In essence *The Beverly Hillbillies* is a class collision comedy but the realities of such a collision are negated by the Clampetts' money. An uneasy and unrealistic premise (again) but ripe for comedy that at once reinforces rural (family) values and satirises 1960s consumer culture. Attallah (2003) points out both the exceptionally low cultural prestige of this show and its exemplary focus on class difference and sexuality as Jed, the non-patriarch of his clan, heads a family of overdeveloped and sexually ignorant youngsters (Elly May and Jethro) while also saddled with an archaically outmoded oldster in the person of Granny. These particularly flat characters produce what Feuer calls 'an almost pure cultural conflict' (1992: 150) but, as we have seen, it is difficult for critics steeped in the values of literature to see it.

The huge success of sitcoms like *The Beverly Hillbillies* came at the expense of the previously dominant form of television comedy: the variety sketch show (see below). As its popularity faltered, one regular sketch show performer, Carl Reiner, wrote a witty family sitcom, based on his own (Jewish) background and intended to star himself. The pilot, titled *Head of the Family*, wasn't taken up but, recast with a WASP star and with the ethnic background removed, it became *The Dick Van Dyke Show* (1961–66) and was a big hit. The set-up combines the family and work lives of Rob Petrie (Van Dyke). It was an important development in the genre since, as Marc observes, though 'The homogeneous suburban family at home is familiar; the heterogenous extended family in the office is new' (1997: 95).

These shifts in focus were pursued in *The Mary Tyler Moore Show* (1970–77) starring the eponymous actress, who had played Rob Petrie's wife, as Mary Richards, a single working woman moving to Minneapolis to work in a television newsroom. The changes in focus on gender, away from family and towards the workplace, were both significant and progressive. The continued portrayal of the traditional family as a place of harmony could not successfully continue in the face of political, generational and gender conflicts in 1960s American culture. These were reflected in a sitcom adapted by producer Norman Lear from *Till Death Us Do Part* called *All in the Family* (1971–79) and which became *Archie Bunker's Place* (1979–83) when the domestic situation was exhausted. Drawing on the successful characteristics of *The Honeymooners* in focusing on a blue-collar blowhard, the show's ethnic insults and intergenerational disharmony were new and more extreme than US television was accustomed to. Like the British version, the show's huge success with audiences was ambivalent and controversial: 'our identification with the ... well-rounded Archie Bunker was likely to outweigh the positive liberal benefits of the show's intended satire of racist beliefs' (Feuer 1992: 150). As ever, audience ratings show only that the set is on, not that it's being watched and certainly not what audiences are taking from it. Lear also successfully adapted *Steptoe and Son* as *Sanford and Son* (1972–77) with a black cast headed by Redd Foxx (see Chapter 10).

Lear's shows, *The Mary Tyler Moore Show* and their spin-offs may be seen as 'relevant' sitcoms, markedly different from the magicoms of the 1960s in apparently dealing with real issues in American society. Attallah (2003: 108) makes a good case for dismissing this as a marketing strategy rather than a genuine change of focus but it has clearly helped some sitcoms to be taken more seriously in American culture. For those audiences less enamoured of even the appearance of relevance, there was *Happy Days* (1974–84), the other major success of 1970s American sitcoms with considerable international success. Set in the 1950s it managed the trick of keeping the traditional father character (Tom Bosley) but adding an alternative role-model biker hero, the Fonz (Henry Winkler), to the mix, comparing and contrasting conventional and 'rebellious' versions of masculinity in a safely non-contemporary setting. Incrementally, the counter-cultural representative is gradually absorbed into the family, becoming a valued member of society and, as Attallah (2003: 111–12) notes, his virility consequently decreases.

In Britain the decade 1970–80 tends to be seen as a classic period for sitcoms, leading in with *Dad's Army* (1968–77), and generating *Are You Being Served?* (1973–85), *Whatever Happened to the Likely Lads* (1973–74), *Fawlty Towers* (1975, 1979), *The Good Life* (1975–78), *Porridge* (1974–77), *Open All Hours*

(1976–85), and *Yes Minister* (1980–82). In the BBC's 2003 sitcom poll six of the above come in the top ten and all are top twenty-five. *Only Fools and Horses*, the poll's eventual winner, had its a shaky start just afterwards in 1981, before becoming a massive mainstream success and continuing, in various formats, until 2002, and *Last of the Summer Wine*, beginning in 1973, ran until 2010. In some senses these 1970s sitcoms were beneficiaries of increased demand for product in the 1980s caused by longer broadcasting hours, the rise of video and the appearance of cable and satellite channels (very few of which originated their own content).

Dad's Army, to take one example, is a much repeated period-set sitcom focused on a platoon of the Home Guard during the Second World War, a situation that allowed an array of social classes and types to be brought together in the village hall to perform tasks they were almost by definition incapable of performing well (not being available for active service by reason of age or ill-health). The mainspring of the comedy is the desire of Captain Mainwaring (Arthur Lowe), the bank manager, to use the platoon as a way to prove himself and increase (rather than diminish) his social standing. With a sterling ensemble cast (all named in the credits) audiences were keyed to a series of catchphrases. These ranged from the Sergeant Wilson (John Le Mesurier) crippled by his upper-class politeness ('I say, would you mind awfully ...') to the excitable butcher Corporal Jones (Clive Dunn) whose colonial experiences could be a liability ('Don't panic, don't panic!'). To try Mainwaring further there were the elderly Godfrey ('Please may I be excused?') and youthful Pike ('Mister Mainwaring, Mister Mainwaring!') helping to form a group not unlike schoolchildren thrust into an adult world. The loss of the spiv character, Pte Walker (James Beck), in 1973 robbed the situation of its shady trickster but the rest of the cast literally soldiered on, well established in their roles.

6 Dad's Army. From left to right: Private Godfrey, Corporal Jones, Captain Mainwearing, Private Pike, Private Fraser, Sergeant Wilson.

Are You Being Served and *It Ain't Half Hot Mum* (1974–81) followed the *Dad's Army* ensemble cast model though other fondly remembered sitcoms of the mid-1970s were more tightly cast. *The Good Life* has four major characters and very few supporting roles and perhaps the best sitcom of the era, *Porridge*, is set in a prison with four key characters: the seasoned protagonist Fletcher, his youthful cellmate Godber; the tough warden, Mr McKay, and the soft warden, Mr Barraclough. Although *Porridge* might not have dealt with the realities of prison life (Medhurst and Tuck 1982: 51) it is, however, one of the few 1970s sitcoms genuinely subversive of authority (Wagg 1998: 15) though with the subversive element safely jailed its subversion is clearly very cautiously framed.

In contrast the beginning of the 1980s was a time for a changing of the guard in British comedy as the awkwardly termed 'alternative comedy' came to dominate and place itself at the 'cutting edge' of the genre across stand-up, sitcom, one-off and sketch comedy. Taking its cue from Punk that reacted against the excesses of 1970s music, but with a much clearer political focus, alternative comedy sought to change the regular targets of jokes, to move the goalposts of comedy, away from casually supporting racism and sexism and xenophobia and towards a questioning of those values. Ultimately all three remained topics for comedy but in a way that acknowledged they were wrong. In principle this was similar to the way in which Alf Garnett was intended to be understood, but there would be less room for ambivalence about it. Sitcom was perhaps the least likely arena for alternative comedy to succeed but it did and the key text is *The Young Ones* (1982, 1984). Using digressive and surreal animated inserts, irrelevant musical performances, self-reflexivity and performative excess (see Bazalgette, Cook and Medhurst 1985: 63–4), *The Young Ones* destabilised the form in a way that would have a long-term effect (see discussion of Liddiment, below).

Perhaps the biggest influence of alternative comedy on British television comedy was through what it put an end to. Older generations of comedians were swept from the schedules or reduced to hosting game shows. Others clung on to the detriment of their reputation (see Chapter 9). Meanwhile, Alf Garnett returned, now his viewpoint was more clearly outmoded, with *In Sickness and in Health* (1985–92).

By contrast the American sitcom of the 1980s rode the currents established in the 1970s with long-running shows. The splendidly written *Cheers* (1982–93) is set in a Boston bar supporting a range of well-defined supporting characters to be relied upon for comic lines (but *not* catchphrases). The situation allows for diverse social positions to be brought together, the most antagonistic extremes being the barmaids, upper-class intellectual Diane and the working-class Italian-American Carla. The key element of the situation is exactly this juxtaposition as Brown suggests: 'While the characters represent many different levels of education, wealth, and social positions in their individual lives, they all have an equal place at the bar once they enter Cheers'

(Brown 2005: 257). Michelle Hilmes shows how cunningly this artificial family appeals to different audiences: '"high-culture" viewers had to be entertained, but not at the expense of "low-culture" fans' (2003: 218). She suggests that potential conflict is defused because 'class is defined almost entirely in terms of allegiance or "taste"' (219) but, more importantly, the humour is double-coded in that for every humorous intellectual reference there is a topping gag that does not depend on getting the reference and usually highlights its pretentiousness (see Hilmes 2003: 220–1).

The juggernaut of 1980s American sitcom was, however, *The Cosby Show* (1984–92), a truly massive ratings success, which came as 'saviour of the genre' (Wagg 1998: 197). A domestic sitcom set in the harmonious home of a successful doctor, Clifford Huxtable (Bill Cosby) and his lawyer wife (Felicia Rashad), the comedy is centred on raising the kids and, as Marc (1997: 191) notes, learning ritual lessons about life. The significance of the fact that the family is black has been much debated (see Chapter 10) but the success cannot be disputed. Race is such a divisive issue in American culture that it is perhaps unfair that *The Cosby Show* should be criticised for its lack of representation of racial interaction when so many other sitcoms lack any, let alone significant, black characters. Brown (2005: 259) notes that despite its inclusion of a range of social types *Cheers* is equally limited in terms of the representation of race.

Contrasting with *The Cosby Show*, domestic sitcoms *Married with Children* (1987–97), *Roseanne* (1988–97) and *Malcolm in the Middle* (2000–6) offered a different view of American family life as abrasive and dysfunctional with flaring hostilities between members. The antithesis of the Huxtables, the Connors in *Roseanne* were blue-collar strugglers living close to hand to mouth where there were all too many opportunities for things to go wrong. Without rejecting the importance of family, *Roseanne* engages with the reality that domestic chores are still skewed towards being female responsibilities and rejects conventional discourses of female domesticity (see Karlyn 2003). The unruly spirit of these series is continued in cartoon domestic sitcoms like *The Simpsons* and *Family Guy* (see Chapter 7).

The successful sitcoms of the 1990s were typically about unmarried characters in urban settings. *Cheers*' ability to make humorous capital out of pretension spawned the long-running spin-off *Frasier* (1993–2004) that combined family and workplace comedy and developed farce-like structures through titled segments. Frasier (Kelsey Grammar) and his brother Niles (David Hyde Pierce) are both upwardly mobile and very conscious of class status but, unlike similar characters of British sitcoms, have the degrees and income to support their pretensions.

The characters of *Seinfeld* (1990–98) and *Friends* (1994–2004) were similarly free of financial concerns and even more popular. The latter continued to be screened almost daily on some British channels until mid-2011. While *Seinfeld* is centred on its eponymous star who is clearly superior to his eccentric foils, George (Jason Alexander) and Kramer (Michael Richards), *Friends*' great strength is its brilliant ensemble, with six characters given nearly equal weight. Rather than featuring *Seinfeld*'s grotesques, each of the principle cast is remarkably attractive. Mills points out that Joey is treated slightly more broadly than the ensemble's other male cast members in that he is not at all self-aware (2005: 85) but this simply means he gets more (and perhaps funnier) comic lines. The same might be said for Phoebe in the female cast. The ensemble playing allowed the audience to feel they were part of the group, rather like being a patron of *Cheers*, only more select and intimate. *Friends* is clearly not a workplace comedy, but nor is it a guidebook to living in 1990s culture in more than a superficial sense, as Kutulas (2005: 225) points out.

In Britain, with many fewer sustained ratings successes to provide continuity, there are often predictions of the sitcom's demise. The industry insider David Liddiment authored a documentary *Who Killed the Sitcom?* (2006) in which he argued that the traditional sitcom was doomed by the impact of alternative comedy, the resulting consistent critical validation of innovation (see Mills 2009: 27), the quality of American imports, the dominance of (cheap) reality TV and the new multi-channel environment fragmenting audiences and preventing new sitcoms achieving critical mass at a time when the demand for instant ratings success is becoming even more shrill. Though Liddiment's points all carry weight there are, in fact, signs of development and change rather than death in the British sitcom. It is clear that the traditional sitcom can still succeed, as with Victoria Wood's *dinnerladies* (1998–2000), *My Family* (2000–) (written by a team, American style), *Black Books* (2000–2), *The IT Crowd* (2006–), *Miranda* (2009–) and *Rev* (2010–). Though it began with an exclusionary level of crudeness targeted at a youth rather than a mainstream audience, *Two Pints of Lager and a Packet of Crisps* (2001–9) probably also falls into this category. *The In-betweeners* (2008–) has recently combined bad taste and teen-appeal to great effect. Equally, however, the sitcom has shown it is a form capable of benefiting from a variety of innovations, the past decade seeing *Spaced* (1999–2001), *The Office* (2001–2), *Peter Kay's Phoenix Nights* (2001–2), *The Book Group* (2003–4), *Green Wing* (2004–6), *Nighty Night* (2004–5), *The Worst Week of My Life* (2004–6), *Extras* (2005–7), *Peep Show* (2005–), *Ideal* (2005–10), *Pulling* (2007–9) and *Gavin and Stacey* (2007–9).

Mills (2009: 127–34) separates these innovative programmes, or what he calls 'comedies of distinction' (134), into three strands. The first is that of the realist or naturalist style that has a documentary element such as *The Office* or *Marion and Geoff* (2000, 2003). This has been picked up on in America with *The Office: An American Workplace* (2003–). The second is the 'social realist' strand that observes its characters closely without documentary cues such as *The Royle Family*, *I'm Alan Partridge* (1997, 2002), *The Smoking Room* (2004–5), *Early Doors* (2003–4) and *Gavin and Stacey.* In the US *Curb Your Enthusiasm* (2000–) exemplifies this style. These two types are clearly related in that they both use

7 Green Wing: An ensemble cast including key female members: (left to right) Michelle Gomez, Tamsin Greig and Pippa Haywood.

increased naturalism, learning from, if not adopting, the techniques by which docusoaps appeal to audiences (see Linder 2005 and Walters 2005:62–7).

The third strand includes shows that tend to adopt distinctive visual styles and/or use the process of editing creatively such as *Spaced*, *Green Wing* and *Peep Show*. Here there are American examples too, like *Scrubs* (2001–10) and *My Name Is Earl* (2005–9), though both of these examples use voiceovers to keep their audiences attuned to what is going on. *Green Wing*, set in a hospital, used loose plotting, speeded-up and slowed-down footage in fifty-minute episodes to create a sitcom that sometimes feels like a themed sketch show. The comedy on offer ranged from verbal riffing, such as Stephen Mangan and Julian Rhind-Tutt's bickering over and with Tamsin Greig or Michelle Gomez abusing her power as staff-liaison in some improvised sequences, to surreal visual gags such as Gomez appearing on a camel and physical comedy exemplified by Mark Heap's ability to raise the clumsiness of his character to the heights of ineptitude. By concentrating on the performances of its ensemble cast *Green Wing* escaped the tightly plotted half-hour without skimping on character but, as a comparison of its longevity with that of *Scrubs* shows, it remains an experiment. Its 2011 descendant, *Campus*, has been less successful.

An example that proves more contentious through its exploration of where the boundaries of the sitcom lie might be *The Book Group*. Mills calls it a 'sitcom/drama hybrid' (2005: 53), rather than designating it a 'comedy of distinction' but it might fit into the third strand that he defines. Drama tropes, rather than documentary tropes, are used to provide an additional edge so that we cannot predict the register of narrative or performance. To spoil the opening episode: when the lonely American author Clare (Anne Dudek) literally bewails her inability to seduce another member of the group it is a bravura reveal of her incipient mental breakdown which is suddenly undercut when we learn that the unpretentious wheelchair-bound Kenny (Rory McCann) is still in the flat waiting for his brothers to pick him up. Veering from embarrassment for Clare to pity for her, to embarrassment for Kenny and recognition of Clare's emotional self-indulgence, the viewer may be buffeted into laughter. Described as 'A sitcom about people who don't really like books for people who don't really like sitcoms' (Thompson 2004: 210), *The Book Group* might equally be seen as being about desire, rather than books, and to be for audiences hoping for something other than conventional sitcoms centred on English male heterosexuals. Books and reading are a notoriously difficult topic for television but, though it gives its characters' set texts short shrift, *The Book Group* offers a number of insights into authors and authorship, for example, through Ben Miller's role as a self-conscious crime writer, or with the imaginary sequences from the minds of group members writing creatively. Each character is rounded and unpredictable rather than stereotyped and the serial (rather than series) narrative allows them to get together in straight and gay relationships and even to die. In other words its characters' lives can change in ways impossible in the conventional sitcom.

Following up: sitcom history

☞ To what extent are early sitcoms dated by today's standards? To what extent do repeatable sitcom classics outshine contemporary shows? How difficult – and how desirable – is mainstream success in this genre?

☞ Analysing two episodes of the same sitcom, consider both the narrtive and the jokes it gives rise to. What do the episodes have in common? How much difference is there between them?

☞ Explore the significance of class in the humour of any example of television comedy.

What sub-genres are identifiable? Which settings recur?

The BBC poll and our historical survey show considerably more complexity in sitcom sub-genres than the basic models of domestic, family and workplace sitcoms. These sub-genres reveal significant differences and commonalities in British and American cultures. In Britain there have been a number of historical situation comedies, some achieving high prominence in the poll: *Blackadder*, *Dad's Army*, *'Allo 'Allo!* (1984–92), *It Ain't Half Hot Mum*, *Hi-De-Hi*, *Goodnight Sweetheart* (straddling past and present) and *Up Pompeii*. There are fewer significant American examples using a period setting: *Happy Days* and its spin-off, *Laverne and Shirley* (1976–83), and *M*A*S*H* (1972–83), all of which are set in the 1950s, 1960s-set *The Wonder Years* (1988–93) and *That Seventies Show* (1998–2006).

Older person-centred comedies are significant in Britain with ageing the topic of *One Foot in the Grave*, *Last of the Summer Wine*, *Waiting for God* and (more recently) *The Old Guys* (2009–). The American exemplar in this sub-genre is clearly *The Golden Girls*. The US adaptation of *One Foot in the Grave* as *Cosby* (1996–2000) was ill-fated.

There are various examples of fantasy-based sitcoms in American television history (as we have seen) but there is also a particular science fiction strand about aliens coming to Earth: *My Favourite Martian* (1963–66), *Mork and Mindy* (1978–82), *3rd Rock from the Sun* (1996–2001). This situation isn't absent from the British sitcom though it is absent from the list: *My Hero* (2000–7) didn't make it despite being contemporaneous with the poll. The British sci-fi exception is *Red Dwarf* (1988–99) a strong and inventive series (eighteenth in the poll) that did well as an export but whose recipe, capable of withstanding changes to cast and crew, nevertheless seems impossible to recreate.

In Britain the poll shows a clear strand of comedies centred on clergy headed by *The Vicar of Dibley* (third) and *Father Ted* (eleventh) but also including *All Gas and Gaiters* (1967–71) (seventy-second), and now continued by *Rev*. This is a sub-genre with little, if any, counterpart in the US, illustrating a clear cultural difference in sensibilities about religion.

British sitcoms regularly use clear regional settings, especially in the north as opposed to the south. Sometimes this is a product of the regional structure of the BBC. *Rab C. Nesbitt* (1990–9, 2011), Scottish set and made, is a good example in that Rab's dialogue was notoriously difficult for non-Scots speakers to follow. However, within England 'the north' is a recurrent setting for sitcoms with slightly under twenty per cent of the total. The 80 per cent of southern-set material illustrates a southern bias in mainstream television, especially at the BBC, but, conversely, the defiant 20 per cent shows a relatively strong and successful resistance to it (see Russell 2004). While British viewers can identify metropolitan, generic urban and rural settings, in American sitcoms regional differences of East Coast, West coast or Midwest culture appear to matter much less, the specific settings of shows like *Taxi*, *Cheers*, *Frasier* and even *Hot in Cleveland* (2010–) are background.

In terms of gender balance, we can see situations that are skewed one way or the other. There are heavily male-centred situations including all the military sitcoms but even *Porridge*, set in a male prison, finds ways to include female characters. *Whatever Happened to the Likely Lads* and *Men Behaving Badly* particularly focus on masculinity (see Medhurst 2007: 117–23) but can do so only by including significant female characters. Female-centred shows include *The Rag Trade* (1961–63), *Absolutely Fabulous* (1992–2002) and *dinnerladies*. American female-focused shows include *The Mary Tyler Moore Show*,

Laverne and Shirley, *The Golden Girls* and, most spectacularly, *Sex and the City*, which has generated considerable critical literature (see Ross 2005; Akass and McCabe 2004).

As to types of comedy represented in the poll, the sitcom clearly has a realistic bent and social comedy dominates. Surrealist humour is thus extremely rare in sitcoms, especially in comparison with radio and television sketch shows. However, highly exaggerated, non-realistic performances and implausible plotting do exist. *The Young Ones*, *Father Ted* and *Bottom* all appear in the poll but the strand might be extended if long-running *The Goodies* (1970–81) (which began with the situation of a three-man agency prepared to do 'anything, anytime') was included, a few elements of *Blackadder* were considered more closely and the more recent *The Mighty Boosh* (2003–7) had been able to establish itself in time. This sort of humour is key to the success of animated series that are also sitcoms such as *South Park*, *The Simpsons* and *Family Guy* (see Chapter 7). Live action American examples are quite rare except for the magicoms and science fiction shows we have noted earlier, though *Soap* (1977–81) is a significant exception.

A recent example of a British non-realist sitcom is *Ideal*, set in the Salford flat of sometime drug dealer Mos (Johnny Vegas), which generates an environment so surreal that reversions to reality can become the punch lines, such as when Brian (Graham Duff), one of his regular visitors, bemoans Mos's clumsiness in sending his prize piece of iced organ-legging crashing down the stairs: 'You've doomed me to a life with only one penis!' To which Mos replies 'Welcome to my world'.

Following up: sitcom sub-genres

☞ Are any of these sub-genres of the sitcom sufficiently distinct to be valuable modifiers to the domestic and workplace sub-genres defined earlier?

☞ Are there other, more viable, ways to link sitcoms through writers, stars or production staff?

The comedy sketch show

As we have seen, recurrent variety show sketches gave birth to the sitcom on radio. Variety is also the ancestor of the television sketch show which packages, with or without a few remaining variety elements, comic sketches for its audience. Defined as such, the sketch show is a very loose form that may include parody, satire, impressions, slapstick, camp and catchphrase humour.

The sketch show is not a significant form in US television today: 'The variety show, once the staple of television comedy, which rivalled and sometimes outdrew the sitcom, is gone ... Some say this is the result of generational splits in musical tastes, which are certainly a factor' (Grote 1983: 159). The history of the American sketch show on television can be briefly traced from the top-rating Sid Caesar's *Your Show of Shows* (1950–54) and various clones until the early 1960s by which time videotaping made other forms of television comedy appear much slicker than these essentially live performances. There were revivals of the form in the late 1960s in *The Smothers Brothers Comedy Hour* (1967–69) and *Rowan and Martin's Laugh-In* (1968–73), which attempted to contain youth culture within the mainstream, but they were ultimately discarded by the networks as too much effort. Though there have been more recent sketch shows on cable (see Chapter 10), at present sketch comedy on the networks is reduced to a residual though significant presence in *Saturday Night Live* (1975–).

In Britain, with shorter runs commissioned, the sketch comedy show continues, though the larger and grander variety tradition of *Sunday Night at the London Palladium* has not survived, and equivalents to American-style shows, for example *Saturday Live* (1986–87), proved difficult to establish. The British sketch show instead varies considerably in format from mainstream to satirical to surreal, for example, Peter Cook and Dudley Moore's *Not Only ... But Also* (1965–70), Spike Milligan's *Q* series (six from 1969–82), *Monty Python's Flying Circus* (1970–74), *Morecambe and Wise* (1961–76), *The Two Ronnies* (1971–86), *Little and Large* (1978–91), *Three of a Kind* (1981–83), *A Bit of Fry and Laurie* (1989–95), *Not the Nine O'Clock News* (1979–82), *Who Dares Wins* (1983–88), *Alas Smith and Jones* (1984–88), *French and Saunders* (1987–96 and subsequent specials), *The Smell of Reeves and Mortimer* (1993–95), *Smack the Pony* (1999–2001), *Big Train* (1998, 2002) and *The League of Gentlemen* (1999–2002).

Some examples of sketch comedy revel in the absurdity of repetition. The use of the catchphrase, something we have already seen in various sitcoms, is exaggerated in the sketch show format. Mills points out that this type of comedy is 'inexplicable through conventional Humour Theory which requires surprise. Catchphrases work in exactly the opposite way; the pleasure rests not in what is going to be said – it's always the same – but what narrative developments will result in the character uttering it' (2005: 88). Examples of sketch shows employing the catchphrase heavily include *Dick Emery* (1963–80), *Harry Enfield's Television Programme* (1990–92), *The Fast Show* (1994–97), *Little Britain* (2003–8), *The Catherine Tate Show* (2004–7) and examples of their catchphrases would be 'Ooh, you are awful! But I like you'; 'Only Me!'; '... which was nice'; 'Yeah, but, no, but'; 'Am I bovvered?' These catchphrases are about creating and completing stereotypes, pushing those stereotypes to breaking point and still repeating the catchphrase in a way that confirms absurd unbreakability of the stereotype.

Parody of particular forms is important in many sketch shows. Examples include the ongoing serials in *The Two Ronnies*, Morecambe and Wise's musical and epic spoofs, Harry Enfield's Mr Cholmondely-Warner public information sequences and *Little Britain*'s co-option of the reality television show voiceover. Further examples are discussed in Chapter 6.

Earlier and more conventional shows held with a regular format in which the stars introduced their sketches, with these frames also becoming opportunities for comic business in which the performers appear 'as themselves'. *The Two Ronnies*, for example, bookended their shows with themselves seated behind desks as they welcomed the audience and went into a warm-up routine of news headline gags and from which they acknowledged applause as if it were a totally live show before ending with their catchphrase sign-off. Between *Alas Smith and Jones* (which puns on the US western series *Alias Smith and Jones*) and *The Smell of Reeves and Mortimer* (i.e. in the late 1980s) adoption of this convention becomes entirely parodic and the tendency just to present sketches predominated, with *The Fast Show* perhaps epitomising this urge to get on with it. Earlier programmes eager to sever the variety roots of the sketch show had already rejected opportunities to establish or reiterate any stable underlying tone or comedic persona. *Monty Python's Flying Circus* was particularly good at discarding conventional frames by using Terry Gilliam's animated 'links' or, as in the title of the movie version *And Now for Something Completely Different*, what might be called lack-of-continuity announcements. Sketch show structure, whether conventional, repetitive and ordered or not, offers its audiences a mixed bag of content. *That Mitchell and Webb Look* (2006–) throws in a behind-the-scenes sketch that, knowingly, has the performers discussing their 'deliberate' hit and miss approach to structure. The sketch show in general makes a feature of its contempt for the coherent narrative logic of the television drama while, simultaneously, being ideally segmented for twenty-first-century usage.

Following up: the sketch show

☞ Analyse an episode of a sketch show. How much does the humour depend on awareness of the period and culture in which it has been produced? Who, or what, are its targets? How much does the style of humour vary from sketch to sketch? To what extent is the success of the comedic elements down to particular performers? Are the sketches one-offs or are the characters returned to repeatedly through the series?

☞ How do different sketch shows structure their elements?

☞ In sketch shows using catchphrases, consider the variety of ways they generate humour. Why does changing the context for the phrase's delivery make it funny again?

The representation of politics in British television comedy

Rather than subdivide television comedy into separate forms throughout, it is worth looking at the broader context of television comedy and how the medium treats particular comedy targets. Our selected example is the politician. From Peter Cook's impersonation of Prime Minister Harold Macmillan in *Beyond the Fringe* (first performed 1960, broadcast on television 1964), through impression shows featuring Mike Yarwood to Rory Bremner to John Culshaw in which the performers present themselves as their targets, the ruling elite of the country has been satirised with ever less reverence on television. Such programmes tend to be topical and rely on knowledge of the public sphere. More recently a cheaper format for satire has proved to be the comedy quiz show and panel game as in *Have I Got News for You* (1990–) and *Mock the Week* (2007–).

Sitcom representations of politicians follow this trend, too. *Yes Minister* (and later *Yes, Prime Minister*) received the dubious accolade of being Prime Minister Margaret Thatcher's favourite comedy (see Oakley 1982: 69). The situation had politicians as to some extent the dupes of the civil servants who theoretically served them, developing into farcical battle of wits between Jim Hacker (Paul Eddington) and Sir Humphrey Appleby (Nigel Hawthorne). Wagg is insistent that the Whitehall mandarin always wins (1998: 30) and the status quo survives, while Oakley (1982: 67) makes clear the ironic nature of the title. Nonetheless, it is possible to see the programme as manifesting both a cynicism about politicians and a suspicion of the non-elected elements of government (Oakley 1992: 75) and also, in the absence of any engagement with the actual politics of the day, 'a nostalgia for [these] past certainties' (78). Subsequent treatment of politics in the 1980s would be more biting. *The New Statesman* (1987–92) featured Tory MP Alan B'stard (Rik Mayall), a corrupt scheming egotist. *The New Statesman*'s relative ferocity owed something to ITV's long-running satirical puppet show *Spitting Image* (1984–96) where three-dimensional puppet caricatures facilitated aggressive and biting sketches about politicians, celebrities and the royal family. This was an area in which the BBC, dependent of the state for the continuation of its licence fee funding, had a far weaker hand. The BBC's *That Was the Week that Was* aka *TW3* (1962–63), a live, late-night satirical show, had broken new ground and was successful enough to export the format (and host David Frost) to America but 'the BBC was persuaded to keep the show off the air in 1964, the year of a general election, and it never returned' (Lewisohn 2003: 757). Government influence on the BBC continues, and Oakley's words about the BBC in 1982, 'beset as it has been by financial and political pressures' (1992: 78), ring equally true today. The BBC's most recent comedic account of politics has been made for BBC3, a non-terrestrial channel that seeks critical and cult kudos rather than mainstream success. *The Thick of It* (2005–9) features ineffectual politicians as the all-too-fallible cringing dupes of splenetic spin doctors like

Malcolm Tucker (Peter Capaldi) enforcing the party line, and formed the basis for the team's film *In the Loop* (2009).

The changes in attitudes which television programmes document over time parallel the politicians' own shift in self-representation from aloof aristocrats to men, and women, of the people. Unfortunately for politicians, their growing obsession with the medium has converged with a burgeoning celebrity culture and the explosion in reality television. Going much further than Liddiment's idea that reality television was a cheaper option for producers than comedy, Ben Thompson suggests that, from the 1990s onwards, reality television would 'at times threaten to render comedy itself unnecessary' (2004: 433). Thompson fears reality television's exploitation of its victims, which ranges from the culling of wannabes and creation of new celebrities in shows like *The X-Factor* to pandering to the public wish to humiliate, destroy or resurrect faded or marginal celebrities in *I'm a Celebrity Get Me Out of Here*, will lead television comedy to become equally merciless. To some extent the duping of experts, authorities and politicians in the public sphere in programmes such as *Brass Eye* (see Chapter 6) and *Da Ali G Show* (see Chapter 10) contributes to a shift in attitudes towards public figures. In appearing on television, politicians become characters on television, characters in a reality-show-cum-soap-opera, with too many barely distinguishable male characters, that is told through the news and supported by some of the least entertaining programmes on television. Jonathan Gray (2009: 165) terms it 'the celebrification of politics'. Yet these television characters want to rule us, and convince us that they are holier-than-thou and interesting. Inept when appearing on shows that are there to mock them such as *Have I Got News for You* and often outshone in public speaking by the increasingly showbiz guests recently added to the format of the BBC's long-running political discussion programme *Question Time* (1979–), politicians are, in effect, now a dysfunctional mode of celebrity and the diminishing respect in which they are held is a measure of the levelling of the public sphere.

The series of sketches in *Little Britain* with the Prime Minister (Anthony Head) and his devoted assistant Sebastian Love (David Walliams) turn on the idea that power is an aphrodisiac and therefore highest office becomes a likely venue for innuendo and same-sex stalking. It is not far away from J.G. Ballard's 1968 literary spoof of political marketing, later taken seriously by some American practitioners, called 'Why I Want to Fuck Ronald Reagan' (1970). These sketches feature virtually nothing overtly political (Mowatt 2010: 28) but instead show us a politician who is slick and handsome and unscathed by his aide's inappropriate behaviour. Sebastian Love's lust for his leader is funny, perhaps, because politicians in reality have become such a turn-off.

Following up: sitcoms and sketch shows

☞ Do sitcoms and sketch shows broadly share attitudes towards topics or do they give distinct perspectives? Is one genre more conservative and the other more radical?

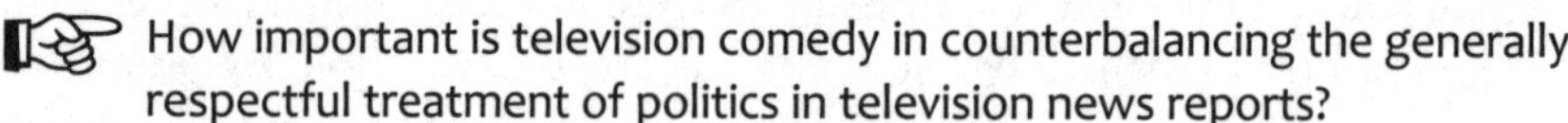

☞ How important is television comedy in counterbalancing the generally respectful treatment of politics in television news reports?

☞ Is it plausible to suggest that successful comedies produced within a particular culture reflect its political and social currents?

What has been left out

There are many examples of comedy on television that we have had no space to give detailed examination. Brett Mills identifies sitcom as a genre defined by its 'comic impetus' (2009: 5–6) and '*a form of programming which foregrounds its comic intent*' (2009: 49, Mills's italics), but it is plain to see that there are other television genres of which might equally be described in this way. Sketch shows, as we have seen, for one and vehicles for stand-up performance, such as *Live at the Apollo*, *Michael McIntyre's Comedy Roadshow* or *Def Comedy Jam*, as another prime example. We have also left out series of one-off comedies using the same performers in different situations such as Ronnie Barker's *Seven of One* (1973), Michael Palin and Terry Jones's *Ripping Yarns* (1976–79), alternative comedy outings under the title *The Comic Strip Presents* (from 1982), *Coogan's Run* (1995), *That Peter Kay Thing* (2000) and *Garth Marenghi's Darkplace* (2004). Other comedy series that are hard to categorise, like *Happy Families* (1985) or *Love Soup* (2005–8), have also been ignored. And there are many other genres on British television that could – in certain examples or specific segments – claim to belong to a discussion about television comedy, including clip shows (*You've Been Framed*), competitions (*Total Wipeout*), quiz shows (*QI*), panel games (*Blankety Blank*), variety shows (*Saturday Night Live*), chat shows (*Jonathan Ross*), reality TV shows (*The Osbournes*), talking heads documentaries (*Grumpy Old Men*), documentary or archive shows about comedians (*Comedy Heroes*) or particular series and comedy dramas (*Fat Friends*). In other words, an enormous amount of popular television will play for comedy and the profusion of such hybrid forms shows just how many ways television can present comedy to its audiences. We simply do not have space to pursue these varieties here, though many examples taken from television comedy inform our subsequent chapters.

Recommended reading

Mark Lewisohn, *Radio Times Guide to TV Comedy*, London: BBC, 2003, 2nd edition.

David Marc, *Comic Visions: Television Comedy and American Culture*, Oxford: Blackwell, 1997, 2nd edition.

Brett Mills, *Television Sitcom*, London: BFI, 2005.

6

Comedy and genre boundaries

It takes quite a lot to ruffle the feathers of the essentially middle-class, reasonably well-educated, concerned, but erring on the side of the staid and conventional, British audience for the BBC's Radio Four, but feathers were certainly flying in 2006 in response to *Down the Line*, a new 'factual phone-in' programme broadcast on Tuesday evenings at 11pm. One listener called it 'regurgitated drivel and crass cringe-worthy antagonistic rubbish', while another said that 'I was appalled by this programme. It was racist, sexist and completely abhorrent' (Moss 2006: 6). It was also, of course, a comedy spoof, written by and featuring Paul Whitehouse and Charlie Higson, a parody of the phone-in programmes that have become a regular format within radio broadcasting. The confusion that many listeners clearly experienced stemmed from the fact that their expectations of what was billed as a 'factual' programme were subverted by material that on first hearing appeared odd, even offensive, but made sense – and became very funny – once listeners realised that this was satirical comedy.

The confusion felt by some listeners to *Down the Line* suggests that the notion of categorisation remains important, even if some film, television and radio examples resist easy classification. The concept of genre has been one of the most useful ways of categorising and classifying a range of popular culture artefacts and has long provided the film industry – producers and exhibitors – with an effective way to promote its product to audiences. It was also found particularly useful in the emerging field of film studies in the 1960s where the attempt to distinguish different films through generic categorisation proved critically productive. On the basis of primarily what were regarded as the core elements of a film, particularly its iconography, typical themes and plot-lines and even typical stars, critics argued for a series of different and distinctive genres, numbering variously between eight and fifteen, by which films could be distinguished. Developing in the study of films from what is now termed classical Hollywood, these generic taxonomies appeared to deliver a coherent way of understanding cultural products.

The development of American independent cinema during the 1960s and 1970s, the growing interest in and awareness of world cinema which did things differently and issues with understanding television through generic constructs have all conspired to render generic criticism increasingly problematic. Early beliefs that films could be categorised through taxonomies of near-scientific rigour have evaporated in the light of developments in film style and content, though attempts to retain the undoubted value of generic categorisation as an 'explanatory cognitive instrument' (Stam 2000: 129) through an emphasis on the fluidity and dynamics of generic structures have proved useful. Rather than seeing genres as mechanistically rigid and static, critics in the 1980s argued for a more organic view, often seeing genres undergoing an almost evolutionary trajectory from 'primitive' to 'mature' to 'decadent'. In this version the 'mature' or 'classical' phase in a genre's evolution constitutes a recognisable set of accepted conventions, before the conventions lose their coherence and descend into either cliché or parody. A view of genre as essentially evolutionary has its limitations, not least because generic hybrids existed even during the so-called 'classical' phase, but, when we are trying to make sense of the eclecticism that characterises aspects of contemporary cinema, genre theory, if taken cautiously, would seem to offer some insight into ways in which generic categories become blurred and generic boundaries crossed.

More recently, the very concept of genre has, for some, become redundant in what they see as a trans- or post-generic cinema which draws upon and mixes meta-generic, modal concepts such as comedy, drama, spectacle or action. Celestine Deleyto, for example, argues that the process of designating a film as belonging to a genre can never be final or complete since: '[g]enres are not discrete units, or categories, but are part of a complex system ... which is constantly mutating through the films themselves and other discourses, both internal and external to the industry' (2009: 9). The ability of films to appeal to spectators through knowing, playful transgression of formerly constraining generic boundaries could be said to characterise much contemporary cinema, a 'logical' development which extends and goes beyond the concept of hybrid films. Such a view has merit when an attempt is made to place, for example, the *Harry Potter* cycle of films (2001–11). However, claims that we have reached a point where generic categorisation has lost all meaning are ultimately too rigid and too ahistorical. While 2010 saw the release of *Jonah Hex*, described as a supernatural western, and *Cowboys and Aliens*, a science-fiction western, one of the most successful films of the year was the Coen brothers' *True Grit*, a generically grounded remake of the 1969 John Wayne western of the same name.

As Andrew Dix usefully points out, understanding the development of any particular genre (and, arguably, changing critical conceptions of that genre) cannot be divorced from historical process and specificity. Both the war genre and the western genre as produced in Hollywood struggled to survive in the context of Vietnam and revisionist histories of the USA. As Dix puts it, 'Like the canary once taken down a mine, a genre is an unusually sensitive instrument for measuring changes in the atmosphere' (2008: 181). Even if talk of a cinema of 'ironic eclecticism' by some contemporary commentators carries resonance, it should not be detached from the historical specificity in which it occurs. Moreover, we can gain an ironic perspective only once we acknowledge the existence and continuing presence of the un-ironic. Put simply, a comedy spoof of a horror film becomes funny only through our awareness of the conventions of the horror genre as they have been exhibited over the years.

The problem for those who like neat theoretical constructions is that such structures often fly in the face of evidence that suggests that things are more messy. What the evidence tells us is that genre theory has been both useful and limited. In television and radio, while some programming such as soap opera and situation comedy can clearly be seen as having strong generic characteristics which make them distinctive, much television and radio programming is described in broader terms such as 'drama', 'light entertainment', 'talk' or 'comedy'. The situation is further complicated when we examine the long history of what we call generic hybrids, a history in which comedy has always been an important element. In this chapter we attempt to examine how genre and generic hybrids have been mobilised and appropriated for comic effect across the decades in radio, film and television.

Playing with audience expectations of genres and formats is not particularly new, but it has become increasingly common in our contemporary media-saturated world. In our Introduction we referred to comedy as a meta-genre, suggesting that it lacks the structures that define other genres. Although it is perhaps true that 'pure' comedy never existed, comedy has been particularly adept at exploiting the potential of crossing borders between and within genres, in creating hybrid forms which combine comedy with other dramatic or generic elements. This is not surprising given the complex relationship between comedy and drama, between laughter and tears. It was Byron who wrote 'if I laugh at any mortal thing / Tis that I may not weep'. As we saw in Chapter 1, silent comedians such as Buster Keaton and Charlie Chaplin dealt in pathos and sentimentality as part of their comedy. Autobiographies written by comedians also emphasise the connection between the joyful and the lachrymose, with titles such as *Crying with Laughter* (Bob Monkhouse) and *No Tears for a Clown* (Les Dawson). Comedy, with its subversive ability to express and explore our deepest fears and anxieties as well as life's ecstatic joys, often makes an effective bedfellow for dramatic material. By subverting generic expectations that audiences have of, for example, thriller, horror, science-fiction or musical films, comedians are able to toy with conventions, play with plot-lines and offer pleasantly visceral, disruptive experiences which we find funny. Often comedy works through parody, in essence the process of imitating, sometimes polemically, another cultural production or practice.

Following Bakhtin, theorists have argued that parodies are more likely to occur at that moment in the life cycle of a genre when its conventions have become so well-known that they lose their impact or become objects of derision. At this stage genres are ripe for spoof treatment. From the early 1970s onwards, when Woody Allen and Mel Brooks made a number of commercially successful parodies of film genres, parody has become a regularly employed mode in comedy feature films. Genres parodied include science fiction (*Flesh Gordon* 1974; *Mars Attacks!* 1996), horror (*Young Frankenstein* 1974; *Scary Movie* 2000; *Shaun of the Dead* 2004), action films (*Airplane!* 1980; *Hot Shots!* 1991; *Tropic Thunder* 2008), crime (*Murder by Death* 1973; *Loaded Weapon 1* 1993; *Hot Fuzz* 2007) and spy films (*Austin Powers: International Man of Mystery* 1997; *Johnny English* 2003). In this chapter we examine some examples including comedy westerns, the Bob Hope and Bing Crosby *Road* series, and the more recent tendency, both in film and on television, to engage with genres associated with 'realism' such as news, current affairs and documentary in order to produce comedy. In these examples it becomes clear that comedy not only playfully spoofs conventions but also calls time on exhausted plots, genres and formats.

Following up: genre

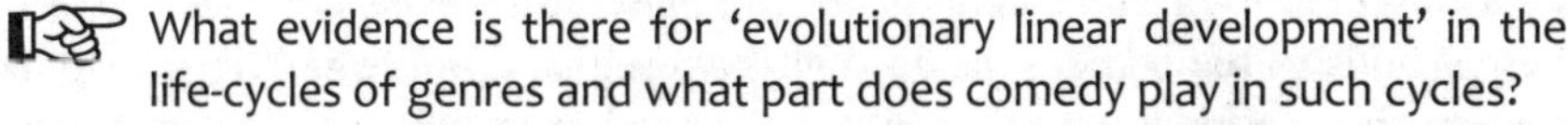

☞ What evidence is there for 'evolutionary linear development' in the life-cycles of genres and what part does comedy play in such cycles?

☞ Can you identify comedy films from sub-genres like the comedian comedy or the romantic comedy which could reasonably be categorised as generically 'primitive', as 'classical' and as 'decadent'?

☞ Evaluate the view that, in postmodern culture, the notion of genre can no longer be taken seriously.

☞ How do you explain the enjoyment that contemporary audiences appear to get from parodies and spoofs?

The comedy western

The western genre, in popular literature, film and television, has been considered one of twentieth-century America's greatest contributions to culture (Kitses 1969, Fenin and Everson 1978, Hardy 1983). Rooted in the historic fact of white colonisation of what we now regard as North America, the western was able to offer a hegemonic narrative of conquest wrapped in a discourse of progress and civilisation. A staple Hollywood genre for decades, at its peak in the 1930s, 1940s and 1950s, the western was eulogised for its epic and mythic version of a rich American history. Yet, even though the western genre was occasionally treated with reverence, it was never immune from treatment which exploited comic potential. Buster Keaton's *The Paleface* (1921) is an oblique social comment on Native American reservations. In *Go West* (1925), Keaton plays Friendless, who, unable to cope with the bustle of New York where he is literally trampled upon, heads west. Surrounded by plot events and iconography typical of the western genre – the ten-gallon cowboy hats, the card sharps and the cattle wrangling – Keaton bumbles his way through a series of misadventures aided by his best friend Brown Eyes, a cow. Determined to rescue Brown Eyes from the Los Angeles slaughterhouse, he succeeds in herding the cattle through the city, in images which resonate ironically with the film's earlier shots of the human 'cattle' stampeding through the streets of New York.

In *Way Out West* (1936), Laurel and Hardy also appropriate western generic iconography to comic effect. Employing the same flimsy plot later used by the Marx Brothers in their *Go West* (1940), Stan and Ollie play prospectors trying to deliver the deeds of a dead friend's goldmine to his daughter. This they do, despite the chicanery of saloon-owner James Finlayson. The gags and comic business are less reliant on generic characteristics than Keaton's *Go West* and perhaps have a less organic relationship with the iconography and 'business' of the western, but the sense of play that the film squeezes from generic settings such as the saloon in Brushwood Gulch is effective. With both Keaton and Laurel and Hardy, a shortfall in the macho masculinity expected from western heroes adds to the comedy, as do their 'civilised' and polite eastern sensibilities which are at odds with the culture of a harsher and more brutal west. *Way Out West* extends its border crossings to include two musical numbers, one of which, 'The Trail of the Lonesome Pine', became a hit in the British charts when it was rereleased in 1975. In the Marx Brother's *Go West* the western iconography acts as an incidental source for their gags as when, on a bumpy stagecoach, Groucho asks a fellow passenger why her baby is always crying; her reply, that it can't stand the jerks on board, is a cue for Harpo and Chico to exit the coach. Whereas Keaton seems embedded in his western landscape, even if he is physically and psychologically overwhelmed by it, Laurel and Hardy and the Marx Brothers retain the essential identities they trade upon in all their films.

In the same way comedians such as W.C. Fields in *My Little Chickadee* (1940) and Bob Hope in *The Paleface* (1948) and *Son of Paleface* (1952) retain their comedic personas largely intact in their comedy westerns. Of course there are comedy westerns in which the leading stars are not conventionally thought of as comedians – *Destry Rides Again* (1939) starring Marlene Dietrich and James Stewart, *McLintock* (1963) starring John Wayne and *Paint Your Wagon* (1969) with Lee Marvin and Clint Eastwood spring to mind – but to an extent the latter examples reflect the growing problems of the western as a sustainable genre, particularly from the 1960s onwards. *My Little Chickadee* relies on the comic personas of Mae West and Fields, she parading her much-vaunted sexuality, he playing the cowardly incompetent con-man Cuthbert

J. Twillie. The film uses and often abuses western genre clichés, as when the pair defeat an Indian attack with a pair of pistols and a slingshot, or when Twillie manages to escape hanging. In *The Paleface* Bob Hope makes an equally unlikely hero. As the incompetent dentist 'Painless' Potter, he is reliant on a strong female character (Jane Russell as Calamity Jane) to propel him to heroic status that his cowardice would naturally deny. With a plot centred on selling guns to the Indians, the film is replete with standard western action such as an attack on the wagon train, but it is Hope's persona as the cowardly dentist that sits at the heart of the film, a hopelessly ineffectual specimen of masculinity who is comically at odds with what he sees as the barbaric west. Having been 'chased by women before, but not when I'm awake', Painless longs to get back east where 'men may not be men, but at least they're not corpses'. The success of the film, including the popularity of the number 'Buttons and Bows', engendered *Son of Paleface*, again with Russell and with Roy Rogers providing the musical number 'A Four-Legged Friend'. Again, much of the comedy is provided by Hope's looks to camera and by his one-line gags, as well as by a quantum of slapstick humour.

Although regarded as a quintessentially American genre, the western has also occasionally been appropriated for comic purposes by British producers. *The Sheriff of Fractured Jaw* (1958), shot in Spain and starring Kenneth More as English gentleman and arms manufacturer Jonathan Tibbs, opposite Jayne Mansfield, raises smiles at the antics of Tibbs who manages against all odds to bring law enforcement to the unruly town. In this he is aided by the previously hostile Sioux Indians who adopt him as a blood brother with the name 'Fleet Iron Hat'. However, the film is no more than wryly amusing as a gentle parody of western genre clichés and More, in no way a comedian, looks rather embarrassed as Mansfield (dubbed by Connie Francis) sings 'The Valley of Love'. Much more raucous is *Carry On Cowboy* (1965), one of a series of *Carry On* films which parodied popular film genres (see Chapter 9). In a plot not unlike *The Paleface* and *Sheriff of Fractured Jaw*, Jim Dale plays Marshall P. Knutt, a British sanitary engineer who is mistakenly sent to the lawless town of Stodge City to restore law and order. The Rumpo Kid (Sid James) rules the town and the ineffective Judge Burke (Kenneth Williams) is powerless to stop him until, after a series of narrow escapes and with help from another female sharp-shooter, Annie Oakley (Angela Douglas), Knutt manages to defeat Rumpo. The film begins by observing the conventions of the western genre, with a ballad sung over the opening titles, the camera following a lone cowboy as he rides into town, and then confronts three gunmen in the main street as the townsfolk scatter. It is only when Rumpo has shot the three gunmen and ponders 'I wonder what they wanted' that the film announces its parodic stance. As a contemporary review of the film noted, 'the introductory scenes make a neat enough send-up of traditional Western routines, situations and dialogue' and, they might have added, music (*Monthly Film Bulletin* 1966: 41–2), but these are coated with incessant puns about characters and events, with a heavy diet of 'near-the-knuckle' double entendres. Told that rustlers have stolen forty cows, Rumpo corrects the statement: 'bullocks' he asserts. When Rumpo is confronted by Belle (Joan Sims) in her saloon she warns 'I don't allow no shooting at my place' to which he replies, looking her up and down: 'Lady, I wouldn't dream of shooting *at* your place.' Less subtly, when he hands over his gun Belle notes 'My, you have a big one', and Rumpo replies, 'I'm from Texas, we all have big ones in Texas.' Fittingly, in a neat comic trope unique in western gunfights, the rookie Marshall manages to defeat Rumpo and his fellow outlaws in the final shoot-out by using the underground sewers as cover.

The late 1960s and 1970s saw a number of comedy westerns produced at a time when the genre was struggling to retain its previous importance in both cultural and commercial terms. The basic plot parodied in *Carry On Cowboy* resurfaced in a number of other comedy westerns, including *Support Your Local Sheriff* (1969) and *Support Your Local Gunfighter* (1971), both starring James Garner, who had found fame in the television western series *Maverick* (1957–60). However, all these comedy westerns were eclipsed when Mel Brooks' *Blazing Saddles* appeared in 1974. This is a film that we will return to in subsequent chapters, one that is regarded by many as the most successful comedy western of all time. Replete with historical anachronisms and spilling beyond its ostensible diegetic world to encompass a 'live' Count Basie orchestra and a wild chase through Hollywood studio sets filming other productions and on to the streets of contemporary Los Angeles, *Blazing Saddles* struck a chord with audiences at a time when revisionist versions of the western genre were gaining ground. *Blazing Saddles* uses comedy to address the issue of racism within the western genre and its partial representation of American history (see Chapter 10) and to excuse its flirtations with the limits of the acceptable (see Chapter 9). In the fight between Lamarr's rowdies and the townsfolk towards the end of the film, an elderly lady is held and punched repeatedly as she turns and addresses the camera, asking if we have ever seen anything like this (though we might have done in *Animal Crackers*). Several complaints were made about the scene in which Mongo, the giant intellectually challenged, indestructible man-beast, punches a horse. The obscenities and the absurdities are constantly underpinned by a sense of the surreal; as the villains ride through the desert to rampage through Rock Ridge, they are held up by a coin-operated barrier, so that Taggart declares that 'somebody's got to go back and get a shit-load of dimes'. The fact that they could simply ride around the barrier, put there by Waco and Bart to buy time, seems not to occur to them.

Blazing Saddles is incessant in its determination to subvert normative expectations of human thought and behaviour. The clichés we have come to associate with the western genre provide the perfect vehicle for such comedy; when Taggart says 'we can head them off at the pass', Lamarr retorts that he hates that phrase and shoots Taggart in the foot to prove it. What makes the film so funny is that it is peppered with incongruities of action, character, language and dialogue as it constantly misaligns levels of awareness of its existence as historical past, familiar fictional genre, film in progress and contemporary reality.

Comedy westerns have been made since, such as *City Slickers* (1991) in which a group of contemporary male urban professionals in mid-life crisis confront the altogether different culture of the west, epitomised by Curly (Jack Palance). Mitch (Billy Crystal) and his two friends finally succeed in driving the cattle to Colorado and in the process find their true selves, returning home having overcome their separate crises, much better men as a result of the experience. However, nothing as funny as *Blazing Saddles* has yet been produced and it is likely to stand as the definitive comedy western for some time. One obstacle to its being dislodged is the overall lack of westerns being made, but maybe *Blazing Saddles* has made audiences so aware of the genre's comic potential that it has become hard to take straight versions of the western seriously.

Following up: the comedy western

☞ Why do you think that the western genre was such an important source for comedy spoofs?

☞ By comparing two or more comedy westerns explain how disruptions to the conventions, plot structures and iconography of the western genre are used to produce comic effects.

Comedy and music: Bob Hope and Bing Crosby in the *Road* films

Putting aside the work of Gilbert and Sullivan, popular musical comedy emerged on stage in the late 1890s. An offshoot of burlesque theatre, musical comedy was 'self-consciously modern, dealing with up-to-date manners and mores' (Pearsall 1975: 18). With the development of synchronised sound in the 1920s (see Barrios 2010) musicals became a staple production in Hollywood and other national cinemas from the 1930s into the 1950s. Few Hollywood musicals of this period are devoid of comedy elements, and British film musicals, especially those produced in the 1930s and 1940s starring the likes of Gracie Fields, often contained a great deal of comedy. However, the comedy vehicles of this period frequently included musical interludes. We have already noted several examples above. Others include those Laurel and Hardy 1930s features based on operettas, and most Marx Brothers films, which build in opportunities for Chico to shoot piano keys and for Harpo to justify his name. In Britain the films of George Formby can be seen as musicals or as comedies depending on the preferences of the audience. The closeness between the two meta-genres of comedy and musical renders problematic any notion of a 'determinist' generic linear development. Neither comedies nor musicals have recurrent iconography or settings and both regularly seem to 'remember' that they appeared together in music hall and variety.

In comedy musicals, the comedy usually exists as a sub-plot to the – usually romantic – main plot in the musical proper. The Warner Bros musicals of the 1930s, including *42nd Street*, *Footlight Parade* and *Gold Diggers of 1933* (all 1933) had strong comic sub-plots, played by an ensemble group of actors (including Guy Kibbee and Hugh Herbert) that existed at the margins of the musical numbers and romantic business. In some later Hollywood musicals, such as *Summer Stock* (1950) and *Singin' in the Rain* (1952), the comedy was provided by all-round entertainers such as Phil Silvers and Donald O'Connor, but they remained supporting players, confined to the sub-plots or comedy numbers that exploited their particular talents. However, many musicals of the 1950s and 1960s including *Carousel* (1956), *South Pacific* (1958), *Sweet Charity* (1960), *West Side Story* (1961) and *The Sound of Music* (1965) largely eschewed comic elements as the genre established a reputation as a vehicle which could carry serious themes and issues. Later successful musicals, such as *Dirty Dancing* (1987), *Evita* (1996) and *Moulin Rouge* (2001), exploit the conventions of the genre but are almost completely devoid of comic sub-plots and comedy business. Beginning with comedy as part of the package and then sidling away from it over the years, the musical seems to have avoided being parodied in the way that the western and other genres have been parodied. This is because the conventional musical, with its basic 'boy meets girl' plot, flimsy 'putting on a show' format and essentially optimistic ideology, is already a self-reflexive comedy in the broadest sense of the term. Adding more comedy pushes the text into becoming a comedy with music, and no longer a comedy musical.

A generic dividing line might still be distinguished between comedies with music and comedy musicals. Songs appear at key moments in the comedies *Life of Brian* (1979) and *The Meaning of Life* (1983), and form a key narrative element of *South Park: Bigger Longer and Uncut* (1999) and the spoof biopic *Walk Hard: The Dewey Cox Story* (2007). Films that are dominated by music but use comedy to link the musical elements include the Beatles' films of the 1960s (see Neaverson 1997), drawing on music hall traditions (see Faulk 2010), and *The Rocky Horror Picture Show* (1975) in which generic spoof and comedic excess intersperse its musical numbers. Then there are comedies that return as musicals because it seems as if they should have had songs in them in the first place, such as *The Producers* (1968/2005) and *Hairspray* (1988/2007). *Mamma Mia* (2008) is ultimately a comedy musical that not only evokes the joys of karaoke engagement with the pure pop of Abba but also delivers knowing shifts of register between narrative, comedic business and the combination of song and spectacle of the early 1930s film musicals. In fact what we tend to see when comedy and music come together is that a third term is needed to provide a focus for the narrative and a butt for the comedy.

The Bob Hope, Bing Crosby and Dorothy Lamour *Road* films are interesting as hybrid films that combine comedy and musical numbers with the appropriation of popular genre film conventions that become the object of comic mockery. A total of seven *Road to ...* films were made between 1940 and 1962: *Singapore* (1940), *Zanzibar* (1941), *Morocco* (1942), *Utopia* (1946), *Rio* (1947), *Bali* (1952) and *Hong Kong* (1962), the last being a spoof of the then newly popular spy film epitomised by the Bond films. Bing Crosby (1903–77) had enormous success in the 1930s and well into the 1950s as a singer, and appeared in a number of Hollywood films, including the musical comedy *A Connecticut Yankee in King Arthur's Court* (1949), which made use of his singing talents. Bob Hope (1903–2003) was one of America's most successful comedians from the 1940s to the 1960s, but he became increasingly unfashionable especially following the debacle of the 1970 Miss World competition where, as compere to the show, his jokes seemed dated and his response to the disruption caused by radical feminists even more so. Yet, in his comedy westerns, in numerous television appearances and in the seven *Road* films, Hope's seminal importance to comedy is clear, as is the influence he had on younger comedians. Calling him a 'pioneer postmodernist', Ben Thompson suggests that 'without Bob Hope's *Road to ...* movies (and *Son of Paleface*), there would have been no Bob Monkhouse and maybe no Farrelly Brothers' (2004: 27). Hope's ability to self-reflexively transcend the material he is dealing with, evident in *The Paleface* and *Son of Paleface*, is especially pronounced in the *Road* films where, for example, he would complain that Crosby has ruined his big scene and his chances of getting an Oscar, or warn the audience that Crosby was about to sing, so now was a good time to go out and get popcorn.

The Road to Bali (1952) was the only one the series to be made in colour. As with the other *Road* films, the songs serve as a showcase for Crosby and have little connection with the plot, which it is merely a flimsy hook on which to hang the comic business. *Bali* both reiterates and parodies Hollywood's orientalist obsessions about an imagined exotic east. The film's comedy relies on a barrage of visual jokes, gags, puns and quick-fire cross-talk between Hope and Crosby, as well as a series of industry in-jokes that knowingly poke fun at the process of filmmaking, not least in the reference to winning an Academy Award; late in the film, Hope physically snatches an Oscar statuette from Crosby's grasp saying 'Give me that: you've already got one'. Later, with the help of special effects, the pair are suspended over water as a tree branch they are leaning on breaks; and Crosby asks 'How come we don't fall?' Hope replies that Paramount wouldn't dare, given Crosby's age. When Hope is asked to explain how he escaped from a diver's suit; he looks at the camera and says, 'It was easy' and then proceeds to 'explain' in pantomime terms, spoofing cinema's conventional need to provide motivation and realism. At the very end of the film, as Crosby walks off with both Lamour and Jane Russell, Hope desperately tries to delay the end of the film, as he physically wrestles with the on-screen graphics announcing THE END.

Never hermetically sealed within the ostensible diegesis, both Hope and Crosby frequently break the fourth wall by turning to camera and directly addressing the audience. At one point Hope declares that 'we've never had any money', then turns to camera and admits this is an effort to stem his tax bill with 'that's for Washington'. Much of the comedy comes from the running gags that populate the *Road* films, not least in the stars' characterisation as two con-men constantly on the lookout for opportunities that invariably lead to near-disaster. The high opinion that Hope, in particular, has of himself (he says of impending romance with Lamour 'I couldn't have happened to a nicer girl') is constantly undercut by events, not least when, in a reference to Darwinism, his face is superimposed on to a monkey.

Dated as they are, the *Road* films are a reminder of Hope's importance as a screen comedian and, given the manner in which they undermine screen conventions across a range of genres, they also offer a powerful corrective to conventional views about the supposed stability of Hollywood genres of the 1940s and 1950s. These films also illustrate how comedy and music, personified by Hope and Crosby respectively, feed off one another.

Following up: comedy and music

☞ Why have comedy and musical numbers been regularly framed together in the same texts? What is the generic logic of the connection between them?

☞ Thompson's description of Bob Hope as a 'pioneer postmodernist' implies that his comedy of the 1940s and 1950s is ahead of its time. By looking at any of the Hope and Crosby *Road* films, consider how Thompson's description might be justified.

Spoofing reality

While cinematic spoofs have a long history, the television spoof is a more recent phenomenon. The surfeit of television across the western world, initially with the advent of satellite and cable, and then with developments in digital technology, has made virtually everyone familiar with television genres, formats, conventions and programmes, to the point where even some 'genuine' programmes appear almost to tumble into self-parodic mode. Because of the differences between cinema and television, spoofs on television have focused mainly, though not exclusively, on factual genres such as news, current affairs and documentary.

The BBC radio series *On the Hour* (1991–92) is a good example of contemporary satirical broadcast material. Chris Morris, Armando Iannucci and colleagues managed to adopt the conventions of radio news presentation in the twelve episodes of *On the Hour* to offer a savage, searingly funny, surrealist broadside aimed at the clichés, conventions and self-serving pomposities of current affairs broadcasting. This programme also offered the first appearance of Steve Coogan's inept sports presenter Alan Partridge (see also *Knowing Me, Knowing You* 1994–95; *I'm Alan Partridge* 1997, 2002).

Morris and many of the same team transferred their spoof format to television in 1994 with *The Day Today*. The programme parodied the lavish seriousness which characterised the worst conventions of television news programming, not least the computer-generated title sequence graphics which here were stretched into comically redundant excess. Fronted by Morris himself who delivered to camera in a brash, direct and aggressively serious manner (based, some have suggested, on the BBC presenter Jeremy Paxman), the programme offered a string of surreal stories in the manner of *On the Hour*. The news often referred to real people, frequently politicians, having behaved in wildly improbable ways, such as the government minister Malcolm Rifkind pulling the legs off live dogs. The comedy works because of the incongruous tension between the footage that we see of politicians, celebrities and others who are frequently seen on television, and the accusation on the soundtrack that they are engaged in absurd activities. Morris, surrounded by computers on his desk, frequently interrupts other reporters, including the business correspondent Collaterlie Sisters, the bearded environmental reporter Rosie May, and the hopelessly incompetent economics correspondent Peter O'Hanraha-hanrahan, as fresh, albeit absurd, news comes tumbling in, such as the infestation of wild horses in the London underground, Marlon Brando being sold at auction, ugly children being banned from school because they put other children off, and the British pound being stolen. The programme's satire culminates in an interview in which Morris manages to provoke a war between Australia and Hong Kong. Much of the comedy springs from the incongruous mismatch between presentational style and subject content, both of them coming to seem equally ridiculous. The wild inaccuracies spouted by Morris as anchorman and his team of reporters amounts to a sustained comic critique of the supposed authority and integrity of television news and current affairs and those who work in the genre.

Morris continued his satirical savaging of television with *Brass Eye*, a series of six spoof documentaries shown on Channel Four in 1997. Like *The Day Today*, *Brass Eye* makes excessive use of computer-generated graphics, offering a satirical comment on their presence within broadcast television and the ways in which programmes could be said to place an over-reliance on them. In the 'Crime' episode Morris physically steps through what we have taken to be a computer-generated graph but is actually a large built one, while another graph (this time computer-generated) shows us statistics about 'crimes we know nothing about'. The episode constructs a view about crime and the supposedly inadequate response of the authorities that simulates a genuine media-generated moral panic. We are told that UK used to stand for United Kingdom, but now it stands for 'Unbelievable Crime Rate', and that prisoners in the high security prison on Dartmoor 'have been running an international airport for over fourteen years'.

Just as *The Day Today* used actual footage to root its comedy in some sort of reality, *Brass Eye* used interviews and comments from celebrities and experts who were asked to voice their opinions on subjects including drugs, crime and sex. It became famous for drawing celebrities into fake charity campaigns that they seemed unable to understand. In the episode 'Science' there is an extended sequence in which a number of actors and presenters are called upon to do their bit for GEFAFWISP and its campaign against the devastating consequences of 'heavy electricity' caused by 'sodomised electrons' falling from wires like 'invisible lead soup' and crushing villagers and animals in Upaveli, Sri Lanka. Richard Briers, Nick Owen, Steven Berkoff and others, though set-up and deceived, willingly lend themselves to presenting supposedly factual material that does not, and cannot, belong to the world as we know it. Ben Walters argues: 'Much of the humour came from the gulf between [the participants'] sophisticated knowledge of media processes and the sheer inanity of the subject matter to which it was applied' (2005: 98). But, as Jonathan Gray points out (2009: 164), however satisfying this mockery is, for every satire there are a dozen flattering media opportunities that allow their celebrities to become detached from the messages they are asked to give voice to.

Brass Eye became particularly infamous in Britain for the 'Paedogeddon' special episode (2001) that parodied the hysterical reaction of the British media to the issue of paedophilia. This choice of subject matter for a comedy programme clearly leads towards a discussion of taste (see Chapter 9). However, much of the immediate reaction to the episode suffered from exactly the same hysteria that was satirised. Newspapers and other media responded not to the programme but simply to the idea that someone had linked comedy and paedophilia on television, and drew in various commentators and politicians as renta-quotes in exactly the same way that the in-show spoofs had been able to get their celebrities to comment without any real understanding of the issues. In clearly targeting the media hysteria and hypocrisy that surrounded the subject of paedophilia at the time, *Brass Eye* represents a brave attack on that hypocrisy through laughter, though Ben Thompson suggests that the *Brass Eye* special also exploits a real problem to make its point: 'Morris should have removed the plank in his own eye before drawing attention to the splinters in everybody else's' (2004: 317). Given his apparent polemical impatience with the pieties of conservative morality, it is no surprise that Morris causes controversy. His film, *Four Lions* (2010), is discussed in Chapter 9.

Brass Eye's attempt to puncture prevalent 'politically correct' social attitudes has perhaps been matched only by Ricky Gervais's piece for *Comic Relief* in March 2007 in which he travestied the very format of charity appeals by revealing an underbelly of commercial and self-seeking promotion. While filming in a mocked-up Kenyan corrugated hut in the BBC's Television Centre, he is told by several celebrities including co-writer Stephen Merchant, chef Jamie Oliver, Bob Geldof and U2's Bono that – morally – he can't fake this; they all then shamelessly proceed to promote themselves and products they are associated with. The piece epitomises an ironic posmodern aesthetic, layered with multiple registers of meaning that the presence of the camera summons up. Both incredibly funny and deeply cynical, it manages to use comedy to make a serious point about the role, place and effect of television charity appeals and yet at the same time prompted viewers to pledge money to the good cause.

Part of the reason for this piece's effectiveness was the reputation that Gervais had built with his earlier fourteen episode BBC series, *The Office* (2001–3). The BBC had already had success with *Operation Good Guys* (1997) and *People Like Us* (1999), comedies which parodied television documentary, and, although initial viewing figures were not spectacular, *The Office* became a cult hit with massive DVD sales and was subsequently sold to over eighty countries, with a number of others producing their own version of the show. Set in a fictitious office in the otherwise unremarkable town of Slough, the programme is, in the words of Jon Plowman, 'basically a sitcom that happens to be filmed quite like a documentary' (Thompson 2004: 414), and purports to show the ordinary, everyday life of those working in the office. However, though the series does have interwoven storylines involving a strong ensemble cast, the main focus is on the central character, office manager David Brent (Gervais), whose lack of self-knowledge is both staggering and embarrassing. Brent wildly overestimates his abilities as a manager but, more damagingly, sees himself as a 'showbiz entertainer' whose opportunity has come, despite the mundane circumstances of his work and life. Though he spouts the language of business and prides himself on his 'people management' skills, Brent is both sexist and racist in his dealings with the office staff. Above all, his constant self-conscious awareness of being looked at and performing for the camera leads him into situations from which he would clearly like to be extricated, such as when, as a practical joke, he pretends to fire receptionist Dawn.

Though some of the comedy arises from more conventional situations, such as the running feud between Tim and the nerdy, pompous 'assistant junior area manager' Gareth, it is the egotistical Brent and his misplaced attempts to control both his staff and the camera that sits at the heart of the comedy. As Walters notes, 'Brent relies on gags and tropes lifted from TV comedians as the basis for his own generally calamitous attempts at humour' (2005: 105). It is this ill-fated co-option of catchphrases and comic tropes and the strained attempt to use humour to resist the takeover by the Swindon branch that finally make Brent a defeated, almost sympathetic character, forced to beg for his own job. In the end *The Office* is as much *about* television comedy as it *is* television comedy, a rich, multi-layered, multi-registered treatise not just on the place and status of work in our contemporary lives but on the place, meaning and impact of both comedy and television too.

Audience familiarity with the tropes and conventions of popular television suggests that comedy parodies will remain a feature of television for some time to come. Peter Kay's *Britain's Got the Pop Factor and Possibly a New Celebrity Jesus Christ Soapstar Superstar on Ice* was broadcast in 2008, a parody of the numerous talent shows such *The X-Factor*, *American Idol* and *Britain's Got Talent* that have proliferated on British and American television in recent years. Adopting the genre's contemporary format, complete with mawkish back-story vignettes of the contestants, Kay's show featured the excruciatingly un-PC singing group '2 Up 2 Down', two men and two wheelchair-bound women who engaged in ever increasingly bizarre settings as the show progressed. Another finalist, R. Wayne, is kicked off the show, but is brought back when his Granny dies from a heart attack after hearing the news of his elimination. Kay himself played Geraldine, a bizarre character from a dysfunctional background who has undergone a gender reassignment operation, and who goes on to win the contest. Ironically, the fictional character Geraldine appeared on a number of actual radio shows and 'her' rendition of 'The Winner's Song' reached number two in the UK song charts. To date the promised sequel, *Celebrity Fiddler on the Roof in the Jungle*, has not materialised.

It may be, as Ricky Gervais argues, that 'there is nothing funnier than real life, real documentaries' (Walters 2005: 15) and at times many contemporary television programmes unintentionally descend into cliché and close approximation of parody. Yet there is little to suggest that programmes which deliberately base their comedy on parodying 'proper' programmes will disappear from television screens. After the exhaustive worldwide success of their reality-television-inflected sketch show *Little Britain* (2003–6), David Walliams and Matt Lucas adopted a new format for *Come Fly With Me* (2010–11), a mock documentary series in which they play all the main characters working for the low-cost airline 'Flylo' and the airport it operates from. Complete with authoritative fly-on-the-wall documentary voiceover, *Come Fly With Me* relies on comic characterisation, particularly the camp cross-dressing that both Lucas and Walliams have become associated with. The series has plausibly been accused of trading in sexual and racial stereotypes, though this is not all that it does. One of the most vicious characterisations is reserved for the bigoted white immigration officer and the gags at the expense of real-life low-cost airlines sometimes offer barbed critiques of business practices, not least when airline boss Omar Baba quells a strike, fires all his staff and replaces them with Vietnamese children. *Come Fly With Me* lacks the comic depths of

The Office, but its comic parody of the docusoap might nevertheless bring the end of that format closer.

The target satirised by the mock-documentary *Twenty Twelve* (2011–12) is the London Olympics of 2012, with a supposedly candid look behind the scenes at the preparations for what is often described as a global event. However, whatever global significance the Olympic Games has is undercut for comic purposes by the sheer incompetence and inefficiency of the planning team, including the web designer who cannot even spell 'Olympics' and a countdown clock that has a major design fault which has gone unnoticed until the very last moment. As Euan Ferguson commented in *The Observer* on 24 July 2011, the programme gets 'way too close for comfort on the excruciations of political correctness, our modern failure to organise a cup of tea without a flowchart and the impossibility of getting athletes to say anything interesting, ever.' Although the comedy ostensibly targets a specific event, it successfully satirises the wider, and wilder, excesses of politically correct, media-conscious contemporary western society.

Following up: spoofing reality on television

☞ To what extent is the presence of a known comic performer such as Peter Kay important for coding a programme as a spoof?

☞ Why has the work of Chris Morris has aroused such controversy? What aspects of his work have caused opposition from authority figures, including politicians?

Rockumentary / Mockumentary: *This Is Spinal Tap* (1984)

Comedic parodies of the documentary genre, often called 'mockumentaries', are now an established format in film and television comedy (see Roscoe and Hight 2001; Hight 2010) in which documentary techniques are imitated for comic effect. A particularly strong strand of mockumentary targets the conventions of documentaries about rock music (so-called rockumentaries) established by films such as *Don't Look Back* (1967) about Bob Dylan, *Gimme Shelter* (1974) with the Rolling Stones and *The Song Remains the Same* (1974) featuring Led Zeppelin. Sometimes, as in Eric Idle's *The Rutles: All You Need Is Cash* (1978), the comedy stems from the parodic resemblances to real-life groups and events, in this case the Beatles. Tracking the rise of 'Rutlemania' and famous albums such as 'Sgt Rutters Only Darts Club Band', the film squeezes comic moments from the discrepancy between what we know about the Beatles and the less-than-successful career of their comically-imagined counterparts. The film takes every opportunity to exploit and subvert what have become clichéd conventions of documentary style, undermining pretensions of seriousness by highlighting comic ineptitude.

One of the most popular and successful mock-rockumentaries has been *This Is Spinal Tap* (1984), Rob Reiner's spoof which purports to chart the comeback of 'England's loudest heavy metal rock group' Spinal Tap as they tour America to promote their album *Smell the Glove*. Reiner plays the on-screen director Marty DiBergi, conducting interviews with band members, capturing their on-stage performances, and following the rifts and arguments as they descend into failure and near-oblivion.

The film has a number of running gags. The band's numerous drummers die under mysterious circumstances, including spontaneous combustion, a 'bizarre gardening accident' and choking on an unknown someone else's vomit. As the tour continues, the venues become ever smaller and insignificant, leading to a shared bill with a puppet show. Numerous scenes serve to highlight the ineptitude of the band, as when they get hopelessly lost trying to find the stage at a gig in Cleveland, or when bassist Derek Small gets stuck in the pod-like stage prop as the band perform live. Determined to revive their act, they decide to have an impressive Stonehenge stage set built, but it turns out only to be tiny in practice, fit only for dwarf dancers to circle.

The interviews with 'director' DiBergi reveal the individual band members as ignorant, sexist and devoid of musical taste. Playing a piano piece inspired by Mozart and Bach, Nigel Tufnell tells DiBergi that the number is called 'Lick My Love Pump'. Even when DiBergi reads them some press reviews of their albums, the band appear indifferent to comments that they show 'no musical growth' and are 'treading water in a sea of retarded sexuality and bad poetry'. Even those who surround the band are shown to be crass and ineffective, such as manager Ian Faith and David St Hubbin's disruptive girlfriend Jeanine. The animosity between Jeanine and Tufnell breaks up the band, only for them to reunite when their number 'Sex Farm' gets to number five in the Japanese charts. Spinal Tap seem destined to continue despite being devoid of self-knowledge, humility or even talent. They desire to live the glamorous life of the rock star and to embody rock clichés, but are incapable of seeing themselves as others do. We should have guessed that a band that began life as 'The Originals', but had to change the name because there was already a band of that name, was doomed to failure. Unaware of the ironies of their situation, they plough on with admirable 'the show must go on' doggedness, helped of course by the drugs. Faced with the band splitting, David says he 'would feel worse if I wasn't under such heavy sedation'.

The film draws knowingly on the tropes and conventions of the rockumentary, mixing on-stage numbers with interviews and 'authentic' candid fly-on-the-wall shots of the band members arguing, complaining about the food provided or experiencing problems with hotel bookings. The 'clips' from earlier television incarnations of the band serve to reinforce this apparent authenticity. The comedy in *Spinal Tap* is so effective because its depiction of the band and its milieu, heightened by the documentary form, is so plausible. The insistent presentation of incidents as reality matches the inability of the protagonists to see anything funny or ridiculous about themselves and their performances. Because of the film's refusal to wink at its audience, the individual viewer is caught between acknowledging these poles of plausibility and ridiculousness, constantly uncertain as to whether the comic target is documentary filmmaking, heavy metal music or this particular band. It is this element of 'ambivalence towards its subject' (Roscoe and Hight 2001: 121) that maintains the film's comic currency. Though they are still made, rock documentaries constantly need to check that they have not strayed into *This Is Spinal Tap* territory, or, when they do, to at least admit that they know it.

Following up: mockumentary

☞ How do you account for the enduring popularity of *This Is Spinal Tap*? How does the film try to persuade audiences that it is an authentic documentary and how does this contribute to the comic effect of the film?

☞ Consider the importance of plausibility in the comic effects of other mockumentaries such as *Zelig* (1983), *CB4* (1993), *Fear of a Black Hat* (1993) and *Best in Show* (2000).

☞ Is *Exit Through the Gift Shop* (2010) a mockumentary, or something else?

Earlier in this chapter we noted that some commentators were of the opinion that the notion of genre has become largely redundant in what is often rather loosely termed postmodern culture. Postmodernity, characterised by its loss of distinction between the real and the imagined through the prevalence of media-produced versions, or what Baudrillard (1981) terms 'simulacra', also fails to maintain any distinction between 'high' and 'popular' cultural production, something which may be seen as liberating, inclusive and exciting. Postmodern culture exhibits a tendency towards pastiche and parody, the blurring of generic boundaries alongside aesthetic experimentation and the rejection of apparent objectivity and coherence in favour of fragmentation and discontinuity. This ability to celebrate fragmentation, to play with intertextual elements through parody, pastiche and spoof, to revel in dismantling the barriers between 'high' art and 'low' culture and to cross generic boundaries is something that comedy has been very good at for a very long time. Noting this point, it is not our intention to reject the usefulness of the concept of genre or to dispute the characteristics of postmodern culture; what we highlight instead is that comedy constantly splashes across generic borders and that this refusal of boundaries and undermining of categories is a fundamental and historical characteristic of comedy both as a meta-genre and within its numerous constituent sub-genres.

Recommended reading

Dan Harries, *Film Parody*, London: BFI, 2000.
Ben Walters, *The Office*, London, BFI, 2005.

7

Animated comedy

Animation is a serious business, bedevilled by popular misconceptions that it is: (1) for children; (2) short; and (3) always funny. Beginning in the late nineteenth century, film animation has varied in length from the short to full-length feature, and has been used for a variety of serious purposes, such as propaganda in Winsor McCay's *Sinking of the Lusitania* (1918), Disney's *Victory Through Air Power* (1943) and Jan Svankmajer's *Death of Stalinism in Bohemia* (1990), as anti-nuclear war statement as in Jimmy Murakami's *When the Wind Blows* (1986) and as political meditation such as Halas and Batchelor's *Animal Farm* (1954). Though all animation shares a representational apparatus and a specific vocabulary and is chiefly distinguished by not being 'live action', not all animation is designed to be comedic. Richard Taylor categorises animation into six distinct types: dramatic, lyrical, didactic, commercial, children's entertainment and the comic. His concept of 'comic' animated films, made 'primarily to provoke laughter' includes what many people would regards as cartoons (Taylor 1996).

Until fairly recently it has been too easy to blame Disney for our assumption that animation – 'the cartoon' – is funny kids' stuff. It is true that animation is produced by most cultures and most countries, often but not always for comic purposes. However, it is equally true that American animation has dominated popular perceptions of this particular cultural form. The dominance within the American cartoon tradition of Disney and other American studios including Warner Bros and MGM and, more recently, the computer-generated animation coming from Dreamworks and Pixar, has influenced the aesthetics, technology and commercial production of animation, as well as ways in which animation is perceived and viewed. The common perception is that the American 'cartoonal' idiom is what Wells terms 'an intrinsically comic space' (Wells 2002a: 48).

Questioning whether accepted notions of genre that are applied to live-action cinema can be applied as effectively to animated film, Wells offers instead the view that animation is better understood in terms of the 'deep structures' that underpin animation process and content. He defines seven distinctive animated genres which he feels address its distinctive aesthetic: formal, deconstructive, political, abstract, re-narration, paradigmatic and primal (Wells 2002a: 67–71). This categorisation is useful in enabling us to understand the rich variety of animation, from Disney to the dreamlike surrealism of the Brothers Quay, to Japanese anime. Wells clearly places most animated comedy within his category of 'deconstructive', including Fleischer's *Out of the Inkwell* series, Otto Mesmer's *Felix the Cat* shorts, the work of Chuck Jones and some work from Disney such as *Aladdin* (1992).

Both Taylor and Wells make the assertion that not all animation aimed at children is necessarily designed to be funny. The Green Cross Code road safety campaign on British television in the 1970s and 1980s used animation, most notably Charley the Cat in the *Charley Says* series, to punch home its serious message to children about the dangers posed by traffic. At the same time, not all animated comedy is designed to appeal to children alone. On the contrary, animated comedy is often targeted at a family audience, a trend that has become very evident in contemporary comedy both on television, with series such as *The Simpsons*, and at the cinema with *Toy Story*, *Shrek* and a host of other computer-generated (CGI) films.

As well as CGI, animation includes 'puppet' or 'model' animation, 'drawn' or 'cel' animation and 'clay' animation, all of which have their own distinctive aesthetic and authorial implications, and need not necessarily be co-opted in the use of comedy. Having acknowledged that animation, in all its varieties and purposes, deserves serious critical attention, this chapter is concerned with understanding the contribution that animation has made to comedy in film and television since the early twentieth century through an examination of specific cartoons. Inevitably, the focus is on American animated comedy.

The distinctiveness of animated comedy

Given sound, animated comedy has no limitations other than the imaginations of its makers. In particular it is free of those limitations that constrain live action, even the most frenzied slapstick, in film or television. Put simply, the laws of physics do not apply in the cartoon world of animated comedy. Or if they apply, they are subverted and challenged in ways not possible when live actors are involved. Moreover, animation has no problems overcoming the psychological and emotional laws of nature that constrain live action cinema, with its necessarily limited range of responses and reactions from on-screen actors. Unlike live-action cinema, animation has no need to replace its stars with stunt performers, since animated characters enjoy a physical, emotional and mental plasticity denied even the highest-paid Hollywood star. Animation's ability to subvert and challenge physical, psychological and emotional realities is ideally suited to the comic process, with its desire to subvert and challenge ideological, social, conceptual and perceptual boundaries, to take us into alternative worlds where we find pleasure in incongruity, in making connections, and in seeing anew. Like comedy, animation defies our normalised expectations of a rational world and, in the process, can make us laugh.

Animation has been described as the 'most aesthetically pure' of all forms and as 'virtual reality before virtual reality became a phrase' (Clarke 2004: 8). Beginning with a blank page, animator's cel, or more likely a software programme and a blank computer screen, the animator is free to construct a fictional world inhabited by the implausible, but one which resonates with, and comments upon, a world we recognise. Homer Simpson may be yellow and have only three fingers on each hand, but he remains somehow resolutely human. Animation is, as Paul Wells argues, both depiction and interpretation, employing an aesthetic of pictorial mediation, an 'expression which moves beyond the recognisable limits of the material world in order to comment on them' (Wells 2002b: 7).

Animation can exist on its own or as part of an otherwise live-action film, as a sequence as in Terry Gilliam's animation in episodes of *Monty Python's Flying Circus*, apparently integrated into the action such as in the musical *Anchors Aweigh* (1945) when Jerry the Mouse dances with Gene Kelly, or in the ambitious combination with live-action in *Who Framed Roger Rabbit* (1988). In *Happy Feet* (2006) the CGI animation mixes with live-action choreography. This ability of the animated world to cross over into, to inhabit, comment, subvert and disrupt the 'real' world of live action has been, and remains, an important source of comedy for animated shorts and features.

The abilities and advantages enjoyed by animation, and particularly CGI animation, have had a remarkable impact on contemporary cinema. Since the box-office success of Pixar's *Toy Story* in 1995, the CGI animated comedy feature has come to be an increasingly important attraction for audiences of all ages. It is also changing the cinema industry, as we are now as likely to *hear* the voices of stars such as Tom Hanks or Eddie Murphy in a CGI animated feature as we are to see them on screen. As feature-length CGI animated comedies become big business, it is no surprise to learn that in 2010 *Despicable Me* (with the voices of Steve Carell, Russell Brand and Julie Andrews) earned more at the US box office in a weekend than the live-action feature *Knight and Day*, starring Cameron Diaz and Tom Cruise, did in three weeks. Over its opening three weeks *Despicable Me* grossed $164 million in the US, a sure indication of the popularity of CGI feature-length animated comedy with a mainstream and family audience.

The current importance of feature-length animation to box-office takings has been recognised by the US Academy Awards. Although the animated short film has been recognised at the Oscars since 1932, when it was known as 'Short Subjects: Cartoons', a category known as 'Best Animated Feature' was introduced in 2001 when the award went to *Shrek*. In 2009 *Up* was nominated for both Best Animated Feature and Best Picture at the 82nd Academy

Awards, the first animated film to be so nominated since the creation of the category.

Following up: understanding animation

☞ Using examples that you are familiar with, analyse different types of animation, identifying what makes them distinctive from each other and what elements they share in common.

☞ What do you understand by the notion that in animation 'the laws of physics do not exist'? In what ways is this freedom from the constraints of live action important in creating comedy in animation? Using specific examples that you have seen, to what extent do you think that the development of CGI has narrowed the conventional distinction between animation and live action?

A brief history of animated comedy

Though generalisations need to be treated with caution, it is possible to detect a broad trajectory in the development of American animated comedy which reflects profound changes in American society and an associated comic sensibility. The earliest silent animated comedies relied on the wit and innovatory visual pleasures associated with a newly emerging cultural form, along with considerable doses of slapstick. The urbanisation of the late-1910s and 1920s, fuelled by the huge influx of migrants, changed the American comic sensibility to a more gag-based comedy, often centred in animated shorts around anthropomorphised cartoon characters such as Otto Messmer's Felix the Cat and Disney's Mickey Mouse. As the United States matured as a melting pot society, but grew increasingly wary of social and political fragmentation both within and external to the USA, a comic sensibility that clustered around post Second World War subjectivities (not least of race, religion and geographies) gave way to increasing irony and scepticism about the 'American Dream' and the 'American Way of Life' which finds full expression in contemporary film and television animated comedy.

The self-reflexive pioneers and the comedy of shock and awe

The earliest animated films owed their origins to 'lightning sketch artists' such as James Stuart Blackton (1875–1941) working in music hall and vaudeville, to innovators such as Emile Cohl (1857–1938) who were fascinated by the stop-frame potential of motion cameras and to newspaper comic strips such as those produced by Winsor McCay (1867–1934) for the *New York Herald*. His films *Little Nemo* (1911), *How a Mosquito Operates* (1912) and *Gertie the Dinosaur*

(1914) found instant success. In *Little Nemo* (available on YouTube), the live-action prologue invites us to share the risible cynicism of McCay's friends when he declares that he will produce moving pictures from four thousand drawings within the month. The work involved in producing the drawings is made clear as several huge barrels marked 'INK', together with over-sized parcels marked 'DRAWING PAPER', are trundled into McCay's drawing office. There are moments of slapstick comedy, such as when the office boy falls and sends McCay's carefully ordered drawings flying in all directions, but the interest is in the animation itself, as the drawn characters illustrate, in full colour, the plastic movement that is inherent in the animation process, as the drawn characters are stretched and squeezed as if they were in a hall of distorted mirrors. McCay's work is intensely self-reflexive, its humour and amusement centred on the witty, innovative process of making animated drawings.

The growing popularity of cinema generally and the success of early animation pioneers such as McCay, John Randolph Bray and the Canadian Raoul Barre propelled animation towards more efficient production methods. One of the most significant was rotoscoping, developed by Dave and Max Fleischer in 1917. This involved shooting sequences as live action and then tracing this frame-by-frame as animated drawings, a process that improved the visual quality of the animation. The Fleischers' *Out of the Inkwell* series, mostly featuring Ko-Ko the Clown, enjoyed considerable success well into the 1920s. As the name suggests, the *Inkwell* series, like *Little Nemo*, was reflexive in nature; as Michael Barrier suggests, 'they were always cartoons about what it was like to be a cartoon' (1999: 25). *Modeling* (1921) is a good example, mixing live action with the antics of Ko-Ko as he skates his way through a series of mischievous gags, at one stage becoming part of a clay sculpture bust being made for a deeply unattractive-looking client who complains that the statue will not do as 'it looks too much like me'. As in all the *Inkwell* cartoons, the animated characters return to the inkwell from where they came. Ko-Ko's disruptive, carnivalesque interaction between live action and the animated sequences, focused on that traditional archetype of the comic figure, the clown, explains the appeal to contemporary audiences of a format that 'embodies in it a comical liberation from the dull drudgery of work, the focus of American life' (Frierson 1997: 91).

The Fleischers continued successfully into the sound era of the late 1920s and into the 1930s, notably with their voluptuous character Betty Boop, described as 'not so much a character as a travesty of compliant femininity' (Barrier 1999: 183). Toned down by the introduction of the Hays Code in 1934, some of the Betty Boop cartoons relied on sexual and racial comic stereotypes which would be found unacceptable today. Popeye the Sailor Man was first introduced alongside Betty Boop in 1935 and the *Popeye* series continued into the mid-1950s. Here the comedy was as reliant on the physical characteristics, physical antics and sung catchphrases of the spinach-eating sailor as on the slapstick punishment regularly meted out between Popeye and his adversary Bluto as they compete for the attention of girlfriend Olive Oyl. This basic format is evident even in later *Popeye* cartoons, such as *Cookin With Gags* (1955), where Bluto plays a series of explosive April Fool jokes on Popeye, with even his tin of spinach sprouting a pop-up snake, until Popeye delivers closure with the usual physical *coup de grâce*. Though by this time in colour, the comedy continued to be heavily dependent on physical slapstick and, as such, increasingly limited in its appeal, though the Popeye cartoons were a staple item on 1960s children's television.

Disney

The most famous name to be associated with – and, arguably, to define – the American cartoon tradition is Walt Disney. Although other animators such as Paul Terry (1887–1971) were important in establishing cartoon production on an industrial basis, it was Disney and his early associates, notably Ub Iwerks, who did most, not just to rationalise production methods but to take animated cartoons aesthetics to a new level. As Paul Terry admitted, 'Disney is the Tiffany of this business, and we're the Woolworth's' (Gabler 2006: 427).

With a career that began in 1921 and with a studio empire that survived his death in 1966, Disney looms large over any discussion of animation. Despite the fact that his first animated series was called *Laugh-O-grams*, and that his response to criticism that his 1924 *Alice* cartoons lacked humour was to promise that he would 'make it a point to inject as many funny gags and comical situations into future productions', whilst insisting that they would be 'a little different from the usual run of slap stick and hold to a more dignified line of comedy' (Gabler 2006: 84–5), the output from the Disney studio was never unremittingly funny. Disney shorts and features contain pathos, often verge into the overly sentimental and have been criticised for their saccharine aesthetic. Yet, for many, Disney productions featuring Mickey Mouse, Donald Duck, Pluto and a host of others remain the standard by which other American comedy cartoons are judged.

By the mid-1930s the studio employed specialist gag-men and at the end of that decade the studio held over 1.5 million jokes classified into 124 topics (Gabler 2006: 189). Though gags remained important, Disney's pledge to inject a more dignified comedy into his productions was kept. Slapstick gags increasingly gave way to, or were contained within, stronger story lines and narratives that were designed to elicit emotional responses. Essentially, in what became known as 'personality animation', Disney wanted audiences not just to laugh but to care about the characters they saw on screen.

The move towards personality animation was evident in an earlier Disney creation, Oswald the Lucky Rabbit, but found full expression in the figure of Mickey Mouse and begins to emerge as early as Disney's *Steamboat Willie*

(1928). One of the earliest synchronised sound cartoons, *Steamboat Willie* makes excellent use of the comic potential offered by a soundtrack working in conjunction with animated visuals. The story line is not strong, with Mickey ignoring his duties as mate aboard the steamboat, preferring instead to make music to impress an as-yet-unnamed Minnie Mouse. Some of the gags were recycled from earlier *Oswald* and *Alice* cartoons, but here they are driven by the musical soundtrack in ways which made it a landmark cartoon. Visual gags and slapstick remain important from the beginning, as we see a profile shot of the steamboat with its elasticated funnels squashing and stretching in time to the musical beat, and the smallest of the ship's three whistles having to be reminded to give its off-tune bleat. We see Mickey whistling at the helm of the boat, giving insouciant and apparently inconsequential spins of the ship's wheel. Our assumption that he is the skipper is comically undercut by the appearance of the massive, bullying Peg-leg Pete, the real skipper. Annoyed at Mickey's presumption, Pete physically drags him away, elongating his body into a black string, so that Mickey has to bundle his body back into his pants. With a wave of his hands, Mickey suggests that the raspberry he blows behind Pete's back was in fact flatulence and then disappears to do his work. Later, with Minnie aboard and after the goat has eaten her sheet music 'Turkey in the Straw', Mickey turns the goat into a phonograph and proceeds to 'play' the tune on a number of animals. Were it live action, a number of animals would have been harmed in the making of the film, but this is animation, so Mickey can pull a cat's tail, squeeze a goose, hammer the cow's teeth like a xylophone, pull the piglets' tails and play the sow's teats like an accordion. Changes to comic sensibility led to this latter sequence being pulled from the cartoon, only for it to be restored for the sake of archive authenticity in the mid-1990s.

Steamboat Willie and other Disney cartoons produced at around the same time and into the 1930s signalled the end of that long-standing tradition of the self-reflexive cartoon in which the animator's hand and the live-action world framed the animation. Now, the comedy was bound within the self-contained cartoon diegesis, an animated universe where physical, psychological and emotional laws and expectations could be stretched, but not broken or discredited, where the impossible seemed plausible, all for comic effect. The extent to which Disney wanted both motion and emotion, as well as psychological and emotional realism, is evident in comedy shorts such as *The Three Little Pigs* (1933), one of the numerous Silly Symphonies produced by the studio. Making use of the well-known narrative, Disney imbues each of the pigs with a distinct personality, and the cartoon epitomises the concept of 'personality animation'. Visual gags still have a place in the cartoon; a portrait of the pigs' father hanging on the wall shows a string of sausages, and the wolf goes literally blue in the face in the unsuccessful attempt to blow down the house built of bricks, but these are now less important than the pleasures derived from the character animation. Although Disney was increasingly disenchanted with comedy, arguing in 1938 that 'we've got more in this [animation] medium than making people laugh' (Gabler 2006: 300), *The Three Little Pigs*, an adventure in Technicolor, and with the song 'Who's Afraid of the Big Bad Wolf' sweeping the nation, struck a chord with Depression America and began Disney's dominance within the animation industry. Despite the success of animated comedy shorts, Disney became increasingly interested in feature-length animation; the success of the ground-breaking *Snow White and the Seven Dwarfs* (1937) ensured that this was the direction the studio would follow in following decades.

Warner Bros and MGM

As Disney became more interested in modes of storytelling rather than comedy *per se*, particularly in feature-length animation, it was Warner Bros and then MGM during the 1930s, 1940s and into the 1950s that took on the mantle of comedy animation shorts. Noting their appeal to a 'more streetwise immigrant humour' in what he describes as a 'more urbane, less coherent, cacophonous' cartoon style, Wells argues that the Warner Bros animators 'reinvented the cartoon as a model of incongruity and irony, caricaturing popular figures, satirising institutional conduct and re-exploring graphic and narrative idioms' (2002b: 50). Warner Bros, in their *Looney Tunes* and *Merrie Melodies* series, along with MGM, competed with Disney using the talents of numerous animators, not least amongst them Tex Avery (1908–80) and Chuck Jones (1912–2002).

Avery was associated with cartoon characters including Porky Pig, Daffy Duck, Droopy Dog and Bugs Bunny, whose catchphrase 'What's up, Doc?' came from him. Though the quality of his animation suffered in comparison with others, Avery's prime interest was in its comic potential. Barrier is of the opinion that Avery 'was interested not in animation as such, but only in his gags and how he could use his director's tools – pacing, timing, staging – to make them work' (Barrier 1999: 351). Unsullied by Disney's desire for strong story lines and character, Avery was interested in animation that was full of pacy, rapid-fire exaggerated gags, usually of a highly physical variety, mixed with increasing doses of sexual innuendo. Given that his 'humour was shaped around adult concerns: sex, status, and survival' (Lenberg 1993: 23) it is easy to understand the appeal of Avery's work for Americans and others during the 1930s and 1940s. Beginning with *Gold Diggers of 49* (1936), Avery animated and directed a string of cartoons for Warner Bros *Looney Tunes* and *Merrie Melodies* series, including the Academy Award-nominated *A Wild Hare* (1940), the first short featuring Bugs Bunny. When he joined MGM in 1942, he was able, despite working with the 'humourless' producer Fred Quimby, to fully express his radical, frenzied, style of humour.

Avery's cartoons had sufficient slapstick to ensure an appeal to children, but he was often to be in trouble because of the element of sexual innuendo that inhabits some of the MGM cartoons. One of the most obvious examples, from 1943, was his *Red Hot Riding Hood*, which parodies straitlaced American animation. The cartoon opens with the patronising voiceover 'good evening kiddies' as it begins to tell the story of Little Red Riding Hood in a traditional manner. However, and perhaps influenced by the series of labour disputes and strikes that occurred in the animation industry at this period (Sito 2006), the wolf breaks out of character, directly addresses the camera and declares he is fed up with 'all this sissy stuff' and threatens to quit unless a new way of telling the story is found. Both Riding Hood – in a Brooklyn accent – and Grandma also protest, until the director's off-frame voice agrees to change things. Avery shifts the setting, pitching the cartoon into the 1940s urban swing era and makes the tone of the cartoon overtly sexual. Utilising the slang of the period, the wolf is now a male sexual predator. Grandma lives in a high-rise penthouse, with a Mae West-inspired invite to 'come up and see me sometime' neon sigh high above her penthouse. Red is a swing singer in a nightclub advertising 'gorgeous girls'. The setting allows the wolf to display his heterosexual desire through a series of visual gags, including self-abuse, as he hammers his head, wolf-whistles, and his eyes pop out of his head. Rejecting his advances, Red hurries to Grandma's apartment. As the wolf arrives, sexual roles are reversed as a lipsticked, red-dressed grandma makes a series of sexual advances to the wolf. Now the pursued rather than the pursuer, the wolf finally escapes and declares he is through with women. Back in the nightclub, he shoots himself as Red comes on stage again, only for his ghost to express the same sexual desire. Along the way, Avery makes good use of fast-paced visual gags. In the nightclub a girl is selling cigarettes. Next to her a very tall girl is selling king-size. Most of the visual gags express the wolf's sexual desire, as eyes pop and his body assumes a phallic shape. As in every Avery cartoon, the slapstick action and the gags come thick and fast, but much of the comedy comes from his rejection of cartoon cliché and the consequent appeal to a comic sensibility that is attuned to changes in sexual politics and urban existence.

Avery's *Bad Luck Blackie* (1949) brilliantly exploits the conceit of the traditional rivalry between cats and dogs, a conceit still current in the animated feature franchise *Cats and Dogs* (2001) and *Cats* and *Dogs 2: The Revenge of Kitty Galore* (2010). Sadistic slapstick rules, as a little white kitten is tormented by a huge bulldog who gets pleasure from chasing, throwing and generally pulverising the kitten. Much of the comedy comes from the quick-fire physics-defying contortions that the bulldog adopts in his pursuit of the kitten. Even moments of apparent remorse are not what they seem; when the bulldog gives the kitten a bowl of milk, its tongue is caught in a hidden mousetrap. The kitten's suffering ends when a bowler-hatted black cat offers his protection, promising that, whenever the kitten blows the whistle he is given, the black cat will bring bad luck to the bulldog by walking across his path. It works, and a plant pot drops on the bulldog's head. This process is repeated seven times with great comic ingenuity, the black cat emerging 'impossibly' from empty cans and drainpipes, and air-swimming over telegraph wires held up by a balloon. At one stage we and the bulldog think that he has found the antidote to his bad luck, as he shows the kitten a 'good luck' horseshoe. Having tossed the horseshoe into the air, the bulldog is hit on the head by four horseshoes and the horse. Later, having scared the kitten into dropping the whistle, the bulldog intends to drop a safe from a great height on the black cat only, at the last minute, for the cat to slide across the animated 'x-marks-the-spot' so that the safe falls on to the bulldog. After further implausible skirmishes, the bulldog robs the cat of his powers by painting him white, only for the kitten to dive into a pot of black paint and assume the bad luck powers. Having swallowed the whistle, the bulldog is plagued by a bout of hiccups, each hiccup followed by objects of increasing size, houses, aeroplanes, battleships, falling on his head. The black cat awards the kitten his bowler hat as a mark of their collaborative triumph over the bulldog.

Bad Luck Blackie perfectly illustrates the ability of animation to defy material and emotional realities for comic effect, to 'deliberately juxtapose unusual and unexpected elements within nominally plausible, authentic and fictionally consistent environments' (Wells 2002a: 37). The mutability of the body within animation, whether animal or human, makes slapstick, comic gags and their amusing injuries an abiding stock-in-trade. Nothing in animation enjoys the permanence or suffers from the constraints that mark the world of live action, yet we remain anchored in a morally recognisable universe. What the bulldog inflicts on the kitten is sadistic, but what the black cat inflicts on the bulldog is justified retribution. At the end of *Bad Luck Blackie*, for all the insane injuries, the squashing and squeezing, the mutabilities and distortions, the improbabilities and impossibilities, the world is returned to a version of normal. Within such reassurance it is possible to find the antics not just witty and amusing but downright funny.

Chuck Jones joined Warner Bros in 1933 and became a director in 1939. Until he left them in 1963 to work for MGM, he did the main drawings for over 250 films, and supervised over fifty Bugs Bunny cartoons. His work was nominated fourteen times for an Academy Award and won three times. Jones attracted criticism that his work was too violent, in cartoons such as *To Duck or Not to Duck* (1943) featuring Daffy Duck and in his Wile E. Coyote Road Runner series, and this aspect of his work was given additional attention when it became a staple item on children's television in later decades. He defended himself, arguing that 'our basic goal in these films was to make people laugh ... and we certainly didn't have children in mind' (Lenburg 1993: 51).

Though Jones did use physical gags as stock-in-trade, much of the comedy in his cartoons comes from the strong characterisation of his leading 'stars'. Though Bugs Bunny cartoons had been directed earlier by other animators including Tex Avery and Friz Freleng, Jones makes him a more long-suffering 'counterrevolutionary', 'a little older, a little more subtle, a little more reluctant to get into contests – unmistakably an adult' (Barrier 1999: 489). If Bugs is always triumphant in outwitting enemies such as Elmer Fudd, Daffy Duck is altogether a much more incompetent character. Jones brought the two characters together in a number of cartoons, even if, as Barrier says, 'it was like watching circus aerialists perform without a net' (1999: 492).

One of Jones's most successful cartoons was *Duck Amuck* (1953), a comic meditation on the art of animation itself. Daffy enters dressed as a musketeer, singing against a painted background. Within seconds, the background disappears, fading to white. When Daffy eventually realises, he exits the frame, then pokes his head around the edge of the frame, asking 'whoever is in charge here, where's the scenery?' An animated paintbrush fills in a farm background. Daffy bounces back into frame, still dressed as a musketeer, and continues where he left off, before realising that the background has changed. Improvising, and saying to camera 'OK, have it your way', he changes into farmer's costume and struts along to the song 'Old MacDonald Had a Farm', only for the background to change yet again, causing him to sing 'on this farm he had an igloo'. Again, he turns to camera and asks whether 'we could make up our mind?' After two more such disruptions, Daffy again addresses the camera and starts to explain that 'this is an animated cartoon and in an animated cartoon …' Before he can finish, an animated pencil erases him. As the screen is left blank, Daffy's disembodied voice asks 'OK wise guy, where am I?' A paintbrush makes him reappear, this time as a guitar-playing cowboy, though when he plays a chord there is only silence. He holds up a note asking 'sound please'. The guitar makes a noise like a gun, a factory hooter, a donkey. Even Daffy's voice is replaced by animal noises. His body is erased and redrawn into a strange, concocted creature. As well as sound, Jones plays with other aspects of the cinematic form, extracting gags from the misuse of colour, from different shots including close-ups, from frame slippage and, when Daffy says 'let's get this picture started', by prematurely bringing up a title card announcing THE END. Later, the ease with which the unseen animator erases a parachute and substitutes an anvil and then, with a similar process, replaces the anvil with a bomb, serves to reinforce the instability and artificiality that characterises animation. The explosion leads an exasperated Daffy to demand who is responsible for all that has befallen him, but, even as he voices his demands, a paintbrush encases him with a door, which a pencil then shuts, once again obliterating Daffy. The 'person' responsible, it turns out, is none other than Bugs Bunny, who turns to camera and knowingly announces, 'ain't I a stinker!'

Duck Amuck is in some sense a return to that tradition of the self-reflexive cartoon of the early animation pioneers, although here the comedy stems from audience comfort and familiarity with the medium, not from amazement and novelty. Fragile though he and animation are, Daffy offers an assurance that, precisely because all things are possible, he and the medium are, in

Barrier's words, 'vividly, insistently alive' (Barrier 1999: 493).

Jones's penchant for comedy that springs from incompetence and powerlessness continued in the Road Runner series (1949–64), as Wile E. Coyote's endless attempts to trap the Road Runner end in failure. The gags are formulaic in nature and invariably physical, such as when Coyote gets trapped in the glue on the road that the Road Runner simply splashes through, or when, as he attempts to harpoon the Road Runner, Coyote's foot gets caught in the harpoon rope. Jones explained that 'the coyote is victimised by his own ineptitude … It is out of this mounting frustration that the comedy develops' (Lenburg 1993: 60). Frustration is the basis of Jones's *One Froggy Evening* (1955) when a demolition worker comes across a singing frog. Hoping to make his fortune, the frog resolutely refuses to sing and dance when it matters. Driven nearly insane with frustration, he bricks the frog up again. Years later in 2056, a futuristic 'building disintegrator' uncovers a frog that launches into a song and dance. In addition to the numerous sight gags and the comic sophistication of the frog's routine, the comedy comes from recurrent human folly that imagines it can order the world as we would like it to be.

The Academy Award-winning work of William Hanna (1910–2001) and Joseph Barbera (1911–2006) was significant not only for the *Tom and Jerry* cartoons produced at MGM from 1940 onwards but because they became the most important animation company producing cartoons for television from the late 1950s onwards. Though differentiation within each cartoon was important, *Tom and Jerry* centred on a basic comic formula, the 'natural' antagonism between cat and mouse. The cat, Tom, usually originates the chase, inflicting violence on Jerry the mouse in the attempt to catch him, but in the process Jerry manages to inflict sufficient damage on Tom to escape. The comedy is based on a string of very violent gags, involving Tom using poison, traps, guns, axes and other lethal weapons. Often the violence that Jerry inflicts on Tom involves the appropriation of domestic appliances, such as shutting him in a refrigerator or sticking his tail into an electrical socket.

Usually the effects of the violence inflicted are temporary, as the duo move on to the next gag. In *Heavenly Puss* (1949), however, the result of a piano crushing Tom appears to be fatal, as his spirit ascends the ghostly stairs to heaven. Denied access to the Heavenly Train, and scared by the vision of a hell run by his arch-enemy Spike the bulldog, Tom is given a chance to redeem himself by returning to Earth to seek Jerry's forgiveness. After a series of sight gags involving pens, ink, torn paper certificates and so on, Jerry does forgive Tom and the two are reconciled, only for Tom to awake and realise it has all been a dream. Normal comic, violent, antagonism between them returns. In *The Cat and the Mermouse* (1949) most of the gags occur under water, the 'impossible plausibility' being maintained when at the end of the cartoon Jerry pumps water out of Tom and the two are, once again, reconciled and ready for the next battle.

Following up: the evolution of animated comedy

☞ By looking at some of the earliest animated comedies produced by people such as McCay and the Fleischers, explain what you understand as their 'self-reflexive' quality. Why do you think this appealed to audiences at that time?

☞ By looking at animated cartoons from the late 1920s and early 1930s that introduced characters such as Mickey Mouse, Popeye and Bluto, analyse the extent to which much animated comedy of that period relied on visual gags and physical slapstick. In what ways did the subsequent introduction of 'personality animation' by Disney place greater emphasis on stronger story lines, narrative-based comedy and psychological and emotional realism?

☞ By looking closely at a cartoon such as *Bad Luck Blackie*, *Red Hot Riding Hood* or *Duck Amuck*, explain why such cartoons appealed to a more urban, modernist comic sensibility?

☞ To what extent do visual gags and physical slapstick remain important in animated comedy today?

Television, modernity and animated cartoons

Despite the Oscar-winning success of Hanna and Barbera's *Tom and Jerry* cartoons, the growth of television in the 1950s had a profound effect on the film industry, not least on animated shorts. Disney concentrated on feature-length animation and live-action features. The pared-down, modernist animation style emanating from UPA (United Productions of America) and the more cerebral comedy offered by their Mr Magoo and Gerald McBoing Boing characters enjoyed some success in the 1950s, but animated shorts for theatrical exhibition no longer made economic sense for the film industry. Even *Tom and Jerry* shot in Cinemascope could not stem the tide, and MGM abruptly closed its animation studios in 1957. By 1963 all the studios that had been involved in animation had stopped making shorts for cinemas.

Disney positively embraced the potential of television. So did Hanna and Barbera, though, in order to meet the quantity and cost demands from television, they reduced the animation, characters, dialogue and story lines to bare basics. This more limited animation signalled a shift away from the frenetic, action-packed gag comedy to a comedy that was more situation-based. Existing cartoon series, including a much less violent *Tom and Jerry*, continued to be produced for television and, together with reruns of old Warner Bros. and MGM, short animation cartoons came to be a staple item for children on American, British and western European television from the late 1950s onwards.

Hanna and Barbera enjoyed considerable success in 1958 with their *Huckleberry Hound* cartoons, which were syndicated across US television, and followed this with *Yogi Bear* (1961) and *The Flintstones* (1960–66). Both series incorporated catchphrases, Yogi declaring that he was 'smarter than the average bear', Fred Flintstone crying out 'yabba-dabba-do' when things were going right for him. In essence *The Flintstones* is an animated situation comedy influenced by live-action television shows such as *The Honeymooners* (1955–56) and *I Love Lucy* (1951–60) (see Chapter 5), and comes complete with its own laugh track. Fred and Wilma Flintstone and their friends Barney and Betty Rubble live in the stone-age town of Bedrock, but have all the characteristics, attitudes and desires of contemporary Americans, including a love of labour-saving devices. This incongruity lies at the heart of the comedy and was jarringly evident in the early black-and-white series where Fred and Barney promote the virtues of the programmes' sponsors, Marlborough cigarettes.

The comedy in *The Flintstones* operates at a variety of levels. There are frequent verbal puns throughout, with names such as Rocky, Quarry, Granite and even Stony Curtis. The characters visit 'Hollyrock' and go south of the border to 'Mexirock'. Visual gags ripple through the cartoons, especially in the ingenious ways in which animals are used to provide stone-age equivalents of modern domestic appliances, such as the baby mammoth used as a vacuum cleaner, or the pelican with a beak of soapy water that is used as a washing machine. Fred has a car, but it is propelled by his own legs running on the floor. Though these offer constant comic pleasures, much of the comedy springs from the modern attitudes displayed by these stone-age characters, not least in the realm of sexual politics, as Fred and Barney often engage in activities behind their wives' backs, or try exert their male authority only to be made to apologise to Wilma and Betty later when their ill-fated schemes go wrong. Tellingly, Fred's authority is undermined during the closing credits of every episode when, attempting to put out the sabre-toothed 'cat' for the night, he is himself dumped outside the door of his own house. If Wilma and Betty are not the 'imprisoning wives' that King sees in some silent film comedy (2002: 130), they are representative of the growing power of women in the 1960s, the decade that ushered in the feminist movement. Of course all this is treated light-heartedly, but the incongruous pleasures of a stone-age mirror held up to contemporary attitudes only serves to endorse the American love affair with materialism. The comedy serves to affirm American ideals and culture, so it is not surprising that *The Flintstones* became the first primetime television animated series to last more than two seasons, a record that was not surpassed by another primetime animated series until the third season of *The Simpsons* in 1992. The series was rebroadcast on US and British television for several seasons and *The Flintstones* have been the subject of three feature films and countless spin-offs and specials, generating substantial consumer merchandise.

Throughout the 1960s and 1970s reruns of existing stock cartoons from Disney, Warner Bro and MGM, along with new animated cartoons such as *Top Cat*, *The Jetsons*, *Wacky Races*, *Scooby Doo*, Bob Godfrey's *Roobarb and Custard* and Cosgrove Hall's *Dangermouse* became a staple item on children's terrestrial television and in the 1980s and 1990s, with the coming of cable, satellite and then digital television, on specialist channels such as the BBC's children's channels, Cartoon Network and its offshoot Boomerang.

Following up: animated comedy on television

☞ The Disney studio's concentration on feature-length animation for cinematic theatrical release coincided with the rise of television and the shift towards television as a means of exhibiting shorter animated cartoons. By looking at a series such as *The Flintstones*, analyse to what extent this shift was accompanied by changes in animation aesthetics and a greater emphasis on comedy that was situation-based.

☞ To what extent does the notion of incongruity help to explain the success of *The Flintstones* and its comedy?

☞ Animated cartoons became a staple item on television screens in the 1960s and 1970s. List as many of these programmes and cartoon series as you can. By concentrating on one or two of these, say why you think that 'cartoons' became associated with children's viewing to the exclusion of adult audiences.

Postmodern comedy and the changing audience for animation

The assumption that children were the only audience for animated comedy began to change in the late 1970s as the nature of animated comedy itself was changing. Having produced the witty and whimsical claymation figure of *Morph* for children's television, Aardman studios in the UK produced *Animated Conversations* for the BBC in 1978, *Conversation Pieces* for Channel Four in 1982 and Nick Park's *Creature Comforts* in 1989. In *Creature Comforts* the sardonic humour produced by animals in a zoo speaking in actual human voices about their pleasures, trials and tribulations appealed to adults as much as children. Park went on to produce the enormously successful short claymation series featuring Wallace and Gromit, including *A Grand Day Out* (1989), *The Wrong Trousers* (1993) and *A Close Shave* (1995). Here the comedy is focused on the relationship between the cheese-loving, aspiring inventor Wallace and his intuitively astute and more intelligent dog Gromit. As in *The Flintstones*, much of the comedy lies in cod-technology and the ways in which it gets Wallace into trouble, before having to be rescued by Gromit.

Hollywood money was invested in Park's feature-length *Chicken Run* (2000), the story of a chicken farm told from the perspective of the chickens in a narrative that parodies both live-action Second World War prison camp drama and conventional romantic comedy. The chickens' natural desire to escape is given urgency – and creates comic suspense – when they slowly begin to realise that they are being fattened up for chicken pies. Though the unfolding of the narrative is a major source of the film's comedy, character-based jokes (the dim-witted Babs) and a series of visual and verbal gags (some, but not all, coming from the two cockney-underworld rats), as well as slapstick comedy (as when the pie machine blows up) are all important. Led by Ginger and with the help of an escaped 'American' chicken Rocky (voiced by Mel Gibson), the chickens finally succeed in their escape plan by making use of a cobbled-together flying machine, an ultimate *deus ex machina* for birds that, as we know even if they don't, cannot fly.

In *Chicken Run*, as in the CGI animated features that preceded and followed, narrative structure, and the different hierarchies of knowledge they contain or allow, are used for comic effect. Comic surprises and the comedy that comes from frustration can be delivered by concealing information, either from characters within the diegesis or from the audience. For example, as they attempt their escape, the film reveals that Fowler, who we (and his fellow chickens) have been led to believe is an experienced war veteran, has never flown a plane in his life. In the same way the charming allure of Rocky is undercut by our later knowledge that he has escaped from a circus and is not the heroic figure that he initially paints himself as. Yet, in the final analysis, it is the triumphant efforts of the chickens, all of whom are imbued with characteristics we normally regard as the sole preserve of humans beings, whether the frail, the dim-witted, the boastful or the truly brave, that provide the film's comic appeal. The award-winning success of *Chicken Run* has been followed by other animated comedies from Park, including the feature *Wallace and Gromit: The Curse of the Were-Rabbit* (2005) and *A Matter of Loaf and Death* (2008).

The work of Nick Park contains comedic elements which work at a variety of levels, appealing to a wide-ranging audience, not just children. With the production of television animated sitcoms such as *The Simpsons*, *King of the Hill*, *Family Guy* and *South Park* throughout the 1990s and beyond, animation was no longer regarded as simply children's entertainment. Together such programmes reflect a shift in comic sensibility towards cynicism, irony and often stringent parody, towards a subversive postmodern comedy that reflects a perceived fragmentary, amoral and dysfunctional world populated by complex and often contradictory identities. The most iconic of all contemporary cartoon characters, Homer Simpson, is 'boorish, incompetent, lazy, uncaring, unintelligent and destructive. [He] is also the opposite of all those things' (Ortved 2009: 285).

Beginning life on *The Tracey Ullman Show* in 1987, *The Simpsons* debuted as a series in its own right in 1989. Currently in its twenty-second season, it is now the longest-running television entertainment show, has spawned the feature-length animated *The Simpsons Movie* in 2007 and has had an impact not just on other animated television shows but on culture at large. Though each episode includes a plethora of throwaway jokes and sight gags, as well as catchphrases like Homer's 'D-oh!' and Bart's 'eat my shorts', much of the show's comedy resides in the deluge of cultural references drawn from television, films, music, newspapers, historical events, politics, religion, sport and science, much of which is treated in a sardonically comic fashion, as when Homer tosses a glowing green radioactive nugget out of the car in the opening titles sequence. Serious issues such as race and gender are treated with comic incision which simultaneously raises a laugh and makes a point, as in the 1991 episode from series three, 'Stark Raving Dad'. A temporary inmate of the 'New Bedlam Home for the Emotionally Interesting', as a result of wearing a pink shirt to work, Homer befriends a tall, plump white man who claims to be Michael Jackson. Released from the home, 'Michael' writes a song for Lisa, as Homer has forgotten to buy her a birthday present. Though 'Michael' confesses to being Leon Kompowsky, a bricklayer, the fact that the character is actually voiced by the real Michael Jackson adds a knowingly comic meta-textual element. The understated comment on homophobia is overshadowed by the episode's treatment of Michael Jackson, his well-documented skin pigmentation treatments and the issue of race and colour which these raised, but the fact that Jackson himself is party to the satirical comedy is indicative of the complex postmodern comedy which saturates *The Simpsons*.

'Stark Raving Dad' is also a reminder that much of the comedy stems from the impossibly comic struggle to match the image of the perfect family that the media industry creates. Homer is a dysfunctional father who can inflict terrible neglect upon his children, but can then be immensely proud when Bart improves his grade F in maths to a D. Frequently, Bart's delinquency gets the family in trouble with the law and, in the process, offers a wry comment on how difficult being a parent can be. In 'The Parent Rap' (series thirteen, 2001) Bart steals a police squad car after Homer has made him walk to school. Brought up before a punitive locum judge, the whole family is punished before the regular judge returns from a fishing trip, absolves the family and declares 'boys will be boys'. Apart from the comic ironies of family life, the episode also points home the arbitrary nature of justice. Lisa's intelligence offers continuous comic criticism of the shortcomings of her family, especially Homer. In 'Any Given Sundance' (series nineteen, 2008) her filmic ruminations on her dysfunctional family detract from the initial pleasure that they have from her award-winning documentary screened at the Sundance Festival.

A number of writers have noted the strong self-reflexive quality of *The Simpsons* and the extent to which it is aware of its own status as a television show. Both Krusty the Clown and the brutal, blood-soaked 'in-show' cartoons, Itchy and Scratchy, with their ironic comic reference to animated series such as *Tom and Jerry*, are evidence of this. Another key component of this very postmodern comedy is the use of celebrity voices and animated characters, ranging from film, television and sports stars to rock bands and politicians. This ironic self-referential humour, in which celebrities can joke at the expense of their own image and status, has become less important in recent series, but has made a major contribution to the show's success, a success which encouraged the US television networks in the 1990s to develop other animated comedy series, including *South Park*, *Family Guy*, *King of the Hill* and *Futurama.*

Following up: animated comedy and the family audience

☞ Assess the contribution of Aardman Animation and Nick Park in creating animated comedy that appealed to a wider family audience. Drawing upon theories of comedy that you have encountered, explain how this appeal is constructed either in a Wallace and Gromit vehicle or in *Chicken Run*.

☞ *The Simpsons* is arguably the most successful animated comedy series on television. By analysing aspects of the show's comedy, explain why it is so successful. Concentrating on one or two specific episodes, what does it mean to describe *The Simpsons* as a 'subversive postmodern comedy'?

Feature animated comedies and the triumph of CGI

Toy Story (1995) was the culmination of a series of increasingly sophisticated computer-animated shorts produced by Pixar Animation Studios from 1984 onwards, and marked a landmark in the development of animated comedy. Under the animator John Lasseter, shorts such as *Luxo Jr.* (1986) and *Tin Toy* (1988) picked up awards and led Disney to suggest that Pixar make a feature-length animation and eventually to buy the company. *Toy Story* and its sequels, *Toy Story 2* (1999) and *Toy Story 3* (2010), are all narrative-based comedies designed for a family audience. Strong comedy narratives are evident in these early Pixar shorts such as *Knick Knack* (1989) in which a toy ornament snowman encased in a 'Nome Sweet Nome Alaska' domed plastic bubble tries to respond to the come-on call from a plastic blonde in a bikini who adorns the edge of a 'Sunny Miami' ornamental ashtray. Bounded by his plastic bubble, the snowman tries various ways through a series of sight gags to break free from his imprisonment, without success. When the ornament finally tips off the edge of the furniture and, falling, the snowman appears to break free from the bubble, he lands in a goldfish bowl, where an equally seductive mermaid beckons him. Just as he advances, his old bubble prison lands on top of him and he is frustrated once more. The comedy comes not just from a series of sight gags, the 'Palm Springs' ornament as a swaying plastic palm tree on a spring base, for example, or the snowman's increasingly frenetic and failing attempts to escape using hammers, blow-torches and TNT explosives, but from the cruel narrative symmetry of the snowman's return to his imprisonment and the frustration of his desires, all beautifully and sardonically undercut by the soothing soundtrack from Bobby McFerrin.

All three feature-length *Toy Story* films are more sophisticated than this, but much of the comedy emanates from the basic narrative premise that the toys are alive except when their owner Andy is around. This central conceit provides a treasure chest of comic possibilities which are mercilessly exploited. Like the anthropomorphic animal characters of classic cartoons over the decades, Woody, Buzz Lightyear and all the other toys have distinguishing human characteristics which render them amusing, including the many facial configurations endured by Mr Potato Head. Whilst such slapstick is designed to appeal primarily (though not exclusively, of course) to children, the comic appeal to adults comes partly from the fact that these toys experience metaphysical crises of identity, as when Buzz is forced to confront his reality as a toy, and when they are faced with rejection and possible redundancy when Andy no longer needs them. Unlike *The Simpsons*, the characters across the *Toy Story* franchise do age with time, lending, particularly in *Toy Story 3*, a comic pathos which is moving, redeemed partly by the sense of renewal when the toys are given by Andy to a new owner, Bonnie. There is a knowingness about the comedy and the faux-terror posed by such characters as Lotso, the Care Bear who, for reasons that are explained to us, have gone over to the 'dark side', and the marauding destruction of looming Big Baby, a straight pinch from the early Pixar short *Tin Toy*. This postmodern comic knowingness is epitomised in *Toy Story 3*, when Ken and Barbie declare that 'it's as if we were made for each other', as, of course, they were.

The commercial and critical success of *Toy Story* inaugurated a deluge of feature-length CGI animated comedies, including *Antz* (1998) and *A Bug's Life* (1998). In 2001 a 'Best Animated Feature' category was introduced at the Oscars, with the proviso that the award would be presented only if a minimum of eight animated features had been given theatrical release that year. The winners, including *Shrek* (2001), *Finding Nemo* (2003), *The Incredibles* (2004), *Happy Feet* (2006), *Ratatouille* (2007) and *WALL-E* (2008), suggest the depth and popularity of animated comedy features as a distinctive genre.

Dreamworks' 2001 winner, *Shrek* launched the franchise series *Shrek 2* (2004), *Shrek The Third* (2007) and *Shrek Forever After* (2010), based on a book described by the screenwriters as a 'Jungian journey of self-discovery and self-fulfilment' (Clarke 2004: 212). Exploiting the postmodern comedic potential of classic favourite fairy tales and characters such as Pinocchio, Puss in Boots, the Three Blind Mice, Prince Charming and the Fairy Godmother, the series offers an extended and heartfelt diatribe against intolerance, ignorance and fear of 'otherness'. In the process it employs a wealth of jokes, puns, slapstick, sight gags and narrative shifts, along with strong voiceover performances, music and song. The basis of the comedy is incongruity, not just of the green, over-sized ogre who is actually gentler and more caring than the 'humans' around him but in the dissonance that stems from a thoroughly contemporary sensibility at odds with the fairy-tale setting of the films. In *Shrek 2*, as Shrek and Fiona trundle their way in a horse-drawn cart to meet Princess Fiona's parents in Far Far Away, the loquacious Donkey (voiced by Eddie Murphy) complains that there is no 'in-flight movie'. As they arrive, their destination signalled by a Hollywood hills lookalike sign, they pass a 'Vesarchery' boutique shop and posters for 'Tower of London Records', stopping at a Friar's Drive-In and ordering the 'medieval meal', a clear reference to McDonald's and its 'specialist' fast-food meals. These and other sight gags, such as the recurrent physical mishaps endured by the Three Blind Mice, ripple throughout the film. The film is punctuated by one-off jokes, as when, attacked by Puss in Boots, Donkey tells Shrek not to feel bad since 'almost everyone you meet wants to kill you'. Later, organising the banquet, the King tastes a dish held by a footman and declares it delicious, asking what it is; the footman replies 'that would be the dog's breakfast, your majesty'. Comic incongruous references to the contemporary world abound, as when the Fairy Godmother's answerphone declares 'I'm either away from my desk or with a client'. When captured by the palace guard, Puss in Boots is the victim of planted drugs, clearly placed there by the arresting officers. Prince Charming is anything but charming and his mother, the Fairy Godmother, is a conniving and malevolent force intent on evil self-gain.

Following up: feature-length animated comedy

☞ Compare a drawn or 'cel' cartoon from the 1930s or 1940s with a recent CGI animation. What types of comedy do the different techniques of animation lend themselves to?

☞ Why do you think feature-length animated comedies aimed at a family audience have been so successful at the box office in recent years?

☞ The *Shrek* franchise films rely on jokes, puns, slapstick, sight gags and narrative shifts in ways animated comedy always has done, yet they clearly appeal to a contemporary audience sensibility. What is this appeal?

The *Shrek* films are arguably the most purely comedic of all the recent animated feature-length productions. Though they do have a serious message for those who care to engage with it, they lack the sentimentality and pathos that is a regular component of the majority of such films, including the 2009 Academy Award winner *Up*.

Up (2009)

Produced by Pixar Animation and distributed by Walt Disney Pictures in 2009, *Up* was the first animated film ever to open the Cannes Film Festival. The film won two Academy Awards in 2010, for Best Animated Feature and Best Original Score. The director Pete Docter reportedly felt that the worldview of an elderly protagonist offered considerable comic possibilities, and both Carl and the young Russell speak their minds and react to events in ways that speak of experience and innocence. Both are bounded by physical limitations, which lead to moments of slapstick humour as well as to the growth of a respectful and caring relationship. One critic was of the view that 'there are scenes in *Up* of such beauty, economy and poetic wisdom that they belong in an anthology of great movie moments' (LaSalle 2009) and, to an extent, these threaten to displace the comic moments that pepper the film.

In a wonderfully elliptic opening, *Up* charts the relationship between tomboy Ellie and Carl Fredricksen, both obsessed with the exploits of heroic explorer Charles Muntz and his travel to Paradise Falls in South America. The couple pledge to visit the remote location but, after a childless marriage and Ellie's death, the aged Carl is left bereft, alone and literally isolated, his house surrounded by skyscrapers being built around it. Faced with a move to the Shady Oakes Retirement Village, Carl rebels and, drawing on his experience as a balloon salesman, sails away in his house suspended by a giant bunch of balloons. On board is a child stowaway, the inept Russell, who hopes to become a 'Senior' in the Wilderness Explorers. They make it to Paradise Falls, encounter an aged Charles Muntz who, surrounded by ferocious talking dogs, has gone over to the dark side in his attempt to capture a rare flightless bird, named by Russell as 'Kevin'. Confronted by Muntz and, after some hair-raising moments centred on Muntz's airship, Carl and Russell escape, accompanied by daft but friendly and loyal dog Dug. Back home, Russell achieves his promotion to 'Senior', with surrogate parent Carl in attendance. The two sit on a kerb eating ice-cream, Carl with a purpose in life, Russell with the parental love he has lacked as a result of his parents' divorce.

Amidst the genuinely affecting sentiment and pathos, *Up* interlaces a plethora of comic moments. Some of these are in the form of jokes, as when the men who call to collect Carl to take him to the retirement home are fooled by his request to 'go to the bathroom'. Sight gags ripple through the film. Carl uses a frog as an alarm clock, the overweight Russell labours ineffectually to climb a rope, Carl turns off his hearing-aid in order to cut out Russell's incessant stream of talk, Russell accidentally throws his navigational GPS device out of the window, Muntz's dogs serve food and wine at table and, overcome by a sword-bearing Muntz who tells Carl to 'spit out his last words', Carl gets away by literally spitting out his false teeth at him. Much of the comedy comes from the characterisation of Russell, who at the very beginning is shown as being not very bright, physically incapable and highly inquisitive, but cutely endearing in his childlike innocence. His first contact with Carl is when Carl shuts the door in his face. Undaunted, he simply begins all over again, worming his way into Carl's – and our – affections.

Up perhaps represents something of the current state of feature-length animated comedies, the influence of what has been referred to as the 'Disney aesthetic' ensuring that comedy mixes with sentimentality and pathos, that narrative becomes central and that there is a moralising cuteness at the heart of the film. On the other hand, the history of animated comedy teaches us that, in this most flexible and plastic of all forms, anything is possible.

Following *Up*

☞ Analyse the different types of comedy at work in *Up*. To what extent are they dependent upon the incongruous physical limitations of an elderly man and an obese boy? How typical of contemporary feature animation do you think *Up* is in combining a range of generic references and conventions? What other animated features do this and what does it contribute to the comedy? What do you see as the role of sentiment and pathos in *Up* compared to other animated comedies?

Recommended reading

Michael Barrier, *Hollywood Cartoons: American Animation in Its Golden Age*, Oxford: Oxford University Press, 1999.

Paul Wells, *Animation and America*, Edinburgh: Edinburgh University Press, 2002.

PART II

Themes, effects and impact of comedy

8

Comedy, gender and sexuality

In this chapter we focus on the ways film and television comedy have presented gender and sexuality. These subjects cross over in more ways than one.

Gender is an issue of difference and difference has continually proved difficult for human cultures to negotiate. Patriarchal culture, that is, society which is structured in order to give the male sex many advantages over the female, has only gradually been revised in western nations and its biases still remain in place. The self-interest that informs the continuance of patriarchal power has its ultimate grounding in the difference between the sexes which must, therefore, be rigidly defined. Sexual difference is regulated and reinforced culturally by the societies in which we live: men are supposed to act in a masculine way, women in a feminine way. But while biological sex is, by and large, fixed, gender is culturally constructed *as if* it were both natural and fixed. In fact these artificial distinctions can be questioned, as Judith Butler argues: 'If gender is the cultural meanings that the sexed body assumes, then a gender cannot be said to follow from a sex in any one way. Taken to its logical limit, the sex/gender distinction suggests a radical discontinuity between sexed bodies and culturally constructed genders' (2006: 9). The addition of gender, the attempted association of a set of characteristics to sex, can be seen as a somewhat blatant imposition. As Eve Kosofsky Sedgwick reminds us: 'gender and genitals we have always with us; but ... the meanings and substance of gender and genitals are embodied in times and institutions' (1985: 47).

Patriarchal society's institutions and rules actually shift and adjust over time, in order to maintain hegemony, while continuing to imply a timelessness to their authority. As such they have always been ripe for comedic exploration. The ancient tradition of males performing female roles on stage illustrates the ambivalence of these rules. In Ancient Greek theatre (as well as Shakespearian theatre) men played the female roles because the gender roles assigned to women were such that they were not allowed to act on stage (i.e. were banned from performing anything other than the role society assigned them), but successful imitations expose the artificiality of the particular construction of femininity. Such conventions survive in pantomime with its dames and principal boys and were a device regularly drawn on in music hall, familiar to players from that tradition such as Stan Laurel (see Sanders 1995). Drag performances cause laughter by contradicting the supposed essentialism of gender. In British comedy, dressing as a woman was the mainstay of Arthur Lucan as Old Mother Riley and this tradition has established performers like Norman Evans, Danny laRue, Barry Humphries (as Dame Edna Everage) and Paul O'Grady (as Lily Savage), and has been a resource for television sketch comedians from very varied backgrounds, from Dick Emery and Les Dawson to the performers of *Monty Python's Flying Circus*, *The League of Gentleman* and *Little Britain*. Drag offers a carnivalesque exception to the everyday norms of gender performance, but one which is ambivalent and which ultimately denies permanent conditions (just as carnival shows that there is an alternative to the status quo while returning to it). In mainstream film comedy drag is rare but memorable, including examples in *I Was a Male War Bride* (1949), *Some Like It Hot* (1959), *Tootsie* (1982), *Mrs Doubtfire* (1993) and *Big Momma's House* (2000). In each case there is considerable effort made to stabilise the (hetero-) sexuality of the central character (see King 2002: 141–2). However, *Priscilla, Queen of the Desert* (1994), a smaller film with three male characters in drag, had more room to allow a range of sexualities. Yet, as Butler says: 'no correlation can be drawn ... between drag or transgender and sexual practice, and the distribution of hetero-, bi-, and homo- inclinations cannot be predictably mapped onto the travels of gender bending or changing' (2006: xiv–xv). Gender is performance but sexuality is practice.

Recent examples of cross-gender performance in British sketch comedy include female comics French and Saunders playing fat old men lusting madly after anything in skirt (see Williams 1998: 161), Reeves and Mortimer's middle-aged Geordies in donkey jackets concerned with bras and paranoid about slights to their bust size ('Are you sayin' I've got nowt?') and *Little Britain*'s 'lady' Emily Howard played by David Walliams as a contemporary transvestite in eighteenth-century costume forever giving the game away by succumbing to the temptations of stereotypically male activities.

These examples all present one gender apparently fascinated by the other but adopting their perceived characteristics badly. Drag performance challenges the audience as to what is the correct reaction to the mixed signals of men performing as women and women performing as men. While it may elicit numerous responses, for it to be outright comic it appears essential that the performance is less, rather than more, convincing. Cross-dressing might 'only' be an indicator of the comic nature of the performance in many instances, but the laughter it produces is nevertheless ambivalent. What exactly are we laughing at? Alexander Doty suggests that: 'as a genre comedy is fundamentally queer, since it encourages rule-breaking, risk-taking, inversions and perversions in the face of straight patriarchal norms' (1995: 334). Cross-dressing for comic effect is an exemplar of this aspect of comedy, revealing patriarchal society's obsession with gender and sexuality, and problematising its supposed certainties about masculinity and femininity. To examine what comedy tells us about Anglo-American attitudes to gender and sexuality, we focus initially on the representation of femininity in film romantic comedy, picking up on the genre after the Second World War. From there we move on to discuss masculinity, and representations of sexuality in film and television comedy.

Following up: comedy in drag

☞ Drag demonstrates that one gender can perform as another, but consider how particular examples vary in how they play this comedically. Is male–female drag a celebration of male adaptability or a joke at the expense of male limitations? What is it about undermining the conventions of gender that is funny?

Femininity as represented in film romantic comedy

We have discussed in Chapter 3 the development, conventions and industrial context of the romantic comedy as established in the 1930s and continued into the early 1940s. Here we follow its later development, focusing on its particular portrayals of femininity in the postwar period.

After the Second World War women who had worked during wartime were encouraged back into the home, and film comedy and its romantic sub-genre both reflected and encouraged these changes. The retrenching of conservative attitudes to gender (see Glitre 2006: 93–8) is illustrated in the caricaturing and infantilising of women in their comedic representations. In *How to Marry a Millionaire* (1953) the three female leads play models (that is, they are for looking at) on the make who scam their way into an expensive furnished flat to use it as a base in their quest for millionaire husbands. Although this sounds enterprising, all three characters are written as mercenary and dim, even stupid, though the calibre of the stars playing them (Lauren Bacall, Betty Grable and Marilyn Monroe) tends to dignify them. Bacall, in particular, has a vocal delivery so urbane that she is capable of making virtually any line sound as though it were witty.

How to Marry a Millionaire was a prestige picture and the first comedy in Cinemascope, which explains its unlikely eight-minute orchestral overture and the gratuitous scenes which suit that format (planes landing, mountain snowscapes and model parades). The key sequence, however, is the one in which Grable's character, Loco, is recruited into the scheme. The other girls are broke and they invite her up as long as she can feed them on the 25 cents she has and whatever else she can use her sex appeal to acquire. The guy who helps her, pays for and carries up her groceries is the handsome Tom

Brookman (Cameron Mitchell) whom Schatze (Bacall) immediately dismisses as strictly petrol pump attendant material. The film then shows him returning to the office building he owns, so undercutting Bacall's wisdom. But, despite this, the film doesn't question what her character outlines to her co-conspirators: marriage 'is the biggest thing you can do in life' and 'If you don't marry you haven't caught him, he's caught you'. What it does undermine is 'It's your head you've got to use, not your heart'. Following her head, Schatze almost marries an elderly, widowed Texan millionaire J.D. Hanley (William Powell), but finally gives in to Tom Brookman and marries him, despite still thinking he works as a petrol pump attendant. When he pays for their greasy spoon reception meal of hamburger and onions she faints at the sight of his wad. So do the other girls, though they have ended up with a forest ranger and a short-sighted tax dodger after their excursions with a married millionaire and a fraudster. The intent of the film appears to be to remind us that monetary or class considerations are less important than compatibility. Brookman identifies Schatze as 'strictly a hamburger and onions dame' early on, she just has to realise it, and the man who fits her is *symbolically* a millionaire. Through their *literal* demands the film protrays its female characters as both mercenary and dumb, full of unreasonable expectations that prevent their own happiness. The film's most memorable gag is Monroe's Pola displaying herself, gorgeously dressed in a magenta satin gown, in multiple reflections in a nightclub 'powder room' then walking into a wall as she tries to leave because she won't wear her spectacles, believing they make her look plain. It is a surprisingly direct correlation of the link between the male gaze of the camera and the punishment of its subject and marks a considerable change in attitude from *It Happened One Night* (see Chapter 3) which punished the viewer's representative.

Ed Sikov, writing about the comedies of the 1950s in *Laughing Hysterically*, sums *How to Marry a Millionaire* up in two words, 'slick, forced' (1994: 3), while he focuses instead on an auteur-based grouping of films (from Hawks, Hitchcock, Wilder and Tashlin). He is right to argue for the importance of the comedies of the decade, and its romantic comedies are hugely revealing about contemporary attitudes to gender. Sikov is also right to see 'patriarchy in protracted decline' during the 1950s, lashing out (1994: 244) with what can be a shocking degree of misogyny.

Kathleen Rowe (1995) highlights representations of women from the 1930s to the 1990s and traces key roles which manage to avoid the patriarchal stereotypes of unattainable virgins and madonna figures on the one hand and threatening monsters or femmes fatales on the other. She calls these non-stereotypes 'unruly women': 'the unruly woman often enjoys a reprieve from those fates that so often seem inevitable to women under patriarchy, because her home is comedy and the carnivalesque, the realm of inversion and fantasy where, for a time at least, the ordinary world can be stood on its head' (1995: 10). This is a concept we shall return to, but the 'problem' of such female independence is a constant in mid-twentieth-century comic representations of femininity.

Historical hindsight allows us to see short, recurring cycles within cinema and television comedy in which the sexualised, unconventional woman appears as an uncanny being who needs to be tamed through romance and domesticity. The 1940s films such as *I Married a Witch* (1941), *One Touch of Venus* (1948) in which a statue comes to life, the British film *Miranda* (1948: see Ashby 2000) and *Mr Peabody and the Mermaid* (1948), both featuring mermaids, all show female protagonists as both supernaturally attractive but inhuman. In the 1960s US television offered fantasy sitcoms such as *Bewitched* (1964–72), which played out the logic of *I Married a Witch* with witch as housewife, and *I Dream of Jeannie* (1965–70) (see Chapter 5). Later still, the film *Splash!* (1984) successfully returned to the mermaid and *Weird Science* (1985) resurrected the perfect artificial woman. The representation of gender difference as supernatural is, of course, not the only way to confront it. Film as a medium may be seen to provide invariably iconic images of glamorous and untouchable female sexuality precisely in order to police this power.

Laura Mulvey argued in her seminal 1975 essay 'Visual Pleasure and Narrative Cinema' (1993a) that Hollywood cinema constructed women as passive, to-be-looked-at, presented for the pleasure of the male viewer. There has been much debate and extension of this essay (including Studlar (1988), Doane (1987) and Mulvey (1993b)), but its utility here extends only as far as its relevance to film comedy. Rowe (1995) shifts away from Mulvey's Lacanian analysis of melodrama and looks at the implications of 'the genres of laughter' for her model of spectatorship. Rowe wonders, for example, if laughter is structured, like the male gaze, at female expense or whether enjoying comedy requires a female audience to engage in 'transvestitism' (1995: 6). Because Mulvey's original essay seeks to promote an alternative (Mulvean) cinema as a necessary antidote to mainstream cinema it homogenises that mainstream as part of a single male cultural psyche. The exclusion in Mulvey's argument that gives most concern here is that of the self-awareness of sophisticated filmmakers and performers. The male gaze revealed by psychoanalytic criticism is an artistic or narrative convention within a business practice which, it is argued, has developed and been adopted because it fits in with the psychology of patriarchal culture. This doesn't allow for individual filmmakers and participants seeing the conventions and exploiting or subverting them. Mulvey counters with: 'However self-conscious and ironic Hollywood managed to be, it always restricted itself to a formal *mise en scène* reflecting the dominant ideological concept of the cinema' (1993a: 113). But this tends to fix mainstream Hollywood product as though it were a constant restatement of a position rather than an ongoing negotiation with patriarchal hegemony.

Mulvey's argument suffers from what Butler calls 'the totalizing gestures of feminism' (2006: 18) compounded by its use of critical psychoanalysis which, as Sedgwick complains, 'seemed to promise to introduce a certain becoming amplitude into discussions of what different people are like – only to turn, in its streamlined trajectory across so many institutional boundaries, into the sveltest of metatheoretical disciplines, sleeked down to such elegant operational entities as *the* mother, *the* father, *the* pre-oedipal, *the* oedipal, *the* other or Other' (1990: 24). It is one thing to discuss cultural psychology, but occasionally the slippage is too great; to state that *the* unconscious is 'formed by the dominant order' (Mulvey 1993a: 112) is a step too far. Certainly the dominant order determines much that is to be repressed within the unconscious but not specific contents or drives.

Sikov draws out the ambivalence with which the female stars were depicted in the film comedies of the 1950s. He shows how in the musical romantic comedy *Gentlemen Prefer Blondes* (1953) the male characters remain peripheral and dull and how the two stars at the centre (Jane Russell and Marilyn Monroe) are both fetishised and powerful in their performances as mercenary women. Another take on the plot of *Gentlemen Prefer Blondes* is *The French Line* (1954), a cheaper RKO musical comedy in which Russell is an heiress travelling incognito and being courted by Gilbert Roland. Money isn't the issue here, putting it aside is: Russell is a proactive female character seeking to be valued for herself. Though the Code prohibited costumes that showed cleavage, the spectacle of the show numbers nevertheless focuses on the female form. The film's strap-line was 'JR in 3D: It'll knock both your eyes out'. The Catholic Legion of Decency found the film offensive, even after Russell's pelvic thrusts were hidden behind obtrusive scenery. The number 'Looking for Trouble (If Trouble Looks like a Man)' is a downright violent expression of female sexuality (which the hero largely misses through being elsewhere, on his way to the scene). Even if the mechanical gaze of the camera may continue to fetishise Russell, the male gaze of the audience has different responses available. Sikov, drawing on Studlar (1988), shows how such imagery goes beyond Mulvey's argument about the spectacle of women being held by the male gaze to avoid the psychological threat of castration. Female sex symbols of the 1950s such as Jane Russell or, in Sikov's prime example, Jayne Mansfield in *Will Success Spoil Rock Hunter?* (1957) are the source of numerous gags focusing on the breasts as signifiers of gender. Sikov adds pre-Oedipal (pre-gendered) identification and the concept of 'the breast as screen' to Mulvey's ideas, emphasising the ambivalent experience of 'joy/terror'. In the 'pleasurable blurring of ego boundaries in the cinema' we see that:

> Just as babies enjoy a psychic fusion with the mother as they nurse, so do the limitations of adult object relationships melt away under the authority of the screen's images in general and the image of Mansfield's breasts in particular. Following this psychological model, the men [in the film sequence] not only want Jayne sexually; they want to be Jayne sexually, presexually, at any phase sexually. (Sikov 1994: 219–20)

Comedy films such as the ones mentioned are very conscious of the power of the look, and even highlight its impact. We do not have to accept Sikov's argument in its entirety to recognise that there are at least alternative psychoanalytic readings of audience reactions. In other words, a comic text can often prompt a whole different set of responses to the depiction of gender difference on screen.

Female sexuality (encoded in the female form) becomes not uncanny as in some texts but 'excessive and implausible' in the comedy performances of Marilyn Monroe, 'like Mae West before her' (King 2002: 140). Rowe (1995: 179) sees these two stars as 'antithetical versions of the blonde sex goddess', the brassy, quipping West contrasting with the rich vulnerability of Monroe (178). While West's knowing sexuality exasperated the advocates of the Production Code in the early 1930s, the ambiguous levels of self-awareness of Monroe's characters allowed her to succeed in the 1950s and remain an icon long beyond the period (see Dyer 1998). Yet all the female sex symbols of the decade, including Monroe, Russell (who wears a blonde wig to impersonate Monroe in *Gentlemen Prefer Blondes*) and Mansfield, rode to fame on the crest of 1950s hysteria about gender. Their desirability and its power become simultaneously threatening and ridiculous because a comedic context both recognises the power and defuses the 'threat' of female sexuality with 'it's only a joke'. Looking at representations of women of all ages Laraine Porter argues:

> While masculinity is also understood as a construct, this is understood as the norm, with femininity a perverse deviation. Mocking the woman is also a way of disavowing her threat to masculinity, to freedom, to control, to order – all that masculinity holds dear and needs to maintain in order to shore itself up against all odds. (1998: 93)

Putting women on a pedestal and knocking them off because, on closer examination, they are not men is the game described here. Yet the fetishisation which is meant to constrain the uncanny power of female sexuality reckons without the humanity of its subjects. None of these comedic performers is ultimately contained by the camera. The destabilising effects of comedy on the boundary between spectator and subject (see discussion of on-screen glances in the work of Laurel and Hardy and the Marx Brothers during Chapter 2) mean that while appearing on screen enmeshed in numerous patriarchal discourses (visual, narratorial, historical, cultural, psychological) they are still understood to be (or have been) people who cannot be fully assimilated within those discourses. This is not to deny that the constructions of femininity offered in classical Hollywood cinema are not severely limited or to suggest that the female body is not fetishised and exploited. Yet a restatement of Mulvey's argument in the context of film comedy must recognise that a female star's iconicity is not merely a product of the camera, but depends both on the qualities of the individual actor and on investment in it by an audience composed of individual male and female spectators each with their own particular responses.

Following up: gender on screen

☞ To what extent do Laura Mulvey's ideas about the male gaze of the camera hold true for comedy films made during the classical Hollywood period?

☞ In what ways is comedy used to address gender in films such as *Gentlemen Prefer Blondes*, *The French Line*, *The Seven-Year-Itch* (1956), *The Girl Can't Help It* (1956) and *Will Success Spoil Rock Hunter?*? Is it a disguise, a provocation or a safety valve?

Hollywood romantic comedy on the rocks

The film romantic comedy in the 1950s and early 1960s was still a genre that could challenge the Production Code, quite literally in the case of Otto Preminger's *The Moon Is Blue* (1953), which was released successfully without Code approval (it featured the words 'virgin' and 'mistress'). Such challenges helped shift the focus of the genre from 'romance' to 'sex'. Yet, as sexual and gender politics changed at an increasing rate, the romantic comedy still figured 'sex' as wedlock and children (though alternatives were increasingly acknowledged) and women's independence as a problem (seemingly for both genders). The key to making a successful romantic comedy for producers remained the balancing of a star couple that somehow reflected the times. Doris Day with any significant male star (Cary Grant, James Garner, Rock Hudson) turned out to be the key ingredient as she became the most successful female star at the box office from 1959 to 1964, playing a variety of roles in films that offered audiences a knowing, risqué approach to the genre.

In the first of these hits, *Pillow Talk* (1959), co-starring Rock Hudson, Day plays glamorous unmarried interior designer, Jan Morrow, opposite Hudson's promiscuous songwriter, Brad Allen. They share a party telephone line (meaning they can overhear each other's calls) and argue over the phone about its usage, establishing a bitter relationship. However, once Brad has seen Jan he decides to pursue her, disguising his real identity under the name 'Rex Stetson'. The risqué nature of *Pillow Talk* may be virtually invisible behind its surface gloss for audiences today, but, properly considered, the title track and the song Day sings on the soundtrack over the journey to a secluded Connecticut cottage ('I'm yours tonight ... possess me, make love to me') show that Jan's desire for sex is as pronounced as Brad's (see Glitre 2006: 173–4; McDonald 2007: 53–4). Even though the couple's convergence of interest promises consummation, the Production Code dictates that the film cannot deliver since they cannot be together until the predatory and dishonest aspects of Brad's 'Rex Stetson' identity have been exposed and he has been punished for

8 Doris Day and Rock Hudson, the glamorous stars of Pillow Talk (1959).

it. Women's increasing independence and, in particular, Jan's job appears to offer opportunities to accomplish this. When Brad tries to re-establish contact with Jan, as himself, as a client, she can revenge herself by a grotesque redesign of his bachelor pad. When he makes clear he has changed his ways, cutting off all his other relationships for Jan, and attempts to storm out leaving her to her vindictive makeover, she uses his (frankly sinister) remote door-locking device to keep him there. It is Jan's knowledge and her choices that allow 'the process of compromise' (Glitre 2006: 176) to be completed.

The progressive elements in the context of the romantic comedy genre drawn out here were not, however, identified as the key to the success of the formula as further Day romantic comedies appeared. In *The Thrill of It All* (1963) Day plays Beverley Boyer, a mother of two married to an obstetrician (who delivers babies) played by James Garner. It is a comedy of remarriage as she gets (unsought) very well paid advertising work and this undermines his role as breadwinner. In one sequence the couple have been at odds and are about to be reconciled but Beverley hasn't had the chance to tell her husband about the swimming pool her employers (a soap company) have installed in their back yard as a reward. Once Dr Boyer has driven his car into the pool, their discussion cannot go well. There are still the single beds that had become Hollywood custom, and talk of children is still the only legitimate way to talk about sex. He distinguishes between her money and 'our money' – the household is his, financially, and anything else is topsy-turvy – yet she makes more money than him, is more famous than him (she appears on billboards) and is clearly very good at her job. The film is unable to resolve these problems by its end and cops out. In setting up Dr Boyer as an obstetrician the film partially allows him to beat women at their own game and, unconvincingly, Beverley decides to have another baby. The romantic comedy genre is being renegotiated here. The wife (and the woman), economically viable on her own in a time of virtually full employment, must nevertheless maintain her marriageability. In the 1960s, with the availability of the pill, sexual freedom for women outside marriage was much easier. *The Thrill of It All* shows audiences that a woman can do without a man but implies it is better to sacrifice that option by insisting on marriage, home and children. Clearly, this is a weak message placed against the questioning of masculinity continuing to be 'the norm' implicit in the rise of feminism that would increasingly impact on gender relations in Britain and the US. After nearly a decade repetition, and the inability to continue to adapt in the face of changing times, meant that the Day series began to pall. Romantic comedy was struggling to keep up with social change and box-office returns for the genre as a whole diminished over the decade.

The romantic comedy since new Hollywood

The final collapse of the Production Code in 1966 also brought about a crisis of faith in the genre that had come to prominence in the wake of its imposition. An exception and huge box-office hit (see Krämer 2005) was *The Graduate* (1967), starring Dustin Hoffman and Ann Bancroft, a perverse New Comedy that blames older women for independent female sexuality and has its hero flee with Bancroft's on-screen daughter (see Rowe 1995: 195). With greater freedom to challenge taste and old taboos, filmmakers were once again interested in more anarchistic forms. The 1930s screwball comedy began to gain nostalgic appeal as its anarchistic style was recognised as relatively radical after the fare of the previous two decades, and there were attempts at updated versions such as *What's Up Doc* (1974) with Barbra Streisand and Ryan O'Neal. In 1979 Brian Henderson (2001), somewhat prematurely, contemplated the end of the romantic comedy genre and lamented the abandonment of the Code which left filmmakers nothing to work around. It was Woody Allen who showed what could be done in the changed circumstances with *Annie Hall* (1977), and the phrase used to describe it, 'nervous romance', has been used to designate romantic comedies of the period (though MacDonald (2007) prefers 'radical romantic comedy'). In Allen's reworking of the genre there are a number of alterations; the film is named after the female lead character, and narrated from the male lead's point of view, implicitly acknowledging a level of subjectivity. Increasing elements of drama are added along with elements of postmodernity, too, but more significant is the increased realism of the film which doesn't happen in a glossy never-neverland but (largely) in New York, a city the director knew well. *Annie Hall* accepts that a relationship is a two-way process, a negotiation between adults. It isn't the be-all and end-all of life, and children and marriage are not the only outcome worth having. And this is just as well because the obstacles in the way are legion and very real: from personal neuroses to career development to simple matters of timing. As a result the film adds an extra Boy loses Girl to the end of the classic Hollywood formula, yet it does so while being very funny including humour in the form of traditional one-liners, formal and postmodern reflexivity, and slapstick moments ranging from lobster hunts to inopportune sneezes. *Annie Hall* won almost all the Oscars that *It Happened One Night* had except best actor, but then Allen had two anyway (Director and Screenplay, shared with Marshall Brickman). The potential of the genre to speak to audiences (and critics) clearly remained. Yet *Annie Hall* is somewhat exceptional.

Mainstream Hollywood filmmaking took longer to recuperate the genre. It was beginning to do so in the late 1980s with a rash of varied approaches, many of them studied in detail in Evans and Deleyto (1998). A key film in this cycle is *When Harry Met Sally* (1989) about the title couple (Billy Crystal and Meg Ryan) whose long-running acquaintance eventually becomes a romance after we have seen the couple reacting to other lovers in their lives. The high concept (one-line plot issue) is about whether men and women can be friends rather than potential sexual partners; the film argues that it depends on the circumstances and, more importantly, on the individuals. The film homes in on identity as the key factor, with both characters taking up positions about what it means (or ought to mean) to belong to a particular gender, and then being taken beyond that position through contact with a single individual. The key scene, the equivalent in several ways to *It Happened One Night*'s hitch-hiking scene, is Sally's public imitation of an orgasm in a restaurant. While consciously pushing at the boundaries of the mainstream, the scene manages, bizarrely, to stay on the right side of taste by being a simulation in an inappropriate context. The butt of the joke (and the motivation for the performance) is Harry's misplaced confidence in his sexual performance. The restaurant location removes any shades of grey by bringing the fake orgasm under scrutiny in a situation where it can only be entirely false. This fake/real ambiguity forms the basis of the 'I'll have what she's having' gag that tops the scene, testifying to the effectiveness of the performance and the rarity of what it imitates (you can't buy those in a restaurant). Krutnik (1998: 32–3) points to this simulation as part of the acknowledged 'lie' of post-nervous romances but the meaning, in the context of the film, that Harry cannot know whether he is a good lover or not, is so emphatically put that Sally really wins an argument for the first time. This may be partially counteracted by the expression of sheer pleasure on Sally's face after she and Harry have made love (it's not aimed at him and there would be no need for her to fake it), but it is also there as a contrast to Harry's troubled expression caused by fear that sex has ruined the relationship. He need not worry. In this film: '[s]ex is ... only a metaphor for a more profound intimacy that requires learning' (Williams 2001: 353). Yet marriage is still the way this intimacy is figured as Harry and Sally are added to the series of staged and scripted documentary-style interviews with married couples that separate the film's 'chapters'.

Pretty Woman (1990) is a second example of Hollywood's return to the genre at the end of the 1980s. It stars Richard Gere as corporate raider Edward Lewis and Julia Roberts as prostitute Vivian Ward who, despite their individual specialisms in financial transactions, get together emotionally in the end. In their own ways both characters are hardened professionals, as Edward observes: 'We're such similar creatures, you and I, we both screw people for money.' Their coming together is a reciprocal process. With the Production Code abandoned nearly a quarter of a century before the film's release, sexual innocence is no longer desirable: sexual knowledge is key (Radner 1993: 62). Vivian is an object of exchange but on her terms. Sex, again, is not the problem; it is a given. What this couple need to work towards is intimacy. As in *Bringing Up Baby* and many early comedies, the key point of contact is the lips: Vivian doesn't kiss clients. This is sufficiently clear for her 'I love you' that follows her kiss with Edward to be redundant. Similarly, Edward's rehabilitation from raider to businessman (no longer wanting revenge on his dead father) is signalled when the senior financial rival (screwball romantic comedy stalwart Ralph Bellamy) says, 'I find this hard to say without sounding condescending but ... I'm proud of you'. As Edward draws patriarchal approval, all his worst characteristics are embodied in his lawyer, Phil Stuckey (Jason Alexander), who believes that Vivian's profession gives him the right to attack her (see Rowe 1995: 199). In the end the rich man, a prince among men, fulfils Vivian's fairy-tale fantasy, what her street friend (Laura San Giacomo) calls 'Cinda-fuckin-rella', by coming to collect her in a white limo (for which read white horse). 'And what happens when the Knight has rescued the princess?' he asks. 'She rescues him right back' is the reply. In fact, she has already done so; *Pretty Woman* begins with Edward in a borrowed car he can barely control lost in downtown LA at night in a nightmare-like scenario. Vivian gives him directions, drives, takes control of the stick shift gears he can't operate. It is through Vivian that he learns to make something other than money in his business (perhaps an implication of making babies). *Pretty Woman* accepts the sexually knowledgeable woman but redirects her towards sexual monogamy, which remains the cultural norm. What Edward gives her in return is the spending power that brings out her true worth. The film works because it succeeds in offering a dual address relevant to a late 1980s audience. It combines a successful romance with a prostitute – a male fantasy, prohibited under the Code – with the familiar romantic comedy fantasy of how to marry a millionaire; a wealthy, cultured man. As Krutnik (1998: 30) points out, the film itself recognises that 'This is

Hollywood' rather than reality and the genre has a new self-consciousness about the reciprocal compatibility between genders, though it stops short of *Annie Hall*'s clear subjectivity.

Such self-awareness is embedded in *Notting Hill* (1999), in which one half of the romantic couple is Anna Scott, a Hollywood film star who earns $15 million per picture, played by Julia Roberts. The logical conclusion of this self-reflexivity is two film stars in love as in *America's Sweethearts* (2001). Calculated to build on the success of 1994's *Four Weddings and a Funeral* (see Mather 2006 for context), *Notting Hill* presents the concept 'Film star falls in love with ordinary person' in its most acceptable configuration, that is, so as to empower the female character. Nevertheless, it is Hugh Grant playing William Thacker, a diffident, floppy-haired middle-class British travel bookshop owner, who more closely inhabits his regular star persona. The problems created for the couple are plausibly developed in Richard Curtis's script as the relatively ordinary meets the high-profile ('My whole life ruined because I don't read *Hello* magazine'). Though the woman sets the pace, the final choice is left to the man, as Anna comes into William's bookshop to apologise for summarily dropping him twice previously and offering a gift (which turns out to be an original Chagall painting) and herself. From his side, such an offer is clearly a fantasy made real, but it is equally fantasy from Anna's side as she aspires to an ordinariness that she cannot will for herself, despite her money and industry clout, and can only ever attain in fiction. Though she tells him 'The fame thing isn't really real, you know', William baulks and refuses. In the following inquest scene William's (overly numerous) support network sympathise with his decision but flatmate Spike (Rhys Ifans), bursting in late and initially unaware of the party line, reacts with 'You daft prick', conflating idiocy and male sex. Compelled to replay the previous scene and repeat Anna's line that she is 'just a girl, standing in front of a boy, asking him to love her' the nakedness and risk of *any* profession of desire, from anyone, becomes apparent to all present, along with William's folly. Catching up with Anna during a press conference, William must, even more publicly, confess he is a 'daft prick' and that his romantic, and indeed phallic, destiny lies with her. Anna's spoken response is framed for the pack of journalists, but Julia Roberts's sustained scintillating smile tells us all we need to know. A final scene shows the couple relaxing in a private park packed with kids, unnoticed and undisturbed, she pregnant and he reading fiction (*Captain Corelli's Mandolin*), an urban idyll. It seems that the star has what she wants – ordinary pleasures, normality –but a slight awkwardness remains as the situation of an empowered female character earning $15 million a picture is treated as anomalous, something preventing her happiness. Like Ellie Andrews in *It Happened One Night*, Anna Scott solves her problems with the right man, wherever she finds him, which involves stepping outside of her privileged world.

Tamar Jeffers McDonald suggests we are now in the era of the 'neo-traditional romantic comedy' in which the certainties of the past are presented 'as if movies like *The Graduate* and *Annie Hall* never existed' (2007: 85–6). Given its current lack of invention, the future of the genre might appear to be in doubt but Kathleen Rowe makes a telling point: 'The very conventionality of its message suggests that it endures in art because it speaks to powerful needs to believe in the utopian possibilities condensed on the image of the couple – the wish for friendship between women and men, for moments of joy in relationships constrained by unequal social power' (1995: 212). For patriarchy to continue it has to offer a place for its female subjects, though it often appears do so with bad grace, both in the past and in the present by stressing the perils of remaining 'uncompromised' or, rather, single. Independent female sexuality is something patriarchy has always feared, and such fears are reflected in screen comedy. Some contemporary neo-traditional romantic comedies appear little interested in sex (McDonald 2007: 97–8), because its availability is not a contemporary issue. In fact recent examples such as *Knocked Up* (2007), *Zack and Miri Make a Porno* (2008), *No Strings Attached* (2011) and *Friends with Benefits* (2011) follow on from *Pretty Woman* in suggesting sex first, romance afterwards. Sex itself no longer compromises a woman, but 'romantic comedy [still] depends on the melodramatic threat that the lovers won't get together and that the heroine will suffer the fate of becoming a spinster or marrying the wrong man' (Rowe 1995: 110) as for example in *Bridget Jones' Diary* (2001) (see Chambers 2009). Romantic comedy remains about the core issue of negotiating gender differences to reach that all-important real right and true relationship. Its comedic resilience is invariably about challenging the societal assumptions and conventions that impact upon that negotiation while acknowledging, in the end, its necessity.

Following up: femininity in romantic comedy

☞ Taking a particular example from Doris Day's run of hit romantic comedies made between 1959 and 1967, consider the extent to which the female roles are progressive or retrogressive.

☞ How do the post-classical romantic comedies of the 1970s negotiate the discrepancy between their generic concern with romance and the availability of sex?

☞ How seriously can we take obstacles to partnership in Anglo-American romantic comedy's default affluent middle-class settings?

☞ How much (or how little) nostalgia do contemporary examples of the genre appear to have for earlier examples?

Femininity in other forms of comedy

Clearly, it is problematic that the chief comedy representation of the female sex on film occurs in a genre that specifically pairs its participants off with men. These are the terms in which patriarchal society conceives women to be significant, and outside of this format it seems women are 'on their own' and therefore suspect (see Chambers 2009). Unsurprisingly, given that most gender-based humour has come from men disparaging women, feminist writers have paid increasing attention to this rather striking imbalance. Arguing that comedy theory can make depressing reading for women, Frances Gray notes that 'misogyny is inscribed in some definitions [of comedy], and where this is not so there is a bland assumption that the experience of both sexes is identical' (1994: 13–14). The deficiencies in masculine-dominated comedy theory have largely been matched by the abundance of masculine-dominated films and broadcast programmes on radio and television. Arguably, even those shows which feature women performers at their centre, from *I Love Lucy* in the 1950s, *Roseanne* in the late 1980s, *Absolutely Fabulous* in the 1990s to *Sex and the City* in this century, have tended to inscribe women in terms of feminine excess which renders them as both 'absurd and liberated' (Chambers 2009: 167). Kathleen Rowe's (1995) discussion of exceptional female comedy performers, from Mae West in the 1930s (see also Curry 1995) to Roseanne Barr in the 1990s (see also Karlyn 2003), identifies them as 'unruly women' refusing societally approved standards of femininity. Such figures are all too rarely seen, especially on the big screen (see Chapter 10 for a discussion of Whoopi Goldberg's film career), but the more domestic television screen has offered a number of opportunities for female comic performers, despite the fact that much of its comedy remains male-dominated. Outside of key sitcom roles (see Chapter 5 and Feuer 2001), however, performers who might fit the tradition Rowe identifies are more difficult to track. The following is an outline sketch of some significant players in British television. Victoria Wood has had a long successful career, mainly on her own terms, as singer, record-breaking stand-up, sketch show auteur and award-winning actress (see Medhurst 2007: 178–186). Wood's workplace sitcom *dinnerladies* presents a diverse female cast in a patriarchal factory environment, with her own character, Bren, visited by her distinctly unruly decrepid fantasist mother Petula (Julie Walters). Jo Brand, with her combination of the aggressive and the domestic ('The way to a man's heart is through his hanky pocket with a breadknife' quoted in Littlewood and Pickering 1998: 301), stands out as a panellist and performer. Though her unwieldy stand-up/sketch show *Through the Cakehole* (1993) ran for only one series, her self-penned hospital comedy drama *Getting On* (2009–10) has won awards. Caroline Aherne contributed to *The Fast Show* (1994–97), starred in *The Mrs Merton Show* (1995–98) as the titular impish interviewer, and acted in and co-wrote *The Royle Family* (1998–2000), all significant contributions to the development of television comedy in this period. Dawn French and Jennifer Saunders have had long running-television success since 1987 in their irregular sketch show (*French and Saunders*) and in some of their solo vehicles, though it was a toned-down Dawn French who starred as title character in the sitcom *The Vicar of Dibley* (1994–2007). A genuinely unruly woman-centred sitcom, *Absolutely Fabulous* (1992–2002) with Jennifer Saunders and Joanna Lumley as promiscuous drink- and drug-abusing London fashionistas, has proved impossible to use as a template across the Atlantic. More recently Catherine Tate produced four series of her successful self-titled sketch show (2004–7), featuring unruly characters young and old, before taking up higher-profile acting work. The performers who make it to the mainstream need to be exceptionally industrious and inventive, often originating material for themselves, but the unruly woman's performer can, it seems, achieve popularity. Other recent performances inflected with this archetype include Ruth Jones's Nessa in *Gavin and Stacey*, and *Green Wing* characters Sue White (Michelle Gomez) and Joanna Clore (Pippa Haywood). Julia Davis's monstrous Jill Tyrrell in *Nighty Night* and Miranda Hart's blundering romantic alter-ego in *Miranda* probably represent the outer and inner limits of the unruly woman in relation to mainstream success. The female leads of *Pulling* (2006–9), including Sharon Horgan's Donna who refuses marriage for a messy life of drink and casual sex, are somewhere in the middle, yet this is a sitcom made for a small channel (BBC3) which, despite American interest, has so far been unable to translate into a series there. Unlike some of the performers who embody her, the unruly woman character is, by her very nature, excluded from general acceptance for she remains disruptive of and hostile to the dominance of masculinity and its discourses.

Following up: unruly women on television

☞ In what ways do contemporary female television performers play with and/or subvert gender stereotypes? Do expectations based on gender assist or obstruct the work of female writers and performers?

☞ To what extent are female-led television comedies in longer narrative formats ambivalent about the possibility of romantic fulfilment for their characters?

Masculinity

Though we now turn to explicitly focus on comedy representations of masculinity, this is a topic that has not been invisible in much of the foregoing since the formula of the romantic comedy film, despite its perceived female focus, provides masculine role models as well as feminine ones. We can briefly return to a previously used example of romantic comedy to illustrate this.

In *Pillow Talk* discussions about the nature of manhood take place between Brad and Jonathan Forbes (Tony Randall), who also knows Jan. Together they suggest that a bachelor like Brad is a tree in the forest who will be cut down and turned to lumber by marriage, clearly implying that marriage is a symbolic castration. In so doing they 'highlight the inherent ideological contradiction' between an image of masculine social dominance and romantic fulfilment in domesticity (see Glitre 2006: 171–2). At this mid-point of the film Brad wants Jan and not marriage. Innuendo about masculine performance occurs when Jonathan packs Brad off to his house in Connecticutt because of the deception Brad has been practising on Jan (and because he covets her himself), little imagining that Brad has engineered it so that Jan will accompany him. The wealthy Jonathan has power over Brad because he is paying him $200,000 to write a musical and, to emphasise this, Jonathan packs a fistful of pencils and numerous musical notation sheets 'just to make sure you'll do plenty of scoring up there'. The dialogue is perfectly justified by the plot but the innuendo is there for the audience to read in and all the funnier because the sheer amount of scoring implied would be superhuman. Yet, as we have seen earlier, both soundtrack and character motivation suggest Jan is equally keen to consummate her relationship with 'Rex' outside of (though as a prelude to) marriage. As surrogates for all their audiences' desires, perhaps superhuman scoring is what we expect from well-matched star couples, though it must take place (off-screen) when an acceptable compromise between the characters has been reached.

Though *Pillow Talk* is a thoroughly conservative film in many ways, and masculinity, in its traditional guises, is still manifested powerfully, its flaws are also being measured. Brad responds to Jan's hostile makeover of his flat by carrying her out of her bed and through the New York streets to inspect it. Male star carrying female star presents as fact that men are stronger and implies that it counts for something, and, since no one attempts to prevent this abduction, indicates that patriarchal authority is on Brad's side. Overall, however, the film shows that the active co-operation of women is essential: Jan uses Brad's remote door-locking device (which she has retained) to prevent him leaving the flat. What allows Jan to capture the new Brad is this element of old Brad that remains. To return to the film's tree metaphor, successful compromise requires that not all the limbs be lopped off. Romantic comedy, a genre often thought of as having a feminine focus, addresses both genders in its audience.

A second major sub-genre within film comedy that we have already spent some considerable time discussing is that of the largely male-focused comedian comedy (see Chapter 1), in which the comedian character struggles to conform to society. Very often part of the comedian comedy's plot will at least resemble that of the romantic comedy, with significant sections (and indeed whole films) keyed to the comedian's performance of masculinity. In fact in these elements of comedian comedy, unlike romantic comedy, the obstacles to the union of the couple are not social and psychological blocks but the hero's poor performance of masculinity. When (and if) the comedian comedy hero is united with a female partner at the end it is generally much more perfunctory or comic than the romantic success that closes the romantic comedy because comedian comedy interprets masculinity, much more widely than simply its relation with the opposite sex. In his original development of the comedian comedy genre, by concentrating on single comedian examples from the 1940s and 1950s, Steve Seidman (1979/1981) implictly suggests that it is a more conservative genre than a wider historical sample would indicate (see Jenkins 1992: 11). For example, the comedy pair or team dynamic is an inherently more anarchistic version of the comedian comedy which gives opportunities to show alternative versions of masculinity, and its comedians are thus less likely to achieve successful or unambiguous masculinity than the individual comic. Even the work of some of the leading comedians of the period, such as Bob Hope and Jerry Lewis, has a different dynamic in their films with partners. Hope and Bing Crosby's parodic *Road* movies (see Chapter 6) particularly engage with ideas of masculinity (see Cohan 2003) and Lewis's initial pairings with Dean Martin have a different character to his later, solo work where he does not have Martin's easy masculinity to bounce off (see Bukataman 1991). Since the split of Martin and Lewis in the mid-1950s, we see an eclipse of the comedic pair in film (for reasons we shall discuss below). Meanwhile, the personas of successful individual comedian comedy stars have continued to present inept versions of masculinity since the New Hollywood of the 1960s.

Woody Allen's screen persona in his early starring roles of the late 1960s and into the 1970s (see Kaminsky 1985: 165–6) draws heavily on Bob Hope's solo appearances as a cowardly lothario from the 1940s (see Chapter 6). *Play It Again Sam* (1973) particularly focuses on earlier models of masculinity (Humphrey Bogart) and Allen's character's inability to conform to them. Steve Martin's early starring film roles from the late 1970s and early 1980s, such as *The Jerk* (1979) and *The Man with Two Brains* (1983), also exemplify problems with masculinity. Later leading comedian comedy performers include Robin Williams in the 1980s (see Matthews 2000), Jim Carrey in the 1990s (see Drake 2003), with Adam Sandler then Ben Stiller bringing us roughly up to the present day. Operating after the end of the classical Hollywood studio system, all these performers have taken opportunities to play against type during their careers, sometimes successfully, but all of them also have a comic persona which they can return to that, however many performative skills are associated with it, does not epitomise stable 'normal' masculinity. Inept performance of masculinity is the comedian comedy's stock-in-trade. Excessive performance of masculinity, ultra-masculinity, can also be funny as in *Anchorman: The Legend of Ron Burgundy* (2005) with Will Ferrell. Getting the pitch of masculinity wrong, by the prevailing standards of the day, is an ongoing matter for anxiety (and therefore for comedy) because it clearly impacts upon the ability of the individual to find a place within society. Anxieties about the practice of masculinity, almost invariably seen in terms of male heterosexuality, are built into the following contemporary example.

Performing masculinity

The *American Pie* series (1999–2003) is a trilogy of films centring on a group of teenagers undergoing rites of passage. This is a typical set-up for film with gross-out elements (see Chapter 9). The audience are placed in a privileged position in the hierarchy of sexual knowledge during these films: whether they've experienced these rites or not, they haven't made – or won't be able to make – more embarrassing blunders than the central character, Jim (Jason Biggs).

In the first film, *American Pie* (1999), four male friends enter a pact to have their first full sexual experience on or before their high school graduation (the fact that it will be heterosexual literally goes without saying). In *American Pie 2* (2001), which is our main focus here, they build on their discovery that there is more to sexual activity than the act of sex itself and confront the problem of finding what is right for them within the wealth of sexual possibilities on offer in contemporary society. The four get back together after their first year in university for 'twelve weeks of immortality' while renting a lakeshore property over the summer with Stifler (Seann William Scott), the crass and foul-mouthed jock from the first film who becomes the fifth member of the group. Stifler is an important additional carry-over because he is beyond the anxieties of the others, and his claims ('I got screwed 23 times last year') throw into relief their intervening experiences; Kevin (Thomas Ian Nicholas) can't get over his high school lover Vicki (Tara Reed); Oz (Chris Klein) is continuing a long-distance relationship with his prom date Heather (Mena Suvari); and Finch (Eddie Kaye Thomas) still seems devoted to the memory of his sexual encounter with 'Stifler's Mom' (Jennifer Coolidge). The mainspring of the comedy is, however, Jim whom Stifler tells 'You're the only guy I know whose dick needs an instruction manual'. In the first film, obsessed by finding out what 'third base' (contact with a vagina) felt like, he ended up being caught by his father (Eugene Levy) making out with his mom's apple pie. The Oedipal angle is not accidental. Jim cannot take control of the phallus.

The first film also has him inadvertantly broadcasting his first attempts at sex with Czech exchange student Nadia (Shannon Elizabeth) over the internet. Not only is he sabotaged (twice) by premature ejaculation as his fantasy is about to become true but *everyone* knows about it (even his family: 'it came up at a PTA meeting' his father notes). Jim's successful sexual experience at the end of the first film was short-lived and is described in the second as being 'with a flute fetish band geek who used me then dumped me after the prom'. In the second film, seeking to improve the masturbation which is again the staple of his sex life, Jim attempts to use a lubricant while watching a pornographic film and accidentally glues one hand to his penis and the other to the incriminating videotape, clearly labelled 'Pussy Palace'. These further misadventures mark – quite literally – his failure to move on from auto-sexuality and to escape Oedipal bonds as his predicament leads to Jim being arrested by the police and escorted through the emergency medical treatment by his father. Though played for cringe-making laughs, his injuries nevertheless set up a brake on his renewed relationship with Nadia and, in order to delay consummating things with her until he has healed (rather than explain the glue mishap), Jim pretends to be in a relationship with his former lover, band geek Michelle (Alyson Hannigan). Michelle coaches him in the niceties of kissing and bra removal and identifies his major problem: 'You're so uptight'. Anxiety over masculine performance affects Jim's relationships with women and leads him to obsess about Nadia. Michelle asks: 'What's the big deal with Nadia? She's like 50,000 times more attractive than most girls, but it's just sex' (i.e. something she is equally capable of delivering). Jim needs to understand, in order to negotiate masculinity as an individual, that sexual fulfilment is not dependent on finding some ideal figure but on discovering what works. Finally, Jim realises 'I am a band geek – I just never joined the band' and abandons Nadia for Michelle. The film does not entirely reject fantasy in favour of reality (as we shall see below), but it does indicate that in the heterosexual economy even inept geeks are catered for, as emphasised by the continuation of Jim and Michelle's romance into matrimony in *American Pie: The Wedding* (2003). Having imposed particular gender differences on its subjects – both male and female – patriarchal hegemony must then show how the difficulties it creates can be overcome, and contemporary comedies such as the *American Pie* films reflect that ongoing negotiation.

Following up: performing gender

☞ Evaluate the performance of masculinity by a sample of male film comedians and the performance of femininity by a sample of female film stars in comedy films from the same period. How much comedy is generated by falling short in the performance of gender roles? How much comedy is generated by excessive performance? How much narrative emphasis is devoted to opposite sex relations. How much to same-sex interaction?

☞ How much do the comic elements of romantic comedy film (or romantic elements in comedian comedy films) assist or disrupt the screen couples in generating on-screen chemistry? To what extent are the supporting characters required to provide humour?

Masculinity, homosociality, homosexuality

Given the disheartening lack of flexibility in screen representations of heterosexuality in comedic texts, the prospects for those groups not sharing dominant paradigms of sexuality cannot be optimistic. However, once we understand that gender definitions are constructed, then it becomes clear that valuations of sexuality which follow from them are also open to question. Patriarchal culture, according to Adrienne Rich (1994), operates a system of 'compulsory heterosexuality' in which men must desire women and women must desire men. The existence of homosexuality disrupts the supposedly clear-cut definition of genders and gender roles and problematises the whole system. As the following quotation suggests, this disruption meets resistance:

> Advice on how to make sure your kids turn out gay, not to mention your students, your parishioners, your therapy clients, or your military subordinates, is less ubiquitous than you might think. By contrast, the scope of institutions whose programmatic undertaking is to prevent the development of gay people is unimaginably large. (Sedgwick 1990: 42)

This is a conflict that humour and comedy attempts to negotiate and needs to continue negotiating by reason of the fact that even today there are groups for whom homosexuality does not, should not or can not exist. The presence of homosexuality continues to deny the reductive, licensed 'compulsory heterosexuality' still sought for in many conservative sectors of western society (most insistently on the religious right). In England and Wales, for example, male homosexuality was illegal until 1967 and the pursuit of full and equal legal recognition is ongoing, as is resistance to it.

The history of the use of the terms 'heterosexuality' and 'homosexuality' (see Sedgewick 1990: 10) reveals that the latter term predates the former and its appearance thus required both the definition of 'heterosexuality' and its social redefinition. Once again, we see that the insistences of patriarchal culture are imposed upon a more fluid reality. As Sedgwick points out: 'categories presented in a culture as symmetrical binary oppositions – heterosexual/homosexual in this case – actually subsist in a more unsettled and dynamic tacit relation' (1990: 9–10). Homosocial (same-sex) interaction is privileged in the everyday functioning of contemporary patriarchal society but that society insists that this must never become homosexual interaction. In classical Hollywood cinema, generally, the more overt the character's homosexuality, the more negative their narrative rewards, as Vito Russo's *The Celluloid Closet* (1987) shows, and there still is comedy that continues to follow this actively homophobic tradition. Part of the way this is accomplished is through ridicule, which is used 'to draw a firm line between "us" (straight men who are devoted to each other) and "them" (queer men who have sex with each other)' (Medhurst 2007: 112). The ancient Greeks found it perfectly possible to support a patriarchal system in which homosexuality was also part of everyday life without compromising masculinity (see Sedgwick 1985: 3–4), but not current patriarchy. In homophobic comedy gay men are perceived as threats to masculinity, and the effects of homosexuality are a symbolic castration or feminisation (literalised as effiminacy in the crudest representations). These are myths which attempt to shore up and stabilise a patriarchy troubled by the fact that individuals won't be told what their sexuality should be. Our culture still attempts to prescribe what is 'allowed' within masculinity and, to this end, there is a strand of comedy that mocks male homosexuality and implies that it approaches what is the ultimate weakness in this worldview: femininity. Again this is a particular cultural construction: 'The virility of the homosexual orientation of male desire seemed as self-evident to the Spartans ... as its effeminacy seems in contemporary popular culture' (Sedgwick 1985: 26–7). Having decided that homosexuality is a defective version of masculinity, homophobic culture prescribes against it by representing it as effeminate. Yet, in order to be condemned, homosexuality must be acknowledged to exist.

While male homosexuality wasn't able to be the centre of a mainstream film, let alone a romantic comedy, prior to its legalisation, this is far from indicating that homosexuality was unknown or invisible in film, television and radio. You just had to know where to look. For example, in the camp argot 'Polari' used by Julian and Sandy (Hugh Paddick and Kenneth Williams) in BBC radio's *Round the Horne* (see Chapter 4) or, in fact, at Kenneth Williams's performances in any media which show him, stalled on the brink of actively being gay. Tragic though this seems to have been for Williams in his personal life, it is the key to his success as a performer, since this is exactly the position which generates the most humour, as Mark Simpson argues:

> the official point of these connotations is not to affirm or proclaim homosexuality but to raise the spectre of it so that it can be dismissed ... The 'ticklishness' and the discomfort these images of queerness produce is always released (and denied) in laughter: How *absurd* it all is, thank god, the audience says aloud by laughing, and how absurd of me to think that there was anything funny *peculiar* about this, it says to itself, wiping the tears from its eyes. (1998:139)

This ambivalent position is exactly the one taken up by various comedians, especially pairs, from Laurel and Hardy to Morecambe and Wise. In so doing they shift the homosocial continuum into realms that the less innocent in the audience (male and female) realise are awkward and to be avoided. Vito Russo (1987: 72–4) claims that certain film texts mark Laurel and Hardy as gay while Charles Barr (1967: 57) had already pre-empted and refused this reading. An example cited by both is *Their First Mistake* (1932) in which Laurel and

Hardy's closeness breaks up Hardy's marriage and, having adopted a child (too late) to save it, they stray into a bizarre infantilised version of parenthood in which gender is irrelevant as they share a bed and care for a child. When Laurel instinctively latches on to the child's bottle their masculinity is shown as nothing more than a playground pretence. We laugh that they get it wrong, but also, perhaps, we laugh with recognition since their childlike innocence questions what we have (been made to) become. In rejecting patriarchal norms of behaviour, we once again see comedy drawing on:

> the audience's nostalgia for the easy and less repressed pleasures of infantile sexuality, which are innocent only of Oedipus and sexual differentiation, not of sexuality itself. Male comedy duos play with queerness because they exist in a space which pretends not to know what 'homosexuality' is, or at least where this diagnosis doesn't apply since 'heterosexuality' doesn't really exist here either. (Simpson 1998: 144)

Arguments about whether any particular male comedy team are or are not representing themselves as gay on particular occasions miss the point – the point being that the argument can take place only because the protagonists of such comedy 'are not [straightforwardly] *straight*' (Simpson 1998: 144). As Doty suggests:

> the queerness of comedy consists of far more than the humorous representation of queerness ... Although you could argue that most comic gender and sexuality rule-breaking is ultimately contained or recuperated by traditional narrative closure (as it attempts to restore the straight *status quo*), or through the genre's 'it's just a joke' emotional escape hatch, the fact remains that queerness is the source of many comic pleasures for audiences of all sexual identities. (1995: 334)

Awareness of the 'queerness' of comedy allows for cross-gender readings, a certain sympathy for female characters for example, and a more advanced understanding of the mutability of gender roles than straight society would allow itself. Such 'queer readings' offer ways of interpreting gender and sexuality as represented in mainstream texts that can be defined most broadly as 'non-straight' (Doty 1998: 149). We shall return to the queerness of comedy at the end of the chapter, but some discussion of how mainstream US comedy approaches homosexuality follows, beginning in the late 1950s.

Once more we return to *Pillow Talk.* When Brad manipulates Jan over the telephone by ridiculing her romance with himself as 'Rex', he suggests her Texan may not be the man she thinks he is, effectively implying Rex is gay (no such term is used) in order to embolden Jan to prove the opposite. This ploy is one of rich irony from later historical perspectives when it became clear that Rock Hudson (Brad and 'Rex') had always been gay but had concealed it throughout his long film career. From this perspective *Pillow Talk*'s coda sequence, after the ideal couple have been matched, is particularly interesting. 'Six months later' Brad Allen is going to tell Jonathan of the legitimate triumph of his virility (Jan is pregnant). Here a bizarre running gag, in which an obstetrician with an office on the same corridor as Jonathan has become convinced Brad is able to bear children, pays off with Brad being dragged away by the deluded doctor and nurse. The idea of the pregnant man was later played for laughs by Arnold Schwarzenegger in *Junior* (1994) when medical science made the possibility somewhat more plausible and artificial insemination was generally understood. In *Pillow Talk* the joke is peculiarly contorted; there's no mistaking Rock Hudson for a woman in disguise and a man who can have a baby would be a biological freak but behind this is the implication that a man who could get pregnant would also have to be a man who ... had sex with men. The joke is partly the implausible gullibility of these medical professionals, but the film also smuggles in, through a joke far more bonkers than the rest of the film, the homophobic idea of male homosexuality as comic because it is, by reason of the impossibility of its producing children, non-viable. It is also significant that this is the film's last gag and that therefore its consequences can't be followed through, a positioning which is significant in the next film we consider.

Some Like It Hot (1959), rated by AFI members the funniest film ever, is a beautifully made comedy that gets nearly all its laughs by playing with gender as the two male leads (Tony Curtis and Jack Lemmon) join an all-female band in drag to get out of 1920s Chicago and the dangers of being witnesses to a fictionalised St Valentine's Day Massacre. It isn't a film directly about transvestitism or homosexuality; we understand who, and what, everyone is under their disguises. But it is a film that is subversive of gender stereotypes, showing how much of gender is really performance. The key role, which makes every aspect of the film work, is the character Jerry (Lemmon) who counterpoints his buddy Joe (Curtis) each step of the way but, in terms of masculine status, is clearly second fiddle (or rhythm section to Joe's lead sax). Without Jerry we have one man in drag and a very different film. King points out the significance of Jerry's 'less stable anchorage' in masculinity (2002: 136) and Jerry fulfils the comedian's role in the comedian comedy as the individual trying (and struggling) to fit in. While Jerry is stuck with his female persona and courted by serial-marrying middle-aged playboy Osgood Fielding III (Joe E. Brown), Joe adopts another level of disguise as 'Junior' of Shell Oil through which he is able to romance Sugar (Marilyn Monroe), the band's star. In the end, still fleeing gangsters, Joe and Jerry use the only escape route they have left, leaving the resort in Osgood's speedboat as the latter expects to be eloping with Jerry's female alter-ego, Daphne. After her surprising goodbye kiss from Josephine, Sugar joins them and the four leave in the boat. Joe and Sugar start kissing in the back (providing the conventional romantic comedy closure), leaving Jerry and Osgood in the foreground as the other couple. Jerry comes up with a sequence of excuses for not going through with the marriage, each of which Osgood airily dismisses. Finally Jerry gives up and pulls off his wig with the line 'Aww, what's the use? I'm a man!' to which Osgood replies, unphased, 'Nobody's perfect'.

One of the great closing lines in movies, this is, in Sikov's opinion, 'openly gay' (1994: 146–7). It's certainly possible to read it otherwise, simply as the culmination of Osgood's blasé nature, but Sikov's is certainly an important and significant critical reading, a point made clearer when Sikov shows a number of commentators contorting their arguments to eliminate its possibility. At the very least, the acknowledgement of the existence of homosexuality after two hours of a film treading very carefully around the issues of men in drag and steering its way to a heterosexual resolution offers the audience a sort of comic relief. Jerry's final line of the film is one of despair; unlike Joe he hasn't got the girl – the goal prescribed for him by conventional masculinity. To read the line again, 'What's the use [of anything]? I'm a man!' Jerry finds nothing but unhappiness in his assigned gender role of masculinity; he has enjoyed some of being feminine but can't keep the pretence up any longer. It isn't him. He's a man and, seemingly, one doomed to failure and unhappiness. Yet Osgood doesn't mind: 'Nobody's perfect'. Nobody and no-body, even with the hyperfeminine, 'jello on springs' Monroe on board. Having ridden out Jerry's list of deal breakers, this is just one more: Osgood is willing to do without marriage, without fatherhood and, speaking the unspeakable of the time, without heterosexuality. They can have fun anyway. The joke depends on the delivery; *of course* what Osgood implies is perfectly possible, entirely reasonable and everything that stands behind Jerry's objection *doesn't matter*. After thoroughly problematising gender, the conclusion is wonderfully apt; marriage, the culmination of institutionalised heterosexuality, is not to be an impossibility for any relationship. It is not so much a coming out as a coming home; a comic and a gay ending. It's probably the best that any predominantly heterosexual culture could offer a gay audience and Sikov is right to defend it as such (1994: 148).

Nevertheless, rather than adding entertainingly positive depictions of homosexuality to their attractions, mainstream comedy films have remained largely ambivalent about gay characters. Though, as Robin Wood says, 'It seems at times that no '90s comedy is complete without at least one gay character, however minimal' (2001: 410), the central roles remain stubbornly heterosexual. The gay romantic comedy has yet to score a mainstream box-office success even though Ang Lee's debut *The Wedding Banquet* (1993) was its year's most proportionally profitable film. *The Birdcage* (1996) successfully features a gay couple but the plot is driven by the needs of the younger generation and the potential in-laws, all of whom are straight. But if mainstream entertainment still resists placing homosexual desire centre stage, it is now at least willing to look at other possibilities. The often camp confidant character – epitomised by Tony Randall in *Send Me No Flowers* (1964) (see Glitre 2006: 177–9) – is given a new spin in *My Best Friend's Wedding* (1997) where Rupert Everett's openly gay character is the alternative when Julia Roberts's character contemplates losing her straight male best friend, Dermot Mulroney, to Cameron Diaz. Everett's character is far more charming and funny and promises a lot of dancing for her future. Wood describes 'Everett's ironic detachment [as] the perfect representation of the intelligent gay man surviving (and even flourishing) within a heterosexual dominated social milieu, belonging but never *quite* belonging' (Wood 2001: 413). This is a positive representation but, perhaps because it undermines the conventional pieties of the romantic comedy plot (heterosexual marriage), it has not yet been much imitated. For other gay characters there have been very slim pickings in terms of narrative rewards, illustrating that a particular set of rules still operates for their representation: 'the straight relationships are "serious" (even when comic) and the gay relationships are comic (even when "serious")' and gay characters in comedies since the 1980s (Wood's example is *Happy, Texas* (1999)) are 'rendered "safe" by the film's overall tone' (2001: 410).

A recent example of this is *I Now Pronounce You Chuck and Larry* (2007) starring Adam Sandler (Chuck) and Kevin James (Larry) as firefighters who pretend to be a gay couple in order to secure a pension benefit for Larry's children. In tacitly approving gay partnership the film continues the acceptance of homosexuality seen in Sandler's films (Wood 2001: 414–18), but neither star's character is gay, or becomes gay, and both are carefully positioned as heterosexual: Larry's wife is dead, Chuck is a womaniser who, in getting to know a woman while posing as gay, finally falls in love (a common trope). The film makes clear that the central characters of a mainstream Hollywood comedy, especially stars with established everyman personas, cannot be gay. Chuck and Larry begin the climactic trial trying to prove they are gay but end up by affirming that they aren't, even though they love each other, while making clear it's OK if other men do want to be gay. Homosexuality belongs, the film seems to insist, at the margins, and with a peculiar logic the film ends with the civil partnership of the most macho black fireman (Ving Rhames) and the impressionable Hispanic fireman (Nicholas Turturro) whose recognition of their sexuality has come through Chuck and Larry's pretence of being gay. While comedy seems able to approach homosexuality more readily than other genres, Hollywood seems far too embedded in patriarchal culture to ever totally commit, even in jest.

The same pattern is basically clear on US television. In the rare instances there is a recurrent gay character they are not allowed to challenge the heterosexual status quo. Though Billy Crystal played a gay character in the ground-breaking spoof sitcom *Soap* (1977–81), the character was also found to have fathered a daughter. Rendering gay characters safe is key to the success of the sitcom *Will and Grace* (1998–2006). Will (Eric McCormack), the gay central character, shares an apartment with old friend Grace (Debra Messing) in a way that makes them look like a heterosexual couple, in other words allowing the reverse of a queer reading to occur (see Provencher 2005: 178).

Physical affection is expressed between Will and Grace rather than between male gay characters despite the promiscuity of gay friend Jack (Sean Hayes). While it is easy to expect too much from a network show and to undervalue the effects of the presence on American television of a gay-themed sitcom, the frustrating lack of actual representation shows both how the hegemonic grip of patriarchy on mainstream entertainment continues to contain homosexuality.

Out of the closet: an example of homosociality/homosexuality in mainstream Hollywood comedy

Mainstream Hollywood's ongoing ambivalence towards male homosexuality can also be seen in *American Pie 2*. In a key sequence the five central male characters (see above) are working as housepainters to fund the rental of their lakefront property. One of them, Stifler, becomes obsessed with the idea that the two women living in the house they are painting, Danielle and Amber (Denise Fay and Lisa Arturo), are lesbians. Finch advises, 'It is possible for women to hold hands and not be gay' and suggests Stifler is homophobic but Stifler nonetheless dives in through an open window and begins his search for 'lesbian artefacts'. He finds 'a big blue rubber dildo' and runs around the house waving it in a state of such excited confusion that when Jim and Finch go in to extract him he can't remember where he found it. His first response to the question 'where did you find it' is: 'Finch's ass'. The idea of female homosexuality clearly has a confusing connection with the male variety and in these circumstances the phallus doesn't necessarily mean what Stifler wants it to mean. Moments later, the three are hiding in what turns out to be the wrong bedroom, with Jim under the bed and Stifler and Finch literally in the closet together, spying on Danielle and Amber who are trying on bikinis. 'Stop touching me!' Stifler hisses. 'I'm not touching you' Finch responds but backs away, looking down. Finch's erect penis is always in the wrong place for Stifler, inside his mother, for example, in the series's most recurring gag. Yet here the potential homosexual implications of their intimacy are offset by the voyeuristic scenario. The hiding trio are eventually discovered and are threatened with a 911 call before the women decide to 'mess with them' by pretending to be lesbians. The price the women exact, however, is 'you go, we go'. In order to earn the stimulation of viewing lesbian activity the trio must offer them comparable male interaction. Equating male and female homosexuality in this way is rare in mainstream culture.

Rather as in the comedies of the 1950s there is a high level of hysteria in this sequence. Arousal, rather desperately connected to the women performing lesbianism, is counterpointed for the males by disgust they supposedly feel for each other's bodies. Every time the women say 'Now it's your turn' the boys mistakenly imagine heterosexual interaction is called for. Finch so wants to see the show on offer that he will let a freaked-out Stifler 'touch his ass' because he is 'comfortable with his sexuality'. Later, Jim and Stifler are compelled to kiss – properly – and then proceed to argue about the quality of the other's kiss and whether or not the other was 'trying'. Jim's exasperation at hearing yet again that he is a lousy kisser and his confusion about whether Stifler has any right to judge given the circumstances are exemplary instances of the way the scene breaks down the normal boundaries of homosocial interaction.

As if to assist the audience, the sequence has a male Greek chorus of short-wave listeners. The other members of the painting team, Oz and Kevin, are looking in through the window and, by walkie-talkie on CB setting, convey the scene to the whole of the (male) neighbourhood. The groups shown listening are a cross-section of American society: the clientele of a fast food store, denizens of a sheriff's office, a barbecuing middle-class father and a redneck trucker who converses with his dog, Cooter. Not only does this last character encourage Stifler to 'squeeze his ass, boy, you'll like it', he later describes Danielle and Amber as sounding like 'those two transvestites we picked up in Biloxi'. With Danielle and Amber soon taking control of Jim's walkie-talkie (another symbolic castration) the complexity of the representation is further increased, and cannot be indefinitely sustained. For the trio in the bedroom the show comes to an end when Amber and Danielle want to see mutual male masturbation and Stifler offers to 'take one for the team' as the recipient. At this point Jim and Finch freak out and flee the scene shouting 'put that thing away'. The (unseen) appearance of a real penis has ended the fantasy.

The scene in the bedroom has the male characters all mixed up, shifting from their view of women as objects to themselves as objects for female entertainment and their contact shifting from homosocial to homosexual. It would certainly be possible to argue that their subjection to the female gaze is emasculating and results in unpleasure but the effect is actually much more complex. By destabilising the conventions of what the protagonists will engage in to gain sexual stimulation the scene erases boundaries that patriarchal culture wants to be clear cut. Afterwards, the male group seem deeply troubled by the preceding events and everything in what would otherwise be an ordinary evening seems loaded with other meanings. Holding up some cards Kevin asks the others 'who wants to play some Asshole?' When Jim demurs it is to watch 'the game' on television; American football being the kneejerk signifier of acceptable homosociality (as indicated by Steve Martin and John Candy when they wake up entwined together having been forced by circumstances to share a bed in *Planes, Trains and Automobiles* (1989)). Kevin responds awkwardly 'I just wanted us to do something together'. When Stifler returns he is determined to stamp out the sudden awareness of the homosocial–homosexual continuum. He dishes out porn videos to everyone and states: 'Just so there's no confusion; Santa Porn has brought us some heterosexual entertainment.' But even his resolve is weak as his customary way of answering the phone now needs a caveat: 'Stifmeister's palace of love – straight love.'

The film is ultimately assiduous in putting to bed this whole issue in its final party scenes. There Stifler meets Danielle and Amber again, discovers they are not lesbians ('we never said that') and, like Finch, claims he is comfortable with his sexuality; comfortable enough to touch every male ass in the room and kiss everyone if it will give him a chance with Danielle and Amber. His narrative reward is to bed them both and thus exorcise homosexuality from the film while establishing exactly where the acceptable boundaries of homosociality are. The series's timid flirtation with homosexuality continues in *American Pie: The Wedding* where the flamboyant gay character, Bear, has a dancing contest with Stifler then (blink and you'll miss it) gets up to dance with the increasingly marginalised Kevin at the wedding reception. In its way *American Pie 2* is remarkably willing to play with sexuality because it remembers that homophobic, patriarchal culture constantly needs to define boundaries, and knows too that the licensed play of comedy is where such concerns can be brought to the surface with least apparent risk (see Medhurst 2007: 112).

Lesbianism and comedy

Doubly excluded from patiarchal culture, female homosexual relationships face hostility and rejection and this is also a feature of their representations within that culture. Historically, lesbian characters are seldom explicitly present in comedies. Partly this is to do with censorship, and partly it is because of the predominance (after the end of the Production Code) of grotesque and/or erotic presentations of lesbianism within non-comedic film (*The Killing of Sister George* (1969), *Performance* (1971)). Suspicion of the male gaze of the camera is difficult to circumvent in this case. Screen presentations of lesbianism are ambivalent because there is potential titillation for the male voyeur in being able to see what may be regarded as perverse and otherwise impossible for the male to experience, as we've seen in *American Pie 2*. Furthermore, the lesbian couple may offer twice as much visual appeal along with the voyeuristic attraction of removing male 'competition' from the on-screen scenario.

Yet lesbianism is a topic which, because it makes male heterosexuality superfluous, implictly undermines all patriarchal values. In comedy that is not expressly homophobic, this undermining occurs fairly swiftly from the first mention of the subject. For example, the stand-up comic Eddie Izzard's line in which he claims to be 'a lesbian trapped in a man's body' taps into knowledge of the fantasy appeal of lesbians to men, as well as the language used by transvestites and pre-operative transsexuals about their conditions, to present him as a man fascinated by the female but rejecting what is involved with masculinity. In so doing he denies what patriarchal culture insists about the appropriateness of conventional masculinity for pursuing women and, in the process, wishes away exactly what patriarchal culture tells men to value – the phallus. It is a particularly effective gag in that – however much it is or isn't in earnest – it feeds Izzard's early comedic persona as someone unwilling to play by gender rules, yet the starting point from which the joke is introduced is masculinity. Williams (1998: 157–8) notes London's 1990s lesbian cabaret scene and interviews Amy Lamé, whose claim to be 'a gay man trapped in a lesbian body' superficially mirrors Izzard's remark but actually has very different reference points, reaffirming her sexuality but laying claim to a particular sensibility and acknowledging its relative recognition within culture. As Smelik (1998: 139) records, lesbianism has even been underrecognised within feminism.

Positive representation of lesbianism in a comedic on-screen narrative depends largely on women in the entertainment industry leading the way. The key text here is the American sitcom *Ellen* (1994–48), in which the star, Ellen DeGeneres, eventually came out. After a funny but more conventional first season DeGeneres altered the set-up and moved her character towards making a revelation about her sexuality, on screen and off, that was groundbreaking within mainstream American television. Ellen's televisual coming out was widely welcomed on the mainstream left and resisted by the right but it has also been condemned as insufficiently political in its presentation of lesbian identity as clear-cut and safe, positioned in binary opposition to female heterosexuality as 'latent, preexistent and natural' (Peterson 2005: 168, 172). Being *the* lesbian representative on television formed an impossible challenge; it is obvious that no one person or character can represent an entire group. The series ultimately found being funny and being positive about life as a lesbian somewhat difficult since sitcoms tend to focus on romantically unsuccessful characters and while this worked fine for quirky, ambivalent Ellen it clashed with her celebratory coming out. Like male homosexuality, lesbianism should not be reduced to a single approved version but understood as 'a space of overlapping, contradictory, and conflictual definitional forces' (Sedgwick 1990: 45). The necessary raft of lesbian sitcoms to represent this diversity seems unlikely, especially given a couple of less successful attempts (*The Ellen Show* (US 2001–2); *Rhona* (UK 2000)), but the drama series *The L Word* (US 2006 to present), offering a wider range of characters, seems to be making progress (see Akass and McCabe 2006).

Independent films focusing on lesbian characters exist but very few are comedies capable of shifting paradigms. *Kissing Jessica Stein* (2001) is an interesting attempt though McDonald (2007: 80–81) judges that 'it marginalises the very sexuality it sets out to showcase' when the title character Jessica finds a heterosexual partner. It may seem invidious to revisit *American Pie 2* yet again on this subject especially when, as we have seen, its lesbians turn out not to be lesbians at all, but this is par for the course as Wood briefly notes (2001: 412). However, there is something telling going on in the 'you go, we go' scene. At the risk of using a theoretical sledgehammer to crack a nut, Judith Butler's essay on 'The Lesbian Phallus' describes the ambivalent results of the scene perfectly:

> When the phallus is lesbian, then it is and is not a masculinist figure of power; the signifier is significantly split, for it both recalls and displaces the masculinism by which it is impelled. And insofar as it operates as a site of anatomy, the phallus (re)produces the spectre of the penis only to enact its vanishing, to reiterate and exploit its perpetual vanishing as the very occasion of the phallus (1993: 89)

It is Amber and Danielle literally holding the phallus, symbolized by the big blue rubber dildo, that puts the women in charge when they find the boys in the bedroom. Yet they are also actresses in lingerie who also have a legion of devoted male listeners in the chorus overhearing the exchanges on short wave radio. In the fast food restaurant a cook responds to the first mention of the word 'lesbians' over his microphone with 'Lesbians?' and Oz supplies a key phrase for the visually disadvantaged listeners, 'Hot lesbians'. In other words, lesbians who fit conventional ideals of feminine beauty. This is the type of lesbian that male fantasy is concerned with, irrespective of whether or not actual lesbian desire co-occupies the space or not. The result is that it is apparently acceptable for women to play in the area of homosexuality in a way that is not acceptable for men, especially when they perform such play for men. It is a literal phallus – Stifler's penis – that breaks Amber and Danielle's spell over Jim, Finch and Stifler and it is its bearer who ultimately beds them. After the boys have run away, Amber and Danielle announce to their 'devoted listeners' that they are continuing and ask 'where's that dildo?', bringing a collective cheer from their in-film audience. Not only is the lesbian phallus in action excluded from the screen but, ultimately, lesbianism is allowed to exist only as male fantasy. If it were real, of course, those same troubling flaws in patriarchy's definitions of gender and sexuality which have recurred throughout this chapter would once again be brought to the foreground.

Though Queen Victoria is (apocryphally) thought to have believed female sexual relationships to be impossible, it is just as revealing that her male functionaries were incapable of convincing her that it was. Similarly, contemporary mainstream culture – still dominated by men, whether comfortable with or trapped within their male bodies – finds it impossible to imagine what love between women could really be like. Luckily, however, for those more imaginative than Queen Victoria, there are many opportunities for lesbian and/or queer readings of ostensibly straight female-centred comedies, as Doty (1998; 2000; 2003) shows.

Conclusion: the queerness of comedy

What we've seen in this chapter suggests that comedy texts constantly revisit the issues of gender and that this recurrent interest is sufficient to underpin both the perennial genre of the romantic comedy and numerous comedian comedies and gross-out films focusing explicitly on gender roles. At the same time we have noted comedy texts identifying and making comic observations about the mutability of gender roles by including comedians in drag and scenarios that present, albeit temporarily, gay and lesbian alternatives to straight, patriarchal norms. What remains to be done here is to show the continuity between comedy's abiding fascination with gender and sexuality and its refusal to allow them to be defined and bounded in the clear-cut way that the discourses of patriarchy insist upon.

This is where queer reading comes in. While queerness is an umbrella term for 'gayness, lesbianism, and bisexuality' (Doty 1998: 149), and can be defined both more broadly and more narrowly than this, queer reading is not reserved for audiences defining themselves as queer, nor does it depend on reading through the prism of queer theory (from Butler, Sedgwick and others). Queer reading consists of the reader consciously or unconsciously stepping outside singular and narrowly defined boundaries of gender and sexuality.

It is probably easy enough to see why lesbian viewers of the comedy musical *Gentlemen Prefer Blondes* might find particular enjoyment in the strength of the relationship between Dorothy and Lorelei, despite the normative, heterosexual outcomes of the movie, or why some gay men might enjoy the American Olympic team's physical displays in that film, but: '[q]ueer positions, queer readings, and queer pleasures are part of a reception space that stands simultaneously beside and within that created by heterosexual and straight positions' (Doty 2000: 345). Doty's account of his own changing relationship to *Gentlemen Prefer Blondes* and queer readings of it (2000: 343, 340–1) illustrates that it is an easy step for males to identify with the female characters and that screen paragons of masculinity rejected as images for identification can be reappropriated as images of desire. Queer readings are live to the possibilities of cross-gender identification and queer identification for audiences who would refuse to see themselves as queer. These might range from straight male viewers finding the Dorothy/Lorelei relationship the most interesting aspect of the film to identifying with Dorothy's unsuccessful interplay with the self-regarding male athletes, to female identification with male characters (not so easy in this particular film) whether their masculinity is questioned or not. Simply put, queer readings refuse to see categories of gender and sexuality as fixed when it comes to our relationship with on-screen characters.

Arguments about the extent to which queer readings intersect with the intended meanings of the filmmakers are largely irrelevant, and especially so when the comedic tone and/or humour of the text depends on the ability of comedy to destabilise boundaries. The key point is that: 'Queer readings aren't "alternative" readings, wishful or willful misreadings, or "reading too much into things" readings. They result from the recognition and articulation of the complex range of queerness that has been in popular culture texts and their audiences all along' (Doty 2000: 345). In the potent combination of sympathy, empathy, suspension of disbelief and identification with a range of subject positions that takes place when we consume comedy texts the destabilisation of fixed categories of gender and sexuality is one of the key sources of laughter.

Film narratives, which identify one outcome for the characters and scenario they establish, may ultimately be less rich sources of queer readings than the repetitive sitcom which is able to return to its characters and premise to accumulate a wealth of possibilities. Doty (2003) shows how female/female relationship in television sitcoms can be read queerly, focusing on *Laverne and Shirley*, and suggests these reinterpretations of the homosocial also work for many other texts. In fact, given the difficulty and sometimes crippling responsibility of the 'gay' comedy text to be representative, as we have seen earlier in relation to *Will and Grace*, texts which are not explictly concerned with non-straight relationships but which allow for queer readings make a more inclusive range of interpretations accessible. For example, *Big Bang Theory* (2007–), a sitcom about four nerdy science graduates and the on-off girlfriend of one of them, constantly makes capital out of the deficiencies in masculinity the male characters reveal in relation to the opposite sex when they struggle to set aside their individual idiosyncrasies and the obsessional pieties of their shared subculture. Queer reading of this show is not just the preserve of its gay audience that recognises it as 'gay adjacent' but is as much a factor in its success with its total audience as its fascination with heterosexual relationships. Even *Big Bang Theory*'s senior production stablemate *Two and a Half Men* (2003–) is open to queer readings. It centres on a household without women in which one adult character is domestic and emotional (Jon Cryer), one slovenly and incorrigeably promiscuous (Charlie Sheen / Ashton Kutcher), and the character of the son (Angus T. Jones) constantly evaluates the adults as male role models. While the explicit premise is to place deficient and excessive versions of masculinity side by side in a domestic setting, being live to the possibility of reading one or both the adults as gay means the humour of their accidents and entanglements is enhanced. When it comes to comedy's relationship with gender and sexuality, whatever the explicit answers and outcomes, there are always alternatives, and always have been.

Following up: the queerness of comedy

☞ What difficulties prevent romantic comedies from escaping 'compulsory heterosexuality'?

☞ How explicit is the recognition of the importance of homosociality in screen comedy? Do comedy films and television programmes reinforce or undermine the distinction between homosocial and homosexual relationships?

☞ Taking specific examples of film or television comedies, evaluate the depiction of non-heterosexual characters. What forms does any marginalisation take?

☞ Do queer readings of comedy texts supplement or improve on conventional, straight readings? Are they more, or less, live to the humour of comic situations?

Recommended reading

Alexander Doty, *Making Things Perfectly Queer: Interpreting Mass Culture*, Minneapolis: University of Minnesota Press, 1993.

Peter William Evans and Celestine Deleyto (eds), *Terms of Endearment: Hollywood Romantic Comedy of the 1980s and 1990s*, Edinburgh: Edinburgh University Press, 1998.

Frances Gray, *Women and Laughter*, Charlottesville: University Press of Virginia, 1994.

Kathleen Rowe, *The Unruly Woman: Gender and the Genres of Laughter*, Austin: University of Texas Press, 1995.

9

Comedy and cultural value: from bad taste to gross-out

Comedy raises issues around the politics of representation, about power, control and freedom of speech because, as Sharon Lockyer and Michael Pickering state: 'Humour is only possible because certain boundaries, rules and taboos exist in the first place' (2009: 16). The issues raised are often articulated through discussions about taste. Taste in this sense is about judgements of what is deemed to be funny and, often, humour which falls foul of 'good' taste is criticised as appealing to the lowest common denominator, that is, an audience without taste. In our discussion of romantic comedy in Chapter 3 we have shown how film was regulated with acceptability to public taste in mind. Similar limitations have been imposed upon television and radio, but it is also clear that the standards of taste alter over time. What was once acceptable and funny can become insulting, morally, socially and politically unacceptable and, conversely, subjects that were once taboo can become common sources of comedy. Equally, and perhaps more problematically, things can be funny even if they are acknowledged to be in bad taste, even offensive. Mills states that: 'It's certainly possible to enjoy a ... joke while simultaneously being offended by it, meaning there's a contradiction between the ideologies held outside humour and the lure of pleasure. Enjoyment of such material can function as a sort of "guilty pleasure", in which the transgressive nature of humour is itself part of the satisfaction' (2005: 136). At its most extreme, some comedy can be considered so offensive that censure, if not outright censorship, seems to some to be an appropriate response. A more typical situation, however, is comedy that some find funny and entertaining, but which seems to others crude, vulgar, derogatory, or simply not funny. In this chapter we examine some films and programmes which raise questions about taste and about cultural values.

Comedy works because it engages with boundaries, with treasured perceptions, with rules, conventions and taboos, but there are occasions when the engagement causes offence, even if no offence was intended. Sometimes the response can be extreme in nature. Considerable controversy surrounded Monty Python's film *Life of Brian* (1979) in which a young Jewish man is mistaken for the Messiah. Accused of blasphemy by numerous religious groups, *Life of Brian* was banned by several local councils in Britain, some of whom had not even seen the film. It was banned for eight years in the Irish Republic and for one year in Norway, which allowed the Swedes to market the film as being 'so funny it was banned in Norway'. Ironically, the real object of the film's broad satirical humour was not Christianity itself but religious and political extremism that blinds people to reality.

Such examples suggest that while some topics remain highly contentious, it is crucial to stress the importance of context. Lockyer and Pickering (2009) begin their book on the ethics of humour by recounting the supposedly jocular comment made in 2003 by Italian Prime Minister Silvio Berlusconi about a German member of the European Parliament, likening him to a Nazi concentration camp guard. The furore surrounding the comment and the universal condemnation of Berlusconi's 'joke' were largely based around the inappropriate context as much as the simile itself. Like earlier newspaper reports of Prince Harry's wearing of a Nazi uniform at a fancy dress party, things are not seen as funny if the context is wrong (in this case the issue was a potential heir to the British throne and no stranger to ceremonial uniforms showing ignorance – at best – of what Nazism meant). Both these events raise questions about taste in humour, and suggest that there are limits to what people will find funny. For Lockyer and Pickering the question becomes: 'how do we negotiate the perilous terrain that lies between humour and offensiveness, or free speech and cultural respect, in a pluralist society?' (2009: 6). This question is especially important for politicians, royalty and other celebrities in the public eye whose capacity to give offence seems considerable, but is clearly relevant for comedy that appears in film, on radio and television.

When it comes to actual comedy neither Berlusconi nor Prince Harry has a great track record or a promising future, yet the difficulties of dealing with Nazism have plagued comedy since the movement became a political force in 1930s Germany. Chaplin's satire of Hitler *The Great Dictator* (1940) was approved by critics but Ernst Lubitsch's *To Be or Not to Be* (1942) was seen as a serious lapse in the director and producer's witty oeuvre. Set in Poland after the Nazi invasion, it deals with a troop of actors led by the hammy Joseph Tura (Jack Benny) resisting Nazi occupation (see Deleyto 2009: 55–81 for a detailed contextualisation). While disguised as a Nazi Tura's vanity means he can't stop himself from trying to get appreciation from the villain, 'Concentration Camp' Erhardt (Sig Rumann), whose verdict is: 'He [Tura] did to Shakespeare what we are doing now to Poland.' As deflation of Tura this is funny, as innuendo it can go as far as the audience wishes, but the sticking point is the way it allows the Nazi character to have a sense of humour. As wartime propaganda took hold this was far too human a trait to ascribe to our worst enemy (see also Billig 2009: 31). For Lubitsch the line was funny and thus worked, for his contemporaries it was decidedly unpalatable. Mel Brooks remade the film in 1983, and making comedy out of Nazism was clearly an element in his invention of the surefire failure musical, *Springtime for Hitler*, embedded in *The Producers* (1968), recently remade as a musical (2005). The successful BBC sitcom *'Allo 'Allo* (1984–92) and Roberto Benigni's bittersweet comedy feature *Life Is Beautiful* (1997) suggest that today Nazi occupation and even the concentration camps are not off-limits as comedic material, merely that they must be carefully handled since 'the boundary between humour and offence is elusive' (Lockyer and Pickering 2009: 15).

The media of film, television and radio are subject to, and exercise, institutional constraints which patrol the limits of what is deemed acceptable. This is why some comedians whose material is considered offensive, such as Britain's Roy 'Chubby' Brown, fail to get exposure on television, though many people enjoy his comedy in live performance and on DVD (see Medhurst 2007: 187–203 and below). In the same way 'sick' jokes that circulate via the relatively unregulated technology of the mobile phone (examples include a glut of them about the 33 Chilean miners trapped underground for 69 days, and about the capsizing of the *Costa Concordia*) suggest that the public appetite for obscene, linguistically, morally and politically challenging humour that flirts with the boundaries of taste is considerable. Though broadcasting and film are always under pressure to be novel and innovative, to attract, build and retain audiences, they go to great lengths to create the proper context so that the humour that is screened or listened to does not give offence, though, as we shall see, they don't always get things right. To an extent, taste and judgement remain the responsibility of the individual, a matter of subjectivity. Some people find a television programme amusing, others do not; some find a particular comedian funny, others do not; some people find a film hilarious, others remain unmoved. However, we suggest that there are other, less subjective, factors which are influential in leading to the judgements made by individuals.

Clearly, the culture we live in will be a major determinant. As Michael Billig writes: 'Within all cultures, there will be debates and conflicts about what constitutes appropriate behaviour. Accordingly, there will be debates about the appropriateness, morality and funniness of humour' (2009: 30). As we shall see in the next chapter, these debates rage most fiercely around racial and ethnic humour. Generally though, it is clear that humour and comedy are not necessarily transferable, even across cultures which share much in common. Although US-produced films and, to a lesser extent, television comedy, occupy considerable British screen-time, not all US television comedies succeed in the UK (see Chapter 5). Conversely, despite their success in the UK domestic market, many British comedy films and television shows do not export well to the United States. There are exceptions, such as the film *The Full Monty* (1994), the *Monty Python* 'franchise' and Ricky Gervais and Stephen Merchant's BBC sitcom *The Office* (2001). Of course this imbalance may be as much an issue of industrial muscle as one of taste. It may also be, as Andy Medhurst argues, that while all cultures share the deep structures of what passes as the comic, national humour consists of 'more nuanced "close-ups" relating to context and specificity' (2007: 14). As he recognises, even within a relatively small nation as England (as distinct from Scotland, Wales or Northern Ireland) there are important regional differences in comic sensibility and the success of – or taste for – certain comedians and their material.

Class, gender and taste

In addition to national and even regional determinants, it seems clear that class and gender are important factors influencing attitudes towards comedic taste. Ken Willis makes the point that 'because our positions in social life differ, so will our humour competences, and thus it isn't possible to carry out a blanket assignment of funniness to texts' (2009: 130). This shows exactly where discussions of taste arise. For example, most critical commentary on slapstick comedy tends to regard it as rather a crude and basic form of humour, unlikely to appeal to those who prefer a more 'intellectual' or 'clever' kind of comedy. To what extent is this view of slapstick comedy – and indeed other forms of comedy – influenced by class and gender?

Writing in the 1980s, Pierre Bourdieu (1930–2002) posits that class factions are determined by a combination of economic, social and cultural capital. He argues that symbolic goods such as literature, cinema and the arts are used as 'strategies of distinction' and help delineate the differences between classes. There exists a hierarchy of consumption of all cultural practices and preferences which is closely related to social origin and educational attainment, and as a result ' tastes ... function as markers of "class"' (Bourdieu 1984: 1–2). Using musical examples to illustrate these hierarchies of taste, Bourdieu argues that Bach's *The Well-tempered Clavier* would be considered legitimate good taste, Gershwin's *Rhapsody in Blue* exemplifies middlebrow taste and *The Blue Danube* represents popular taste. Given the low overall reputation of comedy, commensurate examples are not easy to substitute. We might venture a Shakespeare comedy such as *A Midsummer Night's Dream* now represents 'good' taste (though it was designed to appeal to a range of Elizabethan tastes), Woody Allen's *Annie Hall* might represent middlebrow taste and a popular sitcom such as *Friends* could represent popular taste, yet all of these have elements of slapstick and it seems safer to assume that any comedy might be regarded as only middlebrow at best. For Bourdieu what is valorised as legitimate 'good taste' is the taste of the ruling class, which exists in sharp distinction with the 'cruder' tastes of the lower orders. This matters, he argues, because: 'art and cultural consumption are predisposed, consciously and deliberately or not, to fulfil a social function of legitimating social differences' (1984: 7). Though he was writing in a European context, Bourdieu's ideas on the legitimisation of taste are relevant to the American context where social distinctions are reliant on education and money. An example of this distinction made relatively explicit is present in the 1990s US sitcom *Frasier* where the educated, affluent Frasier and his brother Niles have very different interests and tastes from their blue-collar father, a former policeman who, in his turn, is disdainful of what he regards as his sons' effete cultural pretensions (though, of course, the generic positioning of the protagonists as family prevents these differences from getting out of hand).

Bourdieu developed the concept of 'habitus', which he saw as essentially a structure of mind that was developed by a set of acquired ideas, sensibilities, dispositions and tastes. What follows from this, according to Bourdieu, is that individuals learn to want what conditions make possible for them, and not to aspire to what is not available to them. He argues that, because of its ability to generate and regulate the practices that go to make up social life, habitus is a crucial factor contributing to social reproduction, that is the the continuation of society as it is, or maintaining the status quo.

Bourdieu's work is important because it rejects any notion of absolute or genuine good taste, arguing that what passes as good taste is socially determined by those who have accrued most economic, cultural and social capital. Bourdieu's work analyses the acknowledged differences between 'high art' and 'popular culture', between apparent critical disdain and commercial success, distinctions that still operate today. However, although Bourdieu's work may help to explain continuing hierarchies of taste and the consumption and popularity of certain types of comedy for certain sections of society, there is an argument for saying that the growth of the media and the increased accessibility of media texts, combined with the development of what might be termed 'cool' ironic humour in postmodern culture, has rendered the position more complex than Bourdieu implies. In other words it might be that it has become increasingly acceptable for intelligent, educated and fair-minded (i.e. middle-class) people not to take offence, to even admire and laugh at, comic material that might previously have been considered distasteful, even offensive. In practice this might simply mean that popular culture has become more acceptable but it would not ultimately break the system in which there is acceptable and unacceptable comedy: Medhurst is clearly right to insist that the considerable popularity of a comedian such as Roy 'Chubby' Brown as a live performer 'is a flagrant testimony to the persistence of class as a meaningful category, an indispensable tool which English people use in recognising, understanding and placing themselves' (2007: 199). Studying Brown allows Medhurst to make some excellent points about the communality and immediacy of popular comedy (201–2), showing that what makes his success all the more remarkable is Brown's virtual invisibility in broadcast and cinema media, his reputation being built up through record, video and DVD sales and live touring. It becomes clear that our focus on mainstream film, radio and television already reiterates exclusions from that mainstream on the grounds of taste which is ultimately a reflection of class prejudice.

If a consideration of class can develop our understanding of taste and comedy, then so too can a consideration of gender and sexuality. In Chapter 8 we took an extended look at comedy, gender and sexuality, but want to offer some thoughts here about the extent to which these influence the reception of comedy. Given the dominant presence of aggression and sexuality in jokes, it is surprising that more has not been written about the influence of gender and sexuality on the production and consumption of comedy. Put bluntly, women and men respond to different types of comedy in different ways. Of course this ignores the nuances of sexuality which will clearly have an influence, but, as we shall suggest, there is research evidence to support this bald, bold statement.

It has been argued (Rappoport 2005: 102) that it is possible to make three broad generalisations about gender humour. The first suggests that gender humour is universal. The second suggests that men tell jokes which ridicule women far more frequently than vice versa. The third tells us that women are much more likely to laugh at men's jokes than men are at jokes told by women. In identifying this imbalance, we must we careful not to establish the male joke-teller or the male audience as the norm (see Gray 1994: 13–14). In her research Regina Barreca (1991) identified four distinctive characteristics of women's humour. She found that women dislike slapstick humour where people are humiliated or put down in some way. Women are far more likely to enjoy humour that bursts the pomposities of those in positions of authority and power, and far less likely to enjoy humour that ridicules the less fortunate. Women are more likely to use irony in remarks that appear positive. Women are much more likely than men to use self-critical and deprecating humour as a means of gaining acceptance and approval. Barreca's work thus suggests that women are likely to respond to comedy on radio, film and television in different ways from men. Once again this is not to identify a divergence from some male norm but to illustrate that gender makes a difference to *all* reception of humour.

What this allows us to see is that there is no one point of view from which to consider comedy, either as an individual or critically. There are instead groupings of viewpoints. Gender and class are among the most clear, race, ethnicity and nationality are others but who determines what is and is not acceptable, what is and is not in good taste, is, as Jerry Palmer succinctly puts it, 'largely a question of power relations' (2009: 82 and see also Willis 2009:134).

In the rest of this chapter we look at some detailed examples of comedy in radio, film and television that raises issues of taste. We begin by looking at the *Carry On* films and the work of Benny Hill, examples primarily located in the 1960s, 1970s and early 1980s, then move on to trace the origins and development of the gross-out movie from the abandonment of the Production Code in 1966 to the present. Finally we consider *Borat* (2006), a film that pushes at boundaries of 'good taste' and 'political correctness' but which has enjoyed considerable critical and commercial success, and the controversial *Four Lions* (2010). In this way we ask questions about whether tastes in comedy change over time, and why some comedy material finds lasting acceptability while other material comes to be regarded as offensive and unacceptable, and where the boundaries of acceptable taste currently lie.

Following up: taste and culture

☞ Is the work of Bourdieu still helpful when it comes to understanding contemporary comedy? To what extent do specific examples of humour cross class boundaries?

☞ Taking a joke that is currently being circulated on mobile phone, analyse why the joke might be considered both funny and offensive. Would such a joke find its way on to radio, on to television, or into a film?

British 'low humour': *Carry On* ... Benny Hill

British comedy has a long and acknowledged tradition of what is often called 'low humour'. Influenced by music hall and variety, comedy in British films of the 1930s and 1940s often employed an aesthetic which privileged spectacle over narrative coherence. The disruptive, Bakhtinian qualities embedded in the films of George Formby, the Crazy Gang, Gracie Fields and Frank Randle appealed to working-class communities in a society in which class distinctions were paramount. British comedy films presented a populist articulation of what life was like for many, offering what Sutton terms 'a chorus of raspberries' to set against 'the dominant aesthetics of high art and the classical paradigm of narrative film-making' (Sutton 2000: 226). Of course, in film and on radio and television, there were limits to how far the comedy could drift towards what could be regarded as vulgarity. The stand-up comedian Max Miller was known in the late 1930s and 1940s for his routines which included a high degree of sexual innuendo, but was censured by the BBC for his radio joke about going to the optician, which concluded with the line 'when I see F you see K'.

In the 1950s the films of Norman Wisdom, starting with *Trouble in Store* (1953), encouraged audiences to side with the clumsy but well-intentioned little man who battled against authority and a class-saturated culture of deference. Like those of earlier comedians such as Formby, Wisdom's films were hugely popular, but were derided by the critics who disliked the slapstick antics and the comic pathos. This pattern, of commercial popularity combined with critical disdain at what was regarded as vulgar or in poor taste, persisted right through the 1960s, 1970s and 1980s, not least with the *Carry On* films and the television work of Benny Hill. As we shall see, however, while the *Carry On* films remain a cherished part of the British comic tradition, Benny Hill has become a comic pariah.

Making an important distinction between 'popular' culture and 'low' culture, Leon Hunt argues that '[t]he "low" can be distinguished both as a doubly marginalised district within the popular and as an irrecuperable textual community' (1998: 8). In fact the two main examples we examine suggest that, when it comes to taste and comic sensibility, things are perhaps more fickle and complex than this implies, and that, while some examples of 'low' comedy are recuperable and may even come to be treated with a degree of reverence and affection, others appear to place themselves beyond the pale. What might become clear is that context is key.

Beginning with *Carry On Sergeant* (1958) and ending with *Carry On Columbus* (1992), the thirty-one *Carry On* films have attained institutional status in Britain, despite critical despair at the obvious jokes, flimsy plots, execrable puns and excruciating innuendo. For Medhurst 'they are by far the best-known reference point in the entire history of vulgar English film comedy' (2007: 129). In spite of some significant differences in the films across the decades, the humour in the *Carry On* films remained resolutely lowbrow. The early films, including *Carry On Nurse*, *Carry On Constable* and *Carry On Teacher*, gently pilloried British institutions and the people who worked in them. From *Carry On Jack* (1963) to *Carry On up the Khyber* (1968), the films are largely parodies of generic cinema or historic events. The later films are increasingly reliant on sexual innuendo, double entendre and slapstick. *Carry On Camping* (1969) marked a growing acknowledgement of more open social attitudes towards sex, but the *Carry On* films that followed, at least until the unfortunate *Carry On England* (1976), stopped short of more explicit nudity that was increasingly a feature of other British sex comedies of the 1970s, for example the *Confessions of ...* series of films starring Robin Askwith.

Flirtation with matters sexual, lavatorial and scatological had been a feature in all the films, as can be judged by the names of characters who appeared in them. Dr. Tinkle, Sid Boggle, Senna Pod, Miss Bangor, Private Widdle, Francis Bigger, Citizen Bidet, the Khasi of Kalabar and a host of others epitomise the mildly risqué, euphemistic and often corny humour that is central to the films. However, this humour was located in scenarios that ordinary people could relate to, where escape seemed infinitely preferable to reality, whether from the constraints of marriage, of authority, of work, even, on occasions, of gender. There is a sense that we are watching adults constantly searching for the playground, desperate to avoid the maturity that the world appears to demand from them. This Bahktinian rejection of the oppressive normal order of things is evident, for example, in *Carry On at your Convenience* (1971) when the workers from W.C. Boggs' toilet factory go on a day-trip to Brighton, but a sense of refusal, articulated through the possibilities of the comic, of not taking things and each other too seriously, ripple throughout all the films.

From *Carry On Sergeant*, the critical response from the 'respectable' broadsheet newspapers towards these low-budget features was largely dismissive, the *Daily Telegraph* seeing 'stock figures speaking lines rising from the smutty to the banal' (Webber 2008: 41). A year later in 1959 the British Film Institute's *Monthly Film Bulletin* rated *Carry On Nurse* as a 'somewhat stale farce, mixing slapstick, caricature and crudely anatomical humour'. However, other reviewers at least acknowledged that the films had their funny moments. The *Daily Express* liked *Carry On Constable* (1960) precisely because '[T]here are lavatory jokes, there are puns, trousers fall down' (Webber 2008: 61). As the series progressed, the overwhelming view of the press was that the *Carry Ons* were 'good, simple, dirty fun' offering, seemingly contradictorily, 'innocent vulgarity'.

By the mid-1970s the affection felt for the *Carry Ons* was tested by *Carry On England* (1976) and then severely challenged by *Carry On Emmanuelle* (1978). As the films tried to adapt their comedy to changes in social attitudes towards sexuality and demands for female liberation they replaced innuendo and double entendre with outright nudity, and lost the essence of what many considered to be the *Carry On* comic formula. Though there was an attempt to revive the series with *Carry On Columbus* (1992), it could well be that the affection still felt for the films stems from the fact that their material was never really sexually explicit or wholly offensive. As a result, they have become,

9 Benny Hill, from international television star to forgotten man.

as Medhurst puts it, 'part of the nation's cultural furniture ... entrenched in the language as shorthand for naughty, gigglesome, mildly risqué humour' (2007: 129). Whether by good luck or judgement, the *Carry Ons* preserved their reputation by knowing when to stop.

The reputation of Benny Hill (1924–92) is, by contrast, now so tarnished it is difficult to believe that he was the most popular comedian in Britain for nearly two decades. Though often referred to in the 1960s as the first comedian to be made by the new medium of television, Hill also worked in radio from 1947, appeared in a number of films including *Those Magnificent Men in Their Flying Machines* (1965), *Chitty Chitty Bang Bang* (1968) and *The Italian Job* (1969), and made a number of records including 'Ernie, The Fastest Milkman in the West', a novelty song that topped the British record charts at Christmas 1971. Despite this professional dexterity, it was television, first with the BBC from 1955 and then with the commercial channel Thames Television in the 1970s and 1980s, that made Hill such a huge success. His work was given a series of accolades, including BAFTA and other British industry awards throughout the 1970s and into the early 1980s. He gained huge popularity in the United States from the late 1970s onwards and was equally popular globally, garnering a number of international comedy awards. In 1984, of the 142 countries with broadcasting facilities, 127 had screened *The Benny Hill Show* (Ross 1999: 151). Yet, despite continuing popularity abroad, by the time that Mark Lewisohn published his biography of the comedian in 2003 Hill had become not just largely forgotten in Britain but almost a taboo subject. For Lewisohn the reason is clear: 'The prevailing attitude – among women especially – remains the one that dogged his last dozen years: that his work degraded women' (2003b: 439). Arguably, no other comedian or body of work exemplifies the extent to which changes in comic sensibility and taste can occur in a relatively short time.

Like the *Carry On* films, Hill's comedy was determinedly lowbrow. Performing in postwar army camps in the late 1940s, Hill was using material that was 'fruity, raucous and unsubtle' (Ross 1999: 15). Like the radio and stage comedian Max Miller, Hill belonged to the world of saucy postcard comedy and of sexual innuendo. He combined this humour with knockabout slapstick, and skilfully harnessed his corny gags within the framework of newly emerging television and its conventions. He did this through a series of long-serving caricatures, most famously the dim-witted but ever-willing Fred Scuttle with his clumsy salute, through brilliant comic parodies of other then-current television shows and by his cheeky knowing grins to camera which cemented a complicity with the audience that initially allowed him to profess a certain innocence amongst all the innuendo. For example, in a parody of a quiz show, he asks what was the connection between a billiard table and the inside of a man's trousers; the answer, of course, was pockets, and not what he knows was in the minds of the 'contestants' and many of the television audience. Though critics were often unkind and his material caused some concern in what was still, in the late 1950s and early 1960s, a rather stuffy BBC, *The Benny Hill Show* attracted huge audiences, a reputed 12 million in 1957 and 17 million in 1958.

Hill was lured away from the BBC in 1969 by Thames Television, where *The Benny Hill Show* continued for a further twenty years. A number of characters remained, including Fred Scuttle, and new ones were introduced, notably the bespectacled caricature Chinese Chow-Mein with the catchphrase 'shtoopid iriot' who generated a range of rather unsubtle wordplay, such as 'rubbery rady' (for lovely lady), 'tooth-hurtee' (for two-thirty), as well as opportunities for flirting with the unmentionable (erection/election). Though successful, Hill kept with a formula that precipitated a disastrous decline. However, it was not incipient racism that caused the problem at that time, but the sense that Hill's material was overtly sexist during a period of increasing female emancipation and equality. Hill had always been attracted to the comedy of male emasculation that pervades the seaside postcard culture articulated by Donald McGill, arguing that, for men, sex is a snare and a delusion, an area of activity that becomes funny precisely because men are doomed to failure and frustration. From the mid-1960s the characters that Hill played were often archetypes of male sexual frustration. By the mid-1970s his material was increasingly ribald and the shows became increasingly reliant on semi-clad female dance troupes including Love Machine and, from 1980, Hill's Angels. Criticism that the show featured 'smut' and material that was sexually gratuitous came from right-wing organisations such as Mary Whitehouse's Viewers and Listeners Association and from the churches, and growing numbers of women objected to its perceived sexism. Readers of *Woman's Own*, hardly a radical feminist publication, voted *The Benny Hill Show* the most disliked programme of 1986 (Lewisohn 2003b: 370). The defence by the producer Dennis Kirkland that, if the show was sexist, it was because it was totally anti-men fails to explain the increasingly lurid and exploitative camerawork that emphasised in a gratuitous manner aspects of female anatomy. In an age of increased sexual liberation, Hill's comedy fell the wrong side of a very thin line between openness and offensiveness.

The truth is that society and its tastes had changed, and not just in attitudes to sexuality and gender. Increasingly, in the 1980s Hill's type of comedy, the innuendo, the coy puerile gags, the slapstick chases, was seen as old-fashioned. In its place was 'alternative comedy' which had a different view on sexual relationships and a different comic sensibility.

Of course 1980s television shows such as *The Young Ones* (1982–84) were also capable of irritating some, but they were playing to a younger generation who rejected the mores of their parents. If the characters behaved in ways that were seen by some as crude and brutish, they were nonetheless hugely appealing to the generation of students who loved the show for its surreal, anarchic and aggressive style of comedy (see Chapter 5). Hill's later material, by contrast, appears to have no sense of irony but, instead, almost exactly the seedy 'nudge-nudge-wink-wink' humour pilloried by Eric Idle in the well-known early 1970s *Monty Python's Flying Circus* sketch. Hill's continued winks to camera now seem merely to indicate a certain glee at still 'getting away with it'. The result is that Benny Hill is a 'comedian whose more cleverly realised caricatures are now hard to rescue from the long shadow cast by his interminable sexual harassment chases' (Medhurst 2007: 84).

Following up: low humour

☞ To what extent are dated attitudes displayed in screen humour an obstacle to enjoying its comedy? To what extent do such elements now replace this humour's original challenges to taste and propriety?

☞ Taking either a *Carry On* film or television work featuring Benny Hill, assess the extent to which Barreca's research on gender and comedy has substance. Are there more recent examples where gender dictates differential responses to comedy?

American bad taste

This section discusses American gross-out comedies from the 1960s onwards, their sub-generic characteristics and the reasons for their success, all of which rely on taste and, in particular, 'bad' taste. Discerning or 'good' taste frowns on indulgent excess and thus also frowns on pleasure itself with the implication that some types of laughing are bad for you. Gross-out comedy is a sub-genre of comedy that deliberately confronts the acceptable standards of taste within society.

Until the mid-1960s taste in American cinema was regulated by the Production Code that had been written in the early 1930s and enforced since 1934 (see Chapter 3). The lowbrow medium of popular film was to be subject to the moral, class and taste judgements of those who set themselves up as its arbiters and considered that films were made for a general family audience. Those on both the conservative right and the radical left rejected mass taste because it was chosen over those texts and media (i.e. high culture) that they felt the mainstream audience ought to prefer. The right wing appeared to believe it essential that the mass audience were shown nothing to stir them up and the critical left wing raged against what they saw as the successful pacification of the audience. For this reason Hollywood's popular products, perhaps especially comedies, have often been critically despised. The greater the perceived poverty of taste of any given film, the less likelihood of its being dealt with in critical depth. Academia, coming late to film and later to comedy for just such reasons (as we have seen in our Introduction), tends to support and maintain taste through its canonisation of certain films and filmmakers. Just as cinema itself has been found worthy of study, so film criticism must eventually turn to bad-taste comedy and gross-out films. These films are not an obscure byway of cinema but a historically and economically vital area of the industry that won't go away even if it is critically ignored; it makes money and it does so because it has wide appeal.

The 1963 assassination of United States President Kennedy brought about a spike in ongoing concern about the level of fictional violence, especially in television, which had 'caught up' with film in this regard. At the same time the restrictions of the Code with regard to both sex and violence were exposed when American films were seen against European and other international imports screened in cinema clubs and film schools. In 1966 enforcement of the Production Code was suspended following the distribution of the film version of Edward Albee's Broadway play *Who's Afraid of Virginia Woolf?* containing 'bad' language. The high cultural status of this controversial but critically lauded dramatic work helped justify this move. Two years later the ratings system came into force and, for the first time, differentiated American filmgoers into age groups. ('M' (later 'PG'), 'R' and 'X' were designed to police an age border initially set at sixteen but later raised to seventeen.) Recognition that the cinema audience was not homogeneous allowed Hollywood filmmakers to reflect the stresses of late 1960s America, its economic recession, political, generational and racial strife, in different ways to different audiences. The gross-out genre could not come into being under the Code, but the necessary elements for its development are in circulation from the late 1960s.

The period 1967–77 is an extraordinary one in the film industry as the old guard of the studios realised that they had lost their grip on their most active (youth) audience and turned to new young directors from television and film-school backgrounds who would eventually bail them out with films such as *Jaws* (1975) and *Star Wars* (1977). Peter Krämer's book *The New Hollywood* (1998) offers an excellent way in to analysing this period by considering box-office success as the prime indicator of cultural significance. In focusing on comedy films alone it is not possible to maintain such rigour and, unlike Krämer, we use gross profit figures, not figures adjusted for inflation.

The top five box-office hits included in the top twenty of the New Hollywood period are as in the table below.

What do these successes share? Comic parody of 'serious' genres is apparent in *Blazing Saddles*, *Young Frankenstein* and *M*A*S*H*. *The Graduate* and *American Graffiti* focus on teen heroes; the former an individual, in the second an ensemble (also the case with *M*A*S*H*). Finally, surprisingly, all but *The Graduate* are set in the past. This nostalgic element appears to be significant in that it 'removes' the films from contemporary debates while allowing audiences to read their concerns in to the situation depicted.

Rank	Title	Year	Gross $m	Setting
1	*Blazing Saddles*	1974	119	Spoof western
2	*American Graffiti*	1972	115	Comedy drama with a 1962 soundtrack
3	*The Graduate*	1967	104	Contemporary sex comedy
4	*Young Frankenstein*	1975	86	Spoof of 1930s Universal horror movies
5	*M*A*S*H*	1970	73	Korean War-set and much more raucous than the famous (1972–83) sitcom

The figures show that these films were massive hits, but it remains to be suggested how they pushed the boundaries of acceptable taste. The significance of race in *Blazing Saddles* is discussed in Chapter 10, but the film's use of flatulence was ground – as well as wind – breaking. *Young Frankenstein* has gags involving several types of disability and an obsession with the monster's vital statistics. *M*A*S*H* inserted black comedy and sex in a mobile army surgical hospital setting. *American Graffiti* focused on the clash between adult responsibilities and juvenile pleasures. *The Graduate* played the relationship between a young man (Dustin Hoffman) and the mother of his girlfriend, Mrs Robinson (Anne Bancroft) for laughs. Other films, less wildly successful, nevertheless pushed the boundaries further in this climate with *Harold and Maude* (1971) featuring the relationship between a suicidal teenager and a elderly eccentric, and *Everything You Wanted to Know About Sex...* (1973) included sequences making fun of, among other practices, chastity belts, transvestitism and bestiality. The gross-out movie is clearly not very far away.

The following characteristics of the gross-out comedy film are adapted and summarised from pages 110–12 of William Paul's *Laughing Screaming: Modern Hollywood Horror and Comedy* (1994). They are not exclusive to this sub-genre of comedy, nor are all of them required.

1. A group of characters is featured rather than an individual.
2. The group contains a variety of types.
3. Often the group is teenage.
4. Characters are defined by their sexual desires. Romance is secondary.
5. Characters are defined as good or bad by the positive or negative relationship they have with those desires.
6. The characters are aligned to an institution.
7. There is celebration of the body.
8. The narrative is episodic.
9. There is a basic revenge plot.
10. The narrative pitches 'us' versus 'them'.

With the exception of point three, the above might easily be applied to the *Carry On …* films. There are, however, further key characteristics of the gross-out comedy which Paul draws out by bracketing this type of film with examples of the horror genre:

> Gross-out films are looking for a … strong response from their audience. A gleeful uninhibitedness is certainly the most striking feature of these films … and it also represents their greatest appeal. At their best, these films offer a real sense of exhilaration, not without its disturbing quality, in testing how far they can go, how much they can show without making us turn away, how far they can push the boundaries to provoke a cry of 'Oh, gross!' as a sign of approval, an expression of disgust that is pleasurable to call out …
>
> These films offer a radical challenge to taste and value, but not in the programmatic way of self-consciously avant-garde art that could still make these works acceptable to arbiters of taste and value (1994: 20)

The film generally regarded as initiating the genre is *National Lampoon's Animal House* (1978) which earned almost $142 million and was, at the time, the top grossing comedy ever. Scripted by Harold Ramis and directed by John Landis, it is set in that key nostalgic period of 1962 in a university fraternity house. Most famously it stars John Belushi as Bluto, described by Geoff King as 'a grotesque *spectacle* of transgression' (2002: 69), whose appetite for food and drink and excess is immense. For example, in the cafeteria scene we find Bluto scavenging the clearing area and managing to eat a golfball, immediately showing he does not recognise divisions between waste and food and that, for him, anything may be edible. He moves on to take a tray through self-service, piling it high, stuffing his pockets and sampling the food including inhaling a jelly and stuffing a whole cheeseburger into his mouth. Then, coming to the aid of a delta fraternity brother, he joins a table of killjoy alpha students including the girl he most lusts after, disgusting them with his appetite and, in the course of pretending to be a zit, spitting food over them. This leads to a slapstick chase that ends once Bluto, escaping retribution, has announced 'Food fight!' leading to general mayhem and showing the majority of students taking their lead from him rather than from the self-defining elite students.

Standards of taste promote the suppression and standardisation of the body and its functions (they also engage in the suppression of certain genders and sexualities as we discussed in Chapter 8). Patriarchy, the established order and the standards that it sets form a challenge and a threat to those outside it or not yet assimilated within it. The teen focus of the archetypal gross-out comedy is generated by what our adolescent and teen years necessarily involve: physical and hormonal bodily changes, and the individual addressing societal requirements in terms of gender responsibilities and performance including, though not limited to, sex. All adults have experienced these pressures and their representation therefore has universal appeal. *The Forty Year Old Virgin*

(2005) makes a point of showing that adulthood is not necessarily an escape from such pressures and issues of 'experience'.

Paul imputes an implicit political element to the overturning of taste: 'the aggressive "exposing what should be hidden" is always implicitly a political act because it threatens the social order by contesting proper social behaviour. Challenging what constitutes acceptable public discourse, which is the key to the aesthetics of gross-out, inevitably carries with it deeper challenges' (1994: 52). In appealing to the popular against the dominance of taste and its arbiters (those with negative relations to their desires), film comedy both acknowledges and allows some negotiation with the tensions of becoming adult. For filmmakers the list of characteristics might seem easy to follow but pitching their assault on taste at the right level is fraught with risk. Critics who see gross-out films pandering to the lowest common denominator seem to assume that film producers know exactly what the lowest common denominator wants. Nothing could be further from the truth.

In 1979 Steven Spielberg, creator of massive hits such as *Jaws* and *Close Encounters of the Third Kind* (1977), was given a $35 million budget to make *1941*, a nostalgic comedy about the possible presence of Japanese submarines off the west coast of America causing chaos, with an ensemble cast including John Belushi, Tim Matheson and Dan Ackroyd among others. Though *1941* sounds like a dream combination of *M*A*S*H* and *Animal House*, it flopped and grossed only $6 million. By contrast, in the same year, a cheap vampire spoof starring George Hamilton called *Love at First Bite* took nearly $44 million, and *Meatballs,* a summer camp comedy with Bill Murray, made $43 million, eventually spawning three sequels.

The taste of movie-going audiences in terms of humour is discriminating, in the sense that it knows what it likes, but it is not predictable. Knowing this will, however, never stop film producers trying. The year 1980 did not bring more *1941*s (though *The Blues Brothers*, with Belushi and Ackroyd, might qualify in its excess), but it did bring many more studio pictures trying to get a big success through comedy films either in the gross-out mode or inflected with it. These include *Airplane*, *Caddyshack* and two films with female protagonists for a change, *Private Benjamin* and *9 to 5. Airplane* spoofed the 1970s disaster movies, successfully featured mature actors like Leslie Nielsen and Lloyd Bridges in manic roles and introduced oral sex as a new subject for film comedy. The team behind it went on, not to *Airplane II*, but to *Top Secret* and the innovative though under-appreciated cop show spoof/sitcom *Police Squad* (which led to *The Naked Gun* and its successful sequels). These films combine gross-out gags with a much busier version of Mel Brooks's early 1970s spoofs.

The standard for the small-budget gross-out movie was finally perfected by Bob Clark as writer and director of *Porky's* in 1981. Made for $4 million, it took $105 million and came third in box-office takings for the year, after *Raiders of the Lost Ark* and ahead of the Oscar-winning *Chariots of Fire*. In 2001 it was remembered in a poll of the American public as the funniest comedy ever.

Porky's is about horny teenagers in Angel Beach, Florida in the 1950s, focusing on the sex-starved PeeWee (Dan Monahan) and his attempts to lose his virginity. There is a sub-plot about the Jewish and redneck characters in the group coming to tolerate each other but the main plot is about the humiliation of the enemies of fun, the sports mistress Beulah Balbricker (Nancy Parsons) and the eponymous Porky, a swindling strip-club owner. The film's massive success depends on the effectiveness of a few key scenes: one involving a gym mistress who yodels during sex and, most famously, the shower scene. This is a scene of voyeurism with several Freudian substitutions made literal. While three male characters are spying through holes in the walls of the female showers one of them becomes so excited he replaces his eye with his penis, giving it a voice and name ('Polly Penis') and inviting his shocked audience to approach. He can no longer see that Miss Balbricker has been brought to see what the fuss is about and she seizes the errant organ. Although this is painful for the culprit, Miss Balbricker is compelled to handle the thing she despises and is unable to literally castrate the culprit. The shower scene is followed by a long aftermath scene in the principal's office presided over by a Norman Rockwell portrait of President Eisenhower reminding us of the 1950s setting. With a built-in laugh track of the gym coach's sniggering assistants, it becomes apparent that Miss Balbricker's concerns cannot be addressed because of the dominance of a fragile patriarchal authority. The offending organ is something whose very mention offends the Principal, who tries to insist that it be referred to as a 'tallywhacker'. In a conclusion that sustains sex-based essentialism it is not simply the culprit's penis but the phallus that has slipped through Miss Balbricker's grasp, and the only resolution for the scene, and for the relieved male characters, is to collapse in hysterical laughter.

The teen group formula for the gross-out comedy recurs periodically after *Porky's* but gross-out elements were beginning to feature in a number of other highly successful comedy films. For example, *Ghostbusters* (1984), with Bill Murray, Harold Ramis and Dan Ackroyd under *Meatballs* and *Stripes* (1981) director Ivan Reitman, is an high-budget effects-laden gross-out comedy which became a mega-hit and took $238 million. In the 1990s gross-out specialists the Farrelly brothers established themselves as with the $127 million grossing worldwide hit *Dumb and Dumber* (1994), and the less commercially successful *Kingpin* (1996), but their next effort, *There's Something about Mary* (1998), effectively hybridised the gross-out movie with the romantic comedy and took $176 million. This film manages to get through 'boy meets girl' and 'boy loses girl' stages of the typical romantic plot before the title sequence (see Goldman 2001: 139–51) by presenting the disastrous prom date between Ted (Ben Stiller) and his dream girl Mary (Cameron Diaz). The main body of the film gets them back together with further comic sequences involving various levels of grossness such as Matt Dillon's character accidentally setting fire to a dog in a mad attempt to resuscitate it, Lee Evans's character overacting physical disability and Mary innocently using Ted's semen as hair gel before the classical 'boy gets girl' conclusion. While the Farrelly brothers have continued to make films that test the limits of mainstream taste with somewhat diminishing returns, Stiller has starred in *Meet the Parents* (2000) and its sequel *Meet the Fockers* (2004) which have been able to attract major stars and huge audiences taking $166 and $279 million respectively. By concentrating on the deeply stressful rites of passage of a single individual and involving gross-out elements, such as a mother's ashes and a toilet-trained cat, with the prize of romantic fulfilment, rather than simply sex, the first film in this ongoing series showed gross-out underpinning mainstream comedy and achieving a level of success comparable with more ambitious and critically favoured products; *Meet the Parents* made only $21 million less than *Gladiator*.

It's one thing to gross an audience out, it's another to make it funny too. Audience sensibilities, and therefore opportunities for gross-out comedy innovations, evolve over time, even though the basic ingredients remain universal. The gross-out genre now spans the range of Hollywood production with its cruder, cheaper end represented by the gross-out for gross-out's sake of the *Jackass* films. There appears to be no shortage of ways to challenge taste in film, as the following case studies show in detail.

Following up: grossing-out

☞ To what extent can gross-out films be defined as a sub-genre of comedy? Is the term more useful as a designation for taste-challenging humour that can be used in varous other sub-genres such as romantic comedy or comedian comedy?

☞ Consider the opening eight minutes of *There's Something about Mary* and answer the following questions: What is the funniest point in the sequence? Why is Mary's family constructed as it is? Does the film go too far (i.e. offend all standards of taste) by showing us a close up of what Ted has done to himself? Why is genital misadventure, as in this sequence, or the shower scene in *Porky*'s funny?

Crossing the borders of taste: *Borat* (2006)

Rated the second-best comedy film of all time by the *Guardian* newspaper (*Guardian* 2010), *Borat: Cultural Learnings of America for Make Benefit Glorious Nation of Kazakhstan* (2006) reinforced the reputation of Sasha Baron Cohen, whose emergence and rise from the mid-1990s was as a performer who, on television and on film, tested the limits of contemporary taste. If the number of threatened lawsuits against the film is anything to go by, then *Borat* has a claim to be the most offensive comedy ever. Developed on British television in 1996, Cohen's character Borat, like his other creation Ali G (see Chapter 10), purports to be an innocent abroad, not intending to give offence but doing so through the questions he asks of the unsuspecting real-life people he comes into contact with. The film is a picaresque odyssey as Borat, accompanied by his producer Azamat, travels from his native Kazakhstan across America, ostensibly to garner 'cultural learnings' for his film documentary, though he is soon sidetracked into chasing Pamela Anderson, whom he has seen in an episode of the US beach soap *Baywatch*.

Comically offensive on television, mistaking for example, Amsterdam's canals for a well-organised sewage system, particularly convenient as he has one outside his hotel, in *Borat* Cohen pushes the boundaries ever further. The primary targets for his abusive, critically indefensible comments are women, American cultural habits and Jews, but along the way he has a pop at other subjects often thought too sensitive to make comic material out of, such as when he interviews an African-American politician who is 'a genuine chocolate-face – no make up', scares children with a bear or engages in a

10 Borat (Sacha Baron Cohen) models the mankini at Cannes in Borat (2006).

gross, naked wrestling match with Azamat, ending with the two of them, stark naked, bursting into a mortgage brokers' convention at their hotel. Prostitution, masturbation, bestiality, incest and mental illness are all subject to comic treatment. Able to draw upon an engaging naivety and ignorance that supposedly stem from the cultural attitudes of his native Kazakhstan, Borat makes derogatory remarks about Jews, women and gypsies, as well as Kazakhstan's 'ass-hole' neighbour Uzbekistan (both real countries). His 'own' country has its problems: 'economic, social, Jew'. His attitudes are, of course, abhorrent, as when he expresses his incredulity that Pamela Anderson is campaigning *against* cruelty to animals; this is a man who keeps a live chicken in his luggage.

The comedy based around Borat's 'ignorance' is hugely effective as when, checking in a New York hotel, he unpacks his bag in the lift, believing that it is his room. However, it is in those scenes where he interacts with Americans and their culture that intrigue most. Persuaded that they are contributing to a genuine documentary, Borat inserts himself into the nuances of American life and exposes the limits of their tolerance and behaviour. Being taught dining etiquette leads to him bringing his turd with him back in a bag to the table, to the horror of his southern white hosts, but the cameras are finally shooed away when only Borat's 'guest', an overweight black prostitute, arrives to join the party. At a rodeo, having been introduced to the good-natured fans as a visitor who admires the United States, his version of the Kazakhstan national anthem sung to the tune of the 'The Star-Spangled Banner' gets the crowd on his back. The real offence, however, comes from the interview with the rodeo organiser, who betrays genuine racism. On another occasion, Borat is the guest on a live local television station. Apparently not realising he is on air, he makes some offensive remarks, offering his sister for sex, and says that he is off 'to make urine', much to the discomfort of the presenter. He is hustled away, only to interrupt the live weather forecast. In a wonderfully effective scene of pure slapstick, he parodies American obsession with wealth when he falls and smashes the stock in an antique shop; asked to pay damages, he offers to pay with 'genuine pure' Kazakhstan pubic hair. Staying in a Jewish-run overnight stop, he and Azamat refuse to eat the food and are convinced that the elderly Jewish couple will murder them and have changed their shape to cockroaches in order to get in the room.

Perhaps the most revealing scene occurs towards the beginning of the film, where Borat visits Pat Haggerty, a 'humor coach'. In trying to teach Borat what Americans would find funny – and, more importantly, what they would not find funny – Haggerty lays bare some of the limits to what is regarded as acceptable. Mother-in-law jokes are acceptable, though Borat makes it clear that, when talking about having sex with his mother-in-law, he is not joking. Haggerty is completely unmoved by Borat's amusement at his brother who has 'retardation', and hastens to tell Borat that jokes about the mentally ill are not funny in the USA. Of course, Borat's interactions with American culture confirm the limits of acceptability, but in this early scene we are left in little doubt that comedy is bounded by the culture in which it exists. As one woman guest at the dinner party opines, 'the cultural differences are vast', but Borat 'could be Americanised' if he is prepared to learn. His appearance with his faeces in a bag renders that unlikely.

In the end Borat does take back some American 'cultural learnings' to Kazakhstan. The country has become Christian, though the natives now torment a crucified man rather than the Jews. Borat also brings home some electronic goods such as iPods and plasma TVs, but attitudes have not changed. His despised neighbour has only a mini-iPod and everyone knows, he says, that the mini-iPod is for girls. Though the government of Kazakhstan took offence at his depiction of the country (though these scenes were actually shot in Romania), and a number of American individuals and organisations were equally vocal in their protestations, the real object of Cohen's scathing humour is us, as he forces us to confront our own prejudices and limitations.

Have you heard the joke about the terrorist?: *Four Lions* (2010)

Sensitivities about global terrorism since the attack on the Twin Towers of the World Trade Center in New York in September 2001, and the London bombings of July 2005, have produced a new taboo (or, in Britain, renewing an old one). Anyone who dares to joke about bombs as they attempt to pass through airport security will find out the depths of official concern about terrorism. In this context Chris Morris's comedy *Four Lions* can be seen as a brave attempt to confront deep-seated social anxieties by asking a fundamental question: can terrorism as a subject ever be funny? For Morris the answer, despite the contemporary taboo that precludes discussion of terrorism in any terms other than unblinking condemnation, is yes.

In Yorkshire a group of radical Muslim British Asians, disgusted with the 'godless, consumerist, Paki-bashing, Gordon Ramsey speciality cheddar-cheese-tasting, torture endorsing Disneyland' that is, for them, contemporary Britain, look for an outlet to express their outrage. Londoner Barry, an older, near-paranoid convert, is part of their group, attracted by the possibilities for violence that radical Islam appears to offer. When Omar and Waj return from an abortive trip to a training camp in Pakistan, where they have inadvertently killed Osama Bin Laden, Omar tells the group that they have been instructed to undertake a terrorist attack in Britain. Barry's desire to bomb a mosque, believing that this would ignite a race war, makes it evident that his commitment is to terrorism, not religion. The rest of the group reject Barry's view and finally agree to target the London marathon. Weak-minded Faisal, who has been busy training crows with explosives around their necks, accidentally blows himself up before the attack, but the others get to London. There, unsure whether or not to go ahead with their suicide mission, all four 'lions'

11 In Four Lions (2010) the protagonists argue about their plan, pointedly not dressed as lions.

are blown up, though not in ways in which their search for martyrdom had envisaged.

Director Chris Morris has said that 'terrorist cells have the same group dynamics as stag parties and five-a-side football teams. There is conflict, friendship, misunderstanding and rivalry. Terrorism is about ideology, but it's also about berks' (Morris 2010: 59). Much of the comedy is generated by the incompetence of the 'lions' and their inability to pursue their jihad with logical ruthlessness, The group struggle repeatedly to make jihadist videos that have the requisite sense of threat, as when Waj clutches a small replica rifle suitable, as Barry snorts, only for Action Man. Faisal insists on having a cardboard box over his head, Waj is constantly getting sidetracked into irrelevance, while the newest recruit Hassan is more interested in a combination of rap music video and *X-factor*-style audition tape. The incongruence between terrorist aspiration and the embrace of commercialised modernity is a constant source of comedy. Verbal, physical and conceptual jokes abound, much of them centred around the gap between the serious intent of the terrorists and the mundane, absurd attempts to put this into practice. They communicate, for example, by a children's game site, 'Puffinland'. Barry's ancient car lets them down, the result, he asserts, of the Jewish monopoly of car spare parts, particularly spark plugs, 'invented by the Jews to control global traffic'. The poverty of their efforts to understand complex issues is summed up by Barry's assertion that, whilst you cannot win an argument just by listening to your heart, you cannot win one 'just by being right'. Seeing them dressed in their heavily padded costumes at the London marathon, an unsuspecting policeman tells them that they are 'going to die in those'; he is right of course, but not through the heat exhaustion that he is referring to.

However, if the group's actions descend into farce, so too do the attempts by the authorities to deal with the 'extremists'. For Morris both sides of the 'war of terror' are comically, absurdly, incapable. Both apparently suffer from fear of, and mistaken belief in, the power of the technologies of surveillance. Barry persuades Waj and Hassan to shake their heads vigorously from side to side to avoid the 'space cameras'. Barry also urges the others to swallow their mobile-phone SIM cards unaware, as Omar informs him, that they can still be traced. At the London marathon police marksmen kill an innocent runner because of their inability to intellectually distinguish between a bear, a wookie and Omar's Honey Monster. In the café where Waj has taken the owner hostage, the police also shoot the wrong man, though the MP in charge of terrorism security asserts that 'we shot the right man but the wrong man exploded'. The farcical nature of anti-terrorism activity is stripped bare at the end of the film, where Omar's Qur'an-abiding brother is interrogated at RAF Mildenhall, in a steel container that is 'officially Egypt'.

Ultimately all of the characters are seen as vulnerable in their human frailty. At bottom Morris's film is as much about identity as anything else. It is not just Barry, the convert that Islam would not want, but all the group who are searching for their place in contemporary Britain. Equally, the British authorities are shown not as a model to aspire to but as incompetent and confused as the would-be jihadists. Morris pushes the boundaries of taste in ways that he had previously done through his television programmes such as *The Day Today* and *Brass Eye* (see Chapter 6). In tackling prevalent attitudes towards terrorism, arguably one of society's biggest taboos, and in giving a voice to characters who are shown to be comically inept whatever the depth of their aspirations and intentions, Morris explores through comedy the sad, pathetic and outrageously funny elements that go to make up human experience, especially when engaged at the outer limits of what is deemed acceptable. To reject such comedy on the grounds of taste, echoing the old music hall lines 'I don't wish to know that; kindly leave the stage', continues to mark a refusal to examine one's own point of view and dominant 'common-sense' discourses.

Following up: taste and taboo, Borat and Barry

☞ What contemporary taboos do *Borat* and *Four Lions* take on and turn into comic material?

☞ Are there issues that are somehow too 'distasteful' to be treated as comedy? Analyse why you think that some people might find the work of Sasha Baron Cohen and Chris Morris both unfunny and beyond what is acceptable.

Recommended reading

Sharon Lockyer and Michael Pickering (eds), *Beyond a Joke: The Limits of Humour*, Houndmills, Palgrave, 2009.

William Paul, *Laughing/Screaming: Modern Hollywood Horror and Comedy*, New York: Columbia University Press, 1994.

10

Comedy, race and ethnicity

As the previous chapter suggests, universal agreement as to what is funny is rare, if not impossible. We have also seen how laughter can invoke a temporary suspension of normal mental processes, so that we can often find a joke, a character, a scene or a sketch funny despite ideological concerns we might have. As Schaeffer puts it, '[w]e enter a world of amorality when we laugh, where our moral, practical and rational concerns have a moratorium on their functioning' (1981: 28). If the context is right, comedy provides a vacation away from the intellectual and affective world we inhabit for most of our waking lives. Comedy presents a world full of contradictions, since it can be the voice of both the powerful and the weak, it can be simultaneously subversive and affirming, funny yet offensive or, with or without the passage of time, no longer funny but simply offensive. Arguably, comedy and the laughter it produces are an invitation to a partnership, an invitation to share, even if momentarily, an illusion of complicity and belonging, but comedy has this effect by excluding others. As Andy Medhurst puts it, comedy can be as much a 'fence keeping you out as a gate letting you in' (2007: 20). This notion that comedy can be a Janus-like process, a barrier as well as an entrance, both a 'sword and a shield', is important when we attempt to understand the relationship between comedy, race and ethnicity.

Comic material in broadcasting and film can, as we have seen, have different meanings for different audiences at different times, but it invariably relies a great deal on stereotyping. The term stereotyping was thrust into circulation in 1922 by the American Walter Lippman, who recognised its role in the process of opinion formation and reproduction. Lippman saw stereotypes as inadequate, biased, obstacles to rational thought and resistant to social change but, at the same time, necessary if we are to understand the complex modern world. Though the concept of the stereotype is more complex than many definitions allow, it is useful to accept the broad definition of a stereotype as 'an exaggerated belief associated with a category [whose] function is to justify or rationalise our conduct in relation to that category' (Pickering 2001: 10). Stereotyping is problematic and demeaning for those stereotyped, especially minorities, since it assumes an exclusionary norm. Comedy has an important role in determining attitudes and behaviour towards stereotyped social groups, but the nature and effect of this role is a matter of debate. Karen Ross argues that 'while stereotypes have no basis in reality they are nonetheless real in their social consequences' (1996: 4). Omid Djalili, however, suggests that: 'Stereotypes are only stereotypes, I feel, because they actually have a modicum of truth in them' (Djalili quoted in Lockyer and Pickering 2009: 113). The apparent disagreement here is over the nature of the stereotypes discussed. Ross, writing about representation more widely than in comedy, refers to negative racist stereotypes while Djalili, as a comedian, is referring to recognisable cultural traits suitable for joking about (and undermining) in his act. The inflections of the use of stereotypes are much more complex than they superficially appear (see Malik 2002: 28–9) and their use in comedy complicates them further. As we saw in the introductory chapter, there are those who feel that laughing at others is an expression of a perceived social superiority, so that comedy serves to represent the object of laughter as somehow inferior. Balanced against that is the view that laughter is the enemy of social distinctions, that it helps to eradicate mistaken notions of superiority or inferiority, often by exposing the limitations and prejudices of those who try to maintain such distinctions.

Not surprisingly, when considering ethnic and racial humour we find sharply polarised views about its intent, function and effect. At one end of the spectrum there are those who insist that ethnic and racial humour can only ever serve to assert a presumed superiority of one racial or ethnic group over another. These critics argue that since both racism and jokes are social and cultural products, racial humour is not simply a product of an individual psychology, but is an aspect of racist society. For Howitt and Owusu-Bempah, the consequence is that 'racist jokes ... act as propaganda in support of racist ideology' (2009: 51). They argue that jokes are not merely a passive, harmless reflection of existing social attitudes, but that they perform a much more proactive role in reinforcing and perpetuating social and ethnic prejudice, that they 'are active in the process of the construction of the meaning of "otherness" and inferiority of social groups' (2009: 59). Though Howitt and Owusu-Bempah recognise that jokes about an ethnic minority told by a member of that minority – they cite the prevalence of Jewish jokes told by Jewish comedians, for example – might be seen as 'an opportunity to rejoice in the culture of an ethnic group', they conclude that ethnic jokes can never contribute in a positive and relevant way to contemporary multicultural society (2009: 64).

It is not hard to sympathise with these views when looking at some of the racist jokes on websites which are dedicated to reinforcing ethnic stereotypes and a sense of (almost always) white supremacy. Websites supportive of the Ku Klux Klan and other sites, cited by Michael Billig (2009) and Howitt and Owusu-Bempah, are overtly racist, using categories including 'niggers', 'spics' and 'fags' and listing jokes that offer their users ways of articulating racist propaganda that would be repetitious and moronic as ordinary conversation (see Howitt and Owusu-Bempah 2009: 57). Expressions of overt racism as comedy are now thankfully rare in broadcast media and film, but examples of much more ambiguous racist humour, which depends on how the context is interpreted and meaning is inferred, are not. To condemn all racial and ethnic humour as malignant is, according to commentators such as Davies (1990) and Berger (1993), to misunderstand the ways in which comedy works and suggest that there can be a healing, restorative function of racial and ethnic humour. Their approach has its origins in Freud's theories which suggest that many jokes are motivated by hostile aggression, which is otherwise socially frowned upon or even forbidden. Freud argued that 'the joke will allow us to turn to good account those ridiculous features in our enemy that the presence of obstacles would not let us utter aloud or consciously' (2002: 100). For Freud the ability to deal with the repressed through jokes acts as a mechanism which avoids more draconian responses. His three-dimensional view of human personality, in which primitive, socially unacceptable *id* impulses are inhibited or censored by the moralistic *superego*, while the *ego* or conscious self mediates between them, implies that 'we can get away with making all sorts of insulting, aggressive, or sexual remarks as long as they are delivered in a humorous fashion' (Rappoport 2005: 20). Building upon Freud, Davies (1990) and Berger (1993) argue that stereotype-based humour can enable the harmless release of social-emotional tensions within and between groups, that racial and ethnic jokes do not mean that people hate the object of the joke, but rather offer an opportunity to 'play' with aggression. This is not to deny the potential for racial and ethnic humour and comedy to reinforce prejudice, but to argue for a more complex, and less prescriptive, view of the ways in which comedy works. Films, radio and television programmes provide a context in which audiences may passively transgress the conventional boundaries of both reality and good taste, offering a kind of cognitive and affective playground in which it is possible to stray from normative beliefs and values. The crucial point here is that such films and programmes 'are not inviting us to abandon our moral values, only to rise above them for a moment, take a breather from being good and from the serious work of trying to make a better world' (Rappoport 2005: xiii). It's unfortunate that the logic of humour being a safety valve for society appears to share the logic of racist violence against minorities in times of social unrest. The key factor is whether reference is made to ethnic and racial stereotypes in a way that reinforces them or undermines them.

Sarita Malik (2010: 76) usefully summarises a distinction between racism and racialisation, which is simply when 'a racial character or context is imposed on an individual or group'. The interpretation of the representation of the group marked as 'Other' is ambivalent rather than negative. The point of this distinction is to highlight the fact that to see the issue of race as belonging only to the minority is in itself racist (see Malik 2010: 79–80; Ross 1996: 17–18).

Discussing comedy in the context of race and ethnicity comes down to two basic questions: firstly, what is the relationship between social reality and the comedy's representation of race and ethnicity, and, secondly, who is the comedy for? Many further questions follow from these: Is the comedy addressing a particular minority, the majority or both? The effect of the comedy clearly depends on the extent to which these constituencies feel on the inside or outside of their community. Do they share recognition of any stereotypes used? Do they have experience of racism? Do particular ethnicities see themselves as unique and separate or as part of an inclusive multicultural ethnic continuity?

Hollywood cinema has traditionally downplayed ethnic difference and promoted the idea of the melting pot, thus privileging conformity to US values and homogeneity among American citizens, as Lester D. Friedman (1991a) argues. Friedman (1991a: 3) recounts how his attempts to research Jewish ethnicity in contemporary Hollywood were largely seen as divisive by respondents. In contrast, while studying television comedy, Brett Mills is happy to say that 'Jewish comedy is American comedy' (2005: 126) or at least 'the fact that British audiences can happily consume and enjoy American sitcoms like *Seinfeld* without requiring an understanding of the Jewishness of its content demonstrates how Jewish comedy has become a performance style dissociated from its ethnic, religious and cultural roots' (2005: 127). Mills implies that the ethnicity of the persons in front of and behind the cameras isn't as significant as that of the consumer of the text. Friedman (1991a: 3) initially suggests otherwise but goes on to argue that the ethnic context within which an individual perceives texts 'must be considered an important component of how one gathers meaning from all texts, even those that contain no overt references to ethnicity' (1991b: 21–2). Whether one's ethnicity is determined by 'consent or descent' (1991b: 19), by internal or external factors, chosen or allocated, it is a complex factor in identity. The negotiations involved in reacting to comedy, in deciding what works or doesn't work, is funny or unfunny, inclusive or exclusive, acceptable or unacceptable, or some combination of the foregoing, make it a significant experience for individuals and social groups. Whatever the nature and effect of racial and ethnic humour, it is clear that there have been some significant shifts in the ways in which radio, television and film comedy have presented or inflected it over time. The chapter proceeds with broad case studies of British and American culture.

Following up: race and humour

 To what extent should humour be required to be socially responsible? Is such a concept compatible with humour?

 Is racialised (rather than racist) comedy desirable?

 Is it possible to use stereotypes in ways that counteract and/or resist racism?

Ethnicity in British screen comedy

On British television changes in attitudes are clearly marked in the differences between the 1970s comedy *It Ain't Half Hot Mum*, where the leading Indian character, Rangi Ram, was played by the white British actor Michael Bates, and the series *Goodness Gracious Me*, broadcast on BBC radio from 1996 to 1998 and then on BBC television from 1998–2001, written by and starring Sanjeev Bhaskar and Meera Syal. The latter programme played with British stereotypes, turning the common practices of drunken groups of white British restaurant-goers on their head in the sketch in which Asian characters 'go for an English', asking for 'something really bland' up to and including 'the blandest thing on the menu' and behave in a raucous and boorish manner. The success of *Goodness Gracious Me* was followed by *The Kumars at No. 42* (2001–6), also starring Bhaskar and Syal, a programme that enjoyed considerable international success in India, Malaysia and North America. Whereas Michael Bates played the stereotype, Bhaskar and Syal are confident enough to play with stereotypes in an ironic fashion, unafraid to parody aspects of Asian culture in ways that are funny to a wider multicultural audience. In addition to Bollywood films that play to British Asian audiences, comedy dramas such as *Bhaji on the Beach* (1993), *East Is East* (1999), *Bend It Like Beckham* (2002) and *West Is West* (2010) trace the progress made in multicultural Britain without blinding audiences to the work still to be done. The essential optimism of these works seems justified when looking back at racial and ethnic comedy programmes on British television of the 1960s and 1970s (see Mather 2006).

The difficulties of engaging with the issue of race relations in British television comedy were shown by the inept early *Curry and Chips* (1969) featuring a blacked-up Spike Milligan. However, the BBC's *Till Death Us Do Part* (1965–75) proved a groundbreaking comedy or, at least, 'signalled a drastic break from television's habitually "polite" and awkward response towards racial themes' (Malik 2002: 92). The series spawned two feature films in 1969 and 1972, and a number of international spin-offs including *All in the Family* in the US (see Chapter 5). *Till Death Us Do Part* attracted considerable controversy, with Warren Mitchell playing the opinionated white working-class bigot Alf

Garnett, whose views on politics, women, race and the younger generation were at the forefront in each episode. The production staff, including the writer Johnny Speight, were clearly of the view that the programme was anti-racist and that by ridiculing the main character they exposed him and the nature of his racial prejudices (including animosity towards the 'Jews up at the Spurs', a rival football club to his beloved West Ham) for what they were. However, Garnett's extensive use of the term 'coon' and other derogatory names for minority groups gave offence, particularly as some viewers missed the satirical irony of Speight's writing. Stuart Hood argued that 'If racism is widely spread in a society, as it is in ours, such shows will be seen by a considerable part of the audience as validating their views' (1983: 26). Ross is able to cite research that shows that audiences of *All in the Family* see the character of Archie Bunker appearing to be 'telling it like it is' or to be a bigoted fool depending on their prejudices before watching it (1996: 93). Reception, not the programme makers' intentions, is the important factor.

If *Till Death Us Do Part* attempted to confront racism through the attitudes and arguments of an all-white cast, other British programmes did feature black and Asian actors. *Love Thy Neighbour* (1972–76), produced by Thames, was hugely popular, running to fifty-six episodes in seven series and generating a film based on the programme in 1973. The basic premise is that a black couple, Bill and Barbie Reynolds, move next door to a working-class white couple, Eddie and Joan Booth. For Ross, *Love Thy Neighbour* 'broke new ground in featuring an attractive black couple who were positive and assertive and most definitely not victims' (1996: 94). Eddie's use of abusive terms such as 'nig-nog', 'choc-ice' and 'Sambo' are countered by Bill's references to Eddie as 'honky', 'snow-flake' and 'paleface'. Such exchanges attracted considerable controversy at the time, though the writers of the show argued for the comic irony that they felt lay behind the name-calling. If, as the DVD sleeve notes say, the series 'takes some of the heat out of race relations by showing the funny side of everyday conflict', then this happens largely because it is the white character Eddie who comes off worse in the exchanges. He is shown as less tolerant, less open-minded, less physically capable and much lazier around the house. He is portrayed as being less intelligent than Bill and is more often than not the butt of the jokes. When, in an episode from February 1974, Eddie inadvertently loses the airline ticket that Bill has bought for Barbie so that she can visit her mother in Trinidad, he spends several hours rooting the council rubbish tip looking for it; Bill has already found the ticket, but decides to make Eddie suffer before telling him.

The series exposed the extent to which racist attitudes and racist language permeated Britain in the 1970s. Though Joan and Barbie get on well together and share a sense of female solidarity, Joan can still tell Barbie that, with all that Trinidadian sunshine, 'you'll come back black as a nigger'. In the working man's club frequented by Bill and Eddie, the men rehearse conversations about black immigration from former British colonies that were commonplace in Britain at the time. Arguing that black migration causes unemployment, Eddie refers to the 'nig-nog nurses' that fill the hospitals, contrasting them with those 'white foreigners', the Irish. When Bill stays with them, Eddie rejects the view that Bill is an 'ordinary human being', telling Joan that Bill can't be, because he's black: as he says, 'they've got primitive passions and strange ways'. The live-audience laugh track suggests that all this is deemed to be funny but it is unclear if the laughter is at the views themselves or the crudeness of their articulation. In either case it is left to the plot-lines to make sure that Eddie pays the price for his racist views. Through a dialogue between characters reacting to Britain's changing circumstances, racist views are articulated, examined and exposed but in language offensive to many at the time and unacceptable today. The sitcom form also leaves them doomed to repeat forever their conflictual deadlock (see Mather 2006: 81).

While *Till Death Us Do Part* and *Love Thy Neighbour* reflect the consequences of Empire in an increasingly ethnically diverse Britain, the BBC sitcom *It Ain't Half Hot Mum* (1974–81), set in a British army camp in India in 1944, finds comic material in the colonial experience itself. Much of the comedy comes from the conflict between the professional soldier Sergeant-Major Williams (beautifully played by Windsor Davies) and the diverse bunch of inept, cross-dressing conscripts who make up the Royal Artillery Concert Party and whose main aim is to avoid being sent into action in Burma. Made following the success of *Dad's Army* (1968–77) and at a time when memories of the Second World War and of National Service were still strong, the comedy relies on the incongruous situation of the concert party, whose interests are in putting on a show whatever the limitations, while a war – as well as demands for Indian national independence – rage around them. The Sergeant-Major's efforts to instil some army discipline into the concert party meet with little success, as they offer a carnivalesque resistance to army life, the 'real' business of war and ruling the colony, and frequently rely on the help of the base's Indian servants.

Rangi Ram acts as the focal point for the comedy which springs from ethnic differences between the British and the Indians. He appears overly anxious to please and appease his colonial 'masters', considers himself to be 'British', but also subverts them and exposes their limitations. He invariably offers a perspective on events that apparently spring from indigenous wisdom, often expressed in a pithy utterance delivered straight to camera, but he is also the source of much of the comic word-play, often based on a misunderstanding of English language and culture, citing the song 'Pack Up Your Troubles on the Old Kent Road', or mistaking 'gelatine' for 'quarantine'. His attempts to speak on behalf of his compatriots also generate jokes, as when he declares that the punkah-wallah would most definitely not sell his grandmother for one hundred rupees to help out the concert party, since he sold her last week for two hundred rupees. Until the death of Michael Bates in 1978, Rangi Ram was, nevertheless, a central figure in the sitcom. In the episode 'A Star Is Born', for example, Rangi takes the initiative to stop the Sergeant-Major's efforts to send the gang to the front line. He remains an intriguing figure, offering parodic comment on both British and Indian culture, but undoubtedly supports uncomfortable, patronising stereotypes.

The Fosters (1976–77), based on the US sitcom *Good Times* (see below), was the first British sitcom to feature an all-black cast, including Norman Beaton and a young Lenny Henry, and the later *Desmonds* (1989–94), starring Beaton, achieved sustained success curtailed only by the death of its star. Both these shows, embedded in black British communities, sidestepped comedy based on racial difference, but racial intolerance in Britain of the period remained an issue for not just Afro-Caribbean and Asian ethnic groups but all minorities, as the comedy series *Mind Your Language* (1977–79) shows. Promoted as a 'new multi-racial comedy series', it featured Barry Evans teaching English language to a diverse range of foreign adults in an evening class. As might be expected, the comedy revolved around linguistic misunderstanding, jokes, puns and the sniping that took place between the different national stereotypes. Hugely popular at the time, the show appears banal, inept, pedestrian and, yes, racist today (see Malik 2002: 97), but it does represent something of the ways in which British television was beginning, ineptly as ever, to recognise that it must accommodate diverse ethnicities as Britain became a more multi-racial society. A brief and unfunny revival in 1986 only showed how far that society had changed.

Following up: race and comedy on British television

☞ Consider an episode or episodes from a television comedy series from the twentieth century that includes characters of different races and ethnicities. Does the comedy address issues of race and ethnicity in a progressive, positive way or does it reinforce racism and racist views already embedded in society? Does knowing the history of the text and the time of its production help you understand its particular examples of humour, or not?

☞ How subjective is your response in terms age, gender, class and race?

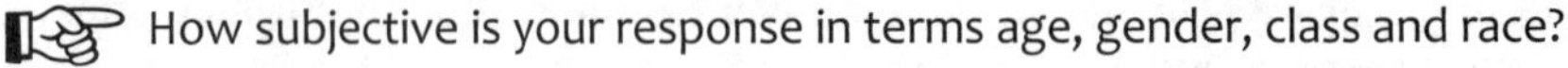

African-American screen comedy

In 2010, out of roughly 309 million Americans, Black or African-Americans made up 12.6 per cent of the US population, a self-ascribing racial minority of roughly 39 million people, a number equal to about two-thirds of the entire UK population. The now well-documented nature of the representation of African-Americans on screen can be seen as giving some indication of the changing status of one particular group in American culture: 'the integration of blacks as equal participants in society remains an official but elusive goal, and the absence of black representation in film [and television] is one manifestation of that problem' (Winokur 1991: 191). The representation of African-Americans in Hollywood and on television has been surveyed in depth by, among others, Donald Bogle (1994, 2001). Karen Ross concludes in her study of Anglo-American film and television that: 'It is the poverty of black images rather than their frequency that constitutes the real problem' (1996: 170). The overall lack of representation merely raises the stakes for examples that do appear: 'any existent representation of blacks will have an enormous amount of social energy cathected on to it. That the bulk of this representation should occur in comedy is an indication of the strength of the attempt to avoid the representation of an enormously difficult subject' (Winokur 1991: 191). Winokur's comments argue that the social tension around race in American society has restricted the representation of black Americans, and that the cultural hierarchy that suggests comedy is relatively trivial allows it to present what might be too problematic for other genres. While we will briefly refer to the larger representation of black culture, our focus on comedy can only give a partial picture of the whole, acknowledging that it is perhaps a disproportionately large part of the picture. Coleman and McIlwain, for example, express frustration that too often 'Black life and culture remain relegated to the comedic' (2005: 133).

Despite the American Civil War (1861–65) leading to the liberation of slaves, soon after 1876 many states enacted laws that racially segregated their society and placed their black citizens in second-class status with separate, and effectively inferior, facilities and rights. During this period entertainment was always a grey area. While white audiences felt themselves entitled to the best in entertainment they were seldom comfortable when that meant freely acknowledging the talents of black performers. This produced the somewhat bizarre and contradictory practice of minstrelsy where white performers blacked up to perform for white audiences (see Carpio 2008: 24). Nevertheless, given music and dance as avenues of success, albeit restricted and based on stereotyping, black performers took their chances. Since black and white culture were ostensibly separate, seeking out genuine black performers added a cachet of 'exotic' otherness to the experience. For example, in the 1920s and 1930s the fashionable Cotton Club in Harlem kept strict segregation between black performers such as Cab Calloway, Count Basie and Duke Ellington and their orchestras, and the white audiences who flocked to see them. But the mainstream music industry these artists competed in was still dominated by white managers, radio and record producers and white competitors.

The same was true in other media. The Nicholas Brothers, for example, are clearly, even given the limited amount of footage available, contenders for the best dancers in America in the 1930s and 1940s, yet dance movies were invariably structured around white stars. *The Pirate* (1948) shows Gene Kelly keen to put himself alongside the Nicholas Brothers for the key number ('Be a Clown') but the film was not welcomed critically and did poorly at box office. The usual procedure for the inclusion of black performers in feature films was to make their appearances non-essential to the plot so that they could be cut out for exhibition in white-only cinemas in the Southern states. Conversely, the presence of their scenes would justify headline billing in black neighbourhood cinemas.

Such restrictions clearly limited black actors too. Though there were black filmmakers serving black audiences, they were only ever able to do so on a financial shoestring, and profits, when there were any, were often siphoned off by white backers. The best-paying opportunities for black actors in the mainstream industry were usually thankless supporting roles as comic relief. Bogle's *Toms, Coons, Mulattoes, Mammies, and Bucks* (1994) summarises the limited number of stereotyped roles available in classical Hollywood. The much-criticised Hattie McDaniel, the first black Oscar winner for her role as Mammy in *Gone with the Wind* (1939), felt it was better to be an actress earning $700 a week for playing a maid rather than earning $7 for being one (see Ross 1996: 15). Ross critiques what she sees as Bogle's 'highly optimistic perspective' in his assessment of the impact of black actors and actresses playing '*against* their roles' (cited Ross 1996: 13), but it seems to us that Bogle is right to the extent that we understand actors to be something more than the roles they inhabit. The ways these issues play out in relation to comedic texts may be illustrated with a specific example from classical Hollywood.

In the 'land yacht' sequence from *Sullivan's Travels* (1940), Sullivan the director is posing as a vagrant but, encumbered by his entourage following in the bus, he hitches a lift with a young whippet tank (or hot rod) driver and attempts to outdistance them. In the slapstick sequence that follows all the ethnically and class marked occupants of the bus are bounced around; the driver, the journalist, the female secretary and the photographer on the front seat; the fixer, radio-operator and doctor at the back; and the cook (Charles Moore, credited as 'Colored Chef') in the galley kitchen. There is a clear hierarchy of slapstick comedy as to who is most humiliatingly shaken, the secretary's stockings add 'a little bit of sex', for example, but it is the cook who comes off worst. One interesting element among the pratfalls is when he gets pancake batter all over his face and is effectively 'whited up'. This echoes an earlier gag in the sequence when a motorcycle policeman is splashed with mud by the passing bus and thus 'blacked up'. The humiliation of an authority figure is in itself comic, the idea of a black policeman in the historical context of the film, might also be meant to be funny, and could clearly be read as racist. However, since he loses contact with the bus (i.e. becomes incompetent), at the moment of wiping the mud away even this may be mitigated. This pair of jokes does, ultimately, ask questions about the fixed nature of racial values and shows whiteness and blackness as accidents, splashed on. While this is not, perhaps, something any of the filmmakers would claim (any more than they might claim racist intentions), it does appear to be a potential of the film's comedy to momentarily shake things up in a time when segregation insisted that racial values were utterly fixed.

If fixed and negative values are upheld by limited stereotypical representations there is clearly an argument to be had as to whether it is better for such representation to exist or not. In reaction to the transfer from radio to television of *Amos 'n' Andy* (1951–53) the National Association for the Advancement of Colored People (NAACP) mounted successful campaigns against its production (see Cripps 2003). This had the unlooked-for effect that there would be no new television shows with black central characters for over a decade (while leaving the two existing seasons of *Amos 'n' Andy* running in syndication until 1966. See Coleman and McIlwain 2005: 127 and Morreale 2003: 302). Other ethnicities did not react in the same way to ethnic shows like *The Goldbergs* (1950–55) and *I Remember Mama* (1949–56) since they portrayed the 'vestiges of a national culture' while, by contrast, the depictions of *Amos 'n' Andy* appeared to the black middle class set on assimilation to be only 'an aberration of white American culture' (Cripps 2003: 34). This attitude undervalued the role of black culture in American culture, particularly that of the Southern states (see Genovese 1975). Winokur, in discussing the sequence of *Back to the Future* (1985) where the white mid-western teenager played by Michael J. Fox 'invents' rock and roll, identifies 'a desire on the part of white America to have been less beholden to black culture (among others) for the structure of its own culture' (1991: 202). That debt was always obscured by segregation which required surrogates to mediate black culture to white audiences. Elvis Presley, for example, emerged as a conduit between black and white music and was found deeply disturbing by the racist white establishment. The presence of black culture in any form might, it seemed, make a difference to attitudes.

The 'subtle integrationist message' of seeing a 'negro family' on television (Cripps 2003: 38) is difficult to evaluate. It clearly helps familiarise the mainstream community with the marginalised one and contributes to the stock of images available to subsequent programme makers. These were somewhat expanded by Bill Cosby co-starring alongside Robert Culp in the spoof spy series *I Spy* (1965–68). Even *Julia* (1968–71), starring Diahann Carroll as a widowed mother and nurse, though widely regarded as excessively bland and irrelevant, is shown by Aniko Bodroghkozy to have been challenging by its very presence: 'the show's "whiteness", middle-classness, and in-offensiveness did not defuse its threat to entrenched racist positions' (2003: 142). Nonetheless, Coleman and McIlwain argue that assimilation is an outdated 'racist ideology' in which 'Black culture was most prized when it approached the norms and values of Whiteness' (2005: 130).

Hollywood's ideology had traditionally been assimilationist in regard to all other ethnic groups and this approach continued in 1960s film production in which the pre-eminent and Oscar-winning black star is Sidney Poitier, whose persona was that of 'the quietly dignified and intelligent urban black man' (Ross 1996: 16). The 1967 comedy film *Guess Who's Coming to Dinner* has him play a Nobel prize-winning doctor courting the daughter of classical Hollywood stars Spencer Tracy and Katherine Hepburn and patiently waiting for them to overcome their unjustifiable racist prejudices against interracial marriage. This was a topical subject. In 1960 when the exceptional dancer, singer and actor Sammy Davis Junior married the Swedish actress May Britt he was threatened personally but also legally as 'anti-miscegenation' laws were still on the statutes of thirty-six states, seventeen of which still enforced them. The Hollywood Production Code of 1930, which specifically banned miscegenation as a subject, was in operation until 1966. But *Guess Who's Coming to Dinner* was not a crusading argument for a change in law: in early 1967 the US Supreme Court had overturned all 'anti-miscegenation' state laws (though Alabama didn't actually amend its state constitution until 2000).

While Poitier's saintly dignity played well with black middle-class audiences, working-class black audiences in downtown cinemas were keen to see less passive heroes of their own colour. It was the novelty of aggressive and masculine black male heroes that drove the blaxploitation cycle of the early 1970s. These films appealed against the background of a number of riots in cities across America in protest against continued police oppression and the lack of tangible change as a result of 1960s Civil Rights legislation (see Carpio 2008: 18).

One significant Hollywood comedy film during this period with direct black input was *Blazing Saddles* (1974), co-written by Richard Pryor and starring Cleavon Little. The basic plot revolves around attempts to dispossess the inhabitants of Rock Ridge so that the railroad can go through the land. When the corrupt Attorney General Hedley Lamarr (Harvey Korman) attempts the land-grab by sending in his thugs to scare the townsfolk away, they demand and get a new sheriff. Lamarr is able to persuade the weak, sex-obsessed Governor Le Petomane (Mel Brooks) to send Bart (Little), a former railroad worker, to Rock Ridge to be the new sheriff, confident that when he gets there he will be lynched. Instead, with the help of the Waco Kid (Gene Wilder) who 'has killed more men than Cecil B. DeMille', Bart manages to rally the townsfolk and defeat Lamarr and his rowdies. This basic summary does nothing to even begin to explain the comedy at work in the film, which mixes gags, comic vulgarity, visual puns, and slapstick with clever one-liners, many of them interrogating the the historical racism of the period depicted and the incipient racism of the western genre. When the white gangmasters ask if the black railroad workers know the song 'Camp Town Ladies', they deny it until roles are comically inverted as the cowboys start stereotypical minstrel dancing in the manner of what their boss Taggart (Slim Pickens) calls 'Kansas

City faggots'. When two of the workers, Bart and Charlie (Charles McGregor), end up in quicksand, Taggart rescues the $400 handcart they rode into it on but leaves them to their own devices. When they have struggled their way out, Taggart tells them 'break's over boys' and to stop lying about getting a suntan, since 'it won't do you no good anyhow'. Bart crowns him with a shovel.

Blazing Saddles allows its black hero to outwit his enemies by playing upon their stupidity, ignorance and stereotypical expectations. When Bart arrives in town as sheriff the residents imagine his first act ('Excuse me while I whip this out') will be to expose himself rather than to read a speech but he evades their immediate armed hostility by taking himself hostage and mimicking the exaggerated fear of previous Hollywood stereotypes. He even gets to break the fourth wall. The film plays upon and subverts a range of racial stereotypes, most of which owe their existence in part to representations of race enshrined in conventional westerns. When the railroad workers offer to join with the townsfolk, they are told that 'we'll give some land to the niggers and the chinks, but we don't want the Irish!' *Blazing Saddles* makes the most of the ethnic continuum of American culture and, by not exclusively dwelling on racism or contemporary black issues (it's smart enough to show that it is ultimately Hollywood hokum), fully justifies Ella Shohat's statement that: 'An awareness of texts as palimpsests of competing ethnic and racial collective discourses is ... critical for a multicultural reading which goes beyond any number of invisible ethnocentrisms' (1991: 246).

The much more scattershot *Kentucky Fried Movie* (1977), directed by John Landis and written by David Zucker, Jerry Zucker and Jim Abrahams, offers a series of sketches some of which have a keen interest in ethnicity and different ethnic stereotypes. One spoof film trailer within the film mocks the sub-genre of blaxploitation films with black female heroines played by Tamara Dobson or Pam Grier by teaming their version, Cleopatra Schwartz (Marilyn Joi), with the definitely un-cool orthodox Hassidic Jew, Schwartz (Saul Kahan), whose only contributions to the violence seem to be breaking a bottle over a man's head and helping with the belt feed of the heavy machine gun Cleopatra is using. The collision plays on 'Schwartz' as a Jewish surname and Yiddish for black and the association of both ethnicities with 'the ghetto', albeit on different continents at different times, and the sheer incongruity of this meeting of stereotypes. It shows, from the outside, both the appeal of blaxploitation and how marginal an understanding of black culture informed non-black Hollywood's engagement with it.

The comedy element in actual blaxploitation films by black filmmakers appears marginal and under-explored. It is present in elements of the key film *Cotton Comes to Harlem* (1970), which re-appropriated old comic stereotypes (see Bogle 1994: 233–4), *Car Wash* (1976) and the micro-budgeted *Dolemite* (1975). The films directed by and starring Poitier with Bill Cosby, *Uptown Saturday Night* (1974), *Let's Do It Again* (1975) and *A Piece of the Action* (1977) were clear-cut comedies, however, and succeeded at the box office. Bogle suggests that: 'because they did not address racial issues, [they] were early crossover hits' (1994: 258). Though it is not often seen in this way, *Blazing Saddles* was perhaps also a crossover hit, appealing to black and white audiences. The vitality of black performers and culture was attractive to white audiences but (with action-oriented blaxploitation suffering rapidly diminishing returns) was increasingly seen as needing to be packaged in an unthreatening manner. No longer limited to removable excerpts, black performances could become integral to the plot, but they were still to be tailored to non-black sensibilities. The potential for comedies with black stars to crossover to white audiences was confirmed by the massive success of *The Silver Streak* (1976) starring Gene Wilder with Richard Pryor in an expanded sidekick role. There is a certain ironic logic to Pryor being successful as a crossover film star. As a stand-up comedian he began by trying to emulate Bill Cosby but, after becoming radicalised in late 1960s California, his live routines (see *Live and Smokin'* filmed in 1971) spoke from his personal experience of 'the ghettoised black underclass' (Wagg 1998: 260). His stand-up validated black experience against white: 'rejecting the pressure to sanitize black culture in the name of integration' (Carpio 2008: 89). His film stardom also meant he reached huge audiences, and tour footage was edited into features *Live in Concert* (1979), *Live on the Sunset Strip* (1982) and *Here and Now* (1983). His film comedy roles such as in *Stir Crazy* (1980), again with Wilder, are surprisingly tame by comparison.

The career of Eddie Murphy, which picked up on and extended Pryor's film success, shows how much more mileage there was in crossover vehicles (see Haggins 2007). The *Saturday Night Live* performer appeared in a string of huge hits: *48 Hours* (1982), *Trading Places* (1983) and *Beverly Hills Cop* (1984). In each film Murphy's character is 'the only significant black man in the film' (Winokur 1991: 200). Only *Trading Places* is an out-and-out comedy though Murphy's performances added a comic element to all of them. In *Trading Places*, Murphy plays a vagrant selected as subject for an experiment in nurture by two elderly commodities traders and given privilege and education in order to show he can perform as well for them as an upper-class white employee played by Dan Ackroyd. Deprived of links to his community, he becomes the successful acquisitive capitalist the Duke brothers want but later collaborates with Ackroyd to undermine their scheme and bankrupt them. His reward is financial success but, while his opposite number gains a girlfriend during the course of the film, a female partner is a final scene afterthought for him. In *Beverly Hills Cop*, where he works mainly alone, rather than with a white 'buddy', he gains a hotel room by posing as a *Rolling Stone* journalist in town to interview Michael Jackson and claiming that the hotel is discriminating against him. While the bravura performance is successful, it suggests that exceptions are made only for entertainers and the media and that claims of racism can be frivolous or used for gain.

Winokur (1991: 199) suggests that in such roles Murphy 'is a black man in blackface, pretending to be black, a fair representation of the classic minstrel paradox. It is blackness passing as itself, wearing the face it is forced to take, re-representing itself as a larger audience conceives of it.' This is somewhat problematic in that it doesn't allow Murphy to own his performances or to be anything other than the role he's playing. It is certainly clear that Murphy's success involves an appeal to a mainstream white audience and that crossover comes with compromises, but, as in our discussion earlier about black actors in classical Hollywood, there's a wider context in which the performer communicates, which includes black audiences. Other successful films like *Beverly Hills Cop II* (1987) and *Coming to America* (1988) ensured that Murphy was the most successful Hollywood star of the 1980s but his attempts at playing more sophisticated characters in *Boomerang* and *The Distinguished Gentleman* (both 1992) were less successful at the box office. Murphy has since fallen back on remakes (*The Nutty Professor* (1996), *Dr Doolittle* (1998)), multiple roles as broad stereotypes (*Nutty Professor II: The Klumps* (2000), *Norbit* (2007)) and memorable vocal work (Donkey in *Shrek* (2001) and sequels).

Whoopi Goldberg's career illustrates a similar situation for black female performers (see Haggins 2007). Introduced to audiences in a dramatic role in *The Color Purple* (1985), though an established stage comedy performer, Goldberg struggled to find adequate vehicles as a star (rather than a supporting actress as in her Oscar-winning role in *Ghost* (1990)). Her greatest box-office success to date came in *Sister Act* (1992), a comedy musical virtually without reference to race in which she played a singer forced to live in a convent as a (bogus) nun to avoid vengeful criminals. In this role, Geoff King suggests, she offers 'the figure of an African-American as a source of renewal of a desiccated white culture' (2002: 146) but is allowed to do so only in an especially de-sexualised and unthreatening way (see Haggins 2007: 155–6). King goes on to argue that '[t]he very fact that comedy – coded as ultimately unthreatening, unserious – has been the primary realm in which black performers have consistently achieved superstar status in film speaks volumes about the racial politics of American society' (2002: 150).

American broadcast television in the 1970s offers a number of parallels to developments in film. In the mid-1970s after the success of the combination of variety and comedy sketches in *The Flip Wilson Show* (1970–74) had topped ratings in 1971, there were a number of sitcoms with black casts: *Sanford and Son* (1972–77), a Norman Lear adaptation of *Steptoe and Son* starring the seasoned stand-up comic Red Foxx as Sanford; *Good Times* (1974–79), set in Chicago housing projects; and *The Jeffersons* (1975–86), a spin-off from Lear's *All in the Family*. The contentious protagonists were shown as disadvantaged by 'racism, public policy and discrimination' and angry about it, but the dramatic stability of the sitcom form prevented them addressing issues in depth, being 'largely distracted by their own poverty and disenfranchisement' (Coleman and Mcllwain 2005: 130). These shows were doing well enough to hang on as sitcoms began to fall in popularity, but it would be a slightly different take on the black family, *The Cosby Show* (1984–92), which came as 'saviour of the genre' (Wagg 1998: 197). Unlike the Lear shows, *The Cosby Show* 'takes an assimilative position on race issues' (Wagg 1998: 197) and it was a ratings-topper for much of its run, clearly appealing to the breadth of American (and international) audiences. It forms a touchstone of the difficulties in discussing race and comedy in that, while there are several ways to critique its middle-classness (though standard for non-black sitcoms), its lack of recognition of racism and its concern not to offend audiences, *The Cosby Show* manages to connect across different ethnic audiences, to replace negative stereotypes with Cosby's 'incarnation of the perfect father figure' (Real 2003: 233) and to entertain without any loss of dignity on the part of the performers (see Real 2003: 236 and Mills 2005: 81). Ross notes that: 'The show allows black and white audiences alike to relate to the Huxtables, perhaps even to aspire to their lifestyle' (1996: 101). Opportunities to affirm black pride are taken but without making racism an issue. The episode when Cliff helps his daughter write about Martin Luther King is often cited (Season 3.6), but a later episode (3.11) in which Cliff's father and his buddies recount Second World War stories is equally potent, focusing on the racism of their enemies and the African-American contribution to the war rather than racism and segregation in the US army. For Real, '*The Cosby Show* recodes blackness, but it fails to address directly class and group conflict within American society' (2003: 241). As such, Amanda Dyanne Lotz notes, *The Cosby Show* 'embodied the high-water mark in terms of integrated audience success' (2005: 143).

Since the success of *The Cosby Show*, the critical consensus is that the black community has been ill-served by television. Though it helped bring a lot of other black-centred shows to the screen, their attempts to find alternative ways

12 The Cosby Show. Bill Cosby's hit 1980s sitcom communicates an assimulationist message.

of doing things produced what Coleman and McIlwain call the 'neo-minstrelsy era' with *The Wayans Brothers* (1995–59) getting its own NAACP boycott (2005: 132–3). Several of these shows appeared on the upstart network Fox which 'sought a foothold with a regular audience of any size' and noted that the African-American audiences making up 11 per cent of American households kept their sets on longer than other demographics. Fox went on to shift their attention to a young white male audience that was tuning in to black sitcoms, 'allowing Fox to "trade up" for a demographic advertisers valued for its perceived cultural capital and buying power, while abandoning the black viewers who helped the network compete with the Big Three [ABC, CBS, NBC]' (Lotz 2005: 143). Subsequently, new networks UPN and The WB (both beginning in 1996) took up where Fox left off and deliberately catered to black audiences, making the Big Four less likely to do so and essentially ghettoising black performers in American television. In fact their policies were so similar that UPN and The WB merged (as CW) in 2006. Lotz concludes that 'what audiences see on television is often a reflection of society at large. Despite changes in the past fifty years, American society remains very segregated' (2005: 149).

Kentucky Fried Movie, referred to earlier, has a segment titled 'Danger Seekers', a spoof of television programmes during the 1970s fad for stunt men, in which a character called Rex Kramer in a white jump suit puts on a crash helmet against a nondescript white wall. He then steps across a railway track (to the 'wrong' side presumably), interrupts a group of large black men playing craps against a wall and yells 'Niggers!' at the top of his voice before running off. The men, initially baffled, give chase and the scene fades out. This cheap and minimal sketch breaks a taboo and uses stereotypes, but the butt of the humour is not obviously the black characters but the nerdish danger seeker who can expect to pay the consequences for his actions. It points to the contentiousness of racist insults and who can use them (which we shall return to) and it attempts to make humour from the basic and fundamental fact that difference exists. It ought not to matter, but it continues to do so.

To what extent should film and television material made by black professionals be oriented towards the white-dominated mainstream audience whose tastes place restrictions upon them? Outside mainstream concerns, Spike Lee's self-produced *She's Gotta Have It* (1986) was able to address black sexuality head on and comically, though in the punishment of its female central character's promiscuity and bisexuality Ross detects 'misogynistic and homophobic sub-themes' (see 1996: 65–6). Nonetheless, the break-out success of Lee's low-budget film, and to a lesser extent Robert Townsend's *Hollywood Shuffle* (1987), showed 'that black-oriented films can appeal to a mixed audience and make serious money' (Ross 1996: 81). The New Black Cinema of the late 1980s and early 1990s was financed on this evidence though the comedic impetus of the initial films was swamped, as in the blaxploitation cycle, by contemporary violent urban thrillers. Nevertheless, the low-budget *House Party* (1990) was a significant hit, spawning two sequels, and showing that black-centred comedy could make an impact, and there now appears to be a consistent international as well as domestic market for broad, black-centred comedies, or what Bambi Haggins calls 'comedies of color-coded color-blindness' (2007: 103), such as *Big Momma's House* (2000), *Barber's Shop* (2002), *Barbershop 2* (2004), *Beauty Shop* (2005), *Daddy Day Care* (2003), *Daddy Day Camp* (2007), *Are We There Yet?* (2005) and *Are We Done Yet?* (2007). Comedy films that mix black and white stars like *Bringing Down the House* (2003) and *Guess Who?* (2005) still tend to nullify the issues they raise, especially about interracial romance (see McDonald 2007: 36–7).

Black American comedy for black audiences is at its most vital in televised stand-up comedy. When Chris Rock's 1996 *Bring the Pain* routine was broadcast nationally it had a significant impact through addressing a black audience and, instead of opposing black culture to white, homing in on divisions within that audience:

> Because black people hate black people, too. Everything white people don't like about black people, *black* people don't like about black people. It's like our own personal civil war.
>
> One one side, there's black people. On the other, you've got niggers.
>
> The niggers have got to go. Everytime black people want to have a good time, niggers mess it up. You can't do anything without some ignorant-ass niggers fucking it up. (Rock 2002: 344)

For Rock's appreciative black audiences there appears to have been a sense of relief at overcoming political correctness or burdensome essentialist racial solidarity (see Haggins 2007: 80). In striking against community tradition Rock anticipates (and impersonates) objections:

> Man, why you got to say that? ... It isn't us, it's the media. The media has distorted our image to make us look bad. Why must you come down on us like that, brother? It's not us, it's the media.
>
> Please cut the shit. When I go to the money machine at night, I'm not looking over my shoulder for the media.
>
> I'm looking for niggers. (Rock 2002: 346)

In the mouth of a white comedian this would be an extremely troubling, racist gag especially in its terminology, and, as Haggins (2007: 84) suggests: 'Rock constantly treads the thin line between humor and heresy.' In his stand-up comedy Richard Pryor was noted for using the term about himself and his audience in a commonplace, affectionate way, reappropriating it for black use. Yet this was something Pryor backtracked on in 1982 after a trip to Africa reminded him of everything the term represented (see Haggins 2007: 55–7). Chris Rock explains his use of the term later in the routine:

> Any black person can say 'nigger' and get away with it. It's true. It's like calling your kid an idiot. Only you can call your kid that. Someone else calls your kid an idiot, there's a fight.

> Yet some white people still wonder why black people can say 'nigger' and they can't. (2002: 346)

While not giving up on its 'team shirt', the black community was ready to acknowledge its lack of homogeneity and its internal diversity. Ultimately Rock's routine is an acknowledgement that class is an issue in American society that is often obscured by race.

Rock's success was a harbinger of things to come. From 1998 the Original Kings of Comedy (Bernie Mac, Cedric the Entertainer, D.L. Hughley and Steve Harvey) played to huge stadium audiences and became the most successful comedy tour ever. The film of the same title, directed by Spike Lee (2000), shows their comedy to be uncompromising in its focus on black experience in America, and took their material to new, even larger audiences. This was 'crossing over' without compromise, showing that comedy was capable of communicating across the fault lines in a culture. The question remains as to whether it also reinforces them.

Chappelle's Show (2003–5), the cable sketch show fronted and co-written by Dave Chappelle, was 'one of the funniest and most incendiary series on American television in the early 2000s' (Haggins 2007: 206), offering a number of challenging takes on race (the blind, black, white supremacist) and exploitation of taboos (the 'Niggar family' sketches). During production of the third series Chappelle bailed out, 'allegedly troubled by the possibility that his play on stereotypes reaffirms racist views' (Carpio 2008: 81). Recognising that some sectors of the audience were laughing at rather than with him, Chappelle deemed his own work 'socially irresponsible' (see Haggins 2007: 231). Humour that plays on the ambivalent stereotypes and contentious terms associated with race in American culture remains powerfully charged. Comedy solves none of the issues around race and ethnicity but it consistently draws attention to them, with unpredictable results.

Following up: representing race

☞ To what extent is representation on screen in comedy film or television desirable for racial or ethnic minorities?

☞ Does public expectation for performers from racial or ethnic minorities to 'represent' their communities restrict them or provide them with comedic opportunities?

☞ What problems are caused by the fact that humour produced by and for one community will be seen by other communities and might be read in different ways?

Pushing British boundaries: ambiguity and ethnic identity

By the late 1990s in Britain it was possible for a white Jewish comic actor to impersonate a black character in ways that reflected the emergence of a multicultural society and the ambiguous attitudes which this change engendered. Of course impersonation of black characters by white actors has been a consistent feature of Anglo-American entertainment since music hall and vaudeville in the nineteenth century, from US radio's *Amos 'n' Andy*, Al Jolson in *The Jazz Singer* (1927) to BBC television's long-running *The Black and White Minstrel Show* (1958–78). A growing awareness that the blackface tradition was inappropriate in the 1970s was evidenced in the musical sketch 'The Short and Fat Minstrel Show' on *The Two Ronnies* in 1973, and by a spoof on *The Goodies* in 1977. However, the emergence of Sasha Baron Cohen's character Ali G on Channel Four's *The 11 O'Clock Show* in 1998, the subsequent *Da Ali G Show* from 2000 and the feature film *Ali G Indahouse* (2002) presented racial impersonation with radically different intent, purpose and effect.

Ali G ('real' name Alistair Lesley Graham) ought not to have been either a sympathetic or a funny character. Ill-educated, if not wilfully ignorant, homophobic and misogynistic, apparently well-versed in the world of illegal drugs, he offered a hilarious (mis)representation of black American hip-hop culture and its appropriation by British youth. Though he speaks the language and struts the stuff associated with the African-American gangs of Compton and Watts, he actually lives in Staines. The comedy stems from the basic incongruity between Ali G's dream and his reality. He boasts that, having tamed the rival gangs of Chertsey and Beaconsfield (both havens of British affluent middle-class suburbia), 'there have been no drive-by killings in West Berkshire'. His talk of the 'Da West Staines massiv' and its 'gangsta' rivalry with 'Da East Staines massiv' is rendered absurd by those who know the sleepy Thames-side town for what it is, its main claim to fame being the place where linoleum was first invented and produced (see Lockyer and Pickering 2009: 187).

Though the persona itself is consistently funny, Ali G is perhaps at his best in the interviews with unsuspecting figures of authority and in the round-table discussions with experts. Unaware that they are being set up, the interviewees and experts get drawn into conversations by Cohen's clever combination of genuine astuteness and apparent naivety. The interviews, in particular, produce their comic effect by a clash of radically different discursive views of the world. Talking with Professor John Henry, an authority on the misuse of illegal drugs, Ali G proves as knowledgeable as the professor, but from the perspective of someone who treats drug use as a legitimate and intimate element of daily existence. Having listened to the effects of drugs on health, on blood pressure, dizziness and palpitations, Ali asks if there 'are any negative effects'. He knows the price of the drugs and asks whether class

A drugs are guaranteed to be better quality. In an interview with the President of the American FBI Association, he manages to get a confession that sometimes interrogations go beyond what is normally acceptable, but 'not as often as in the movies'. Ali takes the hypothetical situation about selling drugs as a personal accusation, wondering whether the Berkshire police have been in touch with the FBI. In a panel discussion with four experts about animal rights, his tale about putting a mouse in a microwave is condemned as 'fiendish' and 'appalling'. In supposedly serious panel discussions on politics, the family, the environment and medical ethics, Ali's views and opinions are greeted with similar outraged responses. Hilariously, when interviewing a minor right-wing politician, Sir Rhodes Boyson, renowned for his ultra-traditional social views, and unaware that the word 'caned' can mean getting high on drugs, Ali manages to get Boyson to admit that he got caned (beaten) at school. As Lockyer and Pickering point out, the less an interviewee gets the joke, the funnier it is (2009: 192).

Sometimes the comedy comes not from Ali's knowledge of his world, a world alien to his 'experts', but from his ignorance. In a discussion about euthanasia, he wonders what it has to do with 'da yoof in Asia'. He is shocked to hear that water is recycled, but is comforted by the implication that it is acceptable to piss in the bath. In a discussion with the Labour politician Tony Benn, he insists that Mrs Thatcher was a communist. He is convinced that dogs can drive, because he 'has seen it on the telly'. His obsession with sex proves an embarrassment for the television personality Gail Porter and even for the seasoned magician Paul Daniels when he tries to upstage Ali by adopting a similar 'home-boy' costume and persona.

Cohen's comic impersonation has its dangers. Noting that all impersonation carries both positive and negative connotations, Pickering and Lockyer assert the importance of context, or what they term the 'comic frame', if comic impersonation is to be funny rather than offensive. They argue that: 'What is specifically peculiar to comic impersonation is not only that it permits offence but also that it makes light of the offence at the same time' (2009: 184). Of course the comedy relies to an extent on ridiculing the guests and interviewees, on setting them up so they parade their own pomposities and pretensions, but it can also serve to expose the fallacies and assumptions on which their worldview rests. It can be unnerving, salutary and funny to watch 'experts' embroiled in questioning their superiority, their power and prestige, to watch puzzlement and uncertainty invading their mindset. What Cohen offers us, through Ali G, is that 'ludicrous context', the sheer comic incongruity when values, beliefs and perspectives collide.

Opinions are divided as to whether the character is racist or not. While Gilroy (2004) argues that Ali G simply exploits that playful manipulation of subjectivities that marks postmodern culture in a youthful multicultural Britain, Malik (2002: 106) identifies Ali G as part of the 'culture of racism' in the British comedy tradition. Lockyer and Pickering suggest that 'Ali G's act was finely balanced on the thin edge between social satire and racist buffoonery' (2009: 199) and argue that his crude obsessions about sex, women, gang rivalry and drugs, and his offensive language, perpetuate negative black stereotypes. Lockyer and Pickering's discussion is shot through with some frustration about their lack of knowledge of Cohen and his intentions (195) and the character himself: 'was he a white, Jewish or Asian wannabe?' (196). In this they resemble the unlucky personalities who encounter him face to face and who are unable to fathom his multiple identities and get beyond the stereotype presented to them. Cohen creates a situation where human foibles are exposed for what they are: something shared by us all since 'we all harbour ethnic stereotypes, and cannot always successfully censor them' (Howitt and Owusu-Bempah 2009: 54). The butt of the joke is not the stereotype itself, but anyone who believes in and wants to live the stereotype.

Following up: Ali G and ambivalence

☞ Does the comedy of Ali G reinforce racism and racist stereotypes or undermine them? Or does it ultimately occupy the more ambivalent area between these two options?

☞ How much does success or failure of the comedy and comedy performance that touches on race depend on audience expectations?

In concluding our chapter on comedy, race and ethnicity with a discussion of Ali G, we return to the same point highlighted by the sudden end of *Chappelle's Show*, noted earlier: a concern about what audiences do with texts. The fact that contemporary comedy offers a range of subject positions from which to interpret its humour becomes troubling for critics and producers when it becomes clear the array offered may include undesirable (racist) ones, as we have seen in earlier discussions of *Till Death Us Do Part* and *All in the Family*. Queer reading (see Chapter 8) focuses on viewpoints that emphasise the mutability of the social conventions of gender and sexuality that are supposed to follow from biological sex. Yet what follows from racial difference in social consensus appears much less clear-cut. The comedy created by Ali G is perhaps most contentious when it appears that his racial identity is willed and chosen when it is surely the key to all aspects, both serious and comic, of our relationship to the issue of race that it is a matter in which our choices are considerably limited. Comedy that makes reference to race may remind us of the fact of our difference, and of the uncomfortable reality that we cannot determine how others will respond to it, but comedy can also cross, blur and break the boundaries built upon difference. In so far as humour retains the power to include and exclude individuals and groups it remains an ambivalent tool, one that illustrates the value of understanding not only how comedy works but also what it does.

Recommended reading

Christie Davies, *Ethnic Humor Around the World*, Bloomington: Indiana University Press, 1990.

Bambi Haggins, *Laughing Mad: The Black Comic Persona in Post-Soul America*, New Brunswick, NJ: Rutgers University Press, 2007.

Leon Rappoport, *Punchlines: The Case for Racial, Ethnic and Gender Humor*, Westport, CT: Praeger, 2005.

Conclusion: 'You had to be there'

Comedy has been intrinsically important in the development, influence and impact of radio, film and television. Its importance for these media industries and its role in their construction of our cultural landscape are clearly linked at all stages of their symbiotic development. Examples of comedy from these media need to be understood in relation to their specific time and place, but we have also suggested that comedy has the capacity to reach out beyond those specifics to appeal to wider audiences and over time. Across the decades there have been countless comedy sequences which remain memorable and which continue to make us laugh. Content is important in successful, lasting comedy, but understanding enduring comedy requires consideration of form, style, performance, consumption and context, too. Analysis of comedy not only allows a means of understanding the specificity of comedy in that medium at that time, but familiarity with the comedy of say, Buster Keaton or the Marx Brothers, or with classic Disney cartoons or even 1970s British television sitcoms, enlarges and deepens our understanding of the genre, and also offers a kind of benchmark, no matter how imprecise, for understanding contemporary comedy.

Though our focus has largely been on successful examples of comedy, which have sometimes had social, cultural, political or ethical impact, it can be as instructive to ask why something no longer amuses or seems funny to us, even though it was felt to be funny when it first appeared. If there are certain universals in human experience which found expression in the Greek comedies of Aristophanes some two-and-a-half thousand years ago, it is also the case that some relatively recent films, television and radio shows now seem desperately unfunny, and embarrassing rather than amusing. No less than interior design, or clothing, or taking snuff, comedy is prone to shifts in fashion, and, no less than any other genre, comedy has raised – and continues to raise – arguments over the representation of identity and difference, of race, gender, sexuality and class, and about what is deemed culturally acceptable on radio and on screen. In order to work, comedy *has* to find such fault lines, contradictions and areas of anxiety or, as Kathleen Rowe puts it: 'it is the genres of laughter that most fully employ the motifs of liminality' (1995: 8). The very existence of different notions of what is acceptable or not in society produces the sort of conflicted and ambivalent areas that contemporary comedy finds ripe for exploration; the partial awareness that David Brent in *The Office* has of his own sexism and racism does not prevent his delusion that, as an 'entertainer', he can negotiate such difficult territory. The truth is, of course, that he can't and this is the basis of the comedy. The sketch show *Little Britain* (see Lockyer 2010) find its laughs by delivering us into this ambivalent, uncomfortable area on the borders of taste in as many ways as possible, with no thought for the return trip.

It is difficult to predict where future frontiers of transgressive taste may lie, but, on the basis of what we have said, it comes as no surprise that a taboo-breaking American sitcom, *The Big C*, based around a central female character diagnosed with advanced skin cancer, hit British television screens in 2010. Should the criterion for judging a comedy about cancer be solely a question of whether it succeeds in making us laugh? As we have argued in this book, with the help of those who have theorised about comedy from a variety of perspectives, identifying the reasons why we laugh is not a straightforward matter. Whether we find joy in being included, are hiding our fears, expressing our sense of superiority, or our relief that such things are happening to other people, it is clear that laughter is a complex business, and that – because of this complexity – the task of trying to make people laugh in response to film, television or radio is undertaken without guarantee of success.

Asked about the function of comedy in a 1979 interview the comedian Chevy Chase, the original *Saturday Night Live* host then on the cusp of a film career, answers 'Comedy is perspective'. There are at least two senses in which this statement applies: comedy is perspective in that it offers us alternative, skewed and sometimes carnivalesque ways of looking at the world; and, in order for it to work, comedy requires the perspectives of joke-teller, comedian or comic actor to connect with those of their audience. The difficulties of pinning down these issues of perspective in comedy are, however, highlighted by an additional element in the context of the interview: Chase's interviewer, on behalf of Australian television, is Norman Gunston (Garry McDonald), an early practitioner of the spoof interview. It's a fascinating meeting in which comedian battles comedian for control of the situation. McDonald is so deep in character that Chase, even if he has an inkling this guy must be a fellow comedian, is utterly unable to penetrate Gunston's façade of disconcertingly ill-prepared ineptitude. The question about comedy craftily follows ones about his favourite colour and which direction he brushes his teeth, but is presented in a way that forbids (any more) flip answers: 'What do you think is the function of comedy, I mean apart from something to look at on TV between the ads.' There will always be those for whom comedy should be nothing but entertainment, but this is always a refusal to see comedy in three dimensions. Whether we do so willingly or under duress, we must see that producing comedy is a matter of finding perspectives that don't quite match. This is why comedy has a way of unsettling fixed worldviews, of asking awkward questions, even of itself, and why the answers remain elusive.

Even those who work in the field cannot seem to agree as to what comedy 'is' or about its effects on us as individuals or collectively as a society. Whilst the British comedian David Baddiel can argue that 'comedy is your conscience taking a day off', Ricky Gervais, co-creator of *The Office*, dismisses the notion that comedy can ever be morally neutral, can ever be 'just a joke', insisting that the material he creates and uses has to be morally justified (Thompson 2004: xv). Perhaps because there is so little agreement about comedy, and there is no comprehensive, totalising theory of comedy to which we can all subscribe, there are still those who argue that trying to understand comedy is a fruitless exercise. Years ago the children's author E.B. White compared analysing humour to dissecting a frog; essentially pointless and fatal to the frog (Mills 2009: 8). Others have likened writing about comedy to trying to dance about architecture. Both perspectives have some merit, but understanding comedy is neither impossible or redundant. We need to take comedy seriously since it is an essential part of being human, it helps shape our relationships with other people and the world around us, and it serves complex social purposes. Given the variety of human experience, there can never be agreement about what the essence of comedy is, how it works, and why some comedy appeals to some people but not others. The competing claims of those who have argued that comedy can be explained by understanding the workings of the subconscious, or the dynamic structural relationships between social beings within hierarchical societies, require us to continually examine specific comedy texts.

The need to keep asking questions seems more important than ever, given the growing presence of – and demand for – material that makes us laugh on radio, on television, in film and through digital technologies such as the internet and mobile devices. US radio comedy has experienced a resurgence through channels such as XM Satellite Radio and programmes such as *The Comedy-O-Rama Show* (featuring the Monty-Python-like *Crunchy Frog Comedy*), *Armstrong & Getty* and *The Bob and Tom Show*, the latter two combining topical talk and comedy. US television sitcoms are enjoying a renewed golden era with programmes such as *Curb Your Enthusiasm*, *How I Met Your Mother*, *Rules of Engagement* and others. Though of differing quality, together they reflect a huge appetite for television comedy, an appetite that is no less extensive in the UK. In Britain television comedy panel shows such as *QI*, *Would I Lie to You*, *Have I Got News for You*, and *Mock the Week* are popular, as are televised stand-up comedy shows such as *Live at the Apollo*, while BBC radio continues to promote comedy in shows such as *Count Arthur Strong's Radio Show!* Meanwhile, the urge to revisit radio and television comedy of the past, through documentaries and archive programmes featuring British comedy talent from across the decades, reveals that public nostalgia for comedy seems to be growing. The expansion of digital media has both stimulated and served this appetite with specialist television channels and radio stations carrying comedy classics whose appeal seems not to diminish. Despite the shrinking shelves of retail shops, DVD box-sets of classic comedy sell as well as contemporary material in a range of other genres. Sales of comedy DVDs have also been fuelled by the growth of internet shopping, which in turn has made previously hard-to-find comedy material readily available. The internet itself has spawned myriad websites devoted to comedy, including some dedicated to particular comedy genres, forms, programmes, series or comedians. To choose just one example, British television and radio material from the 1950s that has previously been difficult to get hold of has become easily accessible through such websites as www.whirligig-tv.co.uk.

The launch of YouTube in February 2005, its subsequent acquisition by Google in 2006 and the ability to access it on mobile devices such as the iPhone and iPad have revolutionised access to radio, film and television programmes and clips, so that comedy material previously held in archives is now readily available through a simple and efficient search engine. This ready availability has in part guided our choice of material to write about, knowing that access to material is now easier than it ever has been.

Digital technology opens up a treasure chest of past and contemporary comedy, and also offers new platforms for comedy. This can be seen on many of the home pages of internet service providers. Amongst the headline and sports news, weather reports, gossip, celebrity culture news and adverts, there is usually a section devoted to the latest 'funniest videos'. Cryptic titles such as 'gymnast falls between the cracks', 'footy prank misfires' and 'child caught out by glass door' indicate that the new technology is currently interested in delivering what is essentially slapstick comedy. However, as the technology develops, original comedy material delivered straight to on-line may well expand, develop and proliferate different modes of comedy in ways that the old analogue technologies did over time.

One of the most significant recent developments has been the use of phone texting to circulate jokes. Given the nature of the medium, many of these jokes seem to rely extensively on stereotyping. Often they push the boundaries of taste, either by being overtly racist or sexist in their content or because there appears to be a clear vogue for jokes which are based on disasters, most recently the Japanese earthquake and tsunami of 2011. Unlike radio, film and television, mobile telephony is currently – at least in terms of content – a relatively unregulated medium, so that jokes many consider offensive are easily put into mass circulation.

Though the technology has changed, the issues remain the same. Do mobile phone jokes reflect Bergson's ideas that laughter is somehow incompatible with emotion or that they spring from our awareness that we live in a crazy machine-like antagonistic world? Do they reinforce Freudian notions that humour provides a particular access to the subconscious, so that the jokes provide some kind of release and relief? To what extent are they a Bahktinian confirmation of the power and necessity of the carnivalesque, a safety valve for the oppressed, a process of licensed transgression? Why is it that some modes of comedy such as slapstick, often thought of as passé, as belonging to a previous era, are now so popular and prevalent? Time and time again in our analyses we have found comedy texts broaching the most fraught issues in our lives and cultures, standards of gender performance, types of sexuality, social, ethnic and cultural difference, only to (almost invariably) close off any radical possibilities. Comedy in our chosen media may often be conservative, but laughter itself is always double-edged: 'for it knows no inhibitions, no limitations. Its idiom is never used by violence and authority' (Bakhtin 1994: 209).

No one book can provide any definitive answers to the questions that trying to understand comedy inevitably poses but, having read this one, we expect that you will be better informed to make critical judgements about the huge variety of comedy produced by the film, radio and television industries, and, consequently, about comedy delivered by newer media such as the internet and mobile devices. The ability to distinguish a range of comic devices, to understand their relationship to narrative, and appreciate a variety of comic modes, deepens our understanding and enjoyment of comedy, enabling us to make distinctions and evaluations. Such a process can never be mechanistic or precise, of course, but the ability to articulate why we find something funny, why a particular programme, film or performer appeals to us, helps us define who we are.

APPENDIX

Writing an undergraduate essay about comedy in film, television or radio

Most important: read the specific instructions given you in your course or programme of study. Pay attention to what you are being asked to do each time, and follow the rules for presenting your work. If you are asked to consider a comedy text from a particular viewpoint, make sure you do so.

Write an introduction and a conclusion to your essay to frame your argument. Do not write the introduction last, though. You may need to alter it somewhat at the end, but it is well worth laying out – for your own benefit as well as that of the ultimate reader – what you intend to tackle in the essay (being careful to relate it to the essay requirements) and how you intend to do so.

Do not attempt to cover too much or many texts in the wordcount available. If wordcount is in short supply, discussing part of a text may be more than adequate.

It is not usually advisable simply to attempt to 'do' a topic (e.g. the Farrelly brothers). It is much better to approach a text with a specific enquiry in mind (e.g. Humour and disability in the Farrelly brothers' *Kingpin*).

Make sure you understand the historical context of the production, including the rules and restrictions that the makers are operating under (e.g. Production Code, running time, live broadcast).

Do not attribute the values of the text to performers, writers, director or producer. Remember that many people are involved in the production of comedy texts.

Don't attribute your own, subjective, response to a general audience.

Question assumptions about what subject(s) the comedy targets. Consider the full range of comedic modes employed. Don't get bogged down in the narrative by either recounting it or assuming that the narrative outcome (the end) embodies all the text has to say about the subject matter.

Always remember you are writing an academic essay and adopt an appropriate tone. This is not your opportunity to try to be funny. When you need to describe comic incidents or dialogue, however, try to do so sympathetically. If you want to write on comedy in an amusing and informative way look for opportunities in fanzines, student newspapers and/or in on-line journalism.

Always include a bibliography referring to the primary text(s) and critical sources you have used. Reference specific quotations in the text and also reference where you have summarised material from other sources in the text.

Don't get frustrated by a lack of specific sources on the comedy text(s) you want to write about. It is important to find them if they exist, but you should be able to find plenty of supporting material on the larger issue(s). You will need to situate your response by drawing on theories of comedy, taste, class, gender, race, performance, identity, stardom. See our Further Reading sections at the end of each chapter and the Bibliography that follows.

Select bibliography

Adorno, Theodor (1999) 'Culture Industry Reconsidered' in Paul Marris and Sue Thornham (eds), *Media Studies: A Reader*, Edinburgh: Edinburgh University Press, 2nd ed., pp. 31–7.

Akass, Kim and Janet McCabe (eds) (2004) *Reading Sex and the City*, London: I.B. Tauris.

Akass, Kim and Janet McCabe (eds) (2006) *Reading the L Word*, London: I.B. Tauris.

Ashby, Justine (2000) 'Betty Box, "the Lady in Charge": Negotiating Space for a Female Producer in Postwar Cinema' in Ashby and Andrew Higson (eds), *British Cinema, Past and Present*, London: Routledge, pp. 166–78.

Attallah, Paul (2003) 'The Unworthy Discourse: Situation Comedy on Television' in Morreale (ed.), *Critiquing the Sitcom: A Reader*, Syracuse: Syracuse University Press, pp. 91–115.

Austerlitz, Saul (2010) *Another Fine Mess: A History of American Film Comedy*, Chicago: Chicago Review Press.

Babington, Bruce and Peter William Evans (1989) *Affairs to Remember: The Hollywood Comedy of the Sexes*, Manchester: Manchester University Press.

Bakhtin, Mikhail (1994) *The Bakhtin Reader: Selected Writings of Bakhtin, Medvedev, Voloshinov*, edited by Pam Morris, London: Arnold.

Ballard, J.G. (1970) *The Atrocity Exhibition*, London: Jonathan Cape.

Barr, Charles (1967) *Laurel and Hardy*, London: Studio Vista.

Barreca, Regina (1991) *They Used to Call Me Snow White ... But I Drifted: Women's Strategic Use of Humor*, New York: Viking Penguin.

Barrier, Michael (1999) *Hollywood Cartoons: American Animation in Its Golden Age*, Oxford: Oxford University Press.

Barrios, Richard (2010) *A Song in the Dark: The Birth of the Musical Film*, New York: Oxford University Press, 2nd ed.

Baudrillard, Jean (1983) *Simulations*, New York: Semiotext(e).

Bazalgette, Cary, Jim Cook and Andy Medhurst (1985) *Teaching TV Sitcom*, London: BFI

Bazin, Andre (1982) *The Cinema of Cruelty*, trans. Saline d'Estrec, New York: Seaver.

BBC (1932) *The BBC Year Book 1932*, London: British Broadcasting Corporation.

Beach, Christopher (2002) *Class, Language, and American Film Comedy*, Cambridge: Cambridge University Press.

Belton, John (ed.), (1999) *Movies and Mass Culture*, London: Athlone.

Berger, A.A. (1993) *An Anatomy of Humor*, New Brunswick, NJ: Transaction.

Bergson, Henri (2008) *Laughter: An Essay on the Meaning of the Comic*, trans. Cloudesley Brererton and Fred Rothwell, Rockville, MD: Arc Manor.

Berman, Garry (1999) *Best of the Britcoms: From* Fawlty Towers *to* Absolutely Fabulous, Dallas: Taylor.

Billig, Michael (2009) 'Violent Racist Jokes' in Sharon Lockyer and Michael Pickering (eds), *Beyond a Joke: The Limits of Humour*, Basingstoke: Palgrave Macmillan, pp. 27–46.

Bodroghkozy, Aniko (2003) '"Is This What You Mean by Color TV?": Race, Gender, and Contested Meanings in *Julia*' in Joanne Morreale (ed.), *Critiquing the Sitcom: A Reader*, Syracuse: Syracuse University Press, pp. 129–49.

Bogle, Donald (1994) *Toms, Coons, Mulattoes, Mammies, and Bucks: An Interpretive History of Blacks in American Film*, Oxford: Roundhouse, 3rd ed.

Bogle, Donald (2001) *Primetime Blues: African Americans on Network Television*, New York: Farrar, Straus & Giroux.

Bourdieu, Pierre (1984) *Distinction: A Social Critique of the Judgement of Taste*, translated by Richard Nice, London: Routledge & Kegan Paul.

Bowes, Mick (1990) 'Only When I Laugh' in Andrew Goodwin and Garry Whannel (eds), *Understanding Television*, Routledge: London, pp. 128–40.

Briggs, Asa (1961) *The History of Broadcasting in the United Kingdom: Volume I, The Birth of Broadcasting*, Oxford: Oxford University Press.

Briggs, Asa (1965) *The History of Broadcasting in the United Kingdom: Volume II, The Golden Age of Wireless*, Oxford: Oxford University Press.

Briggs, Asa (1979) *The History of Broadcasting in the United Kingdom: Volume IV, Sound and Vision*, Oxford: Oxford University Press.

Brown, Robert S. (2005) '*Cheers*: Searching for the Ideal Public Sphere in the Ideal Public House' in Mary M. Dalton and Laura R. Linder (eds), *The Sitcom Reader: America Viewed and Skewed*, Albany: State University of New York Press, pp. 253–60.

Bukataman, Scott (1991) 'Paralysis in Motion: Jerry Lewis's Life as a Man' in Andrew S. Horton (ed.), *Comedy/Cinema/Theory*, Los Angeles: University of California Press, pp. 188–205.

Butler, Judith (1993) *Bodies That Matter: On the Discursive Limits of Sex*, London: Routledge.

Butler, Judith (2006) *Gender Trouble: Feminism and the Subversion of Identity*, Abingdon: Routledge [1990].

Carey, John (2002) 'Introduction' to *The Joke and Its Relation to the Unconscious*, Sigmund Freud, London: Penguin.

Carpio, Glenda R. (2008) *Laughing Fit to Kill: Black Humor in the Fictions of Slavery*, New York: Oxford.

Carroll, Noel (1991) 'Notes on the Sight Gag' in Andrew S. Horton (ed), *Comedy/Cinema/Theory*, Los Angeles: University of California Press, pp. 25–42.

Carson, Diane (1994) 'To Be Seen and Not Heard: *The Awful Truth*' in Carson, Linda Dittmar and Janice Welsch (eds), *Multiple Voices in Feminist Film Criticism*, Minneapolis: University of Minnesota Press, pp. 213–25.

Cavell, Stanley (1981) *Pursuits of Happiness: The Hollywood Comedy of Remarriage*, Cambridge, MA: Harvard University Press.

Chambers, Deborah (2009) 'Comedies of Sexual Morality and Female Singlehood' in Sharon Lockyer and Michael Pickering (eds), *Beyond a Joke: The Limits of Humour*, Basingstoke: Palgrave Macmillan, pp. 164–81.

Chaplin, Charles (1966) *My Autobiography*, London: Penguin.

Clarke, James (2004) *Animated Films*, London: Virgin.

Cohan, Steven (2003) 'Queering the Deal: On the Road with Hope and Crosby' in Frank Krutnik (ed.), *Hollywood Comedians: The Film Reader*, London: Routledge, pp. 156–66.

Collins, Jim (1992) 'Television and Postmodernism' in Robert C. Allen (ed.), *Channels of Discourse, Reassembled*, London: Routledge, pp. 327–49.

Cook, Jim (ed.), (1982) *BFI Dossier 17: Television Sitcom*, London: BFI.

Coward, Mat (2003) *Classic Radio Comedy*, Harpenden: Pocket Essentials.

Crafton, Donald (1995) 'Pie and Chase: Gag, Spectacle and Narrative in Slapstick Comedy' in Katherine Brunovska Karnick and Henry Jenkins (eds), *Classical Hollywood Comedy*, New York: Routledge, pp. 106–19.

Cripps, Thomas (2003) '*Amos 'n' Andy* and the Debate over American Racial Integration' in Joanne Morreale (ed.), *Critiquing the Sitcom: A Reader*, Syracuse: Syracuse University Press, pp. 25–40.

Crisell, Andrew (1986) *Understanding Radio*, London: Methuen.

Crisell, Andrew (1997) *An Introductory History of British Broadcasting*, London: Routledge, 2nd ed.

Curry, Ramona (1995) '*Goin' to Town* and Beyond: Mae West, Film Censorship and the Comedy of Unmarriage', in Katherine Brunovska Karnick and Henry Jenkins (eds), *Classical Hollywood Comedy*, New York: Routledge, pp. 211–37.

Dalton, Mary M. and Laura R. Linder (eds), (2005) *The Sitcom Reader: America Viewed and Skewed*, Albany: State University of New York Press.

Davies, Christie (1990) *Ethnic Humor Around the World*, Bloomington: Indiana University Press.

Deleyto, Celestine (2009) *The Secret Life of Romantic Comedy*, Manchester: Manchester University Press.

Dix, Andrew (2008) *Beginning Film Studies*, Manchester: Manchester University Press.

Doane, Mary-Ann (1987) *The Desire to Desire: The Woman's Film of the 1940s*, Bloomington: Indiana University Press.

Doty, Alexander (1995) 'Queerness, Comedy and *The Women*' in Katherine Brunovska Karnick and Henry Jenkins (eds), *Classical Hollywood Comedy*, New York: Routledge, pp. 332–47.

Doty, Alexander (1998) 'Queer Theory' in John Hill and Pamela Church Gibson (eds), *The Oxford Guide to Film Studies*, Oxford: Oxford University Press, pp. 148–52.

Doty, Alexander (2000) 'There's Something Queer Here' in Joanne Hollows, Peter Hutchings and Mark Jancovich (eds), *The Film Studies Reader*, London: Arnold, pp. 337–47.

Doty, Alexander (2003) 'I Love *Laverne and Shirley*: Lesbian Narratives, Queer Pleasures and Television Sitcoms' in Joanne Morreale (ed.), *Critiquing the Sitcom: A Reader*, Syracuse: Syracuse University Press, pp. 187–208.

Douglas, Susan J. (1999) *Listening In: Radio and the American Imagination*, New York: Times Random House.

Drake, Philip (2003) 'Low Blows? Theorizing Performance in Postclassical Comedian Comedy' in Frank Krutnik (ed.), *Hollywood Comedians: the Film Reader*, London: Routledge, pp. 187–98.

Durgnat, Raymond (1969) *The Crazy Mirror*, London: Faber.

Dyer, Richard (1998) *Stars*, London: BFI, new ed.

Ellis, John (1982) 'Broadcast TV Narration' in Paul Marris and Sue Thorham (eds), *Media*

Studies: A Reader, Edinburgh: Edinburgh University Press, pp. 238–44.

Ellis, John (2000) *Seeing Things: Television in an Age of Uncertainty*, London: I.B. Tauris.

Epstein, Lawrence J. (2004) *Mixed Nuts: America's Love Affair with Comedy Teams from Burns and Allen to Belushi and Ackroyd*, New York: Public Affairs.

Evans, Peter William and Celestine Deleyto (eds), (1998) *Terms of Endearment: Hollywood Romantic Comedy of the 1980s and 1990s*, Edinburgh: Edinburgh University Press.

Everitt, David (2000) *King of the Half Hour: Nat Hiken and the Golden Age of TV Comedy*, Syracuse: Syracuse University Press

Eyles, Allen (1969) *The Marx Brothers: Their World of Comedy*, New York: Barnes, 2nd ed.

Faulk, Barry J. (2010) *British Rock Modernism 1967–1977: The Story of Music Hall in Rock*, Aldershot: Ashgate

Fenin, George N. and William K. Everson (1978) *The Western: From Silents to the Seventies*, London: Penguin.

Feuer, Jane (1992) 'Genre Study and Television' in Robert C. Allen (ed.), *Channels of Discourse, Reassembled*, London: Routledge, pp. 138–60.

Feuer, Jane (2001) 'Situation Comedy Part 2', in Glen Creeber (ed.), *The Television Genre Book*, London: BFI, pp. 67–70.

Foster, Andy and Steve Furst (1996) *Radio Comedy 1938–1968: A Guide to 30 Years of Wonderful Wireless*, London: Virgin.

Freud, Sigmund (2002) *The Joke and Its Relation to the Unconscious*, London: Penguin.

Friedman, Lester D. (ed.), (1991a) *Unspeakable Images: Ethnicity and the Amercian Cinema*, Urbana: University of Illinois Press.

Friedman, Lester D. (1991b) 'Celluloid Palimpsests: An Overview of Ethnicity and American Cinema' in Lester D. Friedman (ed.), *Unspeakable Images: Ethnicity and the Amercian Cinema*, Urbana: University of Illinois Press, pp. 11–35.

Frierson, Michael (1997) 'Clay Animation Comes out of the Inkwell: The Fleischer Brothers and Clay Animation', in Jayne Pilling (ed.), *A Reader in Animation Studies*, London: John Libbey, pp. 82–92.

Frye, Northrop (1990) *Anatomy of Criticism*, London: Penguin [1957].

Gabler, Neal (2006) *Walt Disney: The Triumph of the American Imagination*, New York: Alfred A. Knopf.

Gehring, Wes D. (1996) *American Dark Comedy: Beyond Satire*, Westport, CT: Greenwood Press.

Gehring, Wes D. (1997) *Personality Comedians as Genre: Selected Players*, Westport, CT: Greenwood Press.

Genovese, Eugene D. (1975) *Roll, Jordan, Roll: The World the Slaves Made*, London: Deutsch.

Gilroy, Paul (2004) *After Empire*, Abingdon; Routledge.

Glitre, Kathrina (2006) *Hollywood Romantic Comedy: States of the Union 1934–65*, Manchester: Manchester University Press.

Goddard, Pete (1991) '*Hancock's Half Hour*: A Watershed in British Television Comedy' in John Corner (ed.), *Popular Television in Britain*, London: BFI, pp. 75–89.

Goldman, William (1996) *Adventures in the Screen Trade: A Personal View of Hollywood*, London: Abacus [1983].

Goldman, William (2001) *Which Lie Did I Tell? More Adventures in the Screen Trade*, London: Bloomsbury.

Gray, Frances (1994) *Women and Laughter*, Charlottesville: University Press of Virginia.

Gray, Frances (2009) 'Privacy, Embarrassment and Social Power: British Sitcom' in Sharon Lockyer and Michael Pickering (eds), *Beyond a Joke: The Limits of Humour*, Basingstoke: Palgrave Macmillan, pp. 148–63.

Gray, Jonathan, Jeffrey p. Jones and Ethan Thompson (2009) *Satire TV: Politics and Comedy in the Post-Network Era*, New York: New York University Press.

Gray, Jonathan (2009) 'Throwing Out the Welcome Mat: Public Figures as Guests and Victims in TV Satire' in Jonathan Gray, Jeffrey P. Jones and Ethan Thompson, *Satire TV: Politics and Comedy in the Post-Network Era*, New York: New York University Press, pp. 147–66.

Groch, James R. (1990) '"What Is a Marx Brother?": Critical Practice, Industrial Practice, and the Notion of the Comic Auteur' in *Velvet Light Trap* 26, University of Texas Press, pp. 28–41.

Grote, David (1983) *The End of Comedy: The Situation Comedy and the Comedic Tradition*, Hamden, CT: Archon.

Guardian, The (2010) 'The Best 25 Comedy Films of All Time', *Guardian Supplement*, 18 October.

Gunning, Tom (1995) 'Crazy Machines in the Garden of Forking Paths: Mischief Gags and the Origins of American Film Comedy' in Katherine Brunovska Karnick and Henry Jenkins (eds), *Classical Hollywood Comedy*, New York: Routledge, pp. 87–105.

Haggins, Bambi (2007) *Laughing Mad: The Black Comic Persona in Post-Soul America*, New Brunswick, NJ: Rutgers University Press.

Halas, Vivien and Paul Wells (2006) *Halas and Batchelor Cartoons: An Animated History*, London: Southbank Publishing.

Hamamoto, Darrell (1989) *Nervous Laughter: Television Situation Comedy and the Liberal Democratic Ideology*, New York: Praeger.

Haralovich, Mary Beth (2003) 'Sitcoms and Suburbs: Positioning the 1950s Homemaker' in Joanne Morreale (ed.), *Critiquing the Sitcom: A Reader*, Syracuse: Syracuse University Press, pp. 69-85.

Hardy, Phil (1983) *The Western*, London: Aurum.

Harries, Dan (2000) *Film Parody*, London: BFI.

Hartley, John (2001), 'Situation Comedy Part 1' in Glen Creeber (ed.), *The Television Genre Book*, London: BFI, pp. 65–7.

Harvey, James (1998) *Romantic Comedy in Hollywood: From Lubitsch to Sturges*, New York: Capo [1987].

Haskell, Molly (1989) 'Introduction' to Ed Sikov, *Screwball: Hollywood's Madcap Romantic Comedies*, New York: Crown.

Henderson, Brian (2001) 'Romantic Comedy Today: Semi-Tough or Impossible?' in Gregg Rickman (ed.), *The Film Comedy Reader*, New York: Limelight, pp. 310–26 [1979].

Hight, Craig (2010) *Television Mockumentary: Reflexivity, Satire and a Call to Play*, Manchester: Manchester University Press.

Hilmes, Michelle (1997) *Radio Voices: American Broadcasting 1922–1952*, Minneapolis: University of Minnesota Press.

Hilmes, Michelle (2003) 'Where Everybody Knows Your Name: *Cheers* and the Mediation of Cultures' in Joanne Morreale (ed.), *Critiquing the Sitcom: A Reader*, Syracuse: Syracuse University Press, pp. 213–23.

Hood, Stuart (1983) *On Television*, London: Pluto, 2nd ed.

Horton, Andrew S. (ed.), (1991) *Comedy/Cinema/Theory*, Los Angeles: University of California Press.

Howitt, Dennis and Kwame Owusu-Bempah (2009) 'Race and Ethnicity in Popular Humour' in Sharon Lockyer and Michael Pickering (eds), *Beyond a Joke: The Limits of Humour*, Basingstoke: Palgrave Macmillan, pp. 47–64.

Hunt, Leon (1998) *British Low Culture: From Safari Suits to Sexploitation*, London, Routledge.

Jenkins, Henry (1992) *What Made Pistachio Nuts?: Early Sound Comedy and the Vaudeville Aesthetic*, New York: Columbia University Press.

Kaminsky, Stuart M. (1985) *American Film Genres*, Chicago: Nelson-Hall, 2nd ed.

Karlyn, Kathleen Rowe (2003) '*Roseanne*: Unruly Woman as Domestic Goddess' in Joanne Morreale (ed.), *Critiquing the Sitcom: A Reader*, Syracuse: Syracuse University Press, pp. 251–61.

Karnick, Katherine Brunovska and Henry Jenkins (eds), (1995) *Classical Hollywood Comedy*, New York: Routledge.

Kavanagh, Ted (1949) *Tommy Handley*, London: Hodder and Stoughton.

Kendall, Elizabeth (2002) *The Runaway Bride: Hollywood Romantic Comedy of the 1930s*, New York: Cooper Square [1990].

Kerr, Walter (1975) *The Silent Clowns*, New York: Alfred A. Knopf.

King, Geoff (2002) *Film Comedy*, London: Wallflower Press.

Kitses, Jim (1969) *Horizons West: Studies in Authorship in the Western*, London: Thames and Hudson.

Koestler, Arthur (1949) *Insight and Outlook*, Lincoln: University of Nebraska Press.

Koseluk, Gregory (2000) *Great Brit-Coms: British Television Situation Comedy*, Jefferson, NC: McFarland.

Koszarski, Richard (1994) *An Evening's Entertainment: The Age of the Silent Feature Film 1915–1928*, History of the American Cinema, Volume 3, Berkeley: University of California Press.

Krämer, Peter (1988) 'Vitagraph, Slapstick and Early Comedy' in *Screen*, 29, 2, Spring, pp. 98–104.

Krämer, Peter (2005) *The New Hollywood: From* Bonnie and Clyde *to* Star Wars, London: Wallflower.

Krutnik, Frank (1998) 'Love Lies: Romantic Fabrication in Contemporary Romantic Comedy', in Peter William Evans and Celestine Deleyto (eds), *Terms of Endearment: Hollywood Romantic Comedy of the 1980s and 1990s*, Edinburgh: Edinburgh University Press, pp. 15–36.

Krutnik, Frank (ed.), (2003) *Hollywood Comedians: The Film Reader*, London: Routledge.

Kutulas, Judy (2005) 'Who Rules the Roost?: Sitcom Family Dynamics from the Cleavers to the Osbournes' in Mary M. Dalton and Laura Linder (eds), *The Sitcom Reader: America Viewed and Skewed*, Albany: State University of New York Press, pp. 49–59.

Lahue, Kalton C. (1971) *Mack Sennett's Keystone: The Man, the Myth and the Comedians*, New York: A.S. Barnes.

Landay, Lori (2005) '*I Love Lucy*: television and Gender in Postwar Domestic Ideology' in Mary M. Dalton and Laura R. Linder (eds), *The Sitcom Reader: America Viewed and Skewed*, Albany: State University of New York Press, pp. 87–97.

LaSalle, Mick (2009) '*Up* Soars on Flights of Fancy', *San Francisco Chronicle*, p. E-1, 29 May.

Lenburg, Jeff (1993) *The Great Cartoon Directors*, New York: Da Capo Press.

Lent, Tina Olsin (1995) 'Romantic Love and Friendship: The Redefinition of Gender Relations in Screwball Comedy' in Katherine Brunovska Karnick and Henry Jenkins (eds), *Classical Hollywood Comedy*, New York: Routledge, pp. 314–31.

Lewisohn, Mark (1998) *Radio Times Guide to TV Comedy*, London: BBC.

Lewisohn, Mark (2003a) *Funny Peculiar: The True Story of Benny Hill*, London: Pan.

Lewisohn, Mark (2003b) *Radio Times Guide to TV Comedy*, London: BBC, 2nd ed.

Linder, Laura R. (2005) 'From Ozzie to Ozzy: The Reassuring Nonevolution of the Sitcom Family' in Mary M. Dalton and Laura R. Linder (eds), *The Sitcom Reader: America Viewed and Skewed*, Albany: State University of New York Press, pp. 61–71.

Littlewood, Jane and Michael Pickering (1998) 'Heard the One About the White Middle-class Heterosexual Father-in-law: Gender, Ethnicity and Political Correctness in Comedy' in Stephen Wagg (ed.), *Because I Tell a Joke or Two: Comedy, Politics and Social Difference*, London: Routledge, pp. 291–312.

Lockyer, Sharon (ed.) (2010) *Reading Little Britain: Comedy Matters on Contemporary Television*, London: I.B. Tauris.

Lockyer, Sharon and Michael Pickering (eds), (2009) *Beyond a Joke: The Limits of Humour*, Basingstoke: Palgrave Macmillan.

Lotz, Amanda Dyanne (2005) 'Segregated Sitcoms: Institutional Causes of Disparity Among Black and White Comedy Images and Audiences' in Mary M. Dalton and Laura R. Linder (eds), *The Sitcom Reader: America Viewed and Skewed*, Albany: State University of New York Press, pp. 139–50.

Louvish, Simon (1999) *Monkey Business: The Lives and Legends of the Marx Brothers*, London: Faber & Faber.

Louvish, Simon (2002) *Stan and Ollie: The Roots of Comedy*, London: Faber & Faber.

Louvish, Simon (2003) *Keystone: The Life and Clowns of Mack Sennett*, London: Faber & Faber.

Lovell, Terry (1982) 'Genre of Social Disruption' in Jim Cook (ed.), *BFI Dossier 17: Television Sitcom*, London: BFI, pp. 19–31.

Lynn, Kenneth S. (2002) *Charlie Chaplin and His Times*, London: Aurum Press.

MacCann, Richard Dyer (1993) *The Silent Comedians*, Metuchen, NJ: Scarecrow.

Malik, Sarita (2002) *Representing Black Britain: Black and Asian Images on Television*, London: Sage.

Malik, Sarita (2010) 'How *Little Britain* Does "Race"' in Sharon Lockyer (ed.), *Reading Little Britain: Comedy Matters on Contemporary Television*, London: I.B. Tauris, pp. 75–94.

Maltin, Leonard (1985) *Movie Comedy Teams*, New York: New American Library, [1969].

Marc, David (1997) *Comic Visions: Television Comedy and American Culture*, Oxford: Blackwell, 2nd ed.

Marc, David (2005) 'Origins of the Genre: In Search of the Radio Sitcom' in Mary M. Dalton and Laura R. Linder (eds), *The Sitcom Reader: America Viewed and Skewed*, Albany: State University of New York Press, pp. 15–24.

Mast, Gerald (1979) *The Comic Mind: Comedy and the Movies*, Chicago: University of Chicago Press, 2nd ed.

Mather, Nigel (2006) *Tears of Laughter: Comedy-drama in 1990s British Cinema*, Manchester: Manchester University Press.

Matthews, Nicole (2000) *Comic Politics: Gender in Hollywood Comedy After the New Right*, Manchester: Manchester University Press.

McDonald, Tamar Jeffers (2007) *Romantic Comedy: Boy Meets Girl Meets Genre*, London: Wallflower.

Means Coleman, Robin R. and Charlton D. McIlwain (2005) 'The Hidden Truths in Black Sitcoms' in Mary M. Dalton and Laura R. Linder (eds), *The Sitcom Reader: America Viewed and Skewed*, Albany: State University of New York Press, pp. 125–37.

Medhurst, Andy (2007) *A National Joke: Popular Comedy and English Cultural Identities*, Abingdon: Routledge.

Medhurst, Andy and Lucy Tuck (1982) 'The Gender Game' in Jim Cook (ed.), *BFI Dossier 17: Television Sitcom*, London: BFI, pp. 43–55.

Mellen, Joan (1978) *Big Bad Wolves: Masculinity in the American Film*, London: Elm Tree.

Mellen, Joan (2006) *Modern Times*, London: BFI.

Mellencamp, Patricia (2003) 'Situation Comedy, Feminism, and Freud: Discourses of Gracie and Lucy' in Joanne Morreale (ed.), *Critiquing the Sitcom: A Reader*, Syracuse: Syracuse University Press, pp. 41–55.

Mills, Brett (2005) *Television Sitcom*, London: BFI.

Mills, Brett (2009) *The Sitcom*, Edinburgh: Edinburgh University Press.

Mitchell, Glenn (1997) *The Chaplin Encyclopedia*, London: B.T. Batsford.

Montgomery, John (1968) *Comedy Films 1894–1954*, London, George Allen & Unwin, 2nd ed.

Monthly Film Bulletin (1966) '*Carry On Cowboy*', 33, 386, March, pp. 41–2, London: British Film Institute.

Morreale, Joanne (ed.), (2003) *Critiquing the Sitcom: A Reader*, Syracuse: Syracuse University Press.

Morreall, John (1983) *Taking Laughter Seriously*, Albany, NY: SUNY Press.

Morreall, John (2009) 'Humour and the Conduct of Politics' in Sharon Lockyer and Michael Pickering (eds), *Beyond a Joke: The Limits of Humour*, Basingstoke: Palgrave Macmillan, pp. 65–80.

Morris, Chris (2010) 'Models for Morris', *Sight and Sound*, 20, 6, June, p. 59.

Moss, Stephen (2006) 'Gotcha!', *The Guardian*, 12 May, pp. 6–8.

Mowatt, Ian (2010) 'Analysing *Little Britain* as a Sketch Show' in Sharon Lockyer (ed.), *Reading Little Britain: Comedy Matters on Contemporary Television*, London: I.B. Tauris, pp. 19–33.

Mulvey, Laura (1993a) 'Visual Pleasure and Narrative Cinema' in Antony Easthope (ed.), *Contemporary Film Theory*, Harlow: Longman, pp. 111–24.

Mulvey, Laura (1993b) 'Afterthoughts on "Visual Pleasure in Narrative Cinema" Inspired by King Vidor's *Duel in the Sun* (1946)' in Antony Easthope (ed.), *Contemporary Film Theory*, Harlow: Longman, pp. 125–33.

Musser, Charles (1991) 'Ethnicity, Role-playing, and American Film Comedy: From *Chinese Laundry Scene* to *Whoopee* (1894–1930)' in Lester D. Friedman (ed.), *Unspeakable Images: Ethnicity and the American Cinema*, Urbana: University of Illinois Press, pp. 39–81.

Musser, Charles (1994) *The Emergence of Cinema: The American Screen to 1907*, History of the American Cinema Vol. 1, Berkeley: University of California Press.

Musser, Charles (1995) 'Divorce, DeMille and the Comedy of Remarriage' in Katherine Brunovska Karnick and Henry Jenkins (eds), *Classical Hollywood Comedy*, New York:

Routledge, pp. 282–313.
Neale, Steve and Frank Krutnik (1990) *Popular Film and Television Comedy*, London, Routledge.
Neaverson, Bob (1997) *The Beatles Movies*, London: Continuum
Nelson, Robin (1997) *TV Drama in Transition*, London: Macmillan.
Oakley, Giles (1982) '*Yes Minister*' in Jim Cook (ed.), *BFI Dossier 17: Television Sitcom*, London: BFI, pp. 66–79.
Ortved, John (2009) *Simpsons Confidential*, London: Ebury.
Palmer, Jerry (1987) *The Logic of the Absurd*, London: BFI.
Palmer, Jerry (2009) 'Parody and Decorum: Permission to Mock' in Sharon Lockyer and Michael Pickering (eds), *Beyond a Joke: The Limits of Humour*, Basingstoke: Palgrave Macmillan, pp. 81–99.
Parker, Derek (1977) *Radio: The Great Years*, Newton Abbot: David & Charles.
Paul, William (1991) 'Charles Chaplin and the Annals of Anality' in Andrew S. Horton (ed), *Comedy/Cinema/Theory*, Los Angeles: University of California Press, pp. 109–30.
Paul, William (1994) *Laughing Screaming: Modern Hollywood Horror and Comedy*, New York: Columbia University Press.
Pearsall, Ronald (1975) *Edwardian Popular Music*, Newton Abbot: David & Charles.
Peterson, Valerie V. (2005) '*Ellen*: Coming Out and Disappearing' in Mary M. Dalton and Laura R. Linder (eds), *The Sitcom Reader: America Viewed and Skewed*, Albany: State University of New York Press, pp. 165–76.
Pickering, Michael (2001) *Stereotyping: The Politics of Representation*, Basingstoke: Palgrave.
Pickering, Michael and Sharon Lockyer (2009a) 'Introduction: The Ethics and Aesthetics of Humour and Comedy' in Sharon Lockyer and Michael Pickering (eds), *Beyond a Joke: The Limits of Humour*, Basingstoke: Palgrave Macmillan, pp. 1–26.
Pickering, Michael and Sharon Lockyer (2009b) 'The Ambiguities of Comic Impersonation' in Sharon Lockyer and Michael Pickering (eds), *Beyond a Joke: The Limits of Humour*, Basingstoke: Palgrave Macmillan, pp. 182–99.
Poague, Leland A. (1978) *The Cinema of Ernst Lubitsch*, New York: A.S. Barnes.
Polan, Dana (1991) 'The Light Side of Genius: Hitchcock's *Mr. and Mrs. Smith* in the Screwball Tradition' in Andrew S. Horton (ed), *Comedy/Cinema/Theory*, Los Angeles: University of California Press, pp. 131–52.
Porter, Laraine (1998) 'Tarts, Tampons and Tyrants: Women and Representation in British Comedy' in Stephen Wagg (ed.), *Because I Tell a Joke or Two: Comedy, Politics and Social Difference*, London: Routledge, pp. 65–93.
Provencher, Denis M. (2005) 'Sealed with a Kiss: Heteronormative Narrative Strategies in NBC's *Will & Grace*' in Mary M. Dalton and Laura R. Linder (eds), *The Sitcom Reader: America Viewed and Skewed*, Albany: State University of New York Press, pp. 177–89.
Radner, Hilary (1993) 'Pretty Is as Pretty Does: Free Enterprise and the Marriage Plot' in Jim Collins, Hilary Radner and Ava Preacher Collins (eds), *Film Theory Goes to the Movies*, Routledge: New York, pp. 56–76.
Rappoport, Leon (2005) *Punchlines: The Case for Racial, Ethnic and Gender Humor*, Westport, CT: Praeger.
Real, Michael (2003) 'Structuralist Analysis 1: Bill Cosby and Recoding Ethnicity' in Joanne Morreale (ed.), *Critiquing the Sitcom: A Reader*, Syracuse: Syracuse University Press, pp. 224–46.

Riblet, Doug (1995) 'The Keystone Film Company and the Historiography of Early Slapstick' in Katherine Brunovska Karnick and Henry Jenkins (eds), *Classical Hollywood Comedy*, New York: Routledge, pp. 168–89.

Rich, Adrienne (1994) *Bread, Blood and Poetry*, New York: Norton.

Rickman, Gregg (ed.), (2001) *The Film Comedy Reader*, New York: Limelight.

Rinaldi, Graham (2009) *Will Hay*, Sheffield: Tomahawk.

Robinson, David (1973) *Buster Keaton*, London: Secker and Warburg / BFI.

Rock, Chris (2002) 'From Rock This!' in Mel Watkins (ed.), *African American Humor: The Best Black Comedy from Slavery to Today*, Chicago; Lawrence Hill, pp. 337–54.

Roscoe, Jane and Craig Hight (2001) *Faking It: Mock Documentary and the Subversion of Reality*, Manchester: Manchester University Press.

Rosenberg, Bernard and Harry Silverstein (1970) *The Real Tinsel*, New York: Macmillan.

Ross, Karen (1996) *Black and White Media: Black Images in Popular Film and Television*, Cambridge: Polity.

Ross, Robert (1999) *Benny Hill: Merry Master of Mirth*, London: Batsford.

Ross, Sharon Marie (2005) 'Talking Sex: Comparison Shopping Through Female Conversation in HBO's *Sex in the City*' in Mary M. Dalton and Laura R. Linder (eds), *The Sitcom Reader: America Viewed and Skewed*, Albany: State University of New York Press, pp. 111–22.

Rowe, Kathleen (1995) *The Unruly Woman: Gender and the Genres of Laughter*, Austin: University of Texas Press.

Russell, Dave (2004) *Looking North: Northern England and the National Imagination*, Manchester: Manchester University Press.

Russo, Vito (1987) *The Celluloid Closet: Homosexuality in the Movies*, New York: Harper and Row, revised ed.

Sanders, Jonathan (1995) *Another Fine Dress: Role-Play in the Films of Laurel and Hardy*, London: Cassell.

Schaeffer, Alan (1981) *The Art of Laughter*, New York: Columbia University Press.

Schroeder, Alan (1997) *Charlie Chaplin: The Beauty of Silence*, Danbury, CT: Franklin Watts.

Sedgwick, Eve Kosofsky (1985) *Between Men: English Literature and Male Homosocial Desire*, New York: Columbia University Press.

Sedgwick, Eve Kosofsky (1990) *Epistemology of the Closet*, Berkeley: University of California Press.

Seidman, Steven Barry (1979) 'The Position of the Comedian as an Extra-fictional Performer and a Fictional Figure in a Traditional Hollywood Film Genre.' University of California, PhD Thesis, 1979.

Seidman, Steven (1981) *Comedian Comedy: A Tradition in Hollywood Film*, Ann Arbor: UMI Research Press.

Seidman, Steven (2003) 'Performance, Enunciation and Self-reference in Hollywood Comedian Comedy' in Frank Krutnik (ed.), *Hollywood Comedians: The Film Reader*, London: Routledge.

Sennett, Mack (1954) *King of Comedy*, as told to Cameron Shipp, New York, Doubleday.

Sennett, Ted (1973) *Lunatics and Lovers: The Years of Screwball Comedy*, New Rochelle, NY: Arlington House.

Shohat, Ella (1991) 'Ethnicities-in-Relation: Toward a Multicultural Reading of American Cinema' in Lester D. Friedman (ed.), *Unspeakable Images: Ethnicity and the Amercian*

Cinema, Urbana: University of Illinois Press, pp. 215–50.
Siegel, Scott and Barbara Siegel (1994) *American Film Comedy: From Abbot and Costello to Jerry Zucker*, New York: Prentice Hall.
Sikov, Ed (1989) *Screwball: Hollywood's Madcap Romantic Comedies*, New York: Crown.
Sikov, Ed (1994) *Laughing Hysterically: American Screen Comedy of the 1950s*, New York: Columbia University Press.
Simpson, Mark (1998) 'The Straight Men of Comedy' in Stephen Wagg (ed.), *Because I Tell a Joke or Two: Comedy, Politics and Social Difference*, London: Routledge, pp. 137–45.
Sito, Tom (2006) *Drawing the Line: The Untold Story of the Animation Unions from Bosko to Bart Simpson*, Lexington: University Press of Kentucky.
Smelik, Anneke (1998) 'Gay and Lesbian Criticism' in John Hill and Pamela Church Gibson (eds), *The Oxford Guide to Film Studies*, Oxford: Oxford University Press, pp. 135–47.
Smulyan, Susan (1994) *Selling Radio: The Commercialization of American Broadcasting 1920–1934*, Washington: The Smithsonian Institute.
Spicer, Andrew (2001) *Typical Men: The Representation of Masculinity in Popular British Cinema*, London: I.B. Tauris.
Stam, Robert (2000) *Film Theory: An Introduction*, Oxford: Blackwell.
Stott, Andrew (2005) *Comedy*, New York: Routledge.
Studlar, Gaylyn (1988) *In the Realm of Pleasure*, Chicago: Chicago University Press.
Sutton, David (2000) *A Chorus of Raspberries: British Film Comedy 1929–1939*, Exeter: University of Exeter Press.
Sykes, Eric (2005) *If I Don't Write It, Nobody Else Will*, London: Fourth Estate.
Taylor, Richard (1996) *The Encyclopaedia of Animation Techniques*, Oxford: Focal.
Thompson, Ben (2004) *Sunshine on Putty: The Golden Age of British Comedy from Vic Reeves to The Office*, London: Harper Perennial.
Took, Barry (1998) *Round the Horne: A Complete and Utter History*, London: Boxtree
Wagg, Stephen (ed.), (1998) *Because I Tell a Joke or Two: Comedy, Politics and Social Difference*, London: Routledge.
Walters, Ben (2005) *The Office*, London: BFI TV Classics.
Wasko, Janet (2001) *Understanding Disney*, Cambridge: Polity Press.
Weales, Gerald (1985) *Canned Goods as Caviar: American Film Comedies of the 1930s*, Chicago: University of Chicago Press.
Webber, Richard (2004) *Fifty Years of Hancock's Half Hour*, London: Century.
Webber, Richard (2008) *50 Years of Carry On*, London: Century.
Wells, Paul (1998) 'Where Everybody Knows Your Name: Open Convictions and Closed Contexts in American Situation Comedy' in Stephen Wagg (ed.), *Because I Tell a Joke or Two: Comedy, Politics and Social Difference*, London: Routledge, pp. 180–201.
Wells, Paul (2002a) *Animation: Genre and Authorship*, London: Wallflower.
Wells, Paul (2002b) *Animation and America*, Edinburgh: Edinburgh University Press.
Wertheim, Arthur Frank (1979) *Radio Comedy*, New York: Oxford University Press.
Wexman, Virginia Wright (2003) 'Returning from the Moon: Jackie Gleason and the Carnivalesque' in Joanne Morreale (ed.), *Critiquing the Sitcom: A Reader*, Syracuse: Syracuse University Press, pp. 56–68.
Williams, Frances (1998) 'Suits and Sequins: Lesbian Comedians in Britain and the US in the 1990s' in Stephen Wagg (ed.), *Because I Tell a Joke or Two: Comedy, Politics and Social Difference*, London: Routledge, pp. 146–64.

Williams, Doug (2001) 'Introspective Laughter: Nora Ephron and the American Comedy Renaissance' in Gregg Rickman (ed.), *The Film Comedy Reader*, New York: Limelight, pp. 341–62.

Willis, Ken (2009) 'Merry Hell: Humour Competence and Social Incompetence' in Sharon Lockyer and Michael Pickering (eds), *Beyond a Joke: The Limits of Humour*, Basingstoke: Palgrave Macmillan, pp. 128–47.

Wilmut, Roger (1976) *The Goon Show Companion*, London: Robson.

Winokur, Mark (1991) 'Black Is White/ White Is Black: "Passing" as a Strategy of Racial Compatibility in Contemporary Hollywood' in Lester D. Friedman (ed.), *Unspeakable Images: Ethnicity and the Amercian Cinema*, Urbana: University of Illinois Press, pp. 190–211.

Winokur, Mark (1996) *American Laughter: Immigrants, Ethnicity, and 1930s Hollywood Film Comedy*, New York: St Martin's.

Wood, Robin (2001) '"I Just Went Gay, All of a Sudden": Gays and 1990s Comedy' in Gregg Rickman (ed.), *The Film Comedy Reader*, New York: Limelight, pp. 409–21.

Worsley, Francis (1949) *ITMA: It's That Man Again*, London: Vox Mundi.

Ziv, Avner (1988) *National Styles of Humor*, Westport, CT: Greenwood Press.

Index